The Music and History
of the
BAROQUE TRUMPET
before 1721

The Music and History
of the
BAROQUE TRUMPET
before 1721

Don L. Smithers

Syracuse University Press
1973

First published 1973
Copyright © Don L. Smithers, 1973
First Edition

All rights reserved. No part of this
publication may be reproduced, stored
in a retrieval system, or transmitted,
in any form or by any means, electronic,
mechanical, photocopying, recording or
otherwise, without the prior permission
of the publishers.

Library of Congress Cataloging in Publication Data

Smithers, Don.
  The music and history of the baroque trumpet
before 1721.

  '*An inventory of musical sources for baroque*
trumpet': *p.*
  Bibliography: p.
    1. *Trumpet.*   2. *Trumpet music—History and*
criticism.   I. Title.
ML960.S63   788'.1'09   73–8765
ISBN 0 8156 2157 4

Publication of this book
was assisted by the
American Council of Learned Societies
under a grant from the
Andrew W. Mellon Foundation

Printed in Great Britain
at the
Aldine Press · Letchworth · Herts
for
Syracuse University Press

# CONTENTS

 PLATES

MUSIC EXAMPLES, TABLES, etc.

# FOREWORD

When I read this book in manuscript form some years ago I realized that it was one of considerable importance. What was more, I enjoyed the experience of reading it. This is only remarkable, perhaps, because for a hardened reader (sometimes, under compulsion, of the unreadable) enjoyment in reading is not inevitable. I would like to say that, once having picked up this book, I could not put it down. But that is not true. What is true is that, in every section of the book, large tracts of territory awaiting exploration are effectively and enticingly signposted and admirably described.

Dr Smithers is a musician both before and after he is a musicologist; and his concern is ever with the sounds that come from the trumpet and their wider significance.

In the Baroque era the trumpet was at the high point of its dignity and, on account of its associations and its appearance, it exerted an influence over persons and over communities that in a noise-soused age is difficult to appreciate. One may occasionally begin to feel this when one hears ceremonial music played on State occasions, or from the tower of a German church. A delightful poem quoted on page 122 gives some idea of the influence of a town brass ensemble in Germany in the seventeenth century. On page 158 Dr Smithers analyses the particular use of trumpets in a particular work—the fine Michaelmas cantata, *Er erhub sich ein Streit im Himmel*, by Johann Christoph Bach—and in so doing shows the inviolability of the music-life union in German life in the Baroque era.

Dr Smithers is not one who observes from a distance. He is a participant in his own story. He is, of course, a trumpeter of high distinction, who knows the Baroque repertoire of the instrument better, I suppose, than almost any other person. He also knows trumpeters. His book is not only about an instrument and its capabilities, but about people—about craftsmen who made instruments of great beauty (which are illustrated); about the organizations to which trumpet-players belonged and the matters of prestige and differential that formed the subject of debate within these organizations; about the transmutation of the earlier forms of *Gebrauchsmusik* into symbolic *Kirchenmusik* and hardly less symbolic *Tafelmusik*, or of the fire alarm into sonata and concerto.

Musical history is not a thing apart: it is history. Dr Smithers's understanding of this principle illuminates a narrative which is given additional authority by the multiplicity of his sources. His musical travels—somewhat *à la* Burney—have led him across Europe and far inside the eastern territories, and his conjunction of facts and ideas, of aesthetics, economics and technology, put us all in his debt. What is more, he has given new life to a great mass of music.

Dr Smithers describes the trumpet as the 'most exalted' instrument of the period under scrutiny. He treats it in fitting manner.

PERCY YOUNG

 AUTHOR'S PREFACE

It is remarkable that the majority of books on musical instruments deal with questions of acoustics, construction, and manufacturing methods, and rarely with the intended musical repertory. Some authors frequently ignore the salient fact that a musical instrument was usually made to make music. Discussions of craftsmanship, technology and acoustical principles are necessary in writing the history of an important musical instrument. But no such history can be complete without a thorough examination of the music written for the instrument and the way in which different composers score for it.

I have written this work in the hope of assembling in one place the relevant data about the Baroque trumpet, the most exalted of musical instruments in the seventeenth and early eighteenth centuries. At the same time I have tried to present as large a cross-section as possible of the Baroque trumpet's musical repertory, analysing many of the important pieces scored for the instrument from about 1600 until 1721, the date of Bach's *Brandenburg Concertos*. In addition to the musical and technological considerations, an attempt has been made to give a clear and documented picture of the trumpet and its social position during the first phase of the Baroque era.

For the privilege of allowing me access to original sources, and for the many courtesies extended to me, I would like to express gratitude to the following institutions: the Bodleian Library, British Museum, New York Public Library, Christ Church Library, Fitzwilliam Museum, the National-bibliothek at Vienna, Deutsche Staatsbibliothek, Metropolitan Museum of Art, Germanisches National Museum, and the Bayerisches National

Museum at Munich, the Paris Bibliothèque Nationale, the Universitets-biblioteket at Upsala, the Hudební oddělení národního Muzea at Prague, the Hudební oddělení Moravského Musea at Brno and the Umělecko-historické Muzeum at Kroměříž.

I am particularly grateful to Dr Percy Young, without whose personal interest and generous help this work might never have been published. Thanks are also due to Dr Alexandr Buchner of the Narodní Muzeum at Prague; Professor Sir Jack A. Westrup and Dr Frank Ll. Harrison for their expert counsel; Dr Kurt Wegerer, curator of the Sammlung Alter Musikinstrumente in Vienna; Signor Paganelli for his kindness and help while I was in Bologna, and especially for my visit to San Petronio in the summer of 1965; Dr Malcolm Vale for his generosity in providing me with information about fifteenth-century source material; Dr Helmut Castrop and Eva Wagner for their assistance with the difficult German translations; Margaret Muir for her most appreciated help in the translating of various Italian documents; and Charles Cudworth for making his musical transcriptions available. I am indebted to a long-suffering friend, John King, not only for his having taken the trouble to read the proofs, but for giving so much of his time as a good listener at a stage when thoughts had hardly found their way to paper. Credit for the index is entirely owed to Graham Green, a kindred spirit whose talents have given this work a usefulness it might never have had otherwise. I am very much indebted to John Warrington, a fellow Oxford scholar, for his many suggestions and intelligent editorial amendments while he was with Dent's. But, in the best tradition of the doctrine that 'the last shall be first', there can never be enough words of thanks for my wife and those other loyal and tolerant friends for their encouragement, advice and trust.

DON LEROY SMITHERS

Oxford, 1973

ABBREVIATIONS

A	chorus alto part.
a	solo alto part.
AcM	*Acta Musicologica. Mitteilungen der Internationalen Gesellschaft für Musikwissenschaft* (from 1928 to 1930 called only *Mitteilungen . . .*), 1928 ff. Leipzig, Copenhagen, Basel.
AfMw	*Archiv für Musikwissenschaft*, 1918–26; 1952 ff. Bückeburg, Trossingen, Wiesbaden.
AM	*Annales musicologiques*, 1953 ff. Paris.
B	chorus bass part.
b	solo bass part.
BAMI	*Bolletino dell'Associazione dei Musicologi italiana*, 1909–30, Parma.
BB	*The British Bandsman*, 1887 ff. London.
B.C. *or*	Biblioteca del conservatorio *or*
Bib. d. Cons.	Bibliothèque du conservatoire, Bologna, Brussels, Milan, etc.
Bc	*basso continuo*, i.e. thorough bass.
BJ	*Bach Jahrbuch*, 1904 ff. Leipzig.
B.L.	Bodleian Library, Oxford.
B.M.	British Museum, London.
B.N.	Bibliothèque Nationale, Paris.
BQ	*Brass Quarterly*, 1957 ff. Durham, New Hampshire.
Bsn	Bassoon.
B.V.	Bibliothèque de Versailles.
BWV	*Bach-Werke Verzeichnis* (see SCHMIEDER, 1950, in bibliography).
Chr. Ch.	Library of Christ Church, Oxford.
Clar	clarino, i.e. a high-register trumpet part.
Crn	cornetto, or cornett.

DdT	Denkmäler deutscher Tonkunst, 65 vols., 1892–1931.
D.S.B.	Deutsche Staatsbibliothek, Berlin.
DTÖ	*Denkmäler der Tonkunst in Österreich*, 109 vols., 1894 ff.
EB	*Encyclopaedia Britannica*, 11th edn, 1910–11. Cambridge.
EDM	*Das Erbe deutscher Musik*, two series, 1935 ff.
facs. rep.	facsimile reproduction.
Fl	flute (either a recorder or a transverse flute).
fl.	flourished.
Fw.	Fitzwilliam Museum, Cambridge.
GDMM	*Grove's dictionary of music and musicians*, 5th edn. (ed. Eric Blom), 9 vols. with supplement, 1954. London.
GSJ	*Galpin Society Journal*, 1948 ff. London.
Hn	horn.
JAMS	*Journal of the American Musicological Society*, 1948 ff. Boston, New York, Richmond, etc.
JASA	*Journal of the American Society of Acoustics*, 1929 ff. New York.
KM	*The King's Musick* (see CART DE LAFONTAINE in bibliography).
MAB	*Musica Antiqua Bohemica*, 67 vols., 1949 ff.
MD	*Musica disciplina* (succeeding *Journal of Renaissance and Baroque Music*). 1948 ff. Rome, Amsterdam, etc.
Mf	*Die Musikforschung*, 1948 ff. Kassel.
MfMg	*Monatshefte für Musik-Geschichte* (ed. Robert Eitner), 1869–1905. Berlin, Leipzig.
MGG	*Die Musik in Geschichte und Gegenwart. Allgemeine Enzyklopädie der Musik* (ed. Friedrich Blume), 14 vols. to date, with supplements, 1949 ff. Kassel, Basel.
ML	*Music and Letters*, 1920 ff. Taunton, London.
MMR	*Monthly musical record*, 90 vols., 1871–1964. London.
mod. ed.	modern edition.
MQ	*The Musical Quarterly*, 1915 ff. New York.
MS.	manuscript.
NA	*Note d'Archivio, per la storia musicale*, 1924–43. Rome.
N.B.	Nationalbibliothek, Vienna.
n.d.	no date.
NOHM	*New Oxford History of Music*, 4 vols. to date, 1954–68. London.

Ob	oboe.
Org	organ.
Ov	overture.

P.B.	Proske Bibliothek, Regensburg.
PMA-PRMA	*Proceedings of the (Royal from 1944) Musical Association*, 1874 ff. London.
PR.	print.

QL	*Quellen-Lexicon* (see EITNER, 1900–4, in bibliography).

RBM	*Revue Belge de musicologie . . . Belgisch Tijdschrift voor Muziekweten-schap*, 1946 ff. Antwerp.
R.C.M.	Library of the Royal College of Music, London.
RISM	*Répertoire international des sources musicales*. Vol. i *Recueils imprimés xve–xviie siècles*, 1960; vol. ii *Recueils imprimés xviie siècle*, 1964. Munich-Duisburg.
R.M.A.	Royal Musical Association.
RMARC	*Royal Musical Association Research Chronicle*, 1961 ff. London.
RMFC	'*Recherches*' *sur la Musique française classique.* (*La vie musicale en France sous les rois Bourbons*), 1960 ff. Paris.

S	chorus soprano part.
s	solo soprano part.
SGA	Heinrich Schütz *Gesamtausgabe . . . Sämtliche Werke*, ed. Philipp Spitta and Arnold Schering, 18 vols., 1885–1927.
SIMG	*Sammelbände der Internationalen Musikgesellschaft*, 1899–1914. Leipzig.
S.M.	Library of St Michael's College, Tenbury.
SP	Archives of the Basilica of San Petronio, Bologna.
Str.	strings, i.e. violins, violas, cellos and bass violins.
SWV	*Schütz Werke Verzeichnis* (see BITTINGER in bibliography).
Sym	symphony.
SzMw	*Studien zur Musikwissenschaft. Beihefte der Denkmäler der Tonkunst in Österreich*, 1913 ff. Vienna.

T	chorus tenor part.
t	solo tenor part.
Ti or Timp	timpani.
Tr	trumpet.
Trb	trombone.

U.B. *or* Un.Bib.	Universitäts Bibliothek (university library), Breslau (Wrocław), Upsala, etc.
Va *or* Vla	viola.
Va d'am	*viola d'amore.*
Va d. gam.	*viola da gamba.*
Vc	violoncello.
VjMw	*Vierteljahrschrift für Musikwissenschaft*, 1884–94.
Vl or Vlo	*violone.*
Vn	violin.
Voc	voice *or* voices.
Z.	Zimmerman (q.v. in bibliography).
ZdIM	*Zeitschrift der Internationalen Musikgesellschaft*, 1899–1914. Leipzig.
ZfMw	*Zeitschrift für Musikenwissenschaft*, 1918–35. Leipzig.

To the memory of my father

Friend extraordinary

'We shall not cease from exploration
And the end of all our exploring
Will be to arrive where we started
And know the place for the first time.'

T. S. Eliot, *Little Gidding*

בחצצרות וקול שופר הריעו
לפני המלך יהוה

Psalm xcviii. 6

TABLE OF PITCH DESIGNATIONS

All pitch references in this work are based on the standard of $a = 440$ cycles per second. Inasmuch as the standard of pitch during the seventeenth and eighteenth centuries varied, often considerably, from place to place, trumpets were usually built to a high pitch, i.e. made somewhat shorter, in order to be able to be tuned 'down'. Surviving seventeenth- and eighteenth-century trumpets, trombones and cornettos are mostly somewhat sharp by the present-day standard.

I   THE TRUMPET DEFINED

The late Canon Francis W. Galpin suggested the term 'lip-vibrated aerophone'.[1] He defined a principal sub-section in the class of aerophonic or wind instruments. Simply, any column of air that is 'excited' (i.e. caused to be set into vibration, thus producing a sound) by the player's lips vibrating is a lip-vibrated aerophone. A trumpet is such an instrument. The modern trumpet, a soprano valve trombone, is but one lip-vibrated wind instrument in a family of various sizes and of normally one shape. In the sixteenth and seventeenth centuries, however, a trumpet was any one of many variegated wind instruments with several common characteristics. Referred to at various times and places as a *trompette, busine, tuba, trump, trombetta, trompe, tubecta, tromba, buccina*, the precursor of today's trumpet was lip-vibrated by the use of an implement called a mouthpiece. The tube was made of metal (usually copper, bronze, brass or silver); the air column was a compound acoustical system, and it was capable of producing a series of overblown notes called harmonic overtones or partials.[2] This 'real' or 'classic' trumpet is

[1] Galpin (1910, p. 311 ff.) presented an organically developed classification of musical instruments based to some extent on that of Victor Charles Mahillon. In his later work (1937) he incorporated elements of the Hornbostel-Sachs classification system (from Hornbostel & Sachs (1914, pp. 553–90)). Galpin was the first to propose a classification of musical instruments, applying it for the first time at the International Music Exhibition, London, 1900.

[2] In the strict sense, the acoustical terms harmonic, partial and overtone are not interchangeable. Harmonic and partial are often used interchangeably, defining any of the composite tones, including the fundamental, produced by a vibrating substance. The term overtone, when used correctly, does not include the fundamental tone. Hence the first overtone is actually the second harmonic, or second partial, etc.

differentiated from the modern instrument by virtue of having a longer air column and generally no moving parts.

Bessaraboff (1941, p. 192) indicates the social significance of the Baroque trumpet: 'The real trumpet is the haughty aristocrat of musical instruments. In Western Europe only emperors, kings, great nobles and prominent municipalities enjoyed the privilege of having trumpets. Trumpeters were of "knightly kind" and their calling was considered not a trade but a free and knightly art.' But what was the 'real' trumpet and how did it compare with the assortment of related instruments in the seventeenth century? To understand this and to have some appreciation of the function and repertory of the Baroque trumpet requires an explanation of the physical and acoustical characteristics outlined above. The purpose of this chapter is to define and describe the Baroque trumpet by explaining these acoustical principles, and to describe the related instruments that will be encountered in the course of this work.

Irrespective of its shape, the Baroque or natural trumpet was usually a metal tube between seven and eight feet in length, in two distinct sections. The first section was cylindrical, the predominant length of the bore; the second was conical and terminated in one of two forms, a truncated cone or a bell-shaped flare describing a curve of exact mathematical proportions. After the sixteenth century the latter was the normal form and is known as an exponential bell, following the contour of an exponential curve. The two sections are continuous, the cylindrical bore being normally five times the length of the conical-exponential section.

An expanding section coupled to a long cylindrical tube serves three purposes when the contained air is set into vibration: (*a*) to communicate and radiate the sound waves more effectively into the surrounding air; (*b*) to introduce at a specific level of intensity (depending upon the proportion of cylinder to cone) the even-numbered harmonics, which are almost totally absent in a cylindrical or stopped pipe (the tube is stopped by the player's lips); and (*c*) to reduce the strength of the upper harmonics.

By trial and error European trumpet-makers arrived at the optimum proportions of cylindro-conical-exponential bore. Almost all Baroque trumpets, no matter of what shape or form, have similar proportions. What determine the obvious differences of tone, pitch and many subtle variations from one instrument to another, are the shape of the bore, the thickness of the metal, the diameter of the various sections and the shape and size of the bell. There are two additional factors that are too often ignored in determining the quality of the sound produced: the proportions of the sound generator—the player's vibrating lips and the mouthpiece—and the contributory factors of the performer.

The mouthpiece serves two purposes: to support and contain the vibrating membrane, i.e. the player's lips, which act like a double reed, and to produce a complementary edge-tone. The latter is of particular importance in the sound-production of a trumpet. If the edge-tone, generated by the eddies of air passing through the circular orifice of the mouthpiece, agrees with the frequency of the vibrating membrane, the sound-production will be helped; if these in turn agree with any of the inherent notes of the air column, the resulting tone will be '. . . produced with intensity and brilliance'.[3]

The mouthpiece, then, must be proportionate to the total length of the air column, and must itself be designed to aid the production of particular frequencies. For this reason Baroque trumpet mouthpieces were generally constructed in two or three specific sizes. The bowl or hemispherical cup was shallow, to assist the production of high frequencies; of medium depth for middle register notes; and deep for the lowest frequencies. At the bottom of the hemisphere is the edge-tone-producing orifice or throat, which communicates with an expanding backbore. A correctly constructed mouthpiece will expand the backbore so as nearly to match the diameter of the trumpet bore at the point where the mouthpiece ends and the trumpet begins. Further to enhance the production of high notes, Baroque mouthpieces had a shoulder or grain (the point where the cup and throat intersect) with a very sharp angle. A shoulder that forms such an abrupt transition from the cup to the throat facilitates the production of high frequency edge-tones, which, in turn, assist in the performance of the very high trumpet harmonics.

The sound-production of a trumpet depends upon the frequencies of the vibrating lips reinforced by the mouthpiece edge-tone, and the available notes of the air column. These three elements make a trumpet a three-part coupled acoustical system, but they do not entirely explain the differences of timbre from one instrument to another and the characteristic tone colour of the Baroque trumpet. 'The fact that differences of timbre can be heard shows that the pipe must itself contribute something to the production of the sound.'[4] This contribution, such as that which helps identify one violin as a Stradivarius and another as a cheap imitation, or a trumpet from a trombone when both are playing identical frequencies, is the free

[3] Richardson, 1929, p. 72.
[4] Jeans, 1961, p. 147.

vibrations of the instrument. These vibrations are of high pitch and are generated by the sound body—whether a trumpet, a violin or an organ pipe—set into vibration by the energy of a produced note. Some of these high frequencies may coincide with the harmonics of various notes. When this happens the free vibrations reinforce the coincident harmonics and the resultant is that special quality of a particular instrumental timbre. The band of frequencies, which are these free vibrations reinforcing the equivalent harmonics, is called the formant.

'The formant, which depends only on the structure . . . itself, remains always the same. Clearly the formant has much to do with the characteristic timbre of the instrument; some writers even claim that the timbre of the instrument is completely dominated by it.' [5]

In quoting the experiments of Hermann-Goldap, Jeans (*ibid.*, p. 149) lists the formants of various wind instruments; he also gives a diagrammatic representation to show the range of fundamental notes, and the intensity of the formant tones with respect to the strength of the fundamental. The trombone, trumpet and oboe have the most intense fundamental notes of all wind instruments; the trumpet and horn have the largest formants; but the trumpet alone has the most intense formant in terms of its wide range of fundamental notes. The Baroque trumpet will have a formant somewhere between a horn and a modern trumpet, which, in terms of either instrument, will be rather large.

With these principles contributing to the ultimate sound production, a Baroque trumpet can produce the following notes (Example 1):

Ex. 1. Harmonics of the Baroque trumpet. [6]

Each note represents a particular harmonic, indicated by the corresponding number. Because of the disproportionate length of cylindrical bore and a relatively shallow cupped mouthpiece, the first harmonic or fundamental—shown in parentheses—is impossible to produce and is a theoretical note only. Unless the cylindrical and conical sections are altered

---

[5] *Ibid.*, p. 148.

[6] Although it is just possible to produce a c^2 sharp (harmonic 16+) on a Baroque trumpet, few composers in the seventeenth and eighteenth centuries ever required it.

from their usual proportion of five to one, all Baroque trumpets can produce the series of notes in Example 1, or some transposition relative to the pitch of the instrument.

There is, however, one serious drawback to the Baroque trumpet with its overblown notes: only the octaves (harmonics 2, 4, 8, 16, etc.) are in tune with respect to equal temperament; the harmonics which are factors of 3 or 5 (3, 5, 6, 9, 10, 12, 15, etc.) are notes of just intonation, those shown in black (7, 11, 13, 14) are not in tune in either system and only approximate the representative notes. Nevertheless the Baroque trumpet parts that abound in these out-of-tune partials were dealt with by skilled players. The technique demanded of the relatively few virtuoso players in the seventeenth and eighteenth centuries was not unlike that exhibited by the competent modern jazz musician.

In the next chapter, concerned with the precursors of the Baroque trumpet, we shall discuss various archetypal instruments. One shape, which developed in the late Middle Ages and has persisted until the present day, was the twice folded or closed S shape. This is an obvious form and one that requires the least amount of fuss in manufacture. Almost all surviving seventeenth- and eighteenth-century trumpets were made in this convenient oblong shape.

Putting two reverse bends in a long tube makes it not only more convenient to hold but also, with cordage wound around the two adjacent sections of the bore, a stronger, more durable instrument. Actually the 180° or reverse bends are put into two small segments of tubing which are then joined to the three straight sections, forming a continuous air column from the mouthpiece to the bell. These two elbow sections are called bows, while the long straight sections are called yards.[7] The mouthpiece is inserted into the first yard, which is a length of metal tubing nearly three feet long. This communicates with the first bow, which continues the bore back to the second yard—exactly the same length as the first yard and usually below and parallel to it. The second yard then joins the second bow, turning the bore into the final yard-bell section. The third yard is normally half as long as the first and is fitted to the expanding bell section. The joint of the two sections is always concealed under a decorated but functional cover. This cover is tightly fitted and during the Baroque had a ball-shaped decoration surrounding it. This *boss* serves as a pommel-like

[7] The nomenclature of the Baroque trumpet is that adopted by the Galpin Society. It is based to some extent on the terminology used by James Talbot in the seventeenth-century manuscript on musical instruments found in the library of Christ Church, Oxford (*see* p. 28 and *passim*).

grip to facilitate holding the instrument; it is not a merely decorative, structurally superfluous element. In the Galpin Society nomenclature it is called the *ball*. There are several other such functional decorations: the *garnishes* are engraved or similarly decorated cylinders of metal that cover the joints of the yards and bows and protect the mouthpiece end of the first yard; the *garland* is a band of metal that overlays the bell, adding strength and serving as the important element of decoration where the maker's mark is usually found.

These, then, are the component parts of a Baroque trumpet. They are all made of metal and are shaped in various ways and by various means. The metal most often used was brass, an alloy of zinc and copper. Fanfare or herald trumpets, required for state occasions, were often made of silver with a mercuric amalgamated gold leaf on the ball and garnishes. Mouthpieces were made from a solid bar either of silver or of brass and were fashioned on a lathe. Some mouthpieces seem to have been cast and finished, but these are rare. The decorations found on very ornate instruments were cast in carefully wrought matrices, exhibiting the individual style and design of each maker.

It was mentioned earlier that a trumpet in the Baroque era could have been one of many instruments similar in character and purpose. The Renaissance had a predilection for large families of instruments, some being made in as many as nine different sizes, and the trumpet was no exception. It did not have the proliferate number of sizes and tunings found in the families of recorders, shawms or viols, but it was in several distinct shapes, known by various names, and it existed in a chromatic form well into the eighteenth century. The importance of these variegated forms should not be underestimated. The norm for about 300 years was the oblong trumpet described above, but the other related instruments were used and are the only explanation of some very perplexing scoring requirements.

From the Renaissance until well into the nineteenth century trumpets were in two categories: fixed pitch and variable pitch. Although capable of being tuned with various lengths of tubing known in German as *Krumbogen* and *Setzstücken*, as well as transposed by muting devices, the natural trumpet belongs to the first category. Other fixed-pitch trumpets were the simple straight instruments without any bends and the tightly twice-folded *Clareta* shown in Virdung (1511, fo. C r.) and Agricola (1529, fo. xvi v.). There were also intricately coiled trumpets, which had extra musical significance and are mentioned in Chapters 3 and 5. Trumpets of this sort had no special name; as far as their important acoustical dimensions are concerned they are not unlike the normal oblong trumpet.

In the second category belong the trumpets that were capable of exceeding the few overblown notes of the fixed-pitch trumpets. Pitch variation while playing could be accomplished in three ways: (1) by altering the actual length of the bore, (2) by altering the resonating portion of the bore by including finger or node holes, and (3) by altering the resonance characteristics by hand-stopping. Some Baroque trumpets employed the first of these methods, i.e. the ability to extend or diminish the total length of the vibrating air column. The trombone is the notable example of an instrument with an air column of variable length. The single-slide trumpet (Ger. *Zugtrompete*; It. *tromba da tirarsi*) was similarly constructed. Its overall appearance was nearly identical with the normal fixed-pitch trumpet. The only important difference was the long, extendable mouthpiece pipe that fitted telescopically within the first yard. By holding the instrument in nearly the same manner as a natural trumpet, and maintaining a firm grip on the upper end of the mouthpiece pipe, a performer could vary the length of the instrument sufficiently to produce an almost complete chromatic scale from the middle to the upper registers. Unlike a trombone, however, a player could not move the slide but had to move the whole instrument to and fro, while the slide and mouthpiece remained stationary. Such an instrument was known to have survived until the Second World War. This was the Naumburg *Zugtrompete* made by Hans Veit in Naumburg, Germany. It was dated 1651 and is shown and described in Sachs (1922, pp. 221–2, No. 640, and plate 24). It may well have been one of two instruments mentioned in the inventories of St Wenzel's church in Naumburg,[8] where it was discovered in the nineteenth century. On two separate occasions *Zugtrompeten* are mentioned in the St Wenzel inventories, in 1663 and in 1728. The earlier inventory mentions 'Vier Trompeten mit Mundstücken. Zwey Zugtrompeten mit Mundstücken, gantz neu'.[9] The later 'Inventarium der Musikalischen Instrumente bey hiesiger Stadtkirche, wie sie anno 1728 den 21. Juni befunden worden',[10] itemizes all the instruments and notes whether they are serviceable ('brauchbar') or in the opposite condition ('unbrauchbar'). One

[8] Werner, 1926, pp. 390–415.

[9] *Ibid.*, p. 415: 'Four trumpets with mouthpieces. Two slide trumpets with mouthpieces, brand-new.'

[10] 'Inventory of musical instruments in the local municipal church, as they were found in the year 1728 on the 21st of June.'

more *Zugtrompete* seems to have been added after the 1663 inventory, but one also seems to have lost its slide: 'Nr. 8–9. zwey brauchbare Zug-Trompeten. 10. Eine Trompete, brauchbar, ohne Zug'.[11] Bach required such an instrument in several of his church cantatas. Those parts specifically mentioning 'Tromba da tirarsi' cannot be played on a normal fixed-pitch trumpet; there are just too many notes beyond a single, non-variable harmonic series. As yet there is little information about the earlier history of this kind of trumpet, but there is evidence to suggest that it was a carry-over of a Renaissance instrument of similar design. Such an instrument is discussed in the next chapter.

A possible sixteenth-century version of the *Zugtrompete* was the *Thurner* (modern spelling: *Türmer*, i.e. tower watchman) *Horn*. This was an instrument used by the tower watchmen in Germany and is shown in Virdung (1511). They played various calls and signals on this instrument while keeping a close watch for the outbreak of fire, approaching enemy troops, etc. Some sources imply that a tower watchman's trumpet was drawn ('ziehen') in and out to execute various notes and that such an instrument was used to avoid difficulties with the knightly trumpet guilds. The guild looked upon such instruments with disdain, not regarding them as proper trumpets. It was not until the mid seventeenth century that the guild trumpeters realized that *Zugtrompeten* were actually a threat to their privileged position. The guild petitions to the ruling German noblemen requesting that such instruments be forbidden are discussed in Chapter 5.

Talbot's description [12] of an English variable-pitch trumpet is most illuminating:

In a Flat Trumpet the mouthpiece stands oblique towards right. 2d Crook [bow] placed near left Ear & by it you draw out the Inward yards, whereof one reaches to the Boss [ball] of the Pavillion [bell,] the other to the 1st Crook: its size with the yards shutt the same with common Trumpet. The crook at one end is joynted to an additional yard which incloses the fixed 2d yard from the joynt of the 1st Crook to the beginning of the 2d: at the other [end] it is let into another shorter yard which is inserted into the Pavillion Yard as far as the bottom of the Boss. Longer yd [yard]

[11] Werner, 1926, p. 415.

[12] James Talbot, Regius Professor of Hebrew at Trinity College, Cambridge, from 1689 to 1704, compiled a most interesting and valuable set of notes dealing with musical instruments. Much of his information was gleaned from contemporary sources, as well as from composers and performers of the time. The manuscript is in the library of Christ Church, Oxford (Christ Church MS. 1187). A modern edition of the section on wind instruments is given by Anthony Baines in *GSJ*, vol. i (1948), pp. 9–26.

from bottom of 1st Crook Garnish to its end, 23′ 2″ [23 inches, 2 eighths of an inch, i.e. one half inch] besides 1+ [more than one inch covered]. Shorter from [incomplete sentence].[13]

From the description it is obvious that a flat trumpet was the immediate predecessor of the English slide trumpet. All that had to be added to an instrument of Talbot's description to make it the standard English slide trumpet was the convenient plunger-clock spring return mechanism. The chromatic flat trumpet was used by seventeenth-century English composers and is mentioned in the discussion of Purcell's music.

Talbot very usefully includes a scale of notes for a flat trumpet, beginning on C (its lowest playable note, the 2nd harmonic). Excepting the harmonics of the first or closed slide position, all notes appear with a distance measurement given in inches and eighth parts of an inch. These measurements probably refer to the distance necessary to extend the tubing to produce the desired note. The three-octave chromatic scale as it is found in Talbot's manuscript is given in Example 2.

Ex. 2. Notes and positions for a 'flatt' trumpet.

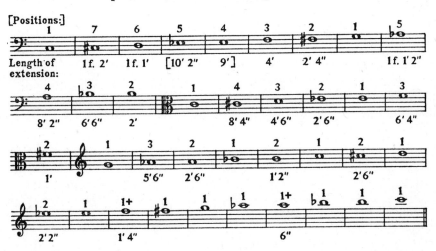

It should be noted that some of the previously mentioned out-of-tune partials are not included as normal overtones of the flat trumpet with the slide closed. For example, the f^1 is shown as a slide extension note, implying that it required correction by extending the slide to lower its pitch.

[13] Christ Church MS. 1187; *see* also Baines in *GSJ*, vol. i (1948), pp. 21–2.

It is doubtful whether there were any other similarly compromising trumpets besides those already mentioned. Since virtually none survive it is difficult to reach any further conclusions until there is more information available.

Concerning the second method of pitch variation, that is, the use of node or finger holes strategically piercing the bore of an instrument, let me say that, despite recent 'theories' and 'reconstructions', no such method seems to have been adopted before the second half of the eighteenth century. The modern Finke-Steinkopf so-called 'clarino', which employs three node holes on a coiled variety of trumpet discussed below, has a number of anomalies which have no precedent in authentic instruments of the seventeenth and eighteenth centuries. The dimensions of bore and bell are wrong and, as a consequence, the timbre is grossly distorted. Because of the fixed position of the holes a further complication is that they are rendered useless when tuning, i.e. 'crooking' the instrument into a higher or lower pitch. Inasmuch as the node holes are placed on the instrument according to a predetermined ratio which is dependent on a given length of air column, shortening or lengthening the bore changes the relative position of the various nodal points of the generated sound wave when the instrument is played. Altenburg (1795, p. 112) mentions the use of node holes, but his remarks seem to reflect speculative and experimental notions on the part of one or two players from the last third of the eighteenth century, rather than anything remotely approaching general practice. His comments about the *Hoftrompeter* Schwanitz at Weimar having an instrument 'using a small leather slide valve across an opening', come remarkably close to describing the William Shaw 'harmonic trumpet' [14] and seem to anticipate the innovations attributed to Anton Weidinger, for whose *Klappentrompete* Josef Haydn supposedly composed his E flat concerto in 1796. The best compromise at a modern reconstruction of a Baroque trumpet that incorporates a single node hole is, in my opinion, the Meinl and Lauber instrument made according to the specifications of a seventeenth-century trumpet provided by Edward Tarr.

The third and probably the simplest method of varying the pitch of the Baroque trumpet was the hand-stopping technique. This was facilitated by the bore of a trumpet being wound into a small coil. Judging from the iconographic sources and the few surviving instruments, the *tromba da caccia*, or *Jägertrompete*, was such an instrument. It had the same bore proportions as the normal 'field' trumpet, it was supposedly of Italian

[14] *See* Halfpenny, 1960.

origin, and it is said to have been preferred by the *Kammertrompeter* (chamber trumpet players) because it was able to correct the out-of-tune harmonics by hand-stopping. The *Stadtpfeifer* Gottfried Reiche, Bach's famous Leipzig trumpeter until 1734, is shown holding such an instrument in his portrait by Elias Gottlob Haussmann. The bell has a wide flange and seems to be as large as any trumpet bell of the period. It points back to the player like a hand horn and is within easy reach for inserting the fingers or hand to 'stop' a particular note.[15] Whether or not this instrument was the so-called 'Clarino' or 'Bach' trumpet is a matter of interpreting the contemporary literary and pictorial sources. Evidence seems to indicate that its use was rather limited. Praetorius compares it with the normal trumpet and makes the following comment: 'Etliche lassen die Trummeten gleich einem Posthorn oder wie eine Schlange zusammen gewunden fertigen: Die aber am Resonanz den vorigen nicht gleich seyn.'[16]

With the gradual implementation of the upper harmonics the natural *Feldtrummet* of the fifteenth and sixteenth centuries emerged from a somewhat obscure history and became the coveted instrument of kings, churches and wealthy municipalities. Once the transition had been made from its unmusical role as a decorative, ceremonial court ornament and a piece of necessary military equipment, the trumpet remained a significant solo instrument for nearly three hundred years. How this transition was made is a matter of guesswork. Possibly the trumpet found its way from the field and battlement into the court chamber and church gallery in two ways: through the imaginative experiments of composers, or as a replacement of similar but variable-pitch instruments that evolved into larger and more unrelated forms. As one type of trumpet became a deeper bass instrument (the trombone), the natural trumpet, by having its range and melodic possibilities extended, became the soprano voice of the brass. But its social significance was never forgotten. Because of its noble status and covert technique the trumpet was set apart from most other musical instruments. This is one reason why it is not found as a normal wind ensemble instrument in the seventeenth and eighteenth centuries. For similar reasons its related chromatic forms were forbidden a normal

---

[15] It should be noted that the bell rim decorations on Reiche's trumpet which Haussmann reproduced are winged angel heads, suggesting the manufacture of J. W. Haas of Nuremberg (*see* Chapter 3, p. 69).

[16] Praetorius, MS. 1619, vol. ii, p. 33: 'Some people have trumpets made like a post horn, or coiled-up like a snake: But those are not equal in resonance to the former [i.e., *Feldtrompeten*].'

existence. It has already been mentioned how the *Zugtrompete* was jealously regarded as a threat to the knightly trumpet guilds; having a difficult technique and being so restricted in its use it gave way to the 'free' and agile cornetto as the normal treble instrument, especially with trombones.

As the trumpet became an established solo instrument in court and church orchestras, some skilled performers obviously tried to convince composers that its melodic limitations could be overcome. In his preface to the earliest published treatise on the trumpet (quoted in full in Chapter 4), Fantini (1638) wrote: 'It will be found that there are some notes, not pointed out at the beginning of the work, which are very imperfect if they are held, but which can be used where they pass quickly.' ('Si trover anno alcune note, che nel principio dell opera non sono accennate, che a voler fermavisi sono imperfette, ma perche passano presto possono servire.') These imperfect notes are non-harmonic tones, frequently found in mid seventeenth-century musical sources. They are usually quick-passing notes, or, if sustained, are a semitone alteration of a harmonic series note. Even though Altenburg (1795, pp. 71-3) mentions the same point over a century and a half later than Fantini, non-harmonic tones are seldom used after the seventeenth century. They were probably very unsatisfactory, and late Baroque composers generally avoid all but the written *b* natural— the lowered eighth or raised seventh harmonic. It most often appears in a second trumpet part and as a very quick neighbouring tone. In Bach's *Mass in B minor*, for example, there are only three natural seventh harmonics in the entire first trumpet part, while there are seventeen in the second trumpet part. Once composers realized that exotic non-harmonic tones were not feasible, it is remarkable what was done with the relatively few trumpet notes available. In Fantini's own country non-harmonic tones were rarely used. Almost none are encountered in the vast seventeenth-century trumpet repertory at Bologna and Modena. By an ingenious combination of repetition of various harmonics, selective short and fragmentary scale patterns limited to the range of existing notes, many Baroque composers managed to create the most exceptional trumpet parts of real musical value.

RENAISSANCE PRECURSORS OF THE BAROQUE TRUMPET

To overlook the contributory elements in the evolution of the Baroque trumpet would preclude a broader understanding of its use, the development of its technique and its musical importance. No work on the history of musical instruments gives sufficient material about the trumpet in Western music before its renowned period. There are, of course, great difficulties in trying to assess the true nature of the instrument before its golden age in the seventeenth and eighteenth centuries. The world before modern times did not share our present-day antiquarian interests. Before the era of museums there was generally little enthusiasm for collecting unserviceable and outmoded objects of art. The survival of pre-Baroque art is by and large accidental.

Decorative and functional art of earlier civilizations fared much better than the utilitarian, easily superseded, and fragile instruments of music. Although fashion in music changes with the same relative frequency as in literature, painting, architecture and sculpture, the products of these arts have always survived in greater numbers and been more carefully preserved. Changes in musical taste and the function of musical instruments require newer but not necessarily better acoustical systems. Most instruments have little value beyond their intended function, so that, historically, when this function changed instruments were discarded or radically altered to cope with the change in fashion.

In attempting to formulate some coherent picture of the function and design of early instruments we must rely on secondary sources, e.g. paintings, carvings and the infrequent instructions set down in treatises and musical compositions. Inasmuch as there are practically no surviving brass instruments made before the sixteenth century, secondary sources are a welcome aid in learning something about pre-Baroque trumpets. Iconographic sources are the best and most reliable evidence of what things were like when the objects themselves are wanting. Fortunately the trumpet enjoyed as celebrated a social and musical position in the fifteenth and sixteenth as in the next two centuries; fortunately, because it was a favourite object for so many drawings, woodcuts, paintings and carvings which were made at the time depicting trumpets in one form or another. The implications are obvious: trumpets were not only regarded as an integral part in a show of splendour, power and magnificence, but were also necessary in demonstrations of adulation and ceremonial-festive activities.

Religious painting is the most fruitful source for representations of Renaissance instruments. Many include arrays of trumpets, stringed instruments and singers—with music sometimes reproduced. In numerous pictures of the Adoration of the Magi, the Coronation of the Virgin and other such themes many kinds of long-lost implements (especially musical instruments) are shown.

The use of realistic details makes Renaissance painting a reliable source of organological information. It seems unlikely that an artist who took pains to represent in exact detail a manuscript of music would not do the same when it came to showing a trumpet, shawm or *lira da braccio*. An informative article by Emanuel Winternitz (1963, pp. 450–63) gives some idea of the role of realistic elements, e.g. musical instruments, in fifteenth-century painting.

Statuary displays the same reliability in determining the shape and form of early instruments. Without the illustrative examples of wood and stone carvings in medieval and early Renaissance buildings, very little would be known about non-surviving instruments of the period. The ceremonial and decorative features of the trumpet made it a favourite instrument in plastic representations of angel musicians.

A comprehensive list of European pre-Baroque instruments, especially trumpets, shown in graphic and plastic works of art, would be enormous. There are some useful compilations of individual collections. Parigi (1951) in particular gives an indication of the vast number of possible sources. Space does not allow an evaluation of even one collection for early trumpet sources, but a descriptive inventory of the most representative fifteenth- to seventeenth-century trumpet iconography will be useful. Some eighteen examples have been selected from various places and cover a period from about 1400 to 1600. Three distinct types of trumpet form are represented: (1) the long straight medieval busine type; (2) the open S shape; (3) the closed, oblong, twice-folded trumpet. None of the examples is 'fantastic', i.e. an imaginary instrument of the artist's own invention. Some seem highly stylized; but when compared with similar or identical instruments depicted more realistically elsewhere, they display all of the same critical features. Several of these iconographic sources suggest that some Renaissance trumpets, like their Baroque counterparts, were chromatic and able to play at least diatonically in their middle and lower registers. The musical possibilities of such instruments (if they were in fact capable of playing more than one harmonic series) are discussed in greater detail later.

The first source to be mentioned is a stone carving above the north wall outside the nave of the church of St Mary the Virgin at Adderbury in Oxfordshire, England. An extremely rare, if not unique, set of figures is shown playing various late medieval instruments. The carving dates from the end of the fourteenth century and, considering its age and the English climate, is in a remarkable state of preservation. At the extreme right are two trumpet-players on either side of a percussion-player performing on what appears to be a pair of timpani. This is an unusual feature, for it would normally be expected that the smaller precursory nakers of the period would have been shown. But the large size of the drums and their appearance with trumpets definitely give the impression that they are a type of kettle-drum. Unfortunately the bell sections of the trumpets have been eroded or knocked off. Both instruments are straight and similar to the medieval busine depicted in various manuscript illuminations. Their occurrence, together with timpani, suggests that trumpets at that date were already playing fanfare figures or melodic passages described in literary sources a century later.

A trumpet from the same period, and of what would then have been of unique design, is shown in a choir-seat carving in the chancel of Worcester Cathedral. Sachs (1940, p. 328) believes that this is the earliest S-shaped trumpet. A reproduction is shown in Galpin (1910, Pl. 49) and in Aldis (1873, Pl. 12). The player, with cheeks puffed out and holding the instrument in his right hand, is to the right of two jousting knights. On the left is a comic figure with a pair of timpani (or very large nakers); he and his instruments have been knocked flying by one of the contenders. Evidently, then, by about 1390 it had become possible to fold the long trumpet back and forth in an S-curve—a notable advance in design and manufacture. About thirty years later (c. 1420) a trumpet of similar shape is included with two straight trumpets in *The Battle*, a painting by the Florentine Paolo Dono (called Uccello), now in the Louvre, Paris. Similarly a trumpet of the same shape is shown being played with two shawms in a *fête champêtre* at the court of Philip the Good. This painting is dated *c.* 1430 and is attributed to Jan van Eyck.

In a series of illustrations depicting the Council of Constance (1414–18) [1] there are a number of scenes with trumpets. As in Paolo Dono's *Battle*, the trumpets are often mixed: straight and S-shaped. There are some interesting features about these illustrations: groups of trumpeters are shown conducted by a figure holding a large baton similar to that of a modern drum-major. For unknown musical reasons, or simply for illustrative variation, the straight trumpets are always held either downward or slightly above a horizontal position; the hand or playing positions are usually one hand under, one over.

Whether or not playing positions are musically significant depends upon the actual design of the instrument. If it is just a straight tube without any moving parts, then it would seem immaterial in what way it was held. But there is fairly strong evidence that this may not always have been the case. A most remarkable detail in a fifteenth-century painting, *The Adoration of the Magi*, attributed to Antonio Vivarini, and preserved in the Staatliche Museen Gemäldegalerie collection at Berlin-Dahlem, shows a long, busine-type trumpet with its mouthpiece separated from the instrument. The mouthpiece is joined to a long piece of tubing, obviously intended for insertion into the trumpet. The piece of tubing is long enough to be a telescopic slide, similar in purpose to the sliding mouthpiece pipe of the *Zugtrompete* described in Chapter 1. The painting shows the Virgin and Child in the stable with the three Magi and a large entourage of men on horseback, nobles, soldiers and fifteen trumpeters. All but one of the trumpets are straight; one is represented in a closed, twice-folded shape. The significant detail (Pl. 1) is to the left of the picture and shows a trumpeter holding an embannered straight trumpet—bell in the air—on his left shoulder; his left hand is holding the mouthpiece end of the instrument and at the same time grasping the above-mentioned mouthpiece and pipe. Curt Sachs (1940, p. 384), the first to comment upon this detail, suggested that the mouthpiece pipe is about ten inches long and intended to alter the harmonic series of the instrument. Since the player is holding the instrument upside-down he may well be holding onto the removable mouthpiece and pipe to keep them from falling out of the trumpet.

[1] *See* Richental, 1874 and 1881.

At the top of the picture is a host of angel trumpeters, one of whose instruments is partially obscured by an overhanging cliff. The playing position is identical with that shown in the Council of Constance illustrations, as well as in most other Renaissance trumpet iconography: each player is holding one hand over the instrument close to the mouthpiece, the other hand, extended palm upwards, holds the body of the instrument. With such a position it would be very easy to secure the mouthpiece against the lips while moving the instrument to and fro to alter its length in the manner of a *Zugtrompete*.

The Vivarini detail, though unique, only substantiates what may be inferred from three other fifteenth-century sources which suggest that variable-pitch trumpets were already in use before 1500. These are Hans Memling's triptych (1480) that once decorated the organ in the Benedictine church at Najera and is now in the Royal Museum at Antwerp; Michael Pacher's altar-piece in the church of St Wolfgang on Lake Aber in Austria, commissioned in December 1471 and finished in 1481;[2] and the *Krönung Mariae* (*Coronation of the Virgin*, c. 1485) by the Meister des Marienlebens, an anonymous fifteenth-century German artist whose paintings of the Virgin are in the Alte Pinakothek at Munich.

In the famous and frequently reproduced Memling triptych, Christ, surrounded by a group of singers, is represented in the centre panel. The left panel shows five instrumentalists (from right to left: a shawm, a twice-folded trumpet, a lute, a tromba marina and a psaltery); the right panel shows five more instrumentalists (from left to right: a long straight trumpet, a folded trumpet, an organetto, a harp and a fidel or rebec). The playing position for each trumpet is the same as that described above: the right hand is extended and holds the instrument, the left hand is close to the mouth and supports the mouthpiece against the lips. The length of extended position of the two folded trumpets is different, however. The trumpet depicted in the left panel is farther from the player than the folded trumpet in the right panel. This does suggest that the instruments could slide back and forth over the mouthpiece pipe. Even the way in which the straight trumpet is being held evokes curiosity. The player is holding the instrument downwards with the right arm fully extended. A normal way of holding such an instrument, if it was not to be moved to and fro, would be simply to grasp it with both hands towards the centre of balance—near the middle. Earlier trumpets of this type that were surely fixed pitch are shown held in such a manner in medieval illuminations.

[2] Stiassny, 1919; *see* also Sachs, 1950, pp. 62–6.

Michael Pacher's altar-piece, depicting the Coronation of the Virgin, includes two angels with compressed but still open S-shaped trumpets (an unimportant difference from the closed form or twice-folded instrument). The artist has taken the trouble to show one instrument extended and the other drawn in towards the player. The difference of extension is much greater than shown by Memling. If the instruments were fixed pitch it does seem rather odd that one should have such a long first yard and the other so short a one by comparison. Since the instruments are identical, except for the difference in length of their first yards, a comparison of their total lengths is in a ratio of just under 9:8. This is corroborated by the findings of Sachs (1950, p. 65), who arrived at this ratio in another way. The ratio of 9:8 is equal to the interval of a major second, which means that while one trumpet is playing in the closed position, the other is playing in a position that will produce an overtone series one tone lower. If it is also possible to assume that these instruments have a sliding mouthpiece pipe within their first yards, it is simple to calculate how far they might extend the bore before the instrument and slide parted. The greatest distance the mouthpiece pipe could be extended is just less than the length of the first yard. Its ultimate extension can only be approximately its own length. Thus, adding the total lengths of the instrument in closed position to the length of its first yard, we arrive at the ratio of 5:4. This is the ratio of the interval of a major third. The implication is that the instrument could lower its primary harmonic series by four semitones. Of course, there are limitations to the possible extension of an instrument, because of the reach of a player's arm; but in this case the player could easily reach to the limits of the instrument itself.

In the *Coronation of the Virgin* by the Meister des Marienlebens we again have the figure of the Virgin surrounded by singers and instrumentalists. Harrison & Rimmer (1964, illustration No. 83) reproduce the left side of the painting, showing three harps, three recorders and three lutes or possibly citterns. An examination of the painting itself shows a remarkable trumpet on the right side being played with three shawms (with pirouettes), two lutes, and a form of bowed stringed instrument resembling a rebec or fidel. With an uncanny anticipation of the flat trumpet described by Talbot,[3] the anonymous fifteenth-century painter has reproduced what is obviously a slide trumpet (Pl. 2). It is actually a single slide archetypal alto trombone; but its mouthpiece, like that of the flat trumpet, 'stands oblique' to the rest of the instrument, allowing the second bow and yards

[3] *See* Chapter 1, footnote 12.

to pass the player's ear in the upper positions. The angel player is holding the instrument in the usual manner: left hand grasping the mouthpiece (and sliding pipe?) close to the lips, the right hand not only holding the second yard but supporting the bell with the index finger around the flange, with the other fingers (partially hidden) on the bell itself. The instrument seems to be shown in an extended position. It is twice folded, but its second yard is longer than the first, with the bell not quite reaching the first bow. This may be the reason why the player is supporting the bell. Without any cordage or other means of making the instrument more rigid, the various bits would be too elastic and could be easily damaged. Since all the other instruments in the painting are normal for the period, there is no reason to suppose that this possible precursor of the trombone was not a reality.

So far, we have mainly discussed trumpets of possible variable pitch. During this time, however, the natural trumpet was beginning to take on its 'classic' dimensions: oblong, twice folded and fixed pitch. Vivarini's *Adoration of the Magi* included one partially obscured folded trumpet, and the two trumpets in the Memling triptych, regardless of their chromatic possibilities, were also folded. A celebrated manuscript in the Musée Condé at Chantilly, known as 'Les très riches heures du duc de Berry', contains a handsome series of illuminations. One of these, entitled *Mai— La Ville de Riom* (folio 5), shows a cavalcade with five trumpets leading the procession. Two of the trumpets are obscured, but there seem to be three oblong folded instruments and two straight. These pictures date from the first quarter of the fifteenth century. The transition from the open S-shape to the closed form was relatively quick.

By the first half of the sixteenth century the natural trumpet had assumed the proportions it was to have for the next two hundred years. In the famous series of early sixteenth-century woodcuts by Hans Burgkmair and other Augsburg and Nuremberg artists, *The Triumphs of Maximilian I*, are a number of illustrations showing carriages filled with musicians playing a large assortment of instruments. The trumpets are all similar to the usual Baroque instrument: oblong, twice folded, with yards of equal length. Similarly, a detail from Hogenberg's *Entry of the Emperor Charles V into Bologna* (Pl. 3) shows two mounted trumpeters and timpanists. The trumpets are again the standard Baroque shape, and shown with flames streaming from their bells (!); unless perhaps the artist has represented the condensation of the players' breath as a vivid reminder of the frigid weather in Bologna during February.

In Albrecht Dürer's magnificent *Triumphal Arch*, commissioned while he was in the service of Maximilian I, and finished in 1515, there are trumpets and timpani. The enormous composition of ninety-two wood blocks shows a trumpet and a pair of timpani at the top of each central column. The trumpets are somewhat 'fantastic', with their bells bent at an upward angle, but the instruments are wrapped with cordage and material in the usual Baroque fashion. They are played with one hand in the typical manner shown in seventeenth- and eighteenth-century illustrations. At the top of the work are two straight trumpets held in the Renaissance manner: one hand at the mouthpiece, the other farther along the instrument. Dürer's reproduction of the two trumpets with the timpani is the earliest with a type of cordage noted by the present writer.

While the natural trumpet was in process of establishing itself in the social complex of Renaissance court and military life, the variable-pitch instrument continued to survive. Besseler (1950, pp. 8–35) has suggested that it was at this time that the trombone had evolved from the chromatic trumpet. The trumpet in the *Coronation of the Virgin* by the Meister des Marienlebens would seem to support this idea. Sachs (1950, p. 66) arrived at the same conclusion: 'The trombone, which, in its modern form with one U-turn reaching behind the player's ear, appeared in the fifteenth century is . . . only a logical development of the slide trumpet.' A curious hybrid slide trumpet appears in a very long and wide woodcut by the Venetian Matteo Pagan. The work is from the early sixteenth century and is called the *Processione dogale*. It is found in the 'Sala Quattro' of the Museo Civico at Venice and shows a large procession of Venetian dignitaries, clerics, musicians and citizens in the Piazza di San Marco. The trumpets are called 'Trombe Pifeari'. One of them closely resembles an alto trombone, but without the second bow and yards projecting behind the player. In some respects it is like the Meister des Marienlebens' trumpet, but there are two braces between the first and second yards near the first bow. From the playing position and the shape of the instrument it is apparently a single slide trumpet of unique design.

A slide trumpet similar in proportions to the 1651 Naumburg *Zugtrompete* is shown in Hermann Finck's *Practica Musica* (1556). The title-page woodcut shows a group of singers around a large open part-book on a lectern with two crumhorn players standing behind and a trumpeter in the foreground. The trumpet resembles an ordinary oblong Baroque instrument, but with a narrow, conically shaped bell. The first yard is elongated, and the player has his left hand on the mouthpiece and is holding the instrument in his other hand midway along the second yard. The open part-book is in the usual sixteenth-century format: the descant, alto, tenor and bass are divided between the two opposing folios. A fixed-pitch trumpet could never hope to perform any of the diatonic parts normally found in Renaissance music. But if such an instrument could alter its harmonic series sufficiently by elongating the first yard, most descant or alto parts could be played. Agricola (1529) may have been alluding to this possibility:

> Etliche aber haben der löcher keyns
> Nur allein oben vnd vnden eyns
> Auff diesen wird die melody allein
> Durchs blasen vnd ziehen gefüret rein
> Als sein Busaun Trumeten vnd Claret

literally translated as:

> But some [instruments] have no holes,
> only one above and one below;
> on these the melody can only be made clear
> through blowing and tugging.
> Such are trombones, trumpets and clarets.

One interesting point emerges from Agricola's doggerel: he applies the same technique ('blasen und ziehen') to all three instruments without any differentiation. Neither he nor Virdung (1511) say what a 'claret' is, but it may have been of variable pitch. The illustation of the *Clareta* in Virdung (1511, fo. C r.) shows an instrument with slight but unimportant differences from the natural trumpet.

A particularly illuminating iconographic source is the title-page woodcut in Elias Ammerbach's *Orgel oder Instrument Tabulatur* (Leipzig, 1571). A copy in the British Museum shows a group of instrumentalists gathered around a table on which has been placed a portative organ. The wind instruments being played are a bass shawm, a flute and, undoubtedly, two *Zugtrompeten*. Wustmann (1909, pp. 72–4) describes the same illustration as 'Leipziger Tischmusik', and theorizes as to the kind of music that was probably played by such an ensemble.

One of the last iconographic sources of the *Zugtrompete* is found in a small anonymous woodcut from the *Nobilita di dame* (Venice, 1605). An original copy in the New York Metropolitan Museum of Art shows ten female figures—eight playing an assortment of wind and stringed instruments, one playing a tambourin, and one with an open book in an attitude of singing. The fourth instrument from the left is a fully extended *tromba da tirarsi* with a very important clue regarding its peculiar design and function. There is a minuscule line at the point where the exposed length of mouthpiece pipe would be expected to join the first yard of the extended instrument. It is almost certain that this line was included to imply that the tube is not one continuous piece, but rather one tube inserted into another. The playing position is as follows: right hand holding the mouthpiece pipe; left hand holding the instrument at the second bow—the one nearest the player. The instrument is pointed downwards and the bell is partially hidden in the folds of the player's garment.

If we assume that some Renaissance trumpets were capable of producing more than the few scattered notes of the harmonic series—and the iconographic evidence would seem to support this idea—it is then important to reach some conclusion as to the possible range and compass of these instruments. Sachs (1950, pp. 62–4) was one of the first to suggest that fifteenth- and sixteenth-century trumpets had a much wider scope than the hitherto assumed triadic 'overblown' notes of the fixed-pitch natural trumpet. He likened the probable variable-pitch trumpets, noted from several quoted iconographic sources, to the *tromba da tirarsi*, formerly belonging to the collection of musical instruments in the Staatliches Hochschule für Musik at Berlin. This is the previously mentioned Naumburg *Zugtrompete*, the kind of instrument specifically required in Bach's cantatas *BWV* 5, 20, 46, 67, 77, 124 and 162. It was an ordinary twicefolded trumpet normally in E flat with the distinctive feature of a telescoping, or sliding, mouthpiece pipe. We have already said that, like the trombone, it was capable of sounding more than one harmonic series, depending upon how far the air column was extended. From the fact that many of the instruments found in fifteenth-century painting and statuary closely resemble the *tromba da tirarsi*, Sachs, Besseler and others concluded that Renaissance composers did avail themselves of variable-pitch trumpets in the performance of polyphonic music.

An interesting question is whether or not Renaissance trumpets had many performance possibilities. This would depend, to some extent, on their tuning. We may suppose that, in addition to the trumpet tuned in F, '. . . the obviously usual variety . . .',[4] there were at least three other possible tunings: C, D and E flat. Although there are no surviving instru-

---

[4] Sachs, 1950, p. 63.

ments to substantiate these tunings, and any measurements taken from contemporary art would only prove inconclusive, it does seem from slightly later practice that the lower tunings would have been the more likely choice. This will be seen from a discussion of the various harmonic series available for the above-mentioned tunings, the few surviving musical examples, as well as the point that almost all late Renaissance-early Baroque brass instruments were tuned in C, D or E flat. The greatest difficulty in trying to assess the extent to which the instruments of the period were chromatic is to determine the number of positions to which the slide could be extended. The greater the length of extended tubing, the lower the pitch. Hence, a larger number of harmonic series are available to the performer. The limits of position number are, of course, the length of telescoping tubing and, more importantly, the distance which the player's arm can reach. The significant technological advance made in the latter half of the fifteenth century, with the development of the trombone, was the implementation of the double slide, or U-slide. There are two definite advantages in this: firstly, it alleviates having to move the heavier of the two components (the slide is moved, not the instrument), while still keeping the mouthpiece placed firmly against the lips; secondly, and most important, it extends the number of playing positions, limited in the case of a single slide by the length of the player's arm. The reason for this is that the player, while moving both parallel sleeves of tubing with one motion, is actually extending or diminishing the total length of the air column by the amount of tubing added or subtracted on each half of the slide. Thus, for a given extension of position by a trombonist, the Renaissance trumpeter would have had to extend his slide twice that length for the same effect.

The next question is concerned with the number of possible slide-extension positions on a Renaissance trumpet. If we mean that each position extends the air column to such a length that it lowers the pitch by one semitone (this is the usual accepted meaning by a trombonist for 'position') and we are talking about an instrument tuned in D, i.e. an instrument of approximately seven and a half feet in its total length, then the distance necessary to lower a given pitch by one semitone would be about five inches. If the playing position of trumpeters in Renaissance painting is the usual one, we can then be certain that the total number of slide positions could not have been more than four. This is substantiated by Sachs's description of the Naumburg *Zugtrompete*.[5] Some measurements

[5] Sachs, 1922, p. 221.

made by the present writer on a natural trumpet in D and an early nineteenth-century English slide trumpet in F by the London maker Charles Pace corroborate Sachs's remarks and the conclusions drawn from Renaissance art: that the total number of slide positions would not have exceeded four on a C or D trumpet.

The measurements obtained from the trumpet tuned in D—a modern German reproduction of an early Baroque natural trumpet—are as follows:

Total length of the air column:	*c.* 91 inches
Ratio of the cylindrical bore to the conical section:	5:1
Inside diameter of the cylindrical section:	$\frac{15}{32}$ inch
Inside diameter of the slide:	$\frac{7}{16}$ inch
Length of extended tubing necessary to lower the fourth harmonic (*d*) by one semitone:	5 + inches

The measurements for the slide trumpet tuned in F were relatively the same, that is, because the total length of tubing is somewhat shorter than the D trumpet (72 inches) the other measurements are proportionately less (the distance from first to second position is $3\frac{3}{4}$ inches). The inverse ratio from first to second position was still 16:15, or the equivalent of a semitone.

If, then, we carry these values to the fourth position, we find that the distance traversed by the sliding portion of the air column is nearly fifteen inches for a trumpet tuned in D. This means that if the right hand is holding a trumpet in the manner suggested by pictorial evidence, where the arm is about half extended in the first position, it will be fully extended in the fourth (assuming that an object held straight out at arm's length, between the right thumb and index finger, is about 30–32 inches for an adult).

In translating the preceding suppositions and data into musical information it will be seen from Examples 3 and 4 that any one of the tunings given can produce in the four available semitone positions a nearly complete chromatic compass of two and a half octaves. Example 3 shows the probable compass for each of the four positions for a single-slide, 8-foot trumpet in C, with the corresponding harmonics indicated by the numbers above and the positions by the numbers to the left. Example 4 gives the full range for the particular tuning; the white notes indicate the available harmonics in the first position (again, numbered above); the black notes are the tones of the extended positions. Each tone has its corresponding position number given below, as well as an alternative position, shown in parentheses, resulting from an overlapping of some pitches in the four harmonic series. The brackets indicate where the gaps occur in the almost complete chromatic compass. The most serious interruption occurs between the second harmonic and the fourth position tone of the third harmonic. The only other interruption is the missing semitone between the third harmonic and the fourth position tone of the fourth harmonic. This, however, could be easily remedied by 'lipping' down, or flatting the latter.

Exs. 3, 4. Available notes and positions for a theoretical Renaissance chromatic trumpet.

Ex. 3.

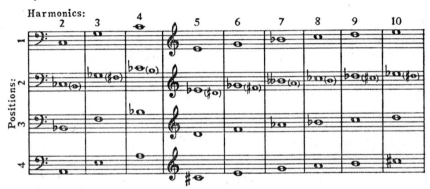

Ex. 4.

Some of the early music itself provides more evidence to support the idea of variable-pitch trumpets having been used in its performance. Before the Baroque era, indications of scoring are almost nil. There are some fifteenth-century sources, however, that do give an indication that trumpets may have been used in the performance of motets, masses and other musical compositions. From the same period as Vivarini's *Adoration of the Magi*, and just prior to the date of Memling's triptych (1480) and Pacher's altar-piece carvings (1481), we have at least seven manuscript musical sources by Arnold de Lantins, Johannes Franchoys, Henricus de Libero Castro, Guillaume Dufay and others which include terms such as 'Contratenor Trompette', 'Trumpetta Introitus' or 'Ad modum tubae'. In the light of contemporary iconography and the Court and church records mentioning trumpets and payment to trumpeters,[6] these terms suggest that trumpets may well have been intended in performances of this kind of music.

How do the ranges and notes required in this music compare with the theoretical performance possibilities of a Renaissance trumpet? The following examples (Ex. 5a–g) give the ranges and inclusive notes of known fifteenth-century pieces with the previously mentioned scoring attributions. Modern transcriptions and editions are noted, as well as bibliographic information about the original sources.

In every case but Dufay's *Et in terra* 'Ad modum tubae' (Ex. 5c), a variable-pitch trumpet would be required. The Dufay example requires only the third, fourth, fifth and sixth harmonics of a fixed-pitch trumpet in C. The presence of a D in Exs. 5d–g presents some difficulty. In terms of the theoretical possibilities of the available positions and notes outlined above, this is the missing interval of a major second between harmonic two and position four of the third harmonic. However, like the frequent non-harmonic tones in seventeenth- and eighteenth-century trumpet parts, this not very frequent note may have been forced or 'lipped' from either of the adjacent notes (up from C or down from E). The only part that presents real difficulties is the version of Pierre Fontaine's *J'ayme bien* in MS. Escorial v. iii (Ex. 5d). A possible explanation of its wide compass is an intended transposition a fourth or fifth higher.

Taking into account the possibilities of transpositions and the not very difficult alteration to produce the infrequent D, all of these pieces from the same period and from the following century may have been composed with similar intentions of performance. The so-called 'sacred song by

[*continued on page 48*]

---

[6] For quotations of payment records to Church and Court trumpeters in Italy during the fifteenth and sixteenth centuries, see *Note d'Archivio* (various articles appearing between 1924 and 1930).

Ex. 5a–g. Ranges and notes required of fifteenth-century music where trumpets are suggested.

5a. Arnoldus de Lantins: *Et in terra pax.*

Contratenor: 'Tuba sub fuga'.

Source: Oxford: B.L. MS. Canonici Misc. 213, fol. 64–64ᵛ. See *Polyphonia Sacra*, ed. by Charles van den Borren, London, 1932, p. 10 (repr. 1962).

5b. Grossim: *Patrem omnipotentem.*

Contratenor: 'Trompette'.

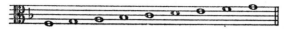

Source: Aosta Seminary Library, MS. Ao, folio 112 recto. See Guillaume De Van, 'A recently discovered source of early fifteenth-century polyphonic music', *Musica Disciplina*, ii, 1948, p. 5 ff.

5c. Dufay: *Et in terra pax.*

Tenor, contratenor: 'Ad modum tubae'.

Tenor   C. tenor

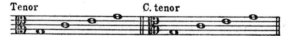

Source: Trento, Castello del Buon Consiglio, Cod. MS. 90, folio 131ᵛ. See *DTÖ*, vol. vii, 1900, p. 145.

5d. Pierre Fontaine: *J'ayme bien.*

Contratenor: 'Trompette'.

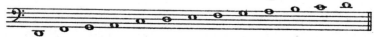

Source: MS. Escorial v. iii; facs. repr. in *Documenta Musicologica*, ed. by W. Rehn, Kassel, 1958. See Pierre Aubry, 1907. See also *NOHM*, vol. iii, pp. 425–6.

5e. Johannes Francho(y)s: *Ave virgo.*

Contratenor: 'Trumpetta Introitus'.

Source: Bologna, B.C. (Liceo Musicale): Cod. 37, folio 240ᵛ–241. See *DTÖ*, vol. xl, 1933, pp. 19–21.

5f. Henricus de Libero Castro (Heinrich von Laufenburg?): *Virgo dulcis.*

Tenor: 'Laudate eum in sono tube'.

Contratenor: 'Tube'.

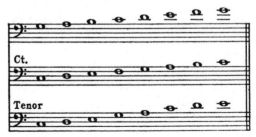

Source: Lost Strasbourg MS. M. 222 C. 22; copy by Edmond de Coussemaker. *See* note 8, below.

5g. Anonymous: *Tuba gallicalis.*

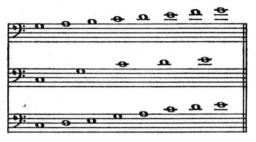

Source: Lost Strasbourg MS. M. 222 C. 22; copy by Edmond de Coussemaker. *See* facsimile in *MGG*, ii, Kassel, 1952, col. 1757. *See* note 8, below.

Henry of Freiburg', mentioned as having trumpet fanfare motives,[7] is, incidentally, the *Virgo dulcis* a 3 by Henricus de Libero Castro (the tenor of which has the psalm text 'Laudate eum in sono tube') given in Ex. 5f, and from the same lost Strasbourg MS. as the *Tuba gallicalis* (Ex. 5g).[8] Susato in 1551 (1936, Heft 1, p. 11) published a 'Mohrentanz' in which the *discantus* noticeably avoids all but one non-harmonic tone of a natural trumpet (except for the natural 7th harmonic, which occurs only twice; all the other notes are within the harmonic series of a C trumpet).

Since a variable-pitch trumpet was a melodic instrument, capable of

[7] Rokseth, 1960, p. 425.

[8] Strasbourg MS. 222 C. 22, destroyed by fire during the war of 1870, contained 207 pieces, of which 52 survive in copies made by Coussemaker; a number of others were known to concord with surviving MSS. *See* Van den Borren, 1924–7.

sounding more than one harmonic series, it is difficult to know in what other fifteenth- and sixteenth-century pieces it could have been intended for performance. The music may not always be the best source of information. Only Dufay's parts (Ex. 5c) and the contratenor of the *Tuba gallicalis* (Ex. 5g) have much trumpet writing in the usual sense of overblown notes. But the examples mentioned previously do serve as further evidence that trumpets were most likely used in a manner long suggested in painting, sculpture and other iconographic sources of the late fifteenth and early sixteenth centuries.

All these sources only confirm a basic concept of evolution theory: that few if any species materialize suddenly and without some relation to earlier forms. The Baroque trumpet did not suddenly appear in seventeenth-century scoring indications without having been part of an earlier musical tradition. The transition from one type of trumpet to the natural Baroque form may have been rapid and may have been precipitated by many causes, but there is little doubt that trumpets were employed in art music before composers thought positive scoring indications were necessary.

3 BAROQUE EUROPEAN TRUMPET-MAKERS AND THEIR INSTRUMENTS

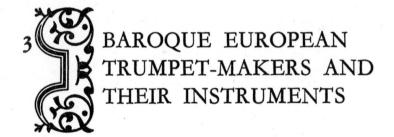

With the advent of protective guilds and clearly defined divisions of labour, specialization in arts and crafts led to the kind of technological expertise associated with the Renaissance. Highly skilled performers and composers made heavy demands upon instrument-makers, and the manufacturing innovations of the fifteenth and sixteenth centuries had great consequences in the performance of music.

Some of the important Renaissance achievements in metal-working, for instance the development of new alloys and new methods of fabricating designs, have special significance in the art of trumpet-making. A seemingly inconsequential innovation, but one which had an enormous effect on brass instrument-making, was the technique of bending a metal tube into a small curve. At first this may not seem very important or a very difficult operation, but one of the reasons for the long straight trumpets before the fifteenth century, and for the wide, sweeping curves of Roman type *lituii*, was the difficulty in bending a thin-walled brass or copper tube into a narrow curve. To achieve this without kinking the tube or flattening its cylindrical shape, some long-forgotten metalsmith hit upon the idea of filling a straight tube with molten lead and, when the latter solidified, shaping the tube to the desired curve.[1] The soft but dense lead, with

[1] In Galpin (*PMA* 1906–7) there is a photograph of a Roman trumpet reproduced in a fresco discovered at Pompeii in 1892. According to Galpin '. . . it clearly shows that the Romans had a form of Trumpet with a "folded" tube similar to the modern military Trumpet—a discovery as interesting as it is novel.' The ancients may have succeeded, by whatever means, in bending a narrow metal tube into a small curve, but it is my opinion that the technique had been completely forgotten and was discovered anew by some European metalworker sometime in the fourteenth century.

a lower melting point than the relatively soft copper or brass, prevents the tube from bending irregularly, i.e. the inside portion of the curve buckling as a result of the formation of unequal radii between the inner and outer curvature of the cylindrical walls. When the desired degree of curvature is achieved, usually 180 degrees, the tube is heated to the melting point of the contained lead, which is then poured out.

Another metallurgical advance was the mercuric amalgamation of copper, silver or brass with gold. This had particular significance in the highly decorated and exquisitely fashioned ceremonial trumpets used for state occasions. Also, the techniques of casting and engraving which reached such perfection in the work of Renaissance artists like Benvenuto Cellini were reflected in the artistically produced state or herald trumpets manufactured at Nuremberg. Precision-made matrices for casting were highly prized and handed down from father to son in a family of master craftsmen.

The most important acoustical development in trumpet-making was the exponential bell. The Italians seem to have made the earliest progress in this direction. The Ubaldo Montini trumpet, to be described later, has such a bell; it is one of the earliest instruments to employ this acoustical principle. As we have seen in the discussion of trumpet acoustics in Chapter 1, an exponential bell, as opposed to the usual sixteenth-century funnel-shaped or cone-section bell, has the property of transmitting sound waves more efficiently into the atmosphere. The curvature of the transmitted sound waves emitted from the open end of a truncated cone is changed abruptly, so that the upper harmonics tend to be distorted.

Having instituted a hierarchical system of apprentices, journeymen and masters, to ensure a continuation of excellence in craftsmanship, the established traditions of the Renaissance guilds were maintained well into the eighteenth century. This is particularly evident in the continuity of production among the Nuremberg makers. In other areas, notably England, the art of trumpet-making was taken up by relatively few craftsmen and at a comparatively later date. Although, as we shall see, trumpet-makers were known in Britain before the seventeenth century, there seems never to have been anything like a guild of brass instrument-makers or an established tradition comparable to that in southern Germany. The important contributions were made by a few individual makers toward the end of the seventeenth century.

The purpose of this chapter is to consider the art of trumpet-making in Europe before the end of the eighteenth century and to discuss the significant instruments that have survived. To analyse the work of every important craftsman, especially in the Nuremberg tradition, would be within the scope only of a special study on the subject. Unfortunately there is as yet no comprehensive publication in any language that deals with the history of brass instrument-makers and their instruments. There are several invaluable studies of specific makers and centres of manufacturing, and these will be mentioned. As regards the long list of important Nuremberg makers, our discussion is limited to one representative family of craftsmen whose instruments are found in many collections and who, it is thought, made the most significant contributions.

One of the oldest trumpets of European manufacture known to have survived until the Second World War was an Italian instrument in the famous Berlin collection at the Hochschule für Musik. Described by Curt Sachs in his comprehensive catalogue [2] of that collection, compiled while he was curator, the trumpet bore a maker's mark and the inscription, *Vbaldo/ Montini/ in Siena/ 1523*. A photograph of the instrument is given as Pl. 24 in Sachs's illustrations. Sachs is probably correct in stating that the Siena trumpet is the oldest known dated instrument. Anthony Baines in his article on the trumpet in *Grove's Dictionary of Music and Musicians* states that 'The oldest surviving specimens are rare sixteenth-century work by the famous Nuremberg maker Anton Schnitzer...' [3] In the list of Nuremberg brass-makers given in Table I (page 64 ff.), it will be seen that Anton Schnitzer the Elder became a master in his art in 1562 and his son, Anton the Younger, in 1591. It is unlikely that either of these famous Nuremberg craftsmen could have made an instrument pre-dating the Montini Siena trumpet of 1523. [4] Inasmuch as Anton Schnitzer the Elder's birthdate is unknown (he died in 1608), it is difficult to fix his age with any precision when he became a master in 1562. The title of master was usually conferred upon an artisan in his late twenties after an unspecified period as an apprentice and journeyman, but it would have been difficult for him to have made an instrument as early as 1523. The oldest members of the Schnitzer family were Erasmus and Hans the Elder, both dying in 1566. It might have been possible for them to have made instruments forty-three years earlier, but it is unlikely that their marks would have appeared

[2] Sachs, 1922, p. 221–2.

[3] *GDMM*, viii, p. 565.

[4] The two instruments, which are in the Vienna Kunsthistorisches Museum, are a silver trumpet with gold ornaments and an intricately coiled brass trumpet, dated 1581 (Pl. 4) and 1598 (Pl. 5) respectively.

on a trumpet made at that time (the master to whom they were probably then apprenticed would have added his own mark).

According to Galilei (1581, p. 146), brass instruments are believed to have been invented and first manufactured in Nuremberg, and Hawkins mentions trumpets by one of the oldest and most respected of Nuremberg brass-makers, Hans Neuschel (*c.* 1465–1533):

. . . and there is extant a memoir which shews that trumpets were made to great perfection by an artist in that city [Nuremberg], who was also an admired performer on that instrument, it is as follows: 'Hans Meuschel of Nuremberg, for his accuracy in making trumpets, as also for his skill in playing on the same alone, and in the accompanyment with the voice, was of so great renown, that he was frequently sent for to the palaces of princes the distance of several hundred miles. Pope Leo x, for whom he had made sundry trumpets of silver, sent for him to Rome, and after having been delighted with his exquisite performance, dismissed him with a munificent reward.' [5]

The association of other members of the Neuschel family with the Holy See and various princes of Europe will be mentioned later in this chapter.

It is doubtful whether Nuremberg produced the first trumpets. The importance of Vincenzo Galilei's observation is, however, that Nuremberg was obviously held in high repute for its manufacture of trumpets and other musical instruments. By the middle of the seventeenth century it was certainly the foremost centre of brass and wood-wind instrument-making. But what of the other European cities whose makers wrought in silver and brass some of the most exquisite examples in the art of trumpet-making? The surviving work of non-German makers is not extensive, but what has come down to us seem to be representative samples from highly skilled and artistic craftsmen.

Judging from the quantity of brass instruments depicted in iconographic sources from the Middle Ages to the end of the seventeenth century, the actual number of instruments was probably very large. Certainly those observed by the painters, poets and chroniclers originated in workshops scattered all over Europe. The work of some makers was prolific, while others seem to have restricted their activities to the local requirements of their own cities. Closson (1935) mentions several makers whose instruments have not survived but who were in all likelihood highly

[5] Hawkins, 1853, vol. ii, p. 612, note 1.

regarded in their own cities in the Netherlands. Perhaps the instruments reproduced in the paintings of Memling and Van Eyck originated in the workshops of the fifteenth-century Flemish makers Pierre Bogaerts, Gui Compains and Jean de Thouraine.[6]

The Italians, who, as we have already seen, had access to Nuremberg instruments, seem to have produced very few brass instruments during the sixteenth and seventeenth centuries. Besides Ubaldo Montini, who worked in Siena, the only other Italian trumpet-maker that has been noted is a fifteenth-century Milanese craftsman by the name of Antonio. He is mentioned by L. F. Valdrighi in the 1888 supplement to his *Nomocheliurgographia*, published in Modena, 1884. But according to Langwill (1962, p. 3) no instruments by this maker have survived.

The French seem to have engaged in the art of trumpet-making at a very early date. A Parisian maker, Roger L'Englois, is said to have made trumpets in 1293.[7] Needless to say we are not so fortunate as to possess any of his instruments, which might have saved much guesswork and *théories nouvelles* concerning the details of medieval trumpets. Another of the medieval French instrument-makers cited by Constant Pierre[8] is Guillaume d'Amiens, who is reputed to have made trumpets. In the sixteenth century, Hanus Malherbe (?–1560) is said to have worked in Sedan, Lorraine, and to have made *trompes de chasse*.[9] Jacquot (1882, p. 60) also mentions a French maker of *trompes de chasse*, Jacques Pichommi, who worked in the city of Nancy in 1564. But none of Malherbe's or Pichommi's *trompes de chasse* has survived.

There are, however, instruments by a seventeenth-century family of French brass-makers. Working in Normandy, the family of Crétien supplied the courts of Louis XIII and Louis XIV with trumpets, horns and bugles. An early seventeenth-century hunting horn by Crétien is in the collection of the Paris Conservatoire (No. 573); a bugle made by R. Crétien is included in the Sachs Berlin catalogue mentioned earlier (No. 3014), as well as three hunting horns also in the Paris Conservatoire (Nos. 575–7). Another Crétien, probably a son of the latter, worked during the reign of Louis XIV. One of his instruments, a *trompe de chasse*, is in the Paris Conservatoire (No. 578). There is enough French music with trumpet parts as well as a significant corpus of iconographic evidence to justify our supposing the existence of many more makers. In all probability there were several French trumpet-makers in the sixteenth and seventeenth

[6] Closson, 1935, pp. 68–74; *see* also Van der Straeten, 1878, vol. iv. p. 196.
[7] Pierre, 1893, p. 8.   [8] *Ibid.*   [9] *Ibid.*, p. 62.

centuries, but, unfortunately, too few instruments survive to allow more than mere speculation.

Before discussing the important contributions of the English and German trumpet-makers, with particular emphasis on the Nuremberg craftsmen, it will be worth noting the legacy of those continental artisans not already mentioned. European collections abound in brass instruments of all ages and from many countries. One of particular interest, though not an instrument collection in the usual sense, is the Armoury within the walls of the Kremlin at Moscow. On a recent trip to the Soviet Union the present writer noticed in one of the Armoury exhibitions a rather odd display of trumpets. Arranged in a floral-like display were several valuable seventeenth-century trumpets by reputable Nuremberg craftsmen, as well as two by a lesser-known Dutch maker, Graft van de Joost. None of these instruments appears to be catalogued or described in any publication; nor are any of the Dutch and German instruments in the Hermitage at Leningrad. It is supposed that the latter were acquired about the time Peter I of Russia purchased the large collections of Flemish art and German silver and pewter toward the end of the seventeenth century.

Trumpet-makers worked as far north as Stockholm and Copenhagen, and the Claudius collection in Copenhagen has a fine specimen by the Swedish maker and *Hof- und Feldtrummeter* Georg Nicolaus Oller, who worked in the mid seventeenth century (Claudius No. 527). Sachs (1913, p. 400) mentions a Danish mathematician, Christian Otter, who designed a curious and as yet unknown type of trumpet, a *tuba hercotectonica*, for Christian IV, King of Denmark and Sweden, 1588–1648.

Although little is known about trumpet-making in the Iberian Peninsula, the catalogue of the instrument collection at Lisbon [10] mentions a trumpet-maker by the name of João Nuñes who worked in Lisbon about 1650. The Spanish seem to have imported brass instruments, for there is little or no information about any Spanish makers during the sixteenth and seventeenth centuries. Since there is a relative correlation between the number of trumpet-makers, the quantity of players and the amount of music written for the instrument in a particular location, a look at the Appendix will show that the Iberian Peninsula was the least productive area of Europe for trumpet music. The almost complete absence of non-military trumpet music in seventeenth-century Spain parallels the dearth of instruments, makers and performers.

A few important trumpet-makers in the Austro-Bohemian principalities,

[10] Lambertini, 1914.

including the musically active centres of Vienna, Prague and Kroměříž, would seem to contradict the correlation of the number of makers with the quantity of music. But from the time of Maximilian I these Hapsburg areas depended largely upon Nuremberg craftsmen, importing instruments, armour and various other items manufactured in that city. Nevertheless, two Austro-Bohemian makers should be mentioned: the seventeenth-century Viennese craftsman Hans Geyer and the seventeenth–eighteenth-century Prague craftsman Josef Wolf. A pair of trumpets by the former, both dated 1690, are found in the Kunsthistorisches Museum at Vienna; another, dated 1684, in Copenhagen's Music History Museum; and a pair of trombones, dated 1676, in the Linz Oberösterreichisches Landesmuseum. The two surviving instruments by Josef Wolf (a trumpet in the Boston Museum of Fine Arts and another in the National Museum at Prague) indicate a style similar to that of the late seventeenth-century Nuremberg trumpet-makers.

The Swiss were not without trumpet-makers. Although they too seem to have relied upon South German makers, especially in the seventeenth and eighteenth centuries, there is evidence of an older tradition. In the Historical Museum at Basel are two trumpets by the late sixteenth-century Basel *Stadtpfeifer*, Jacob Steiger. Both instruments are dated 1578 and are stylistically similar to most other contemporary trumpets. Another trumpet in the Basel collection, also dated 1578, is a silver state trumpet inscribed 'Jacobs'. This is undoubtedly a third instrument by Jacob Steiger. There seem to have been brass instruments made at Zürich during the latter part of the seventeenth century. Langwill mentions a Jakob Balber, 'Zurich, 1671–1725. Coppersmith and Brass Inst. mkr.'[11] None of his instruments, however, seems to have survived.

The art of trumpet-making flourished in seventeenth-century England. The number of instruments that survive is not large, but those that have endured the wear and tear of time indicate a highly developed and rare craftsmanship. By the end of the 1600s there was enough of an industry for Chamberlayne [12] to make this passing comment:

Other late inventions there are, not unworthy to be mentioned. An engine for Rasing of Glass, an Engine for Spinning of Glass, an Engine for Cutting Tobacco, the Rolling Press for Printing off from Copper Plates. . . . The way of separating Gold from Silver. Enamelling in Gold, Silver and Brass; Boulting Mills, Dark Lanthorns, the Trumpet-makers Trade. . . .

[11] Langwill, 1962, p. 4.   [12] Chamberlayne, 1683, Part iii, pp. 267–8.

It is difficult to know if seventeenth-century English trumpet-making techniques were a continuation of an older indigenous tradition. There are scant records of earlier makers. Cart de Lafontaine (1909,[13] p. 27) mentions a George Langdale who received payments for livery as a trumpeter to Elizabeth I in January 1567; he is last mentioned in the court records of James I in 1603 as one of sixteen trumpeters. It was Langdale (or Langdall) who was granted a privilege to make trumpets and sackbuts in about 1585.[14] Apparently this privilege was granted to Langdale by Sir Francis Walsyngham after having been petitioned by the brass-maker Simon Brewer '. . . to be allowed to exercise his trade'.[15] The latter is not mentioned in the court records of Elizabeth I as being a trumpeter. Most sixteenth- and seventeenth-century European brass-makers were also players, and it is possible that Brewer may have been a trumpeter to lesser nobility, which may account for his petition being refused in preference to one of Elizabeth's trumpeters. Unfortunately no instruments of either Langdale or Brewer are known to have survived.

Another English trumpet-maker-player whose instruments no longer exist, but who is mentioned in the court records of Charles I, is Cuthbert Collins. First mention of his name is in March 1625 as having been newly appointed as a trumpeter to Charles I (*KM*, p. 55). In October the following year his half wages were 'admitted' to full wages on the death of another trumpeter, Robert Browne (*KM*, p. 62). In February 1639 a warrant was issued for '. . . Cuthbert Collins to make twenty brass trumpets for his Majesty's service into the northern parts' (*KM*, p. 103); a year later he was paid sixty pounds for the twenty trumpets. His name last appears in a list of 'Trumpettors' in 1641 (*KM*, p. 110).

The oldest surviving English trumpet is by the London maker Augustine Dudley. It is listed in Langwill (1962, p. 28) as a 'Field trumpet' and is dated 1651. It is owned by the London Museum and illustrated in the *Galpin Society Journal* (vol. xv, 1962). The instrument is made of brass and has some silver ornaments. The ball was either removed or was never put on, and the bell is just slightly exponential. Its general appearance is similar to a William Bull trumpet also shown in the *Galpin Society Journal* photograph. Another Dudley trumpet, made of brass with silver mounts, was auctioned at Sotheby's in their 1964 November sale of musical

[13] Referred to in the text as *KM*.

[14] *BB.*, January, 1898, p. 5.

[15] Langwill, 1962, p. 12.

instruments. It was bought by the London Museum for over £400. It is dated 1666 and is more elaborately decorated than the 1651 instrument.

Little is known about Dudley. If he, like his contemporaries, was also a trumpeter, he is not mentioned in the court records before or after the Commonwealth. His two surviving instruments indicate the work of a skilled craftsman and are stylistically similar to other English trumpets whose general characteristics are given below.

Until 1939 there was known to exist a trumpet by a contemporary of Dudley, Simon Beale. The instrument was dated 1667 and was auctioned at Christie's in 1939. It disappeared for many years but turned up again at Christie's in October 1967; its present owner is Mr Michael Dalglish. Photographs of the instrument appear in the *Galpin Society Journal* (vol. xvi, 1963, and xxi, 1969). Beale was not only a maker of trumpets but also a trumpeter-in-ordinary to Charles II. He is frequently mentioned in the court records from the time of his appointment in June 1660 until February 1680, at which time his name appears in a petition '. . . against Joseph Walker, trumpeter' (*KM*, pp. 113–348). In January 1676 there was a 'Warrant for the delivery of one silver trumpett to Symon Beale, as one of the silver trumpets in his custody was lately lost and stolen from off the Horse Guard and cannot be heard of' (*KM*, p. 297). In the September 1675 list of instrument repairs (*KM*, p. 300) Beale was paid two pounds '. . . for mending and altering two recorders. . .'.

There are two references to Beale in Samuel Pepys's Diary:

16th [Dec. 1660] In the morning to church, and then dined at home. In the afternoon I to White Hall, where I was surprised with the news of a plot against the King's person and my Lord Monk's; and that since last night there are about forty taken up on suspicion; and amongst others, it was my lot to meet with Simon Beale, the Trumpeter, who took me and Tom Doling into the Guard in Scotland Yard, and showed us Major-General Overton where I heard him deny that he is guilty of any such things; but that whereas it is said that he is found to have brought many arms to town, he says it is only to sell them, as he will prove by oath.[16]

26th [Sept. 1668] . . . and so I away and walked to Charing Cross, and there into the great new Ordinary, by my Lord Mulgrave's, being led thither by Mr. Beale, one of Oliver's [Cromwell], and now of the King's Guards; and he sat with me while I had two grilled pigeons, very handsome and good meat: and there he and I

[16] Pepys (ed. Wheatley, 1893–9), vol. i, p. 307.

talked of our old acquaintances, W. Clerke and others, he [Beale] being a very civil man, and so walked to Westminster and there parted. . . .[17]

It is not known what became of Beale after his petition against Walker. It would be absurd to judge his work from photographs of one instrument, but that instrument is not typical of surviving seventeenth-century British trumpets.

Trumpet-making was not restricted to the city of London. In 1938 William Blandford examined a pair of seventeenth-century trumpets, both made in Glasgow.[18] The older of the two, a silver trumpet by Thomas McCuir, is dated 1669 with 'Glesgowe' (Glasgow) engraved on the bell. The other instrument is also of silver and made by 'Rot [Robert?] Brock' about 1675. Both are described by Halfpenny (*GSJ*, xxii, 1969, p. 54 ff.).

A late Restoration trumpet-maker was the fife player John Ashbury. One of his trade cards is preserved in the British Museum and indicates that his place of business was '. . . at ye corner of Peter's Court in St. Martin's Lane in the Fields'. On 12th April 1690 Ashbury was '. . . appointed fife, in the place of Clement Newth deceased' (*KM*, p. 399). Newth is shown and mentioned in Charles Sandford's *Coronation of James II* (Pl. 1 and p. 65).

The most important trumpet-maker in seventeenth-century England was William Bull. Like his contemporaries Beale and Collins, Bull was also a court trumpeter. He was appointed a trumpeter-extraordinary to the court of Charles II in July 1666, and attained the rank of trumpeter-in-ordinary in January 1678. Both he and Beale are mentioned by Chamberlayne (1679) as being trumpeters in the Queen's 2nd Troop Horse Guards in 1679. Bull was reappointed a trumpeter-in-ordinary on the accession of James II and is included with Mathias and William Shore in the 1685 list of appointments (*KM*, p. 370). He retained the post of trumpeter-in-ordinary during the reign of William and Mary.

Bull's services were obviously highly regarded, and his ability as a trumpet-player must have been on a par with that of Mathias and John Shore. All three accompanied William III to Holland in 1690, and the court records mention expenses paid to them for '. . . 103 daies . . .' in Holland (*KM*, pp. 404–5). In January 1700 a 'Mr Conrad Richter' was '. . . appointed in the room of Mr William Bull who surrendered' (*KM*, p. 436). On 20th June in the same year an advertisement in the London

---

[17] *Ibid.*, vol. viii, p. 114.
[18] Langwill, 1962, p. 13.

Post Boy gives a possible hint concerning Bull's resignation: 'William Bull, Trumpet Maker to His Majesty, who lately Lived at the Horn and Trumpet in the Hay-Market is Removed to the Horn and Trumpet in Castle street by Leicester-Fields, near the Muse, where all Gentlemen may be furnished with Hunting Horns and Trumpets, both Silver and Brass.'

Bull's trade card in the Banks Collection in the British Museum has the following information:

All Sorts of Trumpetts and Kettle Drums ffrench Hornes, Speaking Trumpetts, Hearing Hornes for Deafe people & all Sorts of powder flasks and allso Wind Gunes made and minded by William Bull Trumpett maker to his Maiestie—Who liveth att the Signe of the Trumpett and Horne in Castal Street Neare the Muyse.

In 1678, the year Bull was admitted as a trumpeter-in-ordinary to Charles II, the *London Gazette* (18th March 1678) stated: 'Trumpets either of Silver or Brass . . . are to be Sold at the Horne and Trumpet in Salisbury street in the Strand near Ivy Bridge. By William Bull, which formerly lived at Towerhill near the Postern Gate.'

During his succeeding years in the service of Charles II, James II and William III, the court records note Bull's services in making and repairing trumpets. For example, on 20th February 1686, Bull is mentioned as having received '. . . Simon Peirson's trumpett, broke to peeces . . .' and '. . . Thomas Barwell's trumpett broke to peeces, which was Culthrops . . .' (*KM*, p. 373). The instruments were given to Bull 'to be new made' and were returned apparently as such in the following May. In April 1688 the official recorder notes that he 'Received Will Shore's trumpett, and delivered it at the same tyme to Bull, to be new made, it being broke . . .' (*KM*, p. 387).

In the period of service as a trumpeter to William III, Bull seems to have had an imbroglio with one of his colleagues. The records of 23rd April 1694 mention a 'Petition of William Bull, trumpeter, to take his course at law against Robert Maugridge, kettle drummer, for scandalous words' (*KM*, p. 416). It is a pity the discourse between Bull and Maugridge (Robert Mawgridge, *see* Charles Sandford's *Coronation of James II*, p. 66 and Pl. II) has not been preserved; but they must eventually have settled their differences since they continued to work together and are mentioned in subsequent lists of court musicians.

There is a discrepancy in the address of Bull's workshop as mentioned in the *London Gazette* advertisement of 1678 (which agrees with one in *The Loyal Protestant* of 7th March 1681) and as it appears on the Haymarket rate books from 1676 to 1696. Langwill (1962, p. 14) suggests that Bull may have had two workshops: one in the Strand and another in the Haymarket. He no longer appears as a ratepayer after 1707, and it is possible that he died sometime prior to that year.

Only four of Bull's instruments have survived: a horn, in E, without a tuning crook, dated 1699 is found in the Carse Collection in the Horniman Museum; a brass trumpet with silver decorations in the London Museum (catalogue No. 292); a silver trumpet formerly owned by Ronald Lee of Hampton Court; and a silver trumpet in C (with crook) in the Ashmolean Museum at Oxford (Pl. 8). All three trumpets have been carefully measured and the specifications of each are given by Eric Halfpenny in the *Galpin Society Journal* (vol. xv, 1962 and vol. xvi, 1963).

It is questioned whether Bull's successor was the early eighteenth-century brass-instrument-maker John Harris. It is supposed that Harris made slide-trumpets, but whether or not he elaborated upon an idea of Bull will probably never be known. From Talbot's description of the 'Flatt Trumpett' (see Chapter 1, p. 28, the 'Flatt Trumpett' and the James Talbot manuscript at Oxford) it would seem that such an instrument was the immediate predecessor of the English slide-trumpet. It is uncertain whether Bull made trumpets of variable pitch, since the kind of instrument Talbot describes has not survived.

Compared with the style of trumpet-manufacturing at Nuremberg (described below) seventeenth-century English trumpets have some unique characteristics. While exhibiting a comparable high degree of workmanship the English makers seem to have preferred a different method of construction. Nearly all seventeenth- and eighteenth-century trumpets made on the Continent display the same constructional elements: twice folded, oblong and narrow, in three parallel sections of equal length and terminating in a wide exponential bell. The decorations are frequently simple; when elaborate they are commonly made of silver with amalgamated gold overlay. The ball or pommel grip is usually small and seldom very elaborate. English trumpets from the same period are twice folded and oblong but are generally wider—the bows having a larger diameter of curvature. There are three sections of tubing in equal lengths on English trumpets, but the first yard is oblique instead of parallel to the second. The reason for this is the chosen method of constructional rigidity. The continental makers either tightly seated or even soldered the tenon-socket, fitted bows and yards, and inserted a small block of wood between the first yard and the bell yard near the mouthpiece end. The two sections of the bore with the intervening block of wood were then firmly over-wrapped and bound with a decorative cordage, thus preventing any movement of the fragile sections of tubing.

The English solution of constructional rigidity is based on leverage. The bows and yards, inserted into one another by a tenon-socket arrangement, appear never to have been soldered. Instead, they are tightly fitted, the tenon being wrapped with a length of waxed string—much in the same way as the joints on a woodwind instrument are fitted. But this alone, without the block-cordage method of securing the first yard to the bell section, would allow too much play and the entire instrument would easily fall to bits (which seems to explain what is meant by 'broke to peeces').[19] This is solved by having a massive and elaborate ball on the bell section with a side hole piercing it at an oblique angle. The first yard is then fitted through this hole to join with the first bow. Thus, with the ball serving as a fulcrum, the first yard is held firmly in place and does not necessitate the use of a block of wood and cordage.

The only drawback to this method is that, because of the large ball, English trumpets tend to be much heavier, and their appearance seems more ungainly due to the obliquely fitted first yard and the oversize ball. The instruments can be quickly dismantled, which is a great advantage in cleaning and in replacing a damaged bow.

Because of the great disparity of surviving instruments it is difficult to compare continental trumpets with those of English manufacture. Since surviving continental trumpets (especially those made at Nuremberg) out-number existing English trumpets by nearly one hundred to one, the only generalizations that can be made are with respect to the differences of construction. But what of the choice of materials, the decorative elements, the acoustical properties, the pitch standards? The only seventeenth-century English trumpets that survive are those highly prized for their obvious decorative value. Most are made of silver, a metal deprecated for its utility by seventeenth-century makers and players alike.[20] It is obvious that silver was chosen by royal dignitaries for a show of splendour and opulence, but the baser 'bastard' brass trumpets of the same period sound better and were preferred by the solo players. We can only guess what happened to the supposed larger number of brass trumpets. The metal was probably used for items of 'higher' priority, which accounts also for the loss of many monumental brasses that once adorned the floors and tombs of English churches and cathedrals. Until there is more conclusive evidence about the standard trum-

---

[19] *See* page 60.　　[20] Talbot (Christ Church, Oxford, MS. 1187).

pet used in English music it can only be assumed that in terms of pitch and timbre it was not unlike the standard trumpet made at Nuremberg.

The list of Nuremberg brass instrument-makers (Table 1, pp. 64–6) gives some idea of just how important and active that city was in manufacturing brass instruments. In a period of about three hundred years there were more Nuremberg craftsmen turning out trumpets and trombones than in all the other cities of Europe before 1800. There are historical as well as geographical reasons for this astonishing activity, and these will be mentioned; but the unparalleled number of makers all living within the walls of a land-locked city would seem to indicate a phenomenon of unique sociological significance.

In addition to listing the makers, their dates (when known) and the important dates when they became journeymen and masters, Table 1 has a diagrammatic representation of the life-spans of the Nuremberg trumpet- and trombone-makers, and gives some idea of the proportion who lived and worked in the seventeenth century. Many of the earlier makers did not restrict their activities to brass instruments. Some made various kinds of woodwind instruments, and there were many craftsmen not included in the list who produced woodwind and stringed instruments only. A list of all Nuremberg instrument-makers and those who worked in allied crafts would be enormous. From Table 1 we also learn that there were at least ten families of brass-makers. That a tradition should exist in a family and be maintained over a period of several generations is not unusual in itself. What *is* unusual is the number of families in the same city engaged in the same activity. This is another feature almost peculiar to Nuremberg. Only among the Cremonese violin-makers do we observe a parallel situation. As the names Amati, Guarneri and Stradivari are synonymous with their superbly made seventeenth-century Cremona violins, so too are the names Ehe, Haas, Kodisch, Neuschel and Schnitzer for Nuremberg trumpets and trombones. We shall restrict our discussion to one of these, the one thought to be most representative of seventeenth- and eighteenth-century Nuremberg trumpet-makers: J. W. Haas.

The cursory information about Haas instruments given in Langwill (1962, p. 45) shows the seemingly abnormal longevity of J. W. Haas: 'Haas, Johann Wilhelm: Nürnberg. Mark: "J.W.H." and a springing hare. There appear to have been three [21] makers using this name: Johann

[*continued on page 67*]

[21] In his 'Addenda and Corrigenda', p. 150, Langwill adds a fourth Haas, Johann Adam (1769–1817).

TABLE I NUREMBERG TRUMPET- AND TROMBONE-MAKERS FROM THE BEGINNING OF THE SIXTEENTH TO THE END OF THE EIGHTEENTH CENTURIES

Barth, Georg	1625–87	J	1642
Baur, Jakob	c. 1565–1612	M	1595
Birckholtz, Wolfgang	c. 1620–1701	M	1650
Doll, Hans	1582–c. 1668	M	1614
D(T)rewelwecz, Anton	c. 1594–?	M	1624
D(T)roschel, Conrad	1596–1645	M	1624
Ehe, Isaac	1586–1632	M.	1607
Ehe, Georg	1595–1668	M	1621
Ehe, Joh. Leonhard	1638–1707	M	1663
Ehe, Joh. Leonhard	1663–1724	M	1690
Ehe, Wolf Magnus	1690–1722	M	1714
Ehe, Friedrich	1669–1743	M	c. 1695
Ehe, Joh. Leonhard	1700–71	M	1722
Ehe, Wolf Magnus	1714–79	M	1742
Ehe, Martin Friedrich	1726–c. 1794	M	1751
Frank, Joh. Christoph	1754–1818	M	1777
Frank, Joh. Jakob	c. 1830–57		
Frank, Joh. David	fl. c. 1850		
Haas, Johann Wilhelm	1649–1723	M	1676
Haas, Wolf Wilhelm.	1681–1760	M	1721
Haas, Ernst Joh. Conrad	1723–92	M	1748

Table 1 (*continued*)

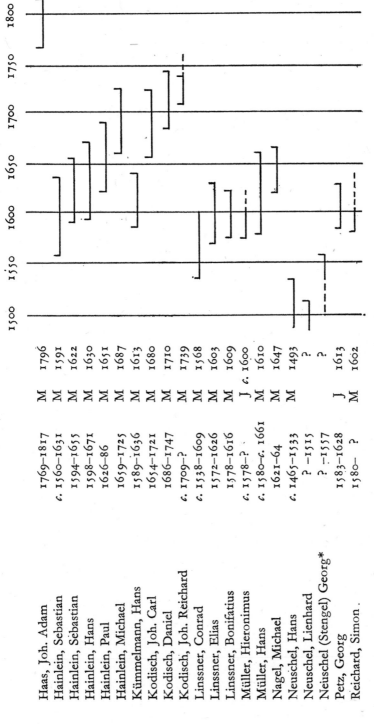

Haas, Joh. Adam	M	1796	1769–1817
Hainlein, Sebastian	M	1591	c. 1560–1631
Hainlein, Sebastian	M	1622	1594–1655
Hainlein, Hans	M	1630	1598–1671
Hainlein, Paul	M	1651	1626–86
Hainlein, Michael	M	1687	1659–1725
Kümmelmann, Hans	M	1613	1589–1636
Kodisch, Joh. Carl	M	1680	1654–1721
Kodisch, Daniel	M	1710	1686–1747
Kodisch, Joh. Reichard	M	c. 1709–?	c. 1709–?
Linssner, Conrad	M	1568	c. 1538–1609
Linssner, Elias	M	1603	1572–1626
Linssner, Bonifatius	M	1609	1578–1616
Müller, Hieronimus	J	c. 1600	c. 1578–?
Müller, Hans	M	1610	c. 1580–c. 1661
Nagel, Michael	M	1647	1621–64
Neuschel, Hans	M	1493	c. 1465–1533
Neuschel, Lienhard		?	? –1515
Neuschel (Stengel) Georg*		?	? –1557
Petz, Georg	J	1613	1583–1628
Reichard, Simon	M	1602	1580– ?

*See Jahn, Fritz: 'Die Nürnberger Trompeten- und Posaunenmacher im 16. Jahrhundert', AfMW, VII, 1925, p. 26.

Table 1 (*continued*)

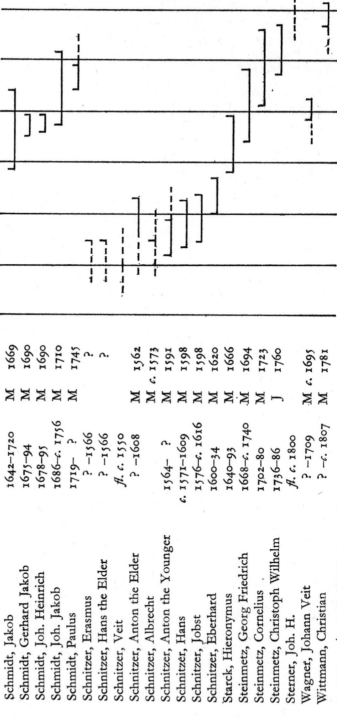

Schmidt, Jakob	1642–1720	M	1669
Schmidt, Gerhard Jakob	1675–94	M	1690
Schmidt, Joh. Heinrich	1678–95	M	1690
Schmidt, Joh. Jakob	1686–c. 1756	M	1710
Schmidt, Paulus	1719– ?	M	1745
Schnitzer, Erasmus	? –1566		?
Schnitzer, Hans the Elder	? –1566		?
Schnitzer, Veit	fl. c. 1550		
Schnitzer, Anton the Elder	? –1608	M	1562
Schnitzer, Albrecht		M	c. 1573
Schnitzer, Anton the Younger	1564– ?	M	1591
Schnitzer, Hans	c. 1571–1609	M	1598
Schnitzer, Jobst	1576–c. 1616	M	1598
Schnitzer, Eberhard	1600–34	M	1620
Starck, Hieronymus	1640–93	M	1666
Steinmetz, Georg Friedrich	1668–c. 1740	M	1694
Steinmetz, Cornelius	1702–80	M	1723
Steinmetz, Christoph Wilhelm	1736–86	J	1760
Sterner, Joh. H.	fl. c. 1800		
Wagner, Johann Veit	? –1709	M	c. 1695
Wittmann, Christian	? –c. 1807	M	1781

J, the year the individual became a journeyman
M, the year he became a master

Wilhelm H., 1649–1723; Wolf Wilhelm H., 1681–1760; Ernst Joh. Conrad H., 1723–92. Minute variations in decoration of bell-rim, stays, etc., enable the work of each to be identified. . . .'[22] A most comprehensive and authoritative source of information on the Nuremberg trumpet and trombone makers appears in a journal dedicated to the history of Nuremberg. Two very important articles by Willi Wörthmüller entitled 'Die Nürnberger Trompeten- und Posaunenmacher des 17. und 18. Jahrhunderts' and 'Die Instrumente des Nürnberger Trompeten- und Posaunenmacher' were published in two issues of the *Mitteilungen des Vereins für Geschichte der Stadt Nürnberg*.[23] Wörthmüller, who also wrote the article on Haas in *MGG* (vol. v, Kassel, 1956, cols. 1175–1177), makes it clear that the name Johann Wilhelm Haas represents a family of master craftsmen for over four generations. Although only one name ever appears on instruments made from the first half of the seventeenth century to the end of the eighteenth century, there are, as we shall see, several characteristics by which the individual maker may be identified, that have in most cases been overlooked, or ignored, in the compilation of many catalogues of instrument collections. But first, a brief discussion about the Nuremberg craftsmen, their city and their instruments.

For almost three centuries the most important centre in the art of musical-instrument manufacturing was Nuremberg. Situated in Middle Franconia, the now Bavarian city of Nuremberg, like so many other German cities at the time, enjoyed the rights of a free imperial city, first conferred upon it in 1219 by Frederick II (1194–1250). This meant that it was responsible only to the emperor for its socio-economic and political activities, and that later it had its own representatives in the *Immerwärende Reichstag*, an imperial diet meeting at Regensburg, which legislated for the various German states and principalities. Like Augsburg, farther to the south, Nuremberg attained great wealth in the Middle Ages as a trade intermediary between the east and northern Europe, retaining that status for some time after the discovery of a sea route to India in the latter part of the fifteenth century. A city of great art, within whose walls were fostered the splendid works of Dürer, Adam Kraft, Veit Stoss and others, Nuremberg was a centre of manufacture, supplying various parts of Europe with furniture, armour, weapons, metal stoves, silver plate and a host of articles in copper, bronze and gold. With this tradition it is understandable that it should have excelled and flourished as a centre of instru-

[22] Langwill, 1962, p. 45.
[23] Wörthmüller, 1954 and 1955.

ment-making, providing numerous courts and cities throughout Europe with superbly made *Rauschpfeifen*, crumhorns, recorders, trumpets and trombones. Jahn (1925, pp. 25–6, 34, 45) mentions the fact that many of the musical instruments supplied to the court of Maximilian I at Innsbruck came from Nuremberg.

Since it seemed likely that some geological-geographical reason accounted for Nuremberg's unusual activity in metal trades, several possible sources of information on this point were examined, and they gave details of the location of various mineral deposits in central Europe. One source revealed that to the north of Nuremberg, at a distance of about one hundred miles, there are several rich copper deposits also capable of producing quantities of silver, zinc, lead and nickel.[24] The Mansfeld copper mines, worked since 1199, are about the richest in Germany, having yielded over one thousand tons of the metal per year in the sixteenth century.[25] Also to the north of Nuremberg, between Leipzig and Kassel, are the Rammelsberg deposits, the second largest in Germany, producing large quantities of copper and various other metals. No wonder that so many of Nuremberg's artisans were metalsmiths, capable of manufacturing some of the most beautiful and treasured objects in pewter, copper, bronze, brass and silver. Among these smith-artists belong the earliest of the brass-instrument-makers. Hans Neuschel the Younger, who plied his trade as a coppersmith, the earliest of the Nuremberg arts, belonged, as did all of the early trumpet- and trombone-makers, to the Guild of Copper Smiths (Zunft des Rotschmieds). He was a master of that guild in 1493.[26] Lienhard Neuschel (d. 1515) worked for the Emperor Maximilian I and also made several silver trombones for Pope Leo X.[27] Georg (d. 1557), son of Hans Neuschel and last of that great name in instrument-making, was not restricted to providing the many courts with whom he dealt—especially the Margrave of Brandenburg—with trumpets and trombones, but also made for them wind instruments of all types. So famous was the name of Neuschel (variants include Meuschel, Neyschel, Neuschl) that even today the Meuschelstrasse, connecting the Löbleinstrasse to the Archivstrasse in the town centre of Nuremberg, bears the name given to it in the sixteenth century by the Stadtbehörder, or city fathers.

[24] Weed, 1907, pp. 90–1.
[25] *Ibid.*, p. 91.
[26] Wörthmüller, 1954, p. 212.
[27] Jahn, 1925, p. 26.

Separating from the Guild of Copper Smiths at the beginning of the sixteenth century, the Guild of Trumpet Makers had a ready market for their products in the various courts, towns, churches and military establishments. Rules and regulations were enacted so as to limit membership; it was even strongly recommended that the arrangement of marriage contracts be restricted to the wives and daughters of the guild or closely allied ones in an attempt to make the guild membership more exclusive; [28] apprentices and journeymen were given a definite period of servitude before becoming eligible for the title of master.

That the art of musical instrument-making and the formation of a strong guild to maintain and protect the interests of its members should have developed in a place such as Nuremberg is not difficult to understand. The social climate generated by a city of so favourable a geographic and economic position, with trades and industries, with diverse professions and members of guilds coming together, exchanging ideas and manufacturing methods and improving upon techniques already highly sophisticated and developed in each particular craft, could lead only to the kind of manufacture that is epitomized by the many surviving instruments.

The master usually associated with this tradition is Johann Wilhelm Haas. His is one of the most prominent names of all the Nuremberg trumpet-makers in the seventeenth and eighteenth centuries. With the mark of the springing rabbit or hare—a descriptive realization or play on the German word *Hase*, a hare—the instruments of this family went to practically every important city and court, not only in Germany but in most other European countries. This is suggested by the comparatively great number of instruments that survive and, like the proverbial iceberg with its greater proportion of mass below the water's surface, indicates a much larger number as having originally been made. The instruments made by the Haas family were not only famous as works of art and for the very high quality of Nuremberg craftsmanship, but were also highly regarded by the players themselves. At the end of the eighteenth century, when the art of trumpet-making, like that of trumpet-playing, was in a definite state of decline, Johann Ernst Altenburg, the last of the *Kameradschaft* trumpeters to write about his art (*see* Chapter 5), comments on Haas instruments in his *Versuch* . . . (p. 10, par. 6): '. . . Indessen hält man die zu Nürnberg von W. Hasen verfertigten und mit Engelsköpfen besetzten gemeiniglich für die besten . . .', which might be translated as: 'In this

---

[28] The famous Nuremberg trumpet-maker Michael Nagel was admitted to the guild in 1647 after marrying the widow of the trumpet-maker Conrad Droschel.

respect it is maintained that those [trumpets] from Nuremberg made by W. Haas and decorated with angel-heads are usually the best.'

Excepting the few items of information gleaned from Nuremberg town and church records, very little is known about the four generations of Haas craftsmen, in spite of their extraordinary fame and reputation. The Nuremberg town council records of 1606 [29] mention Johann Wilhelm Haas's grandfather, the *Nadler* and *Thürmer* (needle-maker and tower watch) Caspar Haas. He received the citizenship of Nuremberg in that year and is said to have come from the small town of Mulfingen in Franken—approximately sixty miles from Nuremberg, between Heilbronn and the beautifully preserved medieval city of Rothenburg. That he worked with metals may be deduced from the information that he was a needle-maker, but of equal importance is the fact that he was also a tower watch and would have had to play a *Türmerhorn*, or trumpet, as did most in that particular community service (*see* Chapter 5, section 'Municipal Trumpeters . . .'). The same town council records mention a brawl involving Caspar Haas, who, as a tower watch on the Tiergärtner Tor (the impressive multi-storeyed tower gate just north of the Albrecht Dürer Haus), apparently had a *Feldtrummet* broken in the mêlée.[30]

Lorenz Haas, son of Caspar and father of Johann Wilhelm, inherited from his father the art of metal-working and was also a tower musician. He married in 1641 and had several children, one of whom was Johann Wilhelm, born in August 1649. It is easy to see how the mixture of professions of his grandfather and father could have resulted in his developing the particular craft for which he is so well known.

The marriage and baptismal records (*Trau-* and *Taufbücher*) of the St Lorenz church give some details about Johann Wilhelm. Following the usual period of about twelve years' apprenticeship, he was married in March 1676 to Ursula Zimmermann, daughter of a sleigh-bell-maker,[31] and by that marriage had four children, two girls and two boys.[32] The youngest, Wolf Wilhelm, born in 1681, was the only one to continue the profession of his father. In 1721 Johann's wife died and was buried in the St Johannis-Friedhof, in the family plot bought by Haas in 1687.[33] Johann died in July 1723, and was laid to rest beside his wife less than a

---

[29] Records of the Nuremberg town council (*Ratsverlässe der Stadt Nürnberg*), 1606/ii, 26th May.

[30] Records of the Nuremberg town council, 1605/xii, p. 36.

[31] Marriage records (*Traubücher*) of the church of St Lorenz at Nuremberg, 1676.

[32] The baptismal records (*Taufbücher*) of St Lorenz, 1677/79/87/89.

[33] Trechsel, 1736, p. 928.

mile from the very place where his grandfather carried out his duties as a *Türmer* for so many years.

After Johann Wilhelm Haas established so solid a reputation as a trumpet-maker and created so successful a business, it is understandable that those who followed him were intent upon preserving its goodwill. Carrying on the inheritance of his father, Wolf Wilhelm Haas continued making brass instruments with the same high degree of craftsmanship and did so at the same place—in the Kreuzgasse, a small street just south of the Pegnitz river, near the Hallertorbrücke. He not only adopted the same name and style as his father, but also improved business relations and added several decorative features to his trumpets. He worked and taught [34] in the house of his father in the Kreuzgasse, and had ten children after his marriage to Magdalena Catharina Hässler in 1721. Wolf Wilhelm died in 1760, and the craft was again continued by his eldest child, Ernst Johann Conrad, born in 1723—the year of his grandfather's death.

Ernst Johann was married twice: in 1762 to Anna Elizabeth Regenfuss, daughter of a uniform-maker, and after her death in 1773 to Magdalena Barbara Möglich, daughter of an interior decorator, by whom he had eleven children. He continued the firm of Johann Wilhelm Haas, and we may see just how successful he was by the probate of his will, shortly after his death in February 1792. His accumulated wealth amounted to about 5,360 guilders with personal possessions valued at another 2,360 guilders. The following partial inventory is given in Wörthmüller (1954):

Real estate	1,400 guilders
Cash	441 ,,
Stocks and investments	2,402 ,,
Precious items, gold rings, silver jewellery and plate, and necklaces	348 ,,
Personal weapons	4 ,,
Tools and machinery	246 ,,
Books	10 ,,
Supplies of tin, copper and brass	83 ,,

Ernst Johann Conrad retained the same high quality of his father's work, but it begins to reflect the tendency toward the classic in the clearer, less elaborate shapes used to decorate his instruments. The only one of his

[34] The city account or audit records (*Stadtrechnungen*) of Nuremberg from 1724, p. 86, 3rd April, show that Wolf Wilhelm was paid three *Reichsthaler* for teaching the trumpet to some of the tower watches (*Türmer*) and children (*junger Leut*) of Nuremberg.

sons to continue in the musical-instrument-making profession was Johann Adam, born in 1769. But already the decline in the art of playing and in the need for these beautifully made instruments is reflected in the fact that there were only two other masters in the profession when Johann Adam himself became a master in 1796. A further demonstration of this rapid decline is that none of Johann Adam's children entered the trumpet-making craft, thus bringing to an end with his death in 1817 a great family tradition and a truly noble art.

Physical Characteristics of Haas Trumpets

With the exception of the makers' marks, the different characteristics of the three Haas craftsmen, discussed earlier, are minute.[35] Both Wolf Wilhelm and Ernst Johann retained not only the trade name established by Johann Wilhelm, but most of the other physical characteristics which distinguish Haas instruments from those of their contemporaries. Generally, there were only two kinds of trumpets made by all three: simple— i.e. without a great deal of decoration—and ornate. Usually the instruments of simple design were made for military use and intended for the field. The ornate trumpets, especially those by Wolf Wilhelm and Ernst Johann, were designed for state or ceremonial use. In both cases, however, the basic construction was nearly the same: bell dimensions were almost identical, the yards were of similar diameter and both types had a *Knauf*, or ball, on the third yard (Pls. 9, 10). The garnishes are the main difference between the simple and ornate trumpets. In some cases the garnishes are soldered to the bore and cannot be removed without heating the metal to melt the solder on the inside.

The garnishes found on most ornate trumpets are usually fluted and have a slight helical, or twisted, appearance. The ends are irregular or scalloped, often with an element of the design found on the garland.[36] The garnish will often have around each end, just before the scroll pattern, an engraved ring with the same pattern found on the bell rim.

Both the simple and ornate trumpets have a decorated garland. In most cases the maker's mark will be given. It is here that identification of maker is possible with little or no difficulty. Depending upon the form of

[35] Smithers, 1965, pp. 23–41, reproducing some of the material included in this section, gives several illustrations showing the makers' marks and various other details found on Haas trumpets.

[36] *See* Smithers, 1965, p. 33, fig. 7.

the hare, an instrument can usually be assigned to one of the three Haas makers. The three forms of the mark of J. W. Haas are all similar and depict a hare in a springing or running position. Only the general character of the hare is different, but in all cases, including the marks of Wolf Wilhelm and Ernst Johann, the letters I W H appear above and to the right of the animal. Perhaps it was a carry-over of the Renaissance artist's predilection for hidden meaning and arcane symbolism, or perhaps it is merely a possible interpretation of a somewhat obvious suggestion, but it may be noted that the hare in the marks of Wolf Wilhelm and Ernst Conrad is in each case looking back to the initials of the founder, Johann Wilhelm. Perhaps the fact that Ernst Johann Conrad's hare is running suggests the lapse of time between his work and that of his grandfather.

Other elements on the bell are indicative of the maker, e.g. the engraved floral pattern of leaves, a flower with the appearance of a tulip and an object resembling a pomegranate.[37] Any or all of these may be found on a Haas instrument. The more ornate instruments will frequently have cast angel heads, either three or four, soldered to the garland.[38] These *Engelköpfen* are winged masks and are often found represented on another part of the instrument, e.g. on the ball. But the absence of the winged angel heads does not preclude an instrument from belonging to the ornate class. Some of the early ornate trumpets by Johann Wilhelm Haas made in silver with gilding lack these decorative features. When an instrument was made of silver and, particularly, with gold leaf amalgamated with various ornaments, it was almost always intended for court or state ceremonial use.

Having supposedly taken over the use of cast-metal decorations from Hans Hainlein, who is reputed to have been Johann Wilhelm's teacher, Haas and his successors made use of this technique with few changes of pattern or design from one generation to the next. It is possible that the matrices used by Johann Wilhelm, and probably made by him, were passed on to Wolf Wilhelm, who in turn left them to Ernst Johann. The kind of uniformity that persists from one generation to the next seems to indicate consistent efforts to preserve the trade name and designs made famous by Johann Wilhelm.

The above-mentioned winged angel heads, usually in silver and overlaid with gold, are extremely consistent from one generation to the next when

---

[37] *Ibid.*, fig. 8.

[38] The trumpet (a *tromba da caccia*) shown with Gottfried Reiche in his portrait by Haussmann has winged angel heads on the bell garland. The particular instrument was in all probability made in the workshop of J. W. Haas at Nuremberg.

they appear on the ball.[39] This decorative as well as functional feature found on most Baroque trumpets is either smooth, or embossed with some kind of design—depending upon whether the instrument is simple or ornate. The ball is often cast and has short lengths of sleeve soldered to each end—it is not pierced by a single length of sleeve. As was the case of the garnishes on the bow-yard joints, the ball sleeve may be fitted over the yard-bell joint and soldered, or it may be merely tightly wedged. If the latter is the case and it is possible to slide the ball back from the bell joint, as could be done with several instruments examined, there is revealed a telescopically fitted joint with the yard inserted into the bell section. In all the cases noted this joint was hammered and brazed and finished with a very smooth and continuous appearance.

The general overall construction of Haas trumpets is nearly the same as that of most other contemporary continental instruments. The twice-folded trumpets are usually coiled to the left of the first yard, with a block of wood inserted toward the mouthpiece end between the first and third yards, with cordage wrapped over it and the tubing. For stability of construction this does not necessitate a series of soldered braces or, as is the case with the English trumpets described earlier, an angular appearance caused by the first yard either partially or totally piercing the ball at an oblique angle.

It is more than likely that most of the trumpet and trombone music discussed in Chapter 6 was originally performed on instruments from Nuremberg. It is doubtful whether the same kind of music could have been written without the availability of high-quality instruments from the shops of the Haas family or the many other Nuremberg trumpet-makers. As in any era, the level of performance depended to some extent upon the reliability and quality of the player's instrument. Baroque trumpet-makers should share some credit when we consider the music that was written for their instruments.

[39] Smithers, 1965, Pl. iv-b, opposite p. 33.

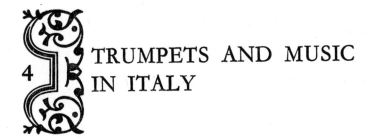

4 TRUMPETS AND MUSIC IN ITALY

1. First Developments

The cities of Northern Italy did much to realize and foster the musical potential of the trumpet. From its first known appearance, in *L'Orfeo/ Favola in Musica/da Claudio Monteverdi* at Mantua in 1607, the trumpet developed rapidly as an orchestral instrument. It is uncertain whether Monteverdi's example was the instigating force that led the way in this rapid development. As far as we know, the only work in which he uses trumpets is *Orfeo*, where they are limited to the opening Toccata. Westrup (1933–4, p. 24) calls this fanfare-like prelude an 'experiment and an astonishing noise, particularly when played the requisite three times; but it is not remarkable as a way of combining instruments'. More than likely, the first noted appearance of the trumpet under such circumstances was not so remarkable either. In rising to the occasion for which *Orfeo* was commissioned, Monteverdi in all likelihood did only that which had been done many times before. The late Renaissance *intermedii* in Italian court entertainments, the pastoral dramas and the spectacular musical banquets often employed the services of resident trumpeters, adding a distinctive touch of splendour.[1]

There are earlier records of trumpets serving in a similar capacity in Italian religious and civic activities. As early as 1395 the city archives of Treviso mention the cultivation of trumpet-playing:

Item: the abovesaid lords, the consuls and the 18 (councillors), being in the abovesaid palace which is the dwelling and habitation of the consuls and of the leaders, by

[1] *See* Weaver, 1961, pp. 363–78.

right of their office resolved that, out of the funds of the community of Treviso, money should be given to Pietro di Bartolomeo Boldrani herewith, in order that he could buy a trumpet and learn to play it: for the presence of artists increases the honour of the whole community; and the said Pietro would then be able also to give evidence of his skill, and thus serve the community. Furthermore, he is above all a very poor person, and so to provide for him mercifully is an act of charity acceptable both to God and to the saints. So it was arranged that he should be given one florin, which he should at once have from the funds of the said community for his legitimate expenses.[2]

At the same city a contract was executed in 1537 to provide trumpet lessons for a willing and able student:

In the same year [1537], during the afore-mentioned Indiction and in the Pontificate of Paul III, on Wednesday September 25th. Scipione di Berardino Pierantoni, of Treviso, willing promised, for himself and for his heirs, and agreed that he was willing to teach, and to demonstrate by performing, the art of playing the trumpet, to Andrea Ciccarelli, of Matigge, near Treviso; this he promised in the presence of Andrea, at his request and with his consent.

And the said Andrea willingly promised and agreed, for himself and for his heirs, that he desired to learn the said art of playing the trumpet, and that he would obey the said Scipione as a good and loyal pupil should.

And the abovesaid Scipione agreed to be bound by this contract and to be obliged to show and demonstrate [his skill] three times on whatever day of that month or afterwards the said Andrea should find most convenient.

And the said Scipione did this because the said Andrea willingly, for himself . . . promised and agreed to give and pay in cash the sum of one florin of the currency of the 'Marchia' for each month in which he, Andrea, had lessons . . . and he promised to obey the commands of Scipione.

And they swore and promised these things to one another. . . .

This agreement was made in the shop of Benedetto di Bartolo Sanctis, which is beside the 'Piazza' of the city next to the road and on the other side; there were also present two discreet and worthy men as witnesses—these were Berardino Celli Ciopti and Thomas Berardino Ser Thomae. . . .[3]

[2] Archives of the city of Treviso, No. 41, 1395, f. 134. Original Latin text quoted by Valenti (1926), p. 63.

[3] Archives *Notarile* of Treviso, To. 361 . . . fol. 193 t. Original Latin again quoted by Valenti (1926), p. 65.

At Turin, where Dufay worked in 1450, there are fifteenth-century payment records to trumpet-players. One dated 20th January 1411 mentions a
'Gift to Petroniat and to two minstrels from Geneva and to a trumpet
player'.[4] Similarly, the fifteenth- and sixteenth-century court and cathedral
records of Urbino abound with references to trumpets and payment to
trumpet-players. In the entourage that accompanied Elizabeth, daughter
of Frederick III, Duke of Urbino, on her way to Rimini in 1475 to marry
Roberto Malatesta, there were lute-players, trumpeters, singers and
'Maestro Pietro the organist'.[5]

Duke Guidobaldi I of Urbino (c. 1507), reputed to have founded the
choir and instrumentalists of the chapel at Urbino, is said to have had on
the first Sunday of each month the Blessed Sacrament carried in solemn
procession around the chapel, accompanied by a great number of dignitaries, citizens and musicians. 'The clerks meanwhile sang praises and
hymns in honour of the Sacrament, accompanied by the trumpeters of the
household of Urbino, who frequently made loud noises, while the
consilarii . . . carried the canopy.'[6]

The statutes of Urbino in 1559 state that on the Feast of Corpus Christi
the procession of city fathers, citizens and clerics '. . . shall be preceded by
trumpets . . .'[7] and '. . . . with a devout and sonorous sound of trumpeters
playing on loud trumpets'.[8]

In 1556 a New Year's gift of half a golden scudo was given to each of
the trumpet-players, 'of whom there are five serving in the *capella* of the
said church of Urbino'.[9]

In a work describing the city of Bologna, a city whose inestimable
contributions to the seventeenth-century trumpet repertory are discussed
below, the author [10] makes the following comments:

*The main piazzas of the city are the great piazza, called the 'Piazza del Comune',
where the 'Legato' and the governor and his 'Auditori' live; also the 'Gonfaloniere*

[4] Borghezio, 1924, p. 221, item 15: 'Strenna a Petroniat e a due menestrelli di Ginevra e ad una
trombetta.'

[5] Ligi, 1925, p. 4.

[6] *Ibid.*, p. 8: 'clericis interim laudes ad eiusdem Sacramenti decus . . . dencantatibus, Urbini
tubicinibus coeuntibus ac saepe sonore clangentibus eiusdem Societatis Consiliariis Baldac-
chinum deferentibus.'

[7] *Ibid.*, p. 41: '. . . cum Tubis praecedentibus . . .'

[8] *Ibid.*, p. 42: '. . . devoto et sonoro Cantu canentibus tubatoribus sonoris tubis . . .

[9] Vale, 1930, p. 106.

[10] Vizani, 1602, pp. 23–4.

di Giustizia' with his 'Signori Antiani'; there the city government meets, and the 'Gonfalonieri del Popolo'; there is permanently on guard there a company of Swiss soldiers, 'Alabarieri', and a company of Italian light cavalry. Above the door of this Palace is placed a very beautiful bronze statue of Pope Gregory XIII, who came from Bologna, which was made by the Bolognese smith Alessandro Mengati . . . and there on a very beautiful arch or balcony of stone, trumpets are played every evening. And after the trumpets have finished, very pleasant music is played on trombones and cornettos at the same Piazza as well as the great building of the church of St. Petronio. . . .

From the same work in the remarks 'Concerning the *Antiani*, the *Consulo* and the *Gonfalonieri di Giustizia*', the author again mentions the social significance of trumpets: [11]

In order to show that this city was in the past ruled and governed by itself as a free state, one still today finds the ancient form of the Republic preserved amongst its citizens, for they are accustomed, as used to happen in other cities, and as is still observed in some cities, to choose from among the number of 'Signori' of the 'Reggimento' [a parliamentary body] a 'Gonfaloniere di Giustizia'; and from among the other noble citizens and the respected merchants, eight 'Signori Antiani', called consuls . . . When they appear in public, these 'Signori' are dressed in rich robes of silk, and during the winter they are muffled up with very precious furs as well. They are accompanied by a very respectable household of eight trumpeters, with a drummer, or player of the nakers, who with these trumpets plays certain Moorish drums. To both the drums and the trumpets are attached banners with the arms of liberty; also eight excellent musicians with trombones and cornettos; a herald; a 'spenditore'; nine pages dressed in scarlet cloaks and stockings in the livery of the city— white and red. . . .

It is obvious from this small sample of contemporary records and descriptions that trumpets had long been an integral part of the socio-musical life of Italian courts and cities. Monteverdi's 'experiment' was neither remarkable nor the innovation some writers have claimed it to be. His association with the Gonzagas, one of the most important families in Italy at the time, would have brought him into close contact with their *trombetteri* and *piffari*, and he would certainly have experienced performances and civic affairs where they are known to have played. His definite prescription of brass instruments in the printed edition of *Orfeo* and their début in opera were, however, novel.

[11] *Ibid.*, pp. 7–8.

The opening music in *Orfeo* is termed a Toccata. Many writers believe that the term is derived from *toccare* (to touch) and was a rhapsodic type of instrumental music normally associated with keyboard compositions. 'The toccata or touch piece was characterized by rhapsodic sections with sustained chords, rambling scale passages, and broken figuration over powerful pedal points which abruptly alternated with fugal sections.' [12] But, interestingly, the Elizabethan term 'tucket', normally associated with fanfares, military trumpet and drum flourishes, seems to be derived from a similar word. Perhaps Monteverdi's understanding of the word as it is applied in *Orfeo* may, like 'tucket', have something to do with *tocco*, meaning a beat or stroke. The connotation is involved with the normal scoring of the bass part in trumpet music at the time, usually played by kettledrums and sometimes doubled by a trumpet with a very large mouthpiece, capable of playing only the most fundamental tonic-dominant figures. Perhaps the toccata, as Bukofzer sees it, developed from an earlier musical genre originally intended for trumpets with their ancillary kettledrums.

In designating the highest to the lowest parts in the 'Toccata', Monteverdi most likely drew upon a long-standing tradition of descriptive terminology. In the Amadino print of 1609 [13] the parts are called 'Clarino, Quinta, Alto e basso, Vulgano, Basso'. This seems to be the earliest source where the term 'clarino' is applied to the upper tessitura of the natural trumpet harmonics.[14] Ten years later Praetorius [15] introduces

---

[12] Bukofzer 1947, p. 47.

[13] Facs. repr. Augsburg, 1927, p. 2.

[14] The term *clarino* in seventeenth- and eighteenth-century trumpet music is, strictly speaking, a register designation and not the name of an instrument. Many Baroque composers seem to have perpetrated a misnomer by an indiscriminate use of the terms *tromba* and *clarino* as instrument designations. There may be significant historical reasons for this. A *clarino* or clarion may have been a very different kind of trumpet during the late Middle Ages and Renaissance and its name, in association with a different timbre and function, may have persisted well into the Baroque era. Horman (1519, folio 255 verso), says that 'A trumpette is streyght: but a clarion is wounde: in and out with an hope' (i.e., wound or bent zigzag in one plane—S-shaped—with a hoop, which was an iron cylinder used for shaping and bending). The clarion, then, may have had military associations, being 'wounde in and out' to facilitate carrying and playing it, especially on horseback. As a consequence, its bore was probably narrower and proportionately more cylindrical than the straight trumpets and sounded considerably brighter. If so, its shriller, more penetrating timbre, a necessity in the field, presumably explains the origin of its name: clarion or *clarino* being derived from the Latin *clarus*, which, when related to hearing, means clear, loud, or distinct.

[15] Praetorius, M., 1619, vol. iii, p. 170. *See* Chapter 6.

the term 'Principale', which, towards the end of the seventeenth century, refers to the register of usually a third trumpet part.

The list of 'Stromenti' in *Orfeo* [16] mentions 'Un clarino con tre trombe sordine' (a clarino with three muted trumpets). The opening music is preceded by the following instructions: 'Toccata che si suona avanti il levar de la tela tre volte con tutti li stromenti, & si fa un Tuono piu alto volendo sona le trombe con le sordine.' [17] Inasmuch as there are four trombones listed with the various continuo, stringed and wind instruments, it must be supposed that the lower four parts were taken by them. Curiously, while the list of requisite instruments for the whole work clearly states 'Quattro Tromboni', the 'Coro de spirti' (chorus of spirits) on page seventy-two of the 1609 edition has the following: 'Coro de spirti, al suono di un Reg. Org. di legno, cinque Tromb. duoi Bassi da ga[m]ba, & un contrabasso de viola.' Why five trombones are not mentioned initially is not clearly understood. Perhaps five also played in the 'Toccata'.

Fantini's work (1638) on the trumpet, discussed below, gives some idea of what is meant by the scoring terms used by Monteverdi in the 'Toccata'. The second to sixth partials of the trumpet are called 'Basso, Vurgano, Striano, Toccata, Quinta'. Fantini does not mention the term 'clarino' in the entire work, but most of the other names do bear a relationship to Monteverdi's designations. Like Monteverdi, Fantini may have been referring to particular trumpet registers, where the above-named notes are simply the mean pitch levels for the highest to the lowest parts. Even though Monteverdi supposedly requires all the instruments to play, it is interesting that the fanfare-like Toccata uses only trumpet terminology in its scoring indications, as well as being written in a definite brass style.

What is meant precisely by a 'clarino' is still a mystery; one explanation has already been given. [18] There are also some possibilities suggested in the next chapter, since the term had wider use in Germany, and on more than one occasion in seventeenth-century German musical sources it is associated with an instrument of smaller proportions than the normal trumpet. In differentiating between 'clarino' and 'tromba', the composer, again possibly drawing upon traditional trumpet terminology, may have been pointing out the difference in musical material associated with the higher

[16] *Op. cit.*, p. 1.

[17] *Ibid.*: 'Before the raising of the curtain the toccata is to be played three times by all the instruments—the muted trumpets are obliged to play a tone lower.'

[18] *See* p. 79, note 14.

1 Detail from *The Adoration of the Magi*, by Antonio Vivarini (*c.* 1444).
By courtesy of the Gemäldegalerie, Berlin-Dahlem.

2 Detail from *Coronation of Virgin*, by the 'Meister Marienlebens' (*c.* 1485). In Alte Pinakothek, Munich; photograph, Don Smithers.

3 Detail from *Entry of the Emperor Charles V into Bologna* (in 1530), by Hogenberg. By courtesy of the New York Public Library.

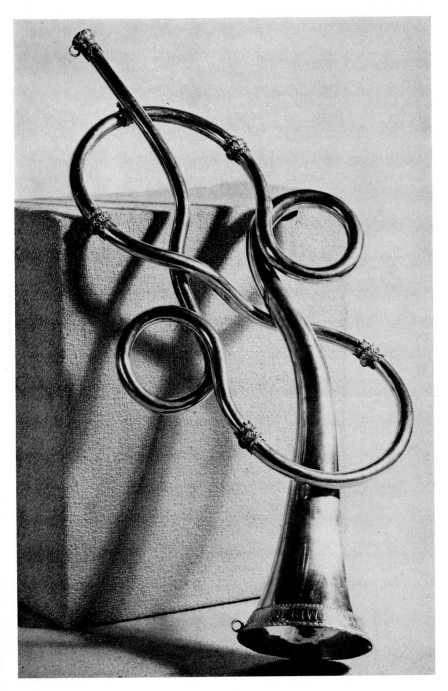

4 Figure-of-eight trumpet by Anton Schnitzer the younger, dated 1598.
By courtesy of the Kunsthistorisches Museum, Vienna.

5 Three silver state or herald's trumpets with elaborate gilded decorations and ornate engraved motifs. *Left:* by Michael Nagel (seventeenth century); *centre:* by Anton Schnitzer (sixteenth century); *right:* by Michael Leichamschneider (eighteenth century).
By courtesy of the Kunsthistorisches Museum, Vienna.

6 Detail of bell sections of trumpets left and centre in plate 5.

7 Double-ended, or reversible, trumpet mute; seventeenth century.
   By courtesy of the National Museum, Prague.

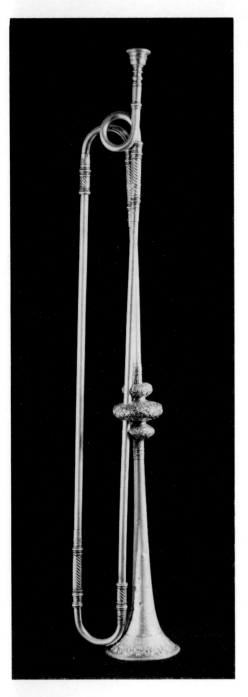

8 Silver trumpet by William Bull.
By courtesy of the Ashmolean Museum, Oxford.

9 (*opposite*). Silver fanfare trumpet with gilded decorations, by Johann Wilhelm Haas dated 1744. Inscribed 'D.G. / CAROLVS / THEODORVS / COMES PAL / ATINVS RHENI / SACRI ROMANI / IMPERII / ARCHI / THESAVRARIVS / ET ELECTOR / ANNO 1744 / I W Haas fec Norib.'

10 (*opposite below*). Detail of *Knauf* (ball) and bell section of trumpet in plate 9.
By courtesy of the Bavarian National Museum.

11 Two silver trumpets by Michael Leichamschneider, 1741.
By courtesy of the Kunsthistorisches Museum, Vienna.

and lower registers: the florid upper partials of the top part as distinct from the simple repeated note tonic-dominant parts, probably for the 'tre trombe sordine'.

Musically, the Toccata in *Orfeo* is nothing more than an elaborate fanfare, and may have been, for all we know, an elaboration of traditional household trumpet fanfare figures. The more elongated and contrapuntal opening of Monteverdi's 'Vespers' of 1610 is a lengthy parody of the Toccata in *Orfeo*, but minus trumpets. With the normal association of drums with trumpets it would not be incorrect to suppose that in the opening music of the opera timpani were included in the term 'Basso'.

With trumpets beginning to flourish in the seventeenth-century orchestras at Venice, Bologna and Modena, composers were quick to recognize their potentialities in church and chamber music. The use of the trumpet seems to have spread rapidly from Northern Italy into Bohemia, Germany, England and Scandinavia by the end of the first quarter of the seventeenth century. The most noteworthy testimony of the trumpet's sudden rise to fame in art music is the appearance in 1638 of the first printed trumpet 'method'.[19] In that year Girolamo Fantini published his *Modo per imparare a sonare di tromba*. . . . The whole of his preface now follows in translation (for the original Italian *see* either of the above, or Sartori (1952, pp. 361–3), where most of Fantini's preface as well as the 'Tavola' are reproduced in the original Italian).

The method of learning to play
The Trumpet,
Both in War
and also musically with an organ, with a muted trumpet, with the harpsichord, and with every other kind of instrument. In addition to this, there are many pieces to be played, such as Balletti, Brandi, Capriccios, Sarabands, Courants, Passages [runs, or studies, or passages on the lines of cadenzas], and Sonatas for trumpet[s] and organ together.

By Girolamo Fantini
of Spoleto
First trumpeter of his serene highness
Ferdinand II, Grand Duke of Tuscany.
Published in Frankfurt by
Daniel Vuastch. 1638.

[19] The earliest trumpet tutor noted so far is a manuscript preserved in the Biblioteca Nazionale at Florence: Cesare Bendinelli, *Tutta l'arte della Trombetta*. It is thought to date from about 1614 but contains pieces dated 1584, 1587 and 1588.

Madrigal by Signor Alessandro Adinari
in praise of the author

O fortunate Flora,
The daughter of ancient Rome,
And Emula, the friendly rival of her [Rome's] ventures,
You now rejoice to have as your king a new Aeneas,
Who has more than one Palinurus on the Tyrrhenian Sea;
But you lacked a Misenus.[20]

And now Girolamo is here, playing every hour
With such amazing art,
That he can by his fiery song arouse Mars;
And (to make such sweet and pleasant sounds) he takes
Fame's trumpet and the winds from the air.

This one, who by the sound of a bellicose instrument
  made helmets tremble at his will,
  and spears clash, and warhorses tremble,
  although they were fiercer than the
  thunder or the wind.

To the author by an unknown writer:

Now, behold, intent on music,
He sweetens his proud sounds,
And makes knights and ladies languish with joy,
His martial talent used for love instead.

Amazing skill and nature together
Enclose in one breast such mighty strength,
That he obscures the fame of ancient Misenus;

The monarch of the trumpet is on earth today,
Who is sure of victory over every heart,
And can cause peace or war.

To his serene highness the Grand Duke

Your serene highness's magnanimous liberality, and the infinite obligation which I
have incurred during the eight years that I have served you, have led me to wish to

---

[20] Misenus was Aeneas' trumpeter.

give some sign of recognition of my debt of gratitude; I confess that this is but a very small token, compared with what I ought to give to so great a prince, my lord and my patron, whose magnanimity has been the reason why I have given birth to this poor work, the result of what little leisure has been granted to me in the past three years; it is the result of my studies, and of such diligence as is possible for me, and despite its weaknesses has caused me considerable trouble. In it I deal with the art of the trumpet, from its first beginnings right up to the extreme perfection which it never reached until our times: I have illustrated every use of it, both in things concerning war and in every other action relevant to the trumpet. I therefore beg your serene highness to accept under your protection this unpolished task of mine, which I present to you and dedicate as a proof of my sincere affection. It would not have been right, and could not have happened, that I should present it to anyone except your serene highness: firstly, because my debt to you required that I should consecrate the fruits of my work to him who had brought it to birth, and also because the increased perfection of trumpet playing is due to nobody but to the monarch of these peoples, who in the past were the inventors of the art. And now, finally, I salute you with due reverence, praying that heaven may grant to your serene highness the fulfilment of your every desire. Your devoted and humble servant, Girolamo Fantini. 20th April, 1638.

The author to his readers

I have sent to the press this poor work of mine for the benefit of those who play the trumpet or who wish to learn to play it—and to play it not in the way that it used to be played in the past, but on the true basis, just as one plays the other perfected instruments; the trumpet has only its natural notes, as is shown at the beginning of the book, although it would not have been possible to make greater efforts to compose works outside this range, it has been necessary to be contented with the existing notes, which by themselves have little charm; thus also there are many basses on which divisions have not been written, because in order to achieve this on such an instrument one would need a vast knowledge of harmony.

Please accept this work with your goodwill, for by so doing you will in time have other works from me, but do send me any discreet criticism that you can offer.

> *Notes for those who wanted to*
> *learn to play the trumpet*
> *musically in harmony with*
> *voices or with other instruments.*

Those who wish to play this instrument should use the tip of the tongue to play it, for a perfect sound cannot be produced by breath alone. When there are notes in the following sonatas which have dots under them, the player should use the tip of the tongue to interrupt the breath, according to the occasion, or rather according to the inclination of whoever professes to play this instrument. And where there is a 'Groppo',[21] this should be played using the tip of the tongue; but a trill should be played by the force of the chest, and should be beaten out with the throat muscles; and this applies to all the notes on the instrument. It will also be found that there are some notes, not pointed out at the beginning of the work, which are very imperfect if they are held, but which can be used where they pass quickly. It should also be noted that when there are notes of any length, that is, of one, or two, or four beats, they should be held in a cantabile manner, starting with a low sound, then increasing the volume until halfway through the note, and then making a diminuendo right to the end of the beat, which should hardly be heard; for by so doing, perfect harmony will be produced. If, at the beginning of the book, 'do' is written underneath C, this should be so, as the trumpet cannot play 'du' or 'ut': these should, however, be avoided, just as a perfect singer will not sing runs on 'i' or 'u'; also in the toccate di guerra *[battle calls], there are words written, which say 'da ton della', 'atta non tano', and 'attanallo', which mean 'buttasella' [prepare to mount, or saddle your horse,] and 'a cavalcare' [ride forward,] and 'a cavallo' [to horse]; 'tinta' means all [tutti]. They are written out in this way because they will sound more clearly on the trumpet, as they will be easier to tongue, which is the proper way to play. And on a muted trumpet one must play [will play] D where C is written.*

Some interesting conclusions may be drawn from Fantini's notes to the reader. He points out the basic musical limitations of the trumpet and its inability to perform successfully any but the notes of the harmonic series. Divisions or florid ornamentation, associated rather with keyboard, stringed and some woodwind instruments, seem to have been beyond the ability of most trumpet-players. As today, emphasis was placed on tonguing and the necessity of developing a flexible tongue properly to execute short and quick ornaments ('Groppi'), as well as attacking notes correctly. The technique of executing trills—today called lip trills—is exactly the same as is demanded of the modern player. Some trills on a modern trumpet are extremely difficult with the use of valves, particularly in the upper register. The difficulty is caused by the harmonic series of one valve combination being too close to another. When using valves for certain trilled notes the same tone will be produced in both combinations, giving

---

[21] A *groppo* or *gruppo* was an Italian sixteenth-century term for ornamentation not unlike our modern trill, but not 'synonymous' as Bukofzer (1947, p. 28) says.

the effect of one continuous pitch, rather than an alternation from one note to another. This necessitates the use of the natural trumpet technique of rapidly slurring from one note to another by using the diaphragm and throat muscles. This is what Fantini means by playing a trill with 'the force of the chest, . . . and beaten out with the throat muscles'.

One of the most illuminating comments is Fantini's remark about imperfect notes (non-harmonic tones). That they can be used as passing or neighbouring tones is corroborated by the number of non-harmonic tones found in seventeenth-century scores. The ability of a proficient player to produce these false notes, at least well enough to give the impression that they were played, is substantiated by Father Marin Mersenne's remarks [22] about Fantini three years before the appearance of the latter's *Modo* (*see* Chapter 10).

Fantini's transference of *messa di voce* vocal technique to the trumpet (like contemporary singers, the trumpet-player is requested to make a crescendo and diminuendo on sustained notes) may not be in agreement with modern concepts of performance, but it is a clear indication of nuance being used by expert players. The remarks about 'do' being written underneath C, and '. . . the trumpet not being able to play "du" or "ut" . . .' are somewhat vague, but possibly refer to correct tonguing and tone production. His closing instructions about using a mute are confirmed by Monteverdi's directions as well as by other contemporary accounts. When a mute was used, especially the long, bored-out ones made of wood, a trumpet's pitch was raised a whole tone. Cazzati's remarks in the preface to his op. 35 collection of sonatas (discussed in the second part of this chapter) make this very clear.

Fantini's 120 musical examples include tonguing passages, duets for two trumpets and several short pieces for one and two trumpets and continuo. Nearly a hundred pieces are dedicated to aristocratic Italian and German families. The work is progressive in its presentation of material, ranging from the simplest exercises to the difficult sonatas towards the end. The sonatas themselves, by far the most interesting pieces, range from the short dance-like pieces to the later technically difficult and orna-mented music in 'detta del Vitelli' (p. 83) and 'detta del Nero' (p. 84). Some of the pieces have changing metre as well as *forte* and *piano* indica-tions of dynamics. Carlo Schmidl (1928, vol. i, p. 519) has suggested that the place of publication may have been Florence instead of Frankfurt. It does seem odd that a work by so illustrious a performer in the service

---

[22] Mersenne, 1635, 1636a, 'De Instrumentis Harmonicis', p. 109

of an important Florentine nobleman should be published so far away in a foreign country. Eichborn (1890, p. 124) suggests that Daniel 'Vuastch' was probably a Frankfurt bookseller.

It has already been noted that Fantini's preface mentions non-harmonic tones; there are several encountered in the course of the work. They frequently appear with a slur connecting them to the real and adjacent notes of the harmonic series. It is felt that Fantini includes some of these notes, 'which are very imperfect if they are held', only to show that the effect of their being played could be impressed on the listener. Such notes are never unprepared, i.e. isolated and to be approached by leap or as an initial tone following a rest. They normally occur, as they do in nearly every Baroque source, as a passing or neighbouring tone of a harmonic series note. Examples of this are found in Fantini's 'l'Accavallo' (p. 13) and the 'Capriccio detta del Carducci' (p. 46). In the latter, the non-harmonic tones d, f and a occur as upper neighbour tones and as a second note in three groups of triplets—between the harmonics c, e and g respectively. In 'l'Accavallo' the non-harmonic tone d is written as a passing note between c and e, and a slur is written over all three notes.

Even though the publication of Fantini's work is comparatively early, the author introduces nearly all the trumpet notes that are to be found in sources from that time until the decline of the instrument at the end of the eighteenth century. It must be assumed that at the time natural trumpet technique was already developed by many players. Fantini may exhibit a certain amount of precocity, especially introducing in 1638 such notes as c^1 sharp in the sonata 'Colloretto' (p. 72) and in the 'Undecima ricercata l'Albergotti' (p. 26); the seventeenth harmonic d^2 in the 'Seconda ricercata detta l'Acciaioli' (p. 23) is certainly an early anticipation of later Baroque virtuoso trumpet parts. But even before Fantini's *Modo*, trumpets were engaged in more complicated parts than Monteverdi's *Orfeo* Toccata. The passages in the anthem *In dulci jubilo* from the *Polyhymnia caduceatrix et panegyrica* (1619) of Michael Praetorius (*see* Chapter 6), although not as altitudinous as some of Fantini's later examples, indicate that trumpet technique was quite sophisticated before 1620. In the same respect the *Buccinate* and the *Iubilate Deo* from the *Symphoniae Sacrae* (1629) of Heinrich Schütz (*see* also Chapter 6) are evidence of a rapidly developing trumpet technique before the appearance of Fantini's work.

By the middle of the seventeenth century the trumpet had found a place in most important musical organizations in Italy and elsewhere. But in Italy some areas seemed more disposed than others to the sound of trumpets and their use in art music. One such area was the duchy of Este with its capital at Modena. Located in north-central Italy, Modena became the ducal residence of the Este on the incorporation of Ferrara with the Papal States in 1598. Historically, the city has tremendous political interest, but, being the capital of the Este duchy, it was also an important cultural centre. Under Francesco II (1660–94) the Biblioteca Estense was founded; earlier, under Alphonso IV (father of Maria Beatrice, who was to become the wife of James II of England), the extensive art gallery was established.

The Estes did a great deal to promote music. During the reign of Francesco II the composers Marco Uccelini, Giovanni Maria Bononcini, Colombi, Reina, Giovanni Vitali (after 1674), his son Tomasso, possibly Stradella, and, for an unknown period of time, Domenico Gabrielli made up the Modena 'school'. The paramount influence Modena and its composers had on the music of other areas was through the medium of chamber music. Operas and church music were produced at Modena, but the important contributions were in chamber-music forms.

Notwithstanding the trumpet's more popular function in the theatre and church music of Modena and the other Este cities, there are a number of surviving examples of chamber trumpet music. The MS. sources of this music are now found in various libraries, notably the Biblioteca Estense at Modena and the Estensischen Musikalien of the Nationalbibliothek at Vienna, and in the works of Stradella from his *Sinfonie a più instrumenti*, which is preserved in the Foà Collection of the Biblioteca Nazionale at Turin. One of the more interesting collections, one that bears more fruit with regard to trumpet music, is the Estensischen Musikalien at Vienna. This collection was fully catalogued and described by Haas (1927) and has a very interesting history. It was found in a castle of the Obizzi branch of the Este family. The name of the castle is Catajo, a handsome building not far from Padua. The Obizzi were descendants of Obizzo I d'Este, *podestà* of Padua towards the end of the twelfth century. In the seventeenth century the Obizzi, like their Este relatives to the south-west in Ferrara and Modena, were patrons of art and music. In the castle was a small private theatre where operas and concerts of chamber music were given by the resident musicians and visiting composers from Modena and Bologna. The theatre contained not only a vast collection of instrumental and vocal music but also a large number of musical instruments. When the Obizzi died out at the beginning of the nineteenth century, Francesco V d'Este of Modena succeeded to the title and lands. The music and instruments at Catajo remained untouched until 1875 when, with the title and estates of the Estes passing to the Archduke Francis Ferdinand, heir to the Austro-Hungarian Habsburg throne, the entire contents of the theatre were sent to Vienna. The instruments are described by Schlosser (1920) and form part of the extensive Vienna collection. The music remained in parcels until Robert Haas managed to sort it out and publish his descriptive catalogue.

In the *Estensischen Musikalien*—or as Haas (1927, p. 11) has rightly put it, the 'Obizzischen Musikalien'—there are at least ten known works with one or two trumpets, and six that are possibly transcriptions of works originally for trumpet but with the parts marked for oboe. There are even two interesting and rare sonatas (really concertos) for cornetto and strings by Pietro Baldessari Bresciano. Except for a printed collection by the Bolognese composer Giuseppe Iacchini (his *Trattenimenti per Camera . . . à una e due Trombe . . .*, Bologna, 1703), which is discussed below, all the trumpet pieces are in MS. parts. The known composers represented are Albinoni, Corelli, a Padre de Castris, Iacchini, Manfredini and Pietro Pignata. Four of the trumpet pieces are anonymous. The works are listed in the Appendix with the Haas catalogue reference. The Corelli pieces are a *Concerto* in D for two trumpets, solo violin and basso continuo, and a *Sonata con Aboe* [sic] *e violini* in C. The former is thought to be spurious, but the latter is an oboe transcription of the D major trumpet sonata. The D major sonata and its concording sources will be discussed in detail later.

At Modena the violinist extraordinary, Marco Uccelini, used the trumpet in various settings in his operas. Trumpet music was also thought to have been associated with his op. 5 collection of violin and continuo sonatas, entitled *Sonate over Canzoni da farsi à violino solo, & basso continuo . . .*, and published in Venice in 1649. The collection is given in Sartori,[23] and an original print is found in the Bodleian Library at Oxford (MS. Mus. Sch. C. 157 a–b). In the continuo part the last piece bears the title 'Trombetta sordina con vn Violino Solo'. It is an unimportant variation of that in the violin part: 'Tromba sordina per sonare con Violino Solo'. It is a most peculiar piece, with the continuo part consisting of various metrical values of a single bass note, D. The range of the violin part is from A to e^2. On page 31 of the violin part there is what appears to be a g^2. It seems to be a mistake, however, for the same note in the basso continuo 'partitura' has e^2. There are many passages which could be trumpet music, and some

[23] Sartori, 1952, p. 405; 1968, p. 117.

writers [24] have assumed that the piece was for violin and trumpet answering one another in antiphony. Unfortunately, as regards our interest in this piece, it seems to be another of Uccelini's remarkable innovations for violin and is a scordatura piece in imitation of a trumpet.[25] Similarly, Giovanni Antonio Pandolfi's 'La Spata Fora, Trombetta due Violini', published in the *Sonate cioe' Balletti* ... of 1669 (Sartori, *Bibliografia*, vol. ii: 1669 i), is a string piece with figures in imitation of trumpet music.

One of Uccelini's students at Modena was Alessandro Stradella, who is also reputed to have studied at Modena under G. M. Bononcini.[26] Stradella was born in 1645; inasmuch as Uccelini left Modena in 1665 to work as the *Maestro di Capella* at the cathedral of Parma, Stradella presumably studied with him some time between 1655 and 1665. Stradella's contribution to the chamber trumpet repertory is a D major *Sonata a 8 viole con una tromba e basso continuo*. It is in score and found in the Biblioteca Nazionale at Turin, along with an interesting concerto-like sonata for two cornettos, two solo violins and continuo. The equally concerto-like trumpet sonata for two choirs of four-part strings and continuo is atypical of many sonatas, concertos and *sinfonie con tromba* of the Bolognese trumpet composers. It is atypical because, like the Corelli sonata and Purcell's trumpet sonata at York Minster, Stradella treats the trumpet part as melodically as possible, giving it the same thematic material as the string parts. Similar pieces by the San Petronio composers at Bologna are often multi-thematic, the string parts having their own melodic material while the trumpet part is usually simpler, more fragmentary and less interesting thematically.

Stradella's trumpet sonata exhibits a precocious inventiveness when compared with Cazzati's op. 35 trumpet sonatas (1665) or Grossi's op. 3 sonatas (1682), the latter published in the same year when Stradella is thought to have been murdered. The work, among others, has been called a *concerto grosso*,[27] and Newman (1959, p. 132) adds that 'here is the Baroque sonata come of age'. Like Torelli, Stradella exploits the full range of the trumpet, taking it from *d* to *d²*. He scores for the trumpet in all four movements, which are given as 'Allegro, Aria, Allegro, Aria'. The trumpet is featured throughout and introduces each movement, beginning the first movement without any accompaniment whatsoever—a rare event during

---

[24] Menke, 1934, Ex. 1 in the appendix.
[25] Schenk, 1964, p. 29; Newman, 1959, p. 123.
[26] Hutchings, 1961, p. 52.
[27] *Ibid.*, p. 54.

this period. The initial statement is fanfare-like, giving the trumpet its most secure harmonics at the outset, and is followed by a diatonic flourish to the repeated a^1. The first choir of strings answers antiphonally with the cello and continuo repeating the opening motive in exact imitation two octaves lower. The rest of the movement continues in a similar fashion, with the second choir of strings answering the first while the trumpet proceeds above them, restating the same thematic material with occasional sequential flourishes.

The second movement, or 'Aria', is in the same abrupt style as the third movement of Corelli's trumpet sonata in D; it begins with trumpet and continuo alone, followed by the strings in very sonorous eight-part writing. It is possible that Stradella may have heard the Corelli sonata, or, like Corelli, he may simply have used the instrument more imaginatively and soloistically than most. This movement is followed by the fugal allegro, which, like the first allegro, introduces the subject in the trumpet. The trumpet continues, playing the counter subject while the first choir of strings enters in the third bar with the dominant statement of the theme—followed two bars later by the second choir restating the subject an octave lower. The trumpet in this movement is an integral part of the overall polyphonic texture, and excepting the restriction to its natural harmonics with the occasional raised 11th partial in the dominant sections, it is given the same material as the other instruments. The movement concludes with a gradual addition of instruments, being accelerated in their successive entries right to the end.

The last movement ('Aria') is a 6/8 gigue with a continuous use of antiphony between the trumpet, the two choirs of strings and the basso continuo. The trumpet is once again given the initial statement. The work is rather sophisticated by contemporary standards in its motivic handling, and yet conservative with respect to the Venetian polychoral style adopted in scoring for two choirs of strings.

About the time Stradella was studying at Modena the Venetians were making their own contributions to the ever-growing trumpet repertory. Opera seems to have provided the most extensive opportunities for trumpet-playing, and judging from the number of works by Venetians that have arias, fanfares, marches and sonata-sinfonia type overtures which make use of the Baroque trumpet, Venice was probably an important centre of trumpet music. It was undoubtedly at Venice that Schütz, as a student of Gabrieli and later of Monteverdi, heard the experiments and musical innovations for trumpet. Before that time a tradition of natural trumpet-playing already existed in Germany and Austria, but it is doubted that its function in art music was very significant.

With the exception of a very few known examples it is curious that the trumpet never found a place in the *concertato* polychoral tradition at Venice, particularly among the composers at St Mark's before Legrenzi. Arnold (1959, p. 104) quotes from some Venetian payment records of 1603 where mention is made of a trumpet-player and several other instrumentalists (trombonists, violinists, a bassoonist, an organist and a cornetto player) who accompanied a mass at St Mark's on Christmas Eve and Christmas morning in 1602 and received a total of twenty-nine *scudi* for their services. But Legrenzi seems to be the first Italian church composer to prescribe a trumpet with choral forces. It is thought that he implemented various scoring devices already established in theatrical forms of entertainment. Descriptions of the large orchestral forces that were organized by Legrenzi at St Mark's do not mention trumpets.[28] But his *Laudate Pueri* scored for SSATB chorus, solo trumpet in D, 2 Vn, 2 Va, Bsn and Bc, indicates that trumpets were used at St Mark's, where the piece was presumably performed. The MS. score of this work, the only known source, is listed in Eitner (1902, vol. vi, p. 116) as Berlin, Königlich Bibliothek MS. 12720. After nearly eighteen months of efforts to track down Legrenzi's only known source of extra-operatic trumpet music, the score was located in the Berlin Deutsche Staatsbibliothek and has a new catalogue number, Mus. MS. 30229. It was one of many manuscripts moved to the Staatsbibliothek at Marburg between 1939 and 1940. It was returned to the Berlin library and recatalogued after the war.

According to Fétis (1878, vol. v, p. 256) Legrenzi is supposed to have published a collection of instrumental pieces with the title *Suonate da chiesa e da camera a 2. 3. 4. 5. 6. e 7. stromenti, con tromba e senza overo flauti, libro sesto, op. 17*, Venice, 1693. To date, there has been no additional information to identify or locate this opus. Fétis may have been mistaken, but the title is definite enough to suppose that he had seen it or had been informed of its existence.

Another Venetian to make use of the natural trumpet was Pietro Andrea Ziani. There is at least one known sonata by him for trumpet, strings and basso continuo. There are two MS. sources [28a] of the work: one in the Christ Church Library at Oxford (Chr. Ch. MS. 771) and the other in the

---

[28] Benvenuti, 1932.

[28a] Two other sources have recently come to light: one in the University Library at Warsaw, incorrectly attributed to Albinoni, the other in Zürich, incorrectly attributed to Bononcini.

Universitets Biblioteket at Upsala (U.B. Instr. mus. i hs. 66:4). Both are in score, the former a seventeenth-century copy and the latter copied some time in the early eighteenth century. The piece is in D major and scored for trumpet, two violins, two violas and basso continuo; the Upsala copy includes a bassoon with the continuo. It was probably composed between 1669 and 1676 while Ziani was employed as second organist at St Mark's. The remarkable thing about this sonata is the unusual anticipation of the type of agitated rhythmic vitality found in Vivaldi's music. The first movement is based on two motives: the energetic semiquaver theme in the strings—first stated in octaves between the violins and the violas and cellos—and the trumpet's simple but 'trumpetistic' fanfare motive. Only the outer movements are scored for trumpet. The unabashed simplicity of the trumpet-writing is actually engaging for both performer and listener. The string-writing more than compensates for the lack of trumpet acrobatics encountered in many of the Bologna sonatas at the end of the century. Whether the trumpet-writing is uncomplicated because Ziani wanted it so, or because a competent player was unavailable, is unknown.

Neapolitans such as Alessandro Scarlatti wrote both simple and florid trumpet parts, depending upon the function of the instrument in a particular piece. The trumpet parts in Scarlatti's serenade *Venere, Adone, Amore* (Chr. Ch. MS. 992 in score) and the *Sinfonia in D* (mod. ed. *Hortus Musicus*, Bärenreiter, vol. 146 [1957]) are simple and archetypes of the later, more rhythmic, less melodic parts of the late Baroque and Classic periods. On the other hand, the trumpet-writing in Scarlatti's cantata *Su le sponde del Tebro* (London: B.M. Add. MS. 31487) and his 'Seven Arias' for trumpet, soprano and basso continuo (Oxford: B.L. MS. Mus. Sch. E 394) is florid and employs the full range of the instrument. The four trumpet parts in his 'Sinfonia avanti l'Opera' in *Il Prigionier[o] Fortunato* (1699) (London: B.M. Add. MS. 16126) are florid, contrapuntal, and with their many repeated notes would make a remarkable sound.

2. The Bolognese 'School'

The most important centre for seventeenth-century trumpet music was Bologna. 'Canite tuba in Sion' [29] appears on a cartouche above the case of Lorenzo da Prato's fifteenth-century organ in the basilica of San Petronio at Bologna. The motto implies the unique contribution of San Petronio's

[29] 'Sound the trumpet in Sion' is the beginning of either Joel ii, 1 ('Canite tuba in Sion, ululate in monte . . .') or Joel ii, 15 ('Canite tuba in Sion, sanctificate jejunium . . .') in the Vulgate edition.

musicians to the art of the Baroque trumpet and the development of new instrumental forms. It was no accident that Bologna fostered these developments; the city had been a centre of intellectual and artistically creative activities since the eleventh century. In that century the oldest and one of the most famous universities in Europe was founded at Bologna. From the twelfth to the fifteenth century the student population numbered between three and five thousand, and among its many illustrious scholars were Dante Alighieri and Petrarch. The university was autonomous but had no fixed residences. Teachers and practitioners of law, medicine and theology lectured in their own houses, and later in rooms hired by the civic authorities. Not until early in the sixteenth century were professors of law given accommodation in a building that belonged to San Petronio. In 1562, by order of Pope Pius IV, the University of Bologna was finally incorporated within its own buildings, built at the direction of the cardinal legate Carlo Borromeo.

Bologna is in the centre of Etruscan Italy. It is surrounded at no great distances by the cities of Florence, Modena, Ferrara and Ravenna. To the north is Mantua, and over the mountains to the west lies Genoa. Through Bologna passed the merchants and their rich wares, the artisans, dignitaries, prelates and also the armies of invading and hostile forces from the north.

For centuries Bologna was torn by the strife of rival aristocratic factions. As a result of the medieval struggles for power between the Estes and other contending forces, Bologna was so weakened that in 1506 Pope Julius II brought the city under the papacy, where it remained until the Napoleonic invasions at the end of the eighteenth century.

The largest church in Bologna is the marvellously preserved Gothic edifice named after the city's patron saint, Petronio. It was begun in 1390, but only the nave and aisles as far as the transepts were finished. While the church measures 384 feet in length and is 157 feet wide, the proposed length of the entire cruciform basilica was to have been nearly 850 feet in length and 460 feet across the transepts. The projected dome was to have been nearly five hundred feet high at the crossing.

Abandonment of this grandiose project may have been due to political turmoil. More probably it was brought about by jealous ecclesiastics in Rome and Milan who feared that a shift in their spheres of influence might follow upon the erection of an edifice larger and more imposing than any in Italy or elsewhere. Like the rest of the impressive architecture within the inner city of Bologna, San Petronio was erected in dark red brick. Its façade was never completely covered by the marble carvings that were intended, so that the church does not have an impressive exterior—it has even been compared to a warehouse.[30]

The serene and spacious interior of San Petronio is another matter. It has few ornaments, and the warm tones of red mixed with greys and sepia enhance the simple but massive design of the structure. The many side-chapels bear witness to the skill and artistic achievements of the Renaissance artists who worked at Bologna. The frescoes and intarsia work in some of the chapels are by Raphael and his contemporaries. One chapel has a remarkable fresco by an anonymous fifteenth-century painter, showing a most unusual view of the Inferno and displaying an imagination comparable to that of Hieronymus Bosch. The chancel is encircled by a horseshoe-shaped balcony (*corretto*) above the choir stalls. On the north and south sides of the chancel and above the *corretto* are the original organs built by Lorenzo da Prato and Baldassare Malamini. The former installed the north gallery organ in the last quarter of the fifteenth century; the opposing Malamini instrument was finished in 1597. Almost all of the surviving woodwork—choir stalls, *corretto*, organ cases and chancel furniture—dates from the second half of the seventeenth century.

Like the *galleria* and *loggia* of St Mark's at Venice, the arrangement of San Petronio's chancel allows imaginative placement of musicians and performances of unusual interest. The two opposing organs, with their possibilities for antiphony and *piano-forte* echo devices, helped to promote the same idea in the instrumental and choral performances given there. Transcriptions of *canzoni* by Gioseffo (Giuseppe) Guami, Floriano Canale and Andriano Banchieri are thought to have been played on the two organs during the early seventeenth century. Many of the *sinfonie* and *sonate* for strings, frequently with trumpets and oboes, require two continuo keyboard instruments. The MS. sets of parts in the archives of San Petronio often have basso continuos specifically marked *organo primo* and *organo secondo*. Similar scoring devices are, of course, found in Venetian music almost a century earlier.

The polychoral-*concertato* style of Gabrieli and his school assumed different proportions at Bologna, especially with the advent of Mauritio Cazzati. When he arrived at Bologna in 1657 to assume his duties as *Maestro di Capella* at San Petronio, Cazzati was well aware of the type of ceremonies described earlier. Trumpets played no small part in Bolognese ecclesiastical and academic convocations. Religious feast days, particularly the Feast of San Petronio (4th October), required music on a grand scale.

[30] Hutchings, 1961, p. 67.

During the celebration of a mass full-length concertos were provided as probable antiphon substitutes between the sections of the Gloria and Credo, the Credo and Sanctus, and following the Agnus Dei.[31] Similar pieces were performed at meetings of the *Accademia Filarmonica*.

Living in a world-renowned centre for the teaching and development of the humanities, it was only natural that Bologna's inhabitants should expect—and indeed they received—the kind of splendid ceremonial sounds that Cazzati and his successors provided at San Petronio. Cazzati's op. 35 *Sonate à due, trè, quattro, e cinque, con alcune per Tromba* (Bologna, 1665 and reprinted at Venice in 1668 and again at Bologna in 1677) are not only the earliest but also the first published full-length sonatas for trumpet. All three pieces 'à cinque' in this collection are for trumpet, strings and continuo. The collection was published in parts for the following instruments: 'Violino I, Violino II, Alto Viola, Tenor Viola, Tiorba o Contrabasso, Organo.' Printed at the end of the first violin part are the words 'Tromba o Violino'. At the back of each part are the composer's remarks about the collection, which here follow in translation:

The Author to the Reader

This work consists of sonatas for two, three, four, and five instruments; where the letters VP are written in the continuo part, this indicates first violin; VS indicates second violin.

It should be realized that the sonatas for trumpet can be played on a violin, if a trumpet is not available; that is, the trumpet part can be played on a violin, and the other parts should be: violin, alto viola, tenor viola, and violone, or trombone.

The sonata called the Caprara should be played on a tromba serrata, *which means a muted trumpet; and if it is to be played on an open trumpet, it must be played a tone lower; this also applies to the other parts.*

The [sonatas] Bianchina and the Zábeccari are played as written on an open trumpet, and if they are to be played on a muted trumpet they must be transposed up a tone. Meanwhile, I beg that you pardon my customary weakness, and pray that you may prosper!

[31] The convincing evidence for and the thoroughly documented work on the subject of instrumental antiphon substitutes in the Roman Rite during the seventeenth century appears in Stephen Bonta's two important articles, 'Liturgical problems in Monteverdi's Marian Vespers' (*JAMS*, xx No. 1, 1967, pp. 87–106) and 'The uses of the *Sonata da Chiesa*' (*JAMS*, xxii No. 1, 1969, pp. 54–84).

Cazzati stresses the point about performing the five-part sonatas on a violin if a trumpet is not available, by adding: 'Per mancanza di Tromba si può sonare con un violino.' The composer undoubtedly wished the collection to have the greatest saleability and was well aware that competent trumpet-players might not have been as plentiful as violinists.

The three trumpet pieces are entitled 'La Caprara', 'La Bianchina', 'La Zâbeccari', and are scored for trumpet, one violin, alto and tenor violas, and continuo, with the possibility of using a trombone instead of a violone and a theorbo instead of a contrabass. The inclusive range of the trumpet part in all three sonatas is from the 4th to the 13th harmonics. The 4th, 5th and 13th harmonics are used sparingly, however, and the raised 11th harmonic occurs with the same infrequency. There are only two non-harmonic tones in all three works (the 7th harmonic c^1 sharp in bar 53 of 'La Caprara' and the unusual raised 8th harmonic c^1 sharp in bar 22 of 'La Bianchina'). The sonatas 'La Caprara' and 'La Bianchina' are in four basic sections, each beginning with a brief toccata-like introduction in which the trumpet plays a simple fanfare motive over a tonic bass; in the case of 'La Caprara', over a rhythmically varied single bass note. In all three sonatas a similar antiphonal formula is used with the strings and trumpet continually answering one another, stating and restating the same material; tuttis occur infrequently. Although there are a number of interesting exceptions, which are discussed below, this echo device is characteristic of many trumpet sonatas. The pieces in which it is used with great economy are generally the most outstanding, other devices having been used to better effect.

The sonatas 'La Bianchina' and 'La Zâbeccari' are in C major and preferably for an unmuted C trumpet. The parts to the sonata 'La Caprara' have no key signature, but it is obviously in D major, since nearly every f and c has a sharp before it. This piece is scored at sounding pitch. Cazzati's directions are specific about using an open trumpet in 'La Caprara', or a muted trumpet in the next two sonatas. If the trumpet is unmuted it sounds its true fundamental, C; if muted it sounds a tone higher. In 'La Caprara' the string parts are already transposed to match the tonality of a muted C trumpet sounding in D. Appropriate transpositions of the string parts must be made if 'La Caprara' is played on an open trumpet, or if the next two sonatas are to be played with a mute.

The use of muted trumpets was not unusual. Monteverdi used them, Cazzati fifty-eight years later; and at the same time as Cazzati, and far to the north in Lübeck, muted trumpets are found in the cantatas of Dietrich

Buxtehude (see Chapter 6). Trichet [32] and Mersenne (1635, pp. 108–9; 1636b, pp. 259–60) mention mutes, and their purpose seems to have been to soften as well as transpose the trumpet (*see* Chapter 10, pp. 232, 233). The modern straight or pear mute does not appreciably affect the pitch of a trumpet, for, unlike its seventeenth-century predecessor, it does not project very far into the bell of the instrument, nor does it completely 'choke' down the end of the bore through a very narrow opening as a Baroque trumpet mute does. After the seventeenth century muted trumpets were almost never used until modern times. After Buxtehude, the last composer to employ muted trumpets until the latter part of the nineteenth century was Johann Philipp Krieger. While at Weissenfels (*c.* 1690) he composed a *Magnificat à 12* requiring six strings, chorus and two 'Trombe Sortino'.[33]

In his excellent survey of Bolognese cultural history, Vatielli (1927, pp. 208–9) remarks on the musical developments at San Petronio with the arrival of Cazzati: 'There coincides with the appointment of Cazzati as *Maestro di Cappella* in 1657 an increase in the size of the choir; there also appears to be a considerable body of instrumentalists who are paid a permanent salary; on special solemn feast-days these were augmented by musicians imported from elsewhere [probably Modena], who were paid a fee for that specific occasion.' [34] Vatielli also adds the following note: 'In the pay-rolls which are preserved in the archives of San Petronio one often finds in the last decades of the seventeenth century and early in the next century the formula: "Paid, on the occasion of the feast of . . . to the [instrumental] musicians hired to augment the orchestra." In 1716, on the occasion of a solemn festival, 123 assorted musicians were hired, in addition to the regular members of the cappella, and the following year 131 were hired.' [35]

Eleven printed collections of Cazzati's works are found among the

[32] Lesure, 1955, pp. 385–6.

[33] Werner, 1911, p. 133.

[34] 'Con l'assunzione del Cazzati a Maestro di Cappella (1657) coincide un ampliamento della cantoria e figura come stabilmente stipendiato un corpo notevole di strumentisti, ai quali in occasione di feste solenni venivano aggiunti sonatori tolti di fuori e rimunerati volta per volta.'

[35] Vatielli, 1927, p. 209, note 1: 'Nei registri di paga conservati nell' Archivio di S. Petronio ricorre frequente negli ultimi decenni del Seicento e nei primi del sequente secolo la formula: "Pagati in occasione della festa di . . . alli musici sonatori pigliati per ripieno." Nel 1716 in occasione di una solennita si presero ben centoventitrè fra musici e sonatori, oltre quelli della cappella, e centotrentano l'anno successivo.'

compositions at San Petronio, including the op. 35 (1665) *Sonate . . . con alcune per Tromba*. The Biblioteca 'G. B. Martini' has copies of most of his extant published vocal and instrumental pieces as well. There are no manuscripts of Cazzati in San Petronio. If the manuscripts were not duplicated by his printed works (they would in all likelihood have perished at the time if they had been duplicates), he may have taken them when he left Bologna in 1671.

In the years following the first publication of Cazzati's op. 35 *Sonate* and before the great surge of trumpet music in the last decade of the seventeenth century, three more publications containing trumpet sonatas appeared in Italy; the third and last of the century, G. B. Bononcini's op. 3 *Sinfonie* will be discussed later. The first two collections to follow Cazzati's op. 35 *Sonate* were Giovanni Buonaventura Viviani's *Sonate a Violino Solo . . . et Sonate per Tromba sola . . . Opera Quarta* (Venice, 1678 and Rome, 1678), and Andrea Grossi's [36] *Sonate a 2. 3. 4. e 5 Instromenti . . . Opera Terza* (Bologna, 1682). The Viviani collection contains twenty pieces for solo violin and basso continuo. The last two works in the collection are sonatas for solo trumpet and basso continuo ('Tromba et Organo ò Gravicembalo'). Besides the short pieces in Fantini's *Modo . . .* , Viviani's two sonatas are the only known Baroque works for trumpet and continuo alone. Neither piece is musically profound, but they are a welcome addition to the repertory and have a certain amount of charm. Although Sartori [37] at one time gave only one source for this collection, a second is found in the Bodleian Library at Oxford (Mus. Sch. C. 164 a–b) and was printed at Rome, but with only the slightest differences from the contents of the Venice print.

Grossi's op. 3 *Sonate* contain three trumpet sonatas. The last three works 'à cinque' are in D major and scored for trumpet, two violins, viola, 'bassetto' (prob. cello) and organ continuo. They are not unlike Cazzati's three sonatas, except that Grossi takes the trumpet up to c^2 sharp and writes b^1 natural quite frequently. His parts are much more florid than Cazzati's and the melodic ideas more fluent. Each sonata is in several movements and most of the allegro sections tend to be fugal, with the trumpet introducing the subject. The first of the trumpet sonatas ('Sonata Decima à 5') is mentioned by Bukofzer (1947, p. 228).

Except for a lull in musical activities at San Petronio between 1695 and *c.* 1701 (probably because of difficulties in meeting the enormous musical

---

[36] Andrea Grossi was probably a grandson of Ludovico Grossi da Viadana (*see* Schmidl, 1928).
[37] Sartori, 1952, pp. 490–1 (*see* second volume with revisions and corrections, pub. 1968).

expenditure), large-scale performances there were frequent, and the demand for instrumental sonatas and concertos is evidenced by the number of surviving parts and scores in the basilica archives. Kept at Number 5 Piazza Galvani is a vast collection of printed and MS. sources mostly of late seventeenth-century Italian vocal and instrumental pieces, many of them scored with trumpet(s). The composers represented for the trumpet pieces are Pirro Capacelli d'Albergati, Matteo Albergati, Giuseppe Alberti (possibly the same as P. C. d'Albergati), Giuseppe Aldrovandini, Giuseppe Coretti, Giovanni Paolo Colonna, Francesco Foggia, Petronio Frances-chini, Domenico Gabrielli, Giuseppe Iacchini (or Jacchini), Ferdinando Antonio Lazzari, Francesco Manfredini, Giacomo Perti, and Giuseppe Torelli; there are twelve anonymous pieces, including two Torelli-like pieces (sonatas) scored for strings, basso continuo and four trumpets. All of the individual pieces will be found in the Appendix under the appropriate composer or among the anonymous compositions.

More than sixty-eight years ago Arnold Schering (1905) drew attention to the significance of the rich treasure of seventeenth-century music at San Petronio and its unsuspected contribution to the development of the *concerto grosso*, the concerto, and the evolution of the sonata. A life-time has passed since Schering's publication and less than 2 per cent of all the pieces in the San Petronio archives are available in modern editions. The number of bibliographic references that have appeared since Schering's observations are tragically few and far between. And yet a published catalogue of the entire manuscript and printed contents of the music archives has been available since 1913. The catalogue of the San Petronio music is only one of many such catalogues of Italian collections that were issued between 1909 and 1942 as part of the *Bolletino dell' Associazione dei Musicologi Italiana*. These are available in many libraries. An interesting but not very comprehensive article by Jean Berger (1951, pp. 354–67) and a chapter in Hutchings (1961, Ch. v) deal with the San Petronio composers and the *Sonate, Sinfonie* and *Concerti* to be found there. Almost none of the writers on Italian church instrumental music ever mention the purpose for which these pieces were intended and when they were performed. It has already been suggested that they were performed during the celebration of masses and on particular feast days.[38] The present keeper of the San Petronio archives, Signor Sergio Paganelli, was quick to remind the author that seventeenth-century Italians, particularly

[38] *See* p. 95, note 31. *See also* Anne Schnoebelen's useful article, 'Performance practices at San Petronio in the Baroque', *AM*, xli, 1969, pp. 37–55.

the affluent and humanist Bolognese, did not share the pious view held elsewhere and by many of the clergy today, that such music is not appropriate to a service of Christian worship. On the contrary, the educated and sophisticated Bolognese—ecclesiastical as well as civic leaders—realized the spiritual and emotional qualities of such theatrically intentioned music. Theatrical elements during the celebration of Mass in most European cities in the seventeenth and eighteenth centuries were far from condemned. What could have been more theatrical than some of Mozart's Salzburg Cathedral anthems, masses and organ sonatas? Present-day conventions should not obscure historical reality. What was done at Bologna in a church that could afford the expense of composers and performers to enrich the service was no different from the comparable situation at St Mark's at Venice with the Gabrielis or in the Protestant liturgy at St Thomas's at Leipzig with J. S. Bach and his predecessors.

The total number of manuscript sources of instrumental pieces with trumpet(s) in San Petronio (in score and/or parts) is eighty-three.[38a] There are thirty-three surviving works for one trumpet, forty-five for two trumpets, and five for four trumpets. There are no compositions for three trumpets. Although the Germans frequently score for three trumpets, Italian, French, English and Bohemian trumpet music is normally scored for one, two and sometimes four trumpets.

The Appendix shows that of the fourteen composers mentioned above, Torelli is represented by the largest number of pieces. There is a total of forty-two trumpet pieces by him in San Petronio, all in manuscript and mostly in parts. Of the forty-two pieces, seventeen are for one trumpet, twenty-three for two trumpets and two for four trumpets. Aldrovandini, Gabrielli, Iacchini and Perti composed the largest share of the remaining pieces. All but two of the eighty-three compositions are in D major and scored for trumpet(s) in D. The two exceptions are Torelli's *Sonata a 4 Trombe in Mi min* (E flat) (now missing), and his *Sinfonia a 4 Trombe in Do maggiore* (C maj.). The reason for these two exceptions may have had something to do with the pitch of the organ when they were first performed, either in San Petronio or at the Accademia Filarmonica.

The terms *sonata*, *sinfonia* and *concerto* seem to have no particular significance. Torelli's pieces with one trumpet are called *Sinfonia* in seven cases and *Sonata* in the remaining ten. Five of his works with two trumpets are entitled *Concerto*, fifteen are entitled *Sinfonia* and each of the remaining three is called a *Sonata*. We have already mentioned that one piece with

[38a] This figure is based on the *BAMI* inventory taken before World War I.

four trumpets was called a *Sonata* while the other was called a *Sinfonia*. Domenico Gabrielli uses the term *Sonata* in all of his pieces, while Iacchini and Perti use both *Sonata* and *Sinfonia* for the same kind of music. Since there is no hard and fast rule about the musical-formal connotations of these terms, all that can be said is that the terms are used indiscriminately, and imply little about the actual construction of a work. 'Whatever name was given to these trumpet pieces at Bologna, many of them were concertos, not merely precursors of concertos. Within the trumpet pieces of one composer we can trace the development from a sonata to a concerto conception.' [39]

A number of the San Petronio trumpet pieces, especially those scored for more than one trumpet, introduce thematic ideas in the first or first principal movement (and often in the last movement) that are not always shared by both trumpets and strings. Fragments of some melodic material may be introduced from one part to another, but quite often the trumpets will have their own melodic material and the strings theirs. Sometimes in an extended movement the secondary thematic material may be stated antiphonally between strings and trumpets. A notable example of this thematic separateness is the first movement of Francesco Manfredini's *Concerto con una o due Trombe* (Bologna: SP Lib. M. 1.). With the exception of thematic material exchanged between trumpets and strings in the second section, the two groups of instruments do not have the same themes.

The first movement principal theme in Manfredini's concerto for two trumpets is the long octave leaping, tonic-dominant statement in the strings—played in octaves between the violins and violas and the cellos and continuo basses. The theme stretches out over nine bars, with the strings breaking into a sequential harmonic progression before the trumpet entry (Ex. 6). The principal thematic material in the trumpet parts is the quaver-semiquaver motive beginning at bar ten. By the use of sequential devices, development of melodic fragments and the usual semiquaver 'violinistic' harmonic sequences, these two ideas are kept in juxtaposition until the statement of the secondary theme by the trumpets (Ex. 7). It is here that both trumpets and strings alternate in presenting this theme. There follows a development of this one idea until the ostinato-like principal theme of the strings is recapitulated. The trumpets once again interject with their first statement while the strings persist with the principal subject. The movement ends with a fragmentary restatement of the secondary motive by the trumpets.

[39] Hutchings, 1961, p. 81.

Ex. 6. Manfredini: *Concerto con una o due Trombe* (1st movement, principal theme).

Ex. 7. Manfredini: *Concerto con una o due Trombe* (1st movement, secondary theme).

This is one of the most attractive of the Bologna pieces, but formally not the most exceptional. Perti's *Sonata a 4 Trombe, Obuè et Violini* (Lib. P. 61 No. 5), with its agitated and scintillating second and fourth movements, is by any standards a show piece for trumpets. The last movement, a brilliant episode for pairs of trumpets in antiphony and bustling semiquavers in a contrasting motive for the strings and oboes with two organs, does not let the orchestra share the same material with the trumpets. The work is not in the usual sense a concerto, nor a sonata in terms of the many contemporary sonatas for one or two stringed instruments and continuo. The inclusive term 'Sinfonia' might have been a better title for this work.

Domenico Gabrielli's D major *Sonata a 6 con Tromba* is a most direct and well-constructed piece. It is essentially in three movements, but it begins with an arresting one-bar declamation marked 'Largo'. This work could easily have been an act overture or scene prelude in any one of many contemporary operas. After the first bar, the Presto begins with a fanfare figure in all the strings, with a *piano* echo repetition in the second and third bars. The trumpet enters with the short, fragmentary subject which is the basis of its entire part. The strings interject with another flourish. Neither they nor the trumpet ever agree on the same thematic material throughout the entire movement. The second movement is basically for solo violin and continuo, with infrequent short cadential entries in the other string parts. The last movement is the extended harmonic episode with a virtuoso first violin part. The trumpet is relegated to reiterating the first and third beat in a bar. With the lower string parts and the continuo filling in the fourth crotchet throughout, a continuous rhythmic pulse is effected by an accentuation of the first, third and fourth beats of every bar.

As frequently as the 'unshared motive' technique is used in the San Petronio trumpet music, most of the pieces follow a precursory *concerto grosso* scheme. The notable exponent of this form is Torelli. His output ranges from contrapuntal two-violin and continuo trio sonatas to the noisy and flamboyant gesture of the *Sinfonia a 4* in C for strings, oboes, four trumpets, timpani, trombone and bassoon. It is difficult to make a chronological arrangement of Torelli's sonatas and concertos. Only five are dated, two in the composer's own hand and three in the manuscript of a copyist.[40] Few of his trumpet pieces were published, but three known to the present writer are found in two posthumous publications. Both were published by Estienne Roger at Amsterdam. The earliest (*c.* 1710) is a collection of *VI Sonates ou Concerts / à 4, 5 & 6 Parties / Composées par / Mrs. Bernardi, Torelli / & autres fameaux Auteurs* . . . (*RISM* ii, p. 368).[41] The first and sixth sonatas in D major are for strings, trumpet and continuo. They are both by Torelli. The 'Sonata 1' is similar in a number of respects to the dated San Petronio MS. *Sinfonia a 4 con Tromba e Violini unissoni 1693* (SP: Lib. T. 1, No. 7), and the 'Sonata VI' is identical with a MS. *Sinfonia con Tromba* in San Petronio (SP: Lib. T. 1; see Giegling: *Torelli*, 'Verzeichnis', No. 10). The second Roger collection (*c.* 1715) is entitled *Concerts à 5, 6, et 7 instruments . . . pour la trompette ou le haubois . . . par Messieurs Bitti, Vivaldi et Torelli* . . . (*RISM* ii, p. 146).[42] The last piece, the D major 'Concerto VI', is by Torelli and is scored for trumpet, strings and continuo.

Despite the difficulties in tracing a chronological order by dating, watermarks, etc., it is possible to see in Torelli's music an evolution from a simple imitative-antiphonal style towards a more mature concerto con-

[40] Giegling, 1949, p. 31.

[41] One of two known copies is in the British Museum, with the shelf-mark g. 914.

[42] One copy is in the Bodleian Library at Oxford: Mus. 183, c. 36 (1–7).

ception. Two of his more full-grown works are the 'Concerto VI' in the *c.* 1715 Roger print and a *Sinfonia con Tromba* in San Petronio (SP: Lib. T. 1 No. 8; *see* Giegling: *Torelli*, 'Verzeichnis', No. 8). Both pieces have quasi-developed, bi-thematic outer movements where the trumpet and strings present and rework the same material. The first movement of the *c.* 1715 'Concerto VI' presents both melodic elements in the introductory section, which is played by the strings (Ex. 8). The trumpet enters at bar seven with the first thematic element (a). The rest of the movement reworks these two ideas and is rounded off with a recapitulation of rhythmically and motivically related material from the opening bars.

The first movement of the *Sinfonia con Tromba* again has both thematic elements contained in the initial statement of the strings (Ex. 9). The four-

Ex. 8. Torelli: Concerto con Tromba, *c.* 1715 (1st movement, introduction).

Exs. 9, 10. Torelli: *Sinfonia con Tromba* (1st movement, string and trumpet motives).

Ex. 9.

Ex. 10.

bar bi-thematic statement is answered by the trumpet (Ex. 10). Not only is the trumpet motive anacrusic like the initial statement, but the quaver-two semiquaver figure is directly related to the second (b) element of the string motive. Later in the movement the trumpet is given the first (a) element. Both elements are developed by strings and trumpet, with the trumpet part being favoured in a soloistic concerto style.

In a style comparable with Torelli's almost mature, full-blown concertos are Giuseppe Iacchini's sonatas for one and two trumpets and strings found in the San Petronio archives (SP: Lib. J. 1. Nos. 1–5). Like his teacher, Domenico Gabrielli, Iacchini played cello in the San Petronio orchestra, wrote many solo pieces for cello and featured it in his *sonate* and *sinfonie* with trumpet(s). Three of his trumpet sonatas were included in his *Trattenimenti* ['entertainments'] *per camera à 3, 4, 5 e 6 Strumenti, con alcuni à una, e due Trombe* .... Contrary to Berger's premise that '. . . San Petronio was, by and large, the only place in Bologna where trumpet works were used', and also that 'printed editions were obviously impractical',[43] the published sonatas of Iacchini and Cazzati, as well as Torelli's posthumous publications, give the opposite impression. One further piece of evidence in this respect is a letter found in Codex No. 67 (item No. 4) in the Liceo Musicale at Bologna. It was addressed to Giacomo Antonio Perti at Bologna, dated 'Florence 8 August 1699', and signed 'Stefano Frilli':

I brought from there [from him(?)] a sinfonia with trumpet written by Signor Iacchini; it was given to me by a scribe, and is very popular—every time that it is played, people ask who wrote it.[44]

Bolognese trumpet sonatas, most likely written for and first performed in San Petronio, were surely played in the concerts of the Accademia Filarmonica. The title page of Iacchini's *Trattenimenti* states that he was cellist at the basilica and at the Accademia.[45] It seems unlikely that he would not have exhibited his works for the approval of his illustrious performer-composer colleagues at the renowned Bolognese musical academy.

[43] Berger, 1951, p. 356.

[44] Mentioned in Gaspari, 1905, vol. iv, p. 118: 'Io portal di costi (datami da un copista) una sinfonia con Tromba del Sig.r Iacchini, quale piace assaissimo, et ogni uolta ne dimandano chi è il nome, rallegrandomi con V.S. per esser egli suo scolare ecc.'

[45] '. . . Giuseppe Iacchini Suonatore di Violoncello nella Perinsigne Collegiata di S. Petronio di Bologna & Accademico Filharmonico.'

It may have been at one of the Accademia Filarmonica concerts that Corelli's one and only trumpet sonata was performed. Although not Bolognese, Corelli had great respect for the musical importance of Bologna and admired the musicians there. Proof of his regard for Bologna and its musical institutions is the fact that on the title-pages of his opus 1–4 *Sonate*, published at Rome, Modena and Bologna, he refers to himself as 'Arcangelo Corelli da Fusignano detto il Bolognese'. Considering his associations with Rome this was a great compliment to Bologna and an indication of that city's musical reputation. The sources of Corelli's unique trumpet piece are given in the Appendix (p. 254). In view of the number of sources that attribute the work to Corelli, there is little doubt that it is authentic; the music itself substantiates Corelli's authorship.

On 16th March 1713 an interesting advertisement appeared in the London *Daily Courant*: '. . . several Pieces of Musick proper for the Trumpet particularly a Sonata Compos'd by Signor Corelli, on purpose for Mr Twiselton when he was at Rome. For the benefit of Mr Twiselton, Trumpet to his Excellency the Duke d'Aumont.' This probably refers to the same trumpet sonata as the one mentioned above. That the piece was known in England is clear from a manuscript set of instrumental parts in the British Museum—possibly in James Paisible's hand—that include an accurate concordance to the other sources of the trumpet sonata.[46]

Whether or not 'Signor Corelli' composed the piece 'on purpose for Mr Twiselton' is a moot point. Tilmouth (1964, pp. 217–21) gives specific references about individual parts that are found in England. He also mentions particular performances where it is supposed to have been played. Considering the publication in the Naples Conservatorio di San Pietro a Majella (see *BAMI*, 'Napoli 2', p. 574), it might be possible to pre-date the work between 1685 and 1690. The manuscript sets of parts,[47] other than the set in the British Museum, indicate that the piece was written some time in the last decade of the seventeenth century.

[46] The instrumental parts are preserved in four part-books, which contain trumpet pieces from Henry Purcell's operas, the 'Suite de Clarke' (*see* Chapter 9), an anonymous trumpet sonata of the Bolognese type, and several suites, overtures, and short pieces for strings, with the occasional addition of oboes and flutes. The shelf marks for the four oblong books are B.M. Add. MS. 39565, 6, 7 (first treble, tenor, bass), and 30839 (second treble). The Corelli sonata is found in the same place in all four books: leaves 52 verso and 53 recto and entitled 'Corelli con duo discando Tromba'.

[47] Tenbury: St Michael's College MS. (parts) SM. 1312; Vienna: Nationalbibliothek (Estensischen Musikalien), MS. 98 b., 'Sonata con Aboe' [sic].

Corelli is supposed to have been at Modena between 1689 and 1690. There he may have composed the trumpet sonata and the pieces previously mentioned in connection with the Este collection now in Vienna. The 'Concerto' in D major for two trumpets, 'Violino Principale' and basso continuo is a curious piece. The manuscript part in Vienna (Haas, 1927, p. 169b) lacks a second movement, which is indicated in the trumpet parts as 'Grave Tacet'. The number of non-harmonic tones in the second trumpet part belies the use of the intended natural instrument. The style and harmony are not Corelli's, and pending further evidence it can only be assumed that the work is spurious.

Besides the purely instrumental pieces at San Petronio there are a number of works for chorus with orchestral accompaniment. Those with trumpet parts are remarkable archetypes of later oratorios. These compositions are usually set to psalm texts and frequently bear the title 'Motetto'. An outstanding exponent of this type of music was Giovanni Paolo Colonna.

In 1659 Colonna was appointed an organist at San Petronio and served under Cazzati until the latter's resignation. Colonna was appointed *Maestro di Cappella* in 1674. He took advantage of the physical attributes of San Petronio, specifying two organs in many of his published collections of 'Motetti Sacri', 'Salmi Brevi' and 'Messi', many of which also require double chorus in eight parts.

Colonna presented to the Emperor Leopold I at Vienna one copy of every composition, which was then deposited in the royal library.[48] For this reason there are eighty-four of Colonna's works in MS. in the National Library at Vienna.[49] At least seven of these works include trumpet(s). There are two settings by Colonna of the text *Beatus vir qui timet dominum* (Psalm cxi in the Vulgate ed.). One is in the Vienna collection [50] while the other is in the library of St Michael's College, Tenbury.[51] The latter is scored for chorus, soloists, solo trumpet in D, five-part strings and basso continuo. It is an extended work with many fugal choruses and instrumental *ritornelli*. The trumpet plays an integral part in the overall polyphonic texture; there are several duet passages for a solo alto and trumpet, where the Bologna trumpet concerto style is in evidence.

Colonna does not seem to have devoted much time to the composing of

---

[48] Eitner: *QL*, vol. iii, p. 19.
[49] *See* Mantuani (1897; 1899).
[50] Vienna: N.B. MS. (score) 15544, dated '1679'.
[51] Tenbury: MS. (score) SM. 1217. Modern ed. by D. Smithers, G. Schirmer, New York.

purely instrumental works; only one such piece attributed to him is found in the archives of San Petronio.[52] However, his brilliant student, G. B. Bononcini, turned his attention to the trumpet sonata at the tender age of fifteen.[53] Like his somewhat older contemporaries Iacchini and Domenico Gabrielli, Bononcini was a cellist in the San Petronio orchestra, the same orchestra in which Torelli was a 'suonatore di violetta'—a violist. Bononcini's knowledge of trumpet music must have been more than casual. In a precocious collection of *Sinfonie a 5. 6. 7. e 8. Istromenti, con alcune à una e due Trombe* (Bologna 1685), Bononcini comes to grips with all the technical problems of the trumpet and shows a mature approach to the art of counterpoint and concerto style. The collection is dedicated to his mentor, Colonna, and contains four trumpet pieces. Two are for solo trumpet and five-part strings with continuo ('Sinfonia Quinta à 6' and 'Sinfonia Ottava à 6') and two more for two trumpets and the same combination of instruments ('Sinfonia Nona à 7' and 'Sinfonia Decima à 7'). All four works are in D major and each is in six sections, with the last movement of the 'Sinfonia Decima' being divided into four changes of tempo, alternating twice from 'Largo' to 'Allegro'. The only known printed source of this collection is at Bologna [54] and most unfortunately lacks the first violin part; there is an almost complete manuscript score in the Paris Bibliothèque Nationale.[55] It was copied by Sébastien de Brossard at the end of the seventeenth century, but the 'Sinfonia Quinta' lacks the last six bars of the third movement ('Grave') as well as the entire last three movements. Using both sources a reconstruction of the missing first violin part in those sections has been possible.

In some respects, Bononcini's trumpet parts are more brilliant and demand greater virtuosity than any of the other Bologna sinfonias and concertos. In the 'Sinfonia Quinta' he restricts the range of the trumpet to the limits of f sharp and b^1, but in the next trumpet piece ('Sinfonia Ottava') he repeatedly takes the trumpet to c^2 sharp and d^2. The works with two trumpets ('Sinfonia Nona' and 'Decima') make enormous demands on the players. In both pieces the range of the first trumpet part is a to d^2, and the second trumpet is relegated to a register not very much

[52] Bologna: S.P. Lib. C. 56 *Sonata a 5 Trombe e Cornetto con Violini.*

[53] Although the composer states in the preface that he is only thirteen ('di tredici anni'), he is known to have been born at Modena on 18th July 1670, fifteen years before the publication of his trumpet sonatas.

[54] Bologna: B.C. X 124 (Vn 1 missing).

[55] Paris: B.N. Vm⁷ 1476.

lower; it must play from *f* sharp to c^2 sharp. The young composer may have been trying very hard to impress his teacher and possibly was showing off, but experience in performing these pieces has shown them to be equal to any by his contemporaries. The last two trumpet pieces are absolutely dazzling.

There is one interesting point about the Bologna manuscript and printed trumpet works: hardly any introduce non-harmonic tones,[56] and the 7th partial (*c* natural in the key of D major) is seldom used. Excepting the few instances in Monteverdi and Fantini, the second and third partials are almost absent in Italian trumpet music. The usual range of Italian trumpet parts is from *d* to b^1. Only in the works of Torelli, Bononcini, and in Corelli's sonata do we find much use made of c^2 sharp and d^2. It is extraordinary what music was made considering the musical limitations of the Baroque trumpet. These limitations may have had more to do with the style and form of the concerto as it evolved in Bologna and Modena than has been hitherto suspected. In circumventing the natural defects of the trumpet, Italian composers were forced to rely on short thematic fragments and succinct musical ideas, rather than the long melismatic phrases found in polyphonic string and vocal compositions of the same period. Such brief statements and the necessary use of antiphony and thematic development in trumpet music soon became the adopted style in other instrumental forms. How much the trumpet directly or indirectly influenced the development of the concerto and the *concerto grosso*, depends upon the importance placed on the Bologna school. Some writers are of the opinion that its importance has been too long underestimated. The ancillary role of the trumpet in the development of the Baroque concerto deserves serious consideration.

[56] Infrequent as non-harmonic tones are in the Italian trumpet repertory, it is interesting that one unusual non-harmonic tone, rarely found outside the Bolognese pieces, appears with some regularity. This is the raised 8th partial already mentioned in connection with Cazzati's *Sonata*, 'La Bianchina'. Bononcini's *Sinfonia nona* of 1685, for example, has one raised 8th partial (d^1 sharp) in the first trumpet part and five (!) in the second trumpet part.

5 THE TRUMPET 'GUILDS'

The development of art trumpet music in Northern Europe followed on the heels of Italian innovations. These developments were inevitable. The social and political conditions of the Northern European kingdoms and principalities were most receptive to Italian forms at the beginning of the seventeenth century. In the north trumpets were already being made and used for ceremonial court activities and in civic affairs. The time was ripe for a transfer of the instrument to more aesthetic enterprises. The transfer was rapid and had some unique results peculiar to those areas with their different individual temperament and their own style of musical composition.

Particularly in Germany trumpet music was shaped by the imported Italian styles at the turn of the sixteenth century. The composers who returned from their studies in Venice, or those who were indirectly influenced by Italian composition techniques, found in the existing tradition of trumpet-playing a ready source of performers and instruments. The first effects were felt in church compositions and in performances of ecclesiastical music. Before discussing these developments and the specific musical sources, let us examine the role of the trumpet in Northern Europe and how its technique gradually evolved into the highly specialized and sophisticated art often associated with the demanding trumpet parts of Bach and Telemann.

Court Trumpeters and the *Kameradschaft*

In Central and Northern Europe the art of trumpet-playing was fostered by two spheres of influence: the court and the municipality. This is not to say that the same influences had not been at work in Italy and elsewhere, but in those areas which now comprise Germany, Austria, Czechoslovakia (Bohemia and Moravia), Denmark, Sweden, Holland, and part of Poland, the duties of court and civic musicians were clearly defined. The activities of each seldom coincided. Rules were enforced by local electors and princes forbidding one group being at cross purposes with the other; each was protected and each guarded their rights jealously.

The court trumpeters belonged to the *Kameradschaft* (fellowship), a knightly class of soldier-performers whose chief importance was leading an army into battle. Most of the trumpets supplied by the Nuremberg makers mentioned in Chapter 3 were sent to the many courts and military organizations in Central Europe. The trumpeters of these military establishments showed the same feelings of comradeship as the troops and officers they led in their various campaigns. Their banding together in what has been called a guild set them apart from other musicians. Their obvious military importance gave them an almost inordinate position of prestige with guaranteed rights and privileges. The *Kameradschaft* trumpeters in most Saxon courts, for example, played signals, cavalry calls, and troop manœuvre flourishes during military exercises and battle campaigns; during times of peace they provided ceremonial music both at the court and in the court *Kapelle*.

The primary importance of court trumpeters, especially during the Thirty Years War (1618–48), was in their military capacity. The superlative few were, however, given the title of *Konzerttrompeter* or *Kammertrompeter* and were frequently asked to join the other household musicians in providing *Tafelmusik* and other forms of musical entertainment. The duties of the *Kammertrompeter* were clearly defined. Their services were required for the noon and evening meals—'zur Tafel zu blasen'.[1] When there were no guests in the court the trumpeters and a timpanist had only one service to perform on weekdays. The entire trumpet corps and the timpani were obliged to perform at special assemblies, tournaments and various sporting events. On the birthdays of the resident nobles as well as on special feast days the *Hoftrompeter* (court trumpeters) were also instructed to provide special ceremonial music. At the beginning of the afternoon and evening meals the *Tafelblasen* often consisted of short pieces for two or three trumpets and timpani. At those courts where music was particularly important, the *Hoftrompeter* were from time to time required to accompany the chapel choir as well as join the court orchestra in

[1] Werner, 1911, p. 87.

theatrical productions. In the lesser courts the duties of the second-rank trumpeters might include assignments of lesser distinction: working in the kitchens or in some similar servile capacity within the court or on the nobleman's estate.

The possession of competent and well-disciplined trumpeters was a matter of pride and personal integrity for the more important Central European courts. Novice trumpeters came from nearby villages or from the ranks of court servants; the minimum period of apprenticeship was two years. A bond or sum of money had to be sworn to the court treasury, and remuneration had to be made to the particular trumpet-master. At the courts of Zeitz, Weissenfels, and at least a dozen other German and Scandinavian courts, the apprentice was required to post a bond of one hundred thalers.[2] Payment was deducted from their menial earnings during apprenticeship as well as from their larger income when the rank of *Hoftrompeter* was eventually granted. The novice was provided with livery and board, and was periodically examined as to his progress. To assure the best possibility of excellence many trumpeters were sent to other courts to learn their art from reputable masters. To improve his 'Capelle' the margrave Georg Friedrich of Ansbach sent a novice to the court of the elector of Württemberg in 1558 to learn from the performers there.[3] Court musicians, especially trumpeters, were frequently exchanged between ruling noblemen, and petitions to local electors were often made by resident trumpeters asking for leave to travel to other courts. Some were granted leave and sent in an official capacity—such as a courier or diplomatic envoy. One such *Hoftrompeter* and *Kammermusiker*, the Berlin court trumpeter Thilemann Hoffmann, was murdered in 1628 while serving in such a dual capacity.[4]

In the Middle Ages Northern European nobles had corps of trumpet players. The kings of Poland had as many as twelve trumpeters, with two timpanists; at the same time the princes of Saxony had at least eight trumpeters and a 'Heerpaukker' (timpanist); and during the Renaissance, until the latter part of the eighteenth century, even the smaller courts of Central Europe had some four trumpeters and a timpanist.[5]

The trumpeters of the free and imperial city of Augsburg were the first

[2] Werner, 1922, pp. 40–3; 1911, p. 87; *see also* Smithers, 1971.

[3] Sachs, 1909–10, p. 106.

[4] *Ibid.*, p. 107.

[5] Altenburg, 1795, p. 26 ff.

to receive privileges, granted by the Emperor Sigismund in 1426.[6] Soon afterwards the nobles and electors of Nuremberg, Frankfurt, Hamburg and Dresden, and the kingdoms of Denmark, Holland and Sweden followed suit regarding the rights, duties and privileges of trumpeters. The 'Holy Roman' Emperor Ferdinand II in 1623, and again at the meeting of the Regensburg *Reichstag* in October 1630, laid down the exact nature of privileges to be enjoyed by the trumpeter *Kameradschaft* in all states of the empire.[7] The imperial mandate reminded court trumpeters of their obligations as true and honourable executants of their art, and of specific circumstances in which the playing of trumpets was forbidden:

Es soll kein ehrlicher Trompeter oder Heerpaucker mit seinem Instrumente sich anders als beym Gottesdienste, Kayser, Könige, Chur- und Fürsten, Grafen, Frey-herrn und Adellichen Ritterschaften, oder sonst hoch qualificierten Personen gebrauchen lassen: Es soll auch in verächtlichen Gelegenheiten mit Trompeter oder Paukken [sic] zu dienen, wie auch das gar lange nächtliche unordentliche Herum-vagiten auf den Gassen, in Wein- und Bierhäusern völlig verboten seyn. Wer sich diesfalls vergreiffen würde, soll nach Erkenntniss des Verbrechens gestraft werden.[8]

These *Vorrechte* or *Privilegi* made various demands on the court trum-peters, but they also guaranteed various rights. They restricted the per-formance of trumpet music to the privileged players; they gave members of the *Kameradschaft* free access to all kingdoms and territories that came under the aegis of the emperor's mandate; and they allowed privileged trumpeters right of appeal to royal authority in cases of dispute or legal actions. Clashes with the non-privileged players (usually the municipal musicians, i.e. the *Stadtpfeifer*) were inevitable. The privileged trumpet players invariably won most disputes—even some involving crimes or

---

[6] Zedler, 1732–54, 'Trompeter', col. 1118.

[7] According to Roman law, which is the legal tradition of continental Europe, a privilege, or a 'Signification', was a special 'ordinance having reference to an individual'. It was a bill or law in favour of *or* against an individual. A privilege was not defined as a special prerogative or right necessarily giving a particular advantage.

[8] Altenburg, 1795, p. 45; *see also* Zedler, 1732–54, vol. xlv, 1734, col. 1120: 'No honourable trumpeter or kettledrummer shall allow himself to be employed with his instrument in any way other than for religious services, Emperors, Kings, Electors and Princes, Counts, Lords and Knights and nobility, or other persons of high quality: It shall also be forbidden altogether to use a trumpet or a kettledrum at despicable occasions; likewise the excessive nocturnal improper carousing in the streets and alleys, in wine- and beer-houses. He who transgresses in this way shall be punished according to the nature of his crime.' For a translation of all twenty-three imperial trumpeter privileges of 1653 *see* Smithers, 1971.

bodily assault against the hapless *Stadtpfeifer*.[9] They usually won because of royal intercession. Most royalty supported the *Kameradschaft*; and in the seventeenth century Johann Georg, *Kurfürst* (electoral prince) of Saxony, went so far as to declare himself the indisputable patron and arbiter in settling disputes involving the *Kameradschaft* throughout the German realm.[10] In March 1661 he also issued a mandate protecting court trumpeters from infringements of their rights by '*ungelernten*' trumpeters, a mandate renewed in 1711 and in 1736.[11] Even the *Stadtpfeifer* were forbidden to play trumpets on most occasions: at weddings of town citizens and local farmers, baptisms, seasonal fairs, church bazaars or similar *Convivien*. The rules were so exacting and stringent that playing a trombone in the fashion of a trumpet ('*mit Posaunen auf Trompetenart*') was enough to incur the wrath of the *Kameradschaft*.[12]

After the Thirty Years War there was a return to more comfortable and civilized living in the courts and towns of Central and Northern Europe. A resurgent interest in the arts took place in the larger cities, with music playing a particularly important role in many municipal organizations. The *Stadtpfeifer* and village musicians had little respect for the restrictions on playing trumpets, or on playing related instruments in the manner of a trumpet. These non-privileged players on more than one occasion showed their disdain for the imperial mandates. Their principal sources of income were fairs, processions and church activities, specifically mentioned in the mandates as being restricted to the *Kameradschaft*. These so-called *ungelernten* performers, many of whom were accomplished virtuosos, naturally resented any loss in revenue and strained the rules and regulations by playing on waldhorns, trumpets with tuning crooks (*Inventionstrompeten mit Setzstücken*) and curiously wound instruments made so as not to resemble trumpets but sounding none the less just the same.[13]

The pettiness of some 'princely' trumpeters and timpanists is revealed by accounts of their puerile behaviour in trying to guard their rights. On 21st May 1671, for example, two court trumpeters from Altenburg lodged a complaint with their prince asking him to put a stop to the degrading kind of activities they had witnessed at a boisterous but convivial feast (*Schmause*) arranged by the apprentice bakers of Altenburg. They seem to

---

[9] *See* Menke, 1934, p. 27.
[10] Altenburg, 1795, p. 47; Fürstenau, 1861–2, vol. i, p. 198.
[11] *Ibid.*, p. 48; Werner, 1911, p. 86.
[12] Werner, 1922, p. 42.
[13] Werner, 1911, p. 89; *see also* Chapter 1, p. 26 and Chapter 3, p. 52, note 4.

have objected to some trombones having been played in the manner of a natural trumpet ('*die Posaunen auf Trompetenart zu blasen*'), particularly as the recalcitrant players had been warned not to do so.[14] Their complaints and tale-telling necessitated a formal response in defence of the situation by the Altenburg city and court musical official, one Herr Uhlich:

. . . . *ahn allen ohrten uff 'Conviviis', Hochzeiten und andern Ehrenzusammen-künfften Ihre Instrumenta als Posaunen und Zincken, auch Geigen und Vieldi-gamben so guth als sie könten, nach der 'Music' gebrauchten, wehre auch ahn allen bräuchlichen, dass sie uff ihren ietztgedachten Instrumenten nach den abgesetzten Noten musicirten, und wenn Bürger und andre Music-Liebhaber ein Stücklein uff Trompetenahrt uff Posaunen, Zincken und Geigen begehrten, könten sie nicht umbhin, ihnen disfals aufzuwartten, so guth sie könten. Welches alles ihrer kunst gemäss von undenklichen Jahren hier und andern orthen gebräuchlichen.*[15]

In 1684, and again some ten years later, a controversy arose in the same city over the playing of timpani by the *Stadtpfeifer*. On both occasions their instruments were taken from them and carried off to the castle. The reason given for this outrageous behaviour was that timpani belonged exclusively to princes and lords ('*da Pauken nur von Fürsten und Herren gehören*').[16]

The same kind of difficulties that arose in Altenburg are also recorded in the court and city archives of Zeitz, Schleiz, Leipzig, Brussels, Antwerp and Amsterdam. The frequent conflicts between the privileged and non-privileged players during the seventeenth century obviously instigated the 1711 and 1730 reissue of mandates strictly forbidding the use of trumpets and timpani by any but the favoured players. The performance privilege was extended to the *Stadtpfeifer*, but only during church services.

Being a court musician and having a royal patron, however, was not always an advantage. The Weissenfels 'Conzert-Meister', Johann Beer

---

[14] *Ibid.*, p. 90.

[15] Landesarchiv Altenburg, *Musici* 3; Werner, 1911, p. 90: 'They used their instruments, such as trombones, cornettos, also violins [and] viola da gambas, according to the music, as well as they could in all places for celebrations, weddings and other honourable gatherings. It is also customary everywhere that they perform, from the music set down, on the instruments discussed here, and if town's people and other music lovers requested a tune in the manner of trumpets on trombones, cornettos and violins, they could not help but oblige them in this way as best they could. All of which has been customary here and in other places according to their art for countless years.'

[16] *Ibid.*

(1655–1700), wrote sardonically in his *Musicalischer Diskurse* ... published posthumously at Nuremberg in 1719, nineteen years after his untimely death at Weissenfels: [17]

Heute muss man mit dem Hof da / morgen dorthin. Tag und Nacht leiden da keinen Unterscheid [sic]. Sturmwind / Regen und Sonnenschein / gilt da eines wie das andere. Heute muss man in die Kirche / morgen zu der Tafel / übermorgen aufs 'Theatrum'. Gegen dieser Unruhe gehet es in Städten etwas ruhiger zu.[18]

Municipal Trumpeters and the *Stadtpfeifer*

Of the many perils against which medieval Europe had to defend itself two were especially harmful to municipal life: (*a*) hostile and invading forces from without; (*b*) the danger of fire from within. To combat the former, stout and precipitous walls ringed most of the cities and towns of Europe, impeding the assault of marauding armies. To guard against the devastations of fire, watchmen were appointed to locate and report any suspicious sources of smoke. To facilitate easier and more reliable observation of both kinds of danger most cities built central towers within the city and high observation towers above the main gates of the surrounding walls. In some European cities the walls and towers still remain. In cities such as Rothenburg, Nuremberg, Bologna, Kraków and Oxford the old fortifications and watch towers may still be seen. As the churches of many cities gradually reached higher than the older defences, their towers and steeples frequently superseded the watch towers as observation posts.

In smaller towns the approach of the enemy or the discovery of fire was easily communicated to the populace by the tolling of a bell, either one in

[17] Zedler (1732–54, vol. iii, col. 900) gives the following biographical sketch of Beer and mentions his accidental death while on a bird shooting party: 'Beer, oder Baehr (Iohann), war bey dem Herzog in Weissenfels Concert-Meister, und war dan 1700 bey einem Vogelschüssen, durch übele Vorsicht eines unweit von ihm mit der Büchse gestandenen Hauptmanns erschossen; Er hat verschiedene Musikalische Schrifften geschrieben, so theils gedruckt, theils ungedruckt sind.' ['Beer, or Baehr (Johann), was a concert master for the Duke of Weissenfels and was then in 1700 shot by a gun during a bird shoot through the carelessness of a captain standing not far from him. He has written various musical works, some of which are printed and some not.']

[18] London: B. M. 785. b. 40., p. 18: 'With the court you've got to be in one place today, tomorrow in another. Day and night, unfortunately, makes no difference. Tempest, rain, sunshine—it's all the same. Today you've got to go into church, tomorrow to the dining hall, the day after tomorrow to the theatre. Compared to all this disturbance life is somewhat more peaceful in towns.'

a centrally located church or one mounted in the town square. In the larger cities information was communicated to the bell ringers by means of horns or trumpets, specially provided for the purpose of sounding alarms and signalling the completion of a round by the watchman of a particular sector. The 1452 *Feuerordnungen* of Cologne, for example, state that when the outbreak of fire is observed the *Feuerwächter* on the town hall tower shall first sound their trumpets and then strike the fire bell.[19] A sixteenth-century chronicler in Amsterdam noted that '. . . from the towers, besides the ringing of bells, there was also the sound of trumpets'.[20]

In England as early as the thirteenth century the security of towns and cities after dark was entrusted to watchmen: 'But for a full remedy of enormities in the night . . . in the yeere of Christ 1253 Henrie the third commanded Watches in Cities, and Borough Townes to be kept, for the better observing of peace and quietnesse amongst his people . . .' [21] The occupation of a watchman in Britain seems to have been somewhat different from that of his continental colleagues. Musical instruments, particularly trumpets, were used, but the night watch did more patrolling than standing about in church or gate towers; the midsummer watch in London must have been particularly impressive: 'Then had yee besides the standing watches, all in bright harnesse, in every Ward and streete of this Citie [London] and Suburbs, a marching watch, that passed through the principal streets thereof . . . The marching watch contained in number 2000 men, part of them being old Souldiers, of skill to bee Captaines, Lieutenants, Serieants, Corporals, etc., Riflers, Drummers, and Fifes, Standard and Ensigne-bearers, Sword-players, Trumpeters on horsebacke, Demi-launces on great horses. . . .' [22]

These marching watchmen with their portable trumpet alarms eventually formed the body of musician-watchmen known in England and Ireland as the town 'Waits'.[23] At Dublin eight waits were chosen in October 1457 '. . . to perambulate the city nightly from curfew to five in the morning . . .' for which they would receive '. . . four pence of every hall

---

[19] Stein, 1894–5, vol. ii, p. 366.

[20] Scheurleer, 1905, p. 38: 'Doch van de torens klonk behalve het klokgelui nog trompetgeschal.'

[21] Stow, 1618, p. 158.   [22] *Ibid.*, pp. 159–60.

[23] A recording of English court and municipal music, directed by the author, has been issued by Argo Records (ZRG 646), entitled 'Music of the Waits'. The author's notes have some of the first published historiography on the 'Waits' to appear in English.

and three pence of every shop within the city bounds'.[24] In 1569 '. . . the same musicians shall three several days or nights every week, as time of year shall require, serve in and throughout the city and suburbs, as the like musicians do in the cities of England, and at the like hours. . . .'[25]

At the north German city of Wismar in 1586 a *Türmer* (tower watch), whose place of observation was on the Nikolaikirche, pledged the following oath before assuming his duties:

Ich Christoffer Westphall schwere das Ich einem Erbarn Rathe der Statt Wissmar trew, gehorsam vndt holdt sein, Ihr vnde der Statt bestes wissen vndt schaden nach meinem vormugen abwenden, auff Sanct Nicolaus Tohrn, worzu Ich fur einen Tuhrnman angenohmen bei tag vndt nachzeiten fleissig wachten, auch mit allem fleisse zu liegt vnde feuer sehen, das dahero der Statt vndt Kirchen kein schade wider fahren muge, mich sonsten auch gegen jedermenniglich bescheidentlich vndt fridtlich norhaldten vndt ein erbarlich vnergerlich leben fuhren will, also mir gott helffe.[26]

Westphall, as most other German *Türmer* by 1500, would have been required to play a trumpet or 'Thurnerhorn' (*see* p. 28).

At Amsterdam in 1608 the town officials came to the conclusion that the surveillance of the 'raetelwaekers' (*Raadwaker*, i.e. town crier or watchman) '. . . was of little satisfaction and that one might better spend the same amount of money by having trumpets play from the town church tower'.[27] In the previous year one Gerrit Tomassen was appointed trumpeter on the 'van bontelbauen' tower with a salary of 100 guilders.[28] At Amsterdam and Hamburg in the seventeenth century it was noted that 'When a Fire happens by Night, the Trumpets [i.e. the trumpet players] plac'd upon the Towers shall sound an Alarm, and hang out two Lanthorns to the Quarter, where the Fire is, and one on the other side'.[29]

[24] Flood, 1909, p. 34.

[25] *Ibid.*

[26] Praetorius, E., 1906, p. 251: 'I Christopher Westphall swear that I shall be true, obedient and loyal to the honourable council of the town of Wismar, to bear in mind their and the town's best interest, and to avert harm to the best of my ability [while] on the tower of St Nicholas, where I have been appointed tower watch. I swear to watch carefully day and night, to look after light and fire with all diligence so that no harm may come to the town and church from them; in other respects I also swear to behave modestly and peacefully with everyone and to lead an honourable and respectable life, so help me God.'

[27] Scheurleer, 1905, pp. 38–9.

[28] *Ibid.*, p. 39,

[29] *The Rules and Orders Establish'd . . . In . . . Hamburgh & Amsterdam for suppressing the Rage of Fire.* Translated from the Original. London, 1715 (no author or translator given), p. 8.

As the medieval towns and cities of Europe came to rely more and more on the sounding of trumpets and like instruments for the warning of fire, rules had to be made to prevent false alarms or the possible misinterpretation of unofficial trumpet playing. As early as 1372 the Paris police regulations made unofficial trumpet blowing a crime after the hour of curfew—except at weddings.[30] In Cologne the *Wachtordnung* of 1604 forbade *Trompetenblasen* after dark, as well as *Feldgeschrei* (shouting).[31]

Such, in brief, is the background of one of the most important musical groups of pre nineteenth-century Europe. From their initial function as civic security guards the trumpet playing *Feuerwächter* and town waits eventually became the municipal musicians, known at various times and places as 'speyllieden', 'Spilut' or 'Spillude' (Modern Ger. *Spielleut*, i.e. musicians, or, more particularly, instrumentalists), 'pijffern', 'Piffari', 'Tibicines Urbis', 'stadspijpers', and, especially in Central Europe, usually known as the *Stadtpfeifer* (literally, city or municipal piper).

Mention has already been made of the Italian *musici civico* and the English waits, but the most important areas to develop municipal music and musicians were the Central European Germanic principalities of the Holy Roman Empire. As their duties became more formalized and their quasi-military capacity acquired greater ceremony (e.g. mounting the watch, changing of the night watch, etc.), the function of Central European *Türmer* changed. What was at first a necessary and utilitarian occupation became a ceremonious and decorative adjunct of civic life. With a gradual development of their musical skills the *Türmer* spent less time fire watching and more time providing musical entertainment at official city proceedings. A tradition was rapidly established, and in some areas the town musicians banded together into a 'bruederschappe' or 'Bruderschaft' (brotherhood). The brotherhoods of civic musicians were the earliest of musical protective organizations, some predating the 1426 *Kameradschaft* privileges mentioned earlier. One such *Bruderschaft* submitted a document of seventeen points for the approval of the Margrave Ulrich von Württemberg in 1458.[32] A type of guild, this particular group consisted of 'Pfeiffer', lute players, trumpeters and other 'Spilut'.[33]

One of the earliest brotherhoods was an English musicians' guild

---

[30] Schletterer, 1884, pp. 29–30.
[31] Hoehlbaum, Konstantin (ed.); *Mitteilungen aus dem Stadtarchiv von Köln*, XI, 28–9, p. 179.
[32] Sittard, 1887.
[33] *Ibid.*

founded in 1350 during the reign of Edward III.[34] The parliament of 1451 annulled the grants and privileges to 'Minstrels and Trumpeters', but because 'certain ignorant rustics . . . falsely represented themselves to be Minstrels', another charter was granted by Henry VI in 1452 and again by Edward IV in 1469.[35]

The group of musicians usually associated with extra court performances of Baroque music were the *Stadtpfeifer*. Throughout what is today Germany, a part of Czechoslovakia, a western area of Poland, the kingdoms of Denmark and Sweden and the Netherlands, the *Stadtpfeifer* were the corporate musicians of nearly every city and town. Descendants of the town watch, or *Türmer*, and to some extent the old unofficial office of the *Hausmänner* (a kind of municipal body of minstrels who played wind and stringed instruments), the *Stadtpfeifer* were indeed the professional musicians of the day. Their services were required by the municipalities for official ceremonies such as parades, the daily *Abblasen* from the *Pfeiferstuhl* on the *Rathaus* (a small gallery on the town hall from which the *Stadtpfeifer* would perform)[36] and for the instrumental accompaniment of the *Sontags Gottesdienst* in the *Hauptkirche* (the main Sunday service in the principal church of the city). The latter was a most important duty in the post-Reformation Lutheran cities, particularly in the north, and in those cities where the Protestant movement took hold. Free-lance playing at weddings, fairs, etc., was, in addition to their municipal income, an important source of revenue for the *Stadtpfeifer*.

Until the seventeenth century the number of *Stadtpfeifer* in the larger cities rarely exceeded six. Nearly all were principally wind players, capable of playing lip-vibrated instruments (trumpets, trombones and cornetts) and double-reed instruments (shawms, dulcians, and the capped reeds, e.g. *Rauschpfeifen* and crumhorns). One or two would have been expert string players, and all would have been on familiar terms with most contemporary musical instruments. In the seventeenth century the number of players, especially in the major cities, increased to the proportions of a small orchestra, with the number of winds and strings being divided almost equally. The wind players retained the title of *Stadtpfeifer* (in some areas they were called *Kunstpfeifer*) while the string players were normally called *Kunstgeiger*.

---

[34] Flood, 1913, pp. 66–7.　　[35] *Ibid.*

[36] Music written for this particular purpose is inappropriately called *Turmmusik* or 'tower music'. The *Pfeiferstuhl* was not remotely like one of the towers where the *Stadtpfeifer* had originally been employed as *Feuerwächter*.

In the sixteenth and seventeenth centuries the *Stadtpfeifer* still had some tower duties, but usually as a matter of ceremony (a last vestige of the originally utilitarian function). Ensemble performances from church or gate towers were rare and were only given on special occasions. The use of a single player as a night watch persisted in some communities until the eighteenth century, however. A charming poem by Jacob Lottich, which appeared in 1679, illustrates the function of the *Stadtpfeifer* in any one of a hundred German cities and towns.[37]

Wann Titans hoher Lauff den Mittag shier will machen /
Die Uhre Zehn schlägt ab / da geht mit seinen Sachen
Der Musicanten Chor / bestimmet sich zu hauff /
Und blaset uns zu Tisch eins mit Posaunen auf.
Die Mittags Music ist vom Raths-Thurn anzuhören /
Fast hoch in freyer Lufft; sie schallet Gott zu Ehren /
Dem Menschen zum Bericht: Dann so weiss jedermann
Ihm täglich um die Zeit / die Glock sey Zehn heran.
Wann nun Latous mit den niemals-müden Pferden
Von uns gereist ab; wann wir von ihm auf Erden
Kein Licht noch Strahlen sehn / so zieht man eine Klock' /
Auf dass ihr süsser Schall zum Abend-Seegen lock' /
Ein Cornetist nimmt dann die beste von den Zinken /
Erwehlt ihm einen Psalm / der ihm schier recht will düncken /
Und pfeiffet nach der Kunst: Er nimmt sein Amt in acht /
Bleibt auf dem Kirchen-Thurn / und wacht die ganze Nacht.
Auf Gassen hin und her gehn auch bestalte Wächter /
Dass Strassen sicher seyn / ergreiffen den Verächter
Der Ordnung und des Rechts; verhüten Feur und Streit /
Dass man bey Schlaffes-Ruh verbleib' in Sicherheit.
So offt der Seyger schlägt / so rufft man aus die Stunden:
An Uhren mangelts nicht: kaum wird dergleichen funden
Von Wercken und von Kunst; komm hier / sieh / wer nicht gläubt /
Dass ein Gewichte nur zwey grosse Uhren treibt.
So bald Aurora blinckt in gold-gefärbter Röthe /
Ergreifft / der ausgewacht / den Wecker / die Trompete /
Macht durch ein Morgenlied die Stadt allard und wach /
*Legt drauf sich selbst zur Ruh / und holt den Schlaff ihm nach.**

[37] Kuster, 1733, pp. 145–6.
* *See* footnote 38 on next page.

In north Germany the cultivation of municipal music began in the fourteenth century. The Hanseatic cities have had a long artistic and musical tradition. Through Bremen, Hamburg and Lübeck, for example, passed some of the most important European musicians, particularly in the sixteenth and seventeenth centuries. The mercantile and political importance of the *Hansastädte*, as well as their geographic proximity to Scandinavia and Britain, meant that many other human activities could thrive besides the commercial interests that were first and foremost.

In Bremen the city records mention 'rades trometer' as early as 1339.[39] In Hamburg the first established group of city musicians was formed in the next century, and first mention of 'Rathstrompeter' in the Hamburg payment records occurs in 1465.[40] At Wismar municipal music was well organized by the middle of the fifteenth century. In 1464 the Wismar *Türmer* Hans Klenske and Jaspar Bausner were mentioned as the *Vorsteher*

[38] When Titan's high course is about to bring midday,
the clock strikes ten;
then the musicians meet with all their odds and ends,
form a group and let us have a tune for lunch on their trombones.
The midday music can be heard from the town hall tower,
almost high up in the open air; it sounds for the honour of God and to inform the people,
so that everyone knows each day at this time it is the tenth hour.
When Latous has departed from us with his never tiring horses
and when we no longer see any light or any rays from him on earth,
then a bell is rung so that its sweet sound entices us to vespers.
A cornettist then takes the best of his *Zinken*,
chooses a psalm which he considers just suitable,
and he pipes in an artful manner;
he does his duty, stays on the church tower and remains awake for the rest of the night.
In the streets guards who have been appointed for this purpose walk up and down and see
to it that the streets are safe; they seize the trespasser against law and order;
they prevent fire and turmoil so that everyone shall be safe while they rest.
As often as the clock strikes the hours are called out.
There is no shortage of clocks: hardly anywhere would you find such ingenious clock works.
Anyone who does not believe this should come here and see for himself that one weight
alone propels two big clocks.
As soon as Aurora gleams in gold and roseate hues the watchman still awake takes his
trumpet, alerts and wakes up the town
with a morning song.
After that he retires and makes up for his lost sleep.

[39] Arnheim, 1911, p. 373.

[40] Sittard, 1890, p. 3.

(directors) of the 'Bruderschaft der Spielleute'.[41] In south-eastern Germany, amalgamation of the *Türmer* and the *Hausmänner* took place in the city of Delitzsch, near Leipzig, in 1580.[42] Werner, quoting from the city archives, made note of the new office as follows:

Der neue Stadtpfeifer hatte 'auf die hohen Feste und sonst der Kantorei zur Zier neben Gesellen mit-Blasen und Pfeifen in dem Figuralgesange sich brauchen zu lassen'. Man gab ihm für das Blasen vom Turme, Wachen und Geigerziehen von früh 3 Uhr bis abends 9 Uhr anfänglich 16 und dann 18 Groschen wöchentlich.[43]

Similarly, at Berlin the trumpet playing *Turmmänner* and the woodwind-string playing *Hausmänner* joined forces somewhat later. The first documentary record of the term *Stadtpfeifer* at Berlin is a payment-book entry on 9th July 1590: 'Steffan Pflugenn Stadtpfeiffer', paid for services '2 Talern'.[44]

But irrespective of the fame and excellence of musicians in many German towns and cities, it was the art of the Saxon *Stadtpfeifer* at Leipzig that was truly remarkable. Nowhere else in Europe did the title of *Stadt-Musicus* have greater significance and musical importance than at Leipzig. The first apparent use of the term *Stadtpfeifer* occurs there in a payment-record entry in the early fifteenth century, and the earliest employment of *Stadtpfeifer* as such was at Leipzig in 1479.[45]

The Leipzig *Stadtpfeifer* were not only required to be excellent performers and to provide suitable music each day (the daily *Abblasen* from a balcony on the town hall was begun in 1599),[46] but many were also accomplished composers. The trumpet music of these composers, particularly that of Johann Pezel, will be discussed in the next chapter.

With the invasions of Saxony, Moravia and Bohemia by Swedish and mercenary troops during the Thirty Years War, Leipzig suffered six sieges. At four different times between 1630 and 1650 the city was occupied by enemy soldiers. From 1648 to 1650 the Swedes retained Leipzig as security

---

[41] Praetorius, E., 1906, p. 229.

[42] Werner, 1918, p. 556.

[43] *Ibid.*: 'The new town musician's duty was "to take part in the concerted vocal music during high feasts and otherwise to adorn the singing, along with the apprentices blowing and piping." He was first given 16 and then 18 *Groschen* per week for blowing from the tower, watching, and winding the clock, from 3 a.m. to 9 p.m.'

[44] Sachs, 1908, p. 56–7.

[45] Wustmann, 1909, p. 31.

[46] Kade, R., 1889, pp. 194–5.

for payment of indemnity, billeting troops and military personnel in many of its homes and public buildings. With the liberation of the city and the withdrawal of Swedish troops on 1st July 1650, Leipzig entered upon an active period of trade, commerce, construction and artistic productivity. As Leipzig's post-war economic situation prospered and its fortifications were strengthened, its municipal music groups were reorganized and enlarged. It was at this time that the *Stadtpfeifer* were divided into two groups: the *Kunstpfeifer* and the *Kunstgeiger*. The former, who were the wind players, enjoyed greater prestige than the latter and were favoured by the civic officials. They were paid more than the string players, they had more privileges, and were often given better playing opportunities.

There were difficulties between the two groups of musicians which resulted in the *Kunstpfeifer* drawing up an 'agreement' ostensibly to protect the interests of each. It consisted of thirteen points, a précis of which may be found in Schering.[47] What it did in reality was reinforce the position of the *Kunstpfeifer*. It gave them the right to choose the better-paid jobs beyond their normal civic engagements, and it gave the *Kunstpfeifer* the prerogative of choosing the music for weddings—an important source of extra-municipal income. The concluding remarks of the thirteen-point agreement must have caused resentment among the string players. In effect, the closing statement said that the *Kunstpfeifer* '. . . should have all these privileges over the *Kunstgeiger*; however, they [the *Kunstpfeifer*] should be indulgent to them [the *Kunstgeiger*]'.[48] The agreement was dated 14th April 1664, and among the signatories was Johann Pezel, who was listed among the *Kunstgeiger*.

Relations between the two groups were probably strained to breaking point shortly after the signing of the thirteen-point agreement. The uncharitable *Kunstpfeifer* demanded of the civic officials the right to employ one of their own *Geselle* (apprentice) as the sixth person in the performance of music from the town hall, or when an extra trumpet was needed in church services. Permission was granted. The infuriated *Kunstgeiger* protested, rightly adding that such stipulations were robbing them of needed income, particularly since most of them could also play trumpets and woodwind instruments.

It is little wonder that many *Kameradschaft* and *Stadtpfeifer* trumpet players were loathed by their fellow musicians. Further evidence of this are the seven articles submitted for the approval of the city fathers of

[47] Schering, 1926, pp. 261 ff.
[48] *Ibid.* p. 262; also cited in Schering, 1921, pp. 26–7.

Leipzig by the *Instrumentalkollegium* in 1662. Members of the famous Leipzig *Collegium Musicum* requested permission of the *Stadtbehörder* to be allowed to carry on their activities unmolested and without interference by the civic or court musicians. Article four reads: 'Weil Stadtpfeifer und musici von Trompetern und Kesselpaukern wo solche sind, oft angefeindet werden, sollen jene befugt sein, auf Erfordern und Begehren Trompeten zu blasen und Pauken zu schlagen, trotz des bestehenden Trompeterprivilegs.' [49]

Many Leipzig *Stadtpfeifer* began their musical activities as *Kunstgeiger*. For economic considerations and for reasons of prestige, many later qualified as expert wind players, especially on trumpet, cornett or trombone. Johann Pezel was a *Kunstgeiger* from 1664 to 1669, qualifying in the latter year as a *Stadtpfeifer* trumpet player and composer. Gottfried Reiche was initially a string player, and little needs to be said about his reputation as a *Stadtpfeifer* trumpeter. Johann Christian Gentzmer, who was a *Stadtpfeifer* from 1679 to 1719, was one of the few to attain that position without first belonging to the organization of string players.

In terms of the performance standards and requirements of today's instrumentalists, it somewhat strains the imagination to realize that most seventeenth- and eighteenth-century *Stadtpfeifer* could demonstrate such a high degree of expertise on several different instruments. That performers such as Pezel and Reiche were competent string players and also expert trumpet players is substantiated by J. S. Bach's adjudication report of 24th July 1745. In it Bach states that the *Stadtpfeifer* apprentice Carl Friedrich Pfaffe '. . . performed quite well and to the applause of all those present [the "Stadt Pfeifer" and other "Stadt *Musicorum*"] on all the instruments that are customarily employed by the Town Pipers, namely: Violin, *Hautbois*, Flute Travers., Trompette, Waldhorn and the bass instruments. . . .' [50]

Although Gottfried Reiche began his work in Leipzig as a member of the string players' 'guild', the list of his effects after his death in 1734 included only brass instruments. Even so, what professional trumpet player today, except possibly a jazz musician, would be expected to play in addition to his normal instrument a waldhorn, a slide trumpet and an alto

[49] Schering, 1921, p. 24: 'Because town pipers and musicians are often victimized by trumpeters and drummers where there are any, the former shall be allowed to blow trumpets and beat drums if it is decided and required, despite the existing trumpeter privilege[s].'

[50] The German text is quoted in its entirety in Schering (1921, p. 44); the translation is from Arthur Mendel (1950, p. 493).

trombone? Some of these instruments were found in Reiche's quarters in the *Stadtpfeifergässlein* after his collapse at the age of sixty-seven. Besides the *Zugtrompete*, 'eine alte im Stadtgraben gefundene Trompete' (an old trumpet found in the city moat), and waldhorn that Schering (1921, p. 34) quotes from the inventory of Reiche's possessions, there were five chorale books and 122 of Reiche's own compositions (probably used for the town hall 'Hora Decima Musik', i.e. the ten o'clock lunch-time music) entitled 'Abblasestücke'.[51]

Reiche must have been a remarkable player. Some of those who followed him were certainly capable of performing Bach's trumpet parts, for example. Bach's post-1734 trumpet parts show little variation from the technical difficulties that are found in his earlier trumpet parts, many of which were written expressly for Reiche. Johann Ludwig Schreiber too must have been a superb trumpet player. He was first trumpet at the court of Köthen while Bach was there, and the difficult 'Tromba' part of the second Brandenburg concerto was probably written for him.[52] But few other trumpet players in the seventeenth and eighteenth centuries had a reputation comparable to that of Gottfried Reiche. Even while he was an apprentice, in 1694, Reiche was paid a substantial sum of money to keep him in Leipzig during the period of mourning for Johann Georg IV, elector of Saxony. With the death of the elector on 27th April 1694 there could be no music-making in public or at weddings for an entire year. Because of this the various Saxon municipalities were not going to pay musicians without services rendered—especially for a year. Had the death been that of a princess or a lesser ranking member of the elector's family, the period of mourning would have been only two months; and the the *Behörder* and *Bürger* of Leipzig, Dresden, Zeitz, etc., might have retained their *Stadtpfeifer* during those eight weeks. But in 1694 the Saxon municipal musicians were told that they were to find other employment during the year-long period of mourning—all except Reiche, who was given a *Gratifikation* '. . . dass er nicht ausser Landes gehen möge' [53] (so

---

[51] It is more than likely that among the 122 'Abblasestücke' were the *Vierundzwanzig Neue Quatricinia* (Leipzig, 1696) for one cornetto and three trombones. These are the only known surviving pieces by Reiche. The unique copy at Berlin was destroyed in World War II, but fortunately Adolf Müller's edition, published at Dresden in 1927, preserves all twenty-four pieces. The original tonality has been altered, but Müller does give the intervals of transposition from the keys of the 1696 print.

[52] *See* Smend, 1952, p. 25.

[53] Schering, 1926, p. 266.

that he would not wish to go elsewhere). It was Kuhnau who remarked that 'nobody will pray more devoutly for a long life for his sovereign than the instrumentalists'.[54] Moreover, trumpets were particularly unsuitable during a lachrymal period, or 'Trauerzeit'. The trumpet is '. . . ad pompam, und nicht ad lamentationem aptirt; und wer sie anders brauchet, verwechselt ihr Natur'.[55]

Until recently it had been assumed that the *Zinken* (cornetto) parts in the works of various seventeenth- and eighteenth-century Leipzig composers (and composers of other European musical centres) had always been played by brass players—more especially trumpet players such as Pezel, Gentzmer and Reiche. It is likely, however, that cornettos were usually played by the double-reed playing *Stadtpfeifer*. One piece of evidence is the list of effects of the oboist Gleditsch.[56] Besides a quantity of *Abblasen* pieces by Gleditsch, apparently similar to those of Reiche, there was also a cornetto. This makes a great deal of sense. It would be easier for an oboist or shawm player to play a cornetto, especially using the traditional side embouchure, than a trumpet player who might seriously disturb his special embouchure with a radically different mouthpiece—even if played from the side of the mouth. The list of Reiche's belongings does not mention a cornetto, and there is no evidence that cornetto playing in Leipzig or anywhere else was the particular province of trumpet players. Specific examples of seventeenth- and eighteenth-century orchestration substantiate this. Scores with cornetto parts may include parts for trumpets, trombones, etc., but not usually oboes or shawms at the same time, and vice versa. The only double-reed instruments one is likely to find scored with cornettos are the lower dulcians or bassoons.

As the seventeenth century progressed the musical activities of Leipzig and of most other Saxon towns and cities continued to expand. Not only was the number of *Stadtpfeifer* increased; music began to flourish also in the coffee houses and the universities, and to some extent among the religious in the outlying monasteries in predominantly Roman Catholic areas. Judging from the number of pieces recently found in Austrian and south German monasteries, such places were not without access to trumpets. The demand for bigger and better musical performances was eventually felt in the city churches. It was in the latter half of the seventeenth century that there was a broadening in the scope of the musical portion of the Sun-

---

[54] Quoted in Bukofzer, 1947, p. 406.
[55] Beer, 1719.
[56] Schering, 1921, p. 34.

day church service. More performers were required than at any time previously. The scoring of many cantatas by German composers between 1660 and 1700 reflects the tendency toward musical bigness and also the demands of consistories and church congregations for an increase in the musical portion of the service. Opera may have had something to do with this.

To meet the needs of larger orchestras all sorts of musical instruments were purchased by Central European churches during the second half of the seventeenth century. The records in the archives of St Thomas's at Leipzig, for example, mention various repairs to instruments and the purchase of several brass instruments and timpani. In 1664 a new pair of trumpets and a trombone were bought; in 1668 a new pair of timpani; in 1675 the trumpet-maker Heinrich Pfeiffer repaired a 'Quart' and a 'Bassposaune' that belonged to St Thomas's; and in 1695 Pfeiffer was paid out of the St Thomas funds 2 florins 20 groschen for each of two new trumpets with matching tuning crooks; the price included the mending of two other trumpets.[57] An inventory dated 1702, signed by Johann Kuhnau and entitled 'In der Kirche zu St. Thomae', includes among several entries of stringed and wind instruments '6 Trompeten, worunter eine kleine aus dem Dis' (probably a *tromba da caccia*).[58]

The instruments purchased by most Central European churches were played by the *Stadtpfeifer*, the supernumerary performers from the local *Collegium Musicum* and, depending upon the size of the orchestra required for a particular work, by other *Stadtpfeifer* from nearby cities. Not unlike the free-lance status of many musicians today, the *Stadtpfeifer* undertook playing engagements in other areas. For a procession during the Feast of St John at Dresden in 1572, four *Stadtpfeifer* were hired from Leipzig.[59] At that time Dresden had only one municipal musician, called the 'Kreuztürmer', and as early as 1522 it is stated in the Dresden records that forty-two groschen were paid to the 'Pfeiffern von Leipzig' for playing at an important wedding; they played ('gepfiffen') during the wedding mass and just before the sacrament of matrimony.[60] The archives of the north German city of Mölln state that in 1667 the 'Musicus Instrumentalis der Stadt Möllen', the *Stadtpfeifer* Andreas Schmidt requested leave to attend rehearsals in Wismar.[61] In the sixteenth and seventeenth centuries muni-

[57] Schering, 1926; 1921, pp. 34–5.
[58] Schering, 1918–19, pp. 275–88.
[59] Kade, R., 1889.
[60] *Ibid.*
[61] Praetorius, E., 1906.

cipal musicians from the German Hanseatic cities travelled to Denmark and Sweden and assisted in performances at Copenhagen, Stockholm, Upsala and Malmö.[62]

When needed, the *Stadtpfeifer* in some German towns were hired to augment local court orchestras. One of the famous *Ratsmusiker* in seventeenth-century Bremen, the *Stadtpfeifer* Ernst Abel, performed with the Hanover *Hofkapelle* in 1636.[63] At the court of Altenburg, where Gottfried Scheidt was organist in the early seventeenth century, the orchestra occasionally consisted of trumpeters, a violinist, a lutenist, a *Stadtpfeifer* and a timpanist—the *Stadtpfeifer* being hired perhaps to play trombone or a double-reed instrument.[64] When Samuel Scheidt was at Halle he made use of a trumpeter who came from another city (probably Leipzig). For his journey and service the trumpeter was paid nine florins and three groschen.[65] In the Königsberg court payment books of 1600 there is a list of the *Kapelle* under the cantorship of Johann Eccard. It consisted of eight basses and tenors, six 'Discantisten' and an organist. Among the fifteen 'Instrumentisten vnd Trommeter' there was a cittern player and the Königsberg 'Törmer' (*Türmer*) Adam Bredhut, who was also a 'Hehrpeücker' (timpanist) and had with him two apprentices, who assisted at table during meals while the *Tafelmusik* was performed.[66]

Between 1613 and *c.* 1625 the records of orchestral players at the Neuburg *Hof* (in Bavaria) mention three *Türmer*: Hans Hammerbach and his two brothers, Christoph and Georg.[67] The same records mention a 'Zinkenbläser von Neumarck auss Bayern', who was employed to play with the court organist, violinists and singers.[68] It is worth mentioning that the two Neuburg *Kapellmeister* during this time were the important early seventeenth-century Italian composers Giacomo Negri and his successor Biagio Marini.

In 1683 the *Hofmusiker* and *Stadtpfeifer* of Ansbach performed together at the court of the Margrave Johann Friedrich. The list of musicians is indeed a conglomeration of talent: one of the trumpeters was also an actor, three were *Stadtpfeifer* (the 'Stadtmusikanten' Tondorff and Hans

---

[62] Arnheim, 1911, pp. 386–7.
[63] Fischer, G., 1903, p. 2.
[64] Werner, 1900, p. 401.
[65] Werner, 1912, p. 302.
[66] Mayer-Reinach, 1904, p. 50.
[67] Einstein, 1908, pp. 341–2.
[68] *Ibid.*

Paul, and the 'Thürmer' Johann Paul Kircher) and one of the more famous performers was the *Hofmusiker* and composer Johann Fischer.[69]

In order to work full time for a royal patron some *Stadtpfeifer* resigned altogether from their municipal employment. The most notable case in the seventeenth century was the Lübeck *Ratstrompeter* Gabriel Voigtländer. From *c.* 1626 to 1638 Voigtländer was a *Stadtpfeifer* at Lübeck and held the respected position of official herald for the *Stadtbehörder*. By 1639 he was in the service of Christian IV of Denmark, but not merely as a trumpeter; Voigtländer was also patronized as a court poet and madrigalist.[70] Soon afterwards, being already recognized as a poet of some distinction, Voigtländer entered the service of Prince Christian at his court in Nykjöbing castle, serving as a trumpeter, poet and composer.[71]

While nearly every large town and city in Europe before the Industrial Revolution had its trumpet blowing, *Stadtpfeifer* watchmen, this long and important tradition was allowed to atrophy in all but one place. The Polish capital of Kraków is a unique exception. It is a tribute to the intelligent preservationists in Poland today that the remarkably preserved medieval city of Kraków still maintains the office of the fire watchmen trumpeters. Kraków still knows the charm and security that towns like London, Nuremberg and Leipzig once did many years ago. Almost unbelievably, the Kraków fire department maintains six tower watchmen trumpeters, who, in pairs, share the endless cycle of twelve-hour morning to noon and twelve-hour noon to midnight watches from the highest point in the old city. This is at the top of the taller, octagonal north tower of the thirteenth-century church of St Mary the Virgin, whose Veit Stoss altar piece is one of the world's rarest treasures. From high up above the equally medieval market square the six fire-brigade trumpeters take turns playing a natural trumpet tune called the 'Hejnał' (pronounced ('hay-now'), which is heard each hour, four times on the hour, twenty-four hours per day, 365 days a year. With the exception of the era during the Napoleonic wars, this is a nearly unbroken tradition since 1241. That was the year when a Kraków trumpeter supposedly had an enemy arrow shot through his neck while in the process of sounding an alarm from his post on top of the city wall to warn the town of approaching Tatar invaders. To commemorate this act, all subsequent Kraków alarm-trumpeters are reputed to have abruptly broken off the melody-signal,

[69] Sachs, 1909–10, pp. 132–3, 135.
[70] Fischer, K., 1910, pp. 20–1.
[71] Hammerich & Elling, 1893, pp. 97–8.

which the hapless trumpeter is said to have been playing at the time. The sudden break in the melody still heard today vividly reminds us of the deadly, however legendary, marksmanship of the Tatar archer and the implications of an invading army.

The 'Hejnał' has most certainly been played this way since the beginning of the nineteenth century. Playing each hour to each of the four corners of the world, but today on modern Czech B flat trumpets, the firewatch trumpeters can be heard all over Kraków within the old city walls. Outside the walls, the Kraków trumpeters are heard *live* all over Poland once each day at noon, again playing the 'Hejnał' four times to the four compass points of the globe, simultaneously broadcast on all programmes of the State radio and television. The effect of this tradition is quite unlike anything now known in the West. It might well be a salutary one if revived, particularly once it is realized that the office of the trumpeter-tower watch is in part ecclesiastical and that the trumpeters are reminding us not only of our safety but of our responsibilities to God and to one another.

THE TRUMPET MUSIC
OF GERMANY

6

There is some difficulty in dating the earliest source of German ensemble music with trumpets. If we exclude the few Renaissance pieces with their possibility of chromatic trumpets and assume that Monteverdi's *Orfeo* (1609) is the earliest trumpet source, then only between three and eight years elapsed before the first trans-alpine appearance of music with specific trumpet parts. The earliest source of German trumpet music is either a work by Schütz that was possibly composed in 1612—his *Danket dem Herrn* (*SWV* 45), about which more will be said in a moment—or Johann Michael Altenburg's *Gaudium Christianum*, published at Jena in 1617. The Schütz and Altenburg works are, incidentally, the earliest musical sources where timpani are specified.

Two MS. collections of trumpet 'fanfares' preserved in the Royal Library at Copenhagen might be called the earliest sources of natural trumpet music. These were compiled by the Saxon court trumpeters Hendrick Lübeck and Magnus Thomsen, both of whom were trumpeters at the court of Christian IV of Denmark.[1] But neither collection contains ensemble music and their musical importance is questionable.

It may seem unimportant where and when the first publication appeared with trumpet parts—or specific parts for any other instrument, for that matter. Early municipal and court records, as well as the accounts of pre-seventeenth-century chroniclers, indicate that trumpets were used in ensemble music long before composers were explicit in their scoring requirements. But the earliest obligatory use of an instrument is relevant to the history of musical instruments and the history of orchestration.

[1] The Lübeck and Thomsen transcriptions appear in Schünemann, 1936.

When the instrumental scoring requirements of composers became more specific and appeared in writing for the first time, an important step was taken in the evolution of the orchestra. The time and place of the event should be noteworthy.

As the orchestra began to assume coherent shape and developed from somewhat arbitrary numbers of instruments, its component parts acquired an individual purpose and a specific function based on timbre, flexibility and range. The musical potential of the natural trumpet began to be realized when composers recognized its melodic possibilities and were no longer satisfied with the improvisatory 'excerpts' of contemporary trumpet players. Praetorius [2] discusses this, and some of his remarks will be explained later. It was some time, however, before the trumpet transcended its historical and social position and could be accepted as a regular orchestral or even solo instrument.

Trumpets in the earliest German sources serve as doubling instruments in the accompaniment of a chorale, and they are frequently used to perform short, episodic fanfare figures, interspersed between the vocal statements. Johann Michael Altenburg is one of the first to use trumpets in this way. His *Gaudium Christianum* is a collection of pieces for three choirs of voices and instruments, each in four parts, plus three trumpets and a pair of timpani. The following precedes *Die Engelische Schlacht*, the fourth piece in the collection:

Nota Diesen Chor, welcher nur auf Trompeten und Paucken gerichtet, mag oder kan ... der Cantor ausslassen. Wo er ihm aber haben kan ... soll er besonders und alleine stehen, und diesem Chor, so oft ein NB. in tiefsten Bass steht, ein Zeichen geben, damit sie sich desto danach zu richten haben und den Ansatz machen. [3]

In suggesting that the trumpets and timpani may be omitted, Altenburg was only expressing the view that competent trumpeters and timpanists might not be available, but that the music was still worthy of performance. Such statements do not imply that the trumpet and timpani parts are of no consequence. As today, saleability and the desire for performance made considerations of orchestration rather flexible.

[2] Praetorius, M., 1614–19, vol. iii.

[3] 'Observe that this choir, which is intended only for trumpets and drums, may or can be left out by the choir director. But where he can have it, he should stand apart and by himself and give a sign to this choir whenever there is a *nota bene* in the lowest bass [part], so that they [the trumpeters] can prepare themselves accordingly [i.e. get their instruments 'set' on their lips] and make their entrance.'

The title of *Die Engelische Schlacht* in the basso continuo part mentions not only the three trumpets but also the specific tuning of the timpani:

No. 4 Die Engelische Schlacht / Apoc. 12 mit 12 oder 16 Stimmen. Darein zugleich 3 Trompeten und zwo Pauken / die eine in das kleine c, die ander in das grosse g gestellet können gebraucht werden.[4]

Die Engelische Schlacht is one of many seventeenth-century pieces based on the allegory of the struggle between the angel Michael and the Devil (from Revelation xii. 7–12). A struggle of such consequence was, naturally, tantamount to a great battle, and great battles were never fought without the accompaniment of trumpet calls, signals and fanfares. In works (to be discussed) where the same text is treated by Schütz, Hammerschmidt and Johann Christoph Bach, trumpets play no small part in setting the appropriate scene.

Altenburg's use of trumpets is conservative by comparison. Nevertheless, his example serves as one of the earliest departures from the traditional, improvised use of trumpets in concerted music. Hammerschmidt, who in the next generation worked at Zittau, more than likely gleaned several ideas from Altenburg's music. Meinecke (1903, p. 44) shows a parallel between *Die Engelische Schlacht* and Hammerschmidt's *Andern Theil geistlichen Gespräche über die Evangelia* (No. 26. Dresden, 1656), which also uses trumpets. Altenburg's 1620 collection, the *Hochzeitliche musicalische Freude . . .* , specifies trumpets, but with a reservation similar to that of the 1617 publication. A complete set of eight parts is in the British Museum and the title-page of each part includes the following:

. . . Darein / zugleich ein / Choral Stimme / beneben 2. Clareten vnd 1. Trom- / bet, gerichtet ist / doch also dass die Claret vnd Trombet / (wo mans nicht haben kan) mögen ausgelassen werden.[5]

The trumpet parts double the soprano parts throughout and are not as interesting as those in *Die Engelische Schlacht*. Both collections are set in the Venetian polychoral style with which Altenburg must have been familiar through the works of Hassler and the imported publications of Andrea and Giovanni Gabrieli.[6]

[4] 'Number 4, the Angelic Battle, from Revelation xii, with twelve or sixteen parts, in which may be used both 3 trumpets and two drums—one tuned to C, the other low G_1.'

[5] 'In which, at the same time, a choral voice is arranged next to two "Clareten" [*clarini?*] and one trumpet, but in such a way that the "Claret" and the trumpet (where they are not available) may be left out.'

[6] Meinecke, 1903, p. 40.

It would be ironic if, as Werner (1905, pp. 119–24) has suggested, Johann Michael Altenburg was the father of the 'Hof-, Feld- und Konzerttrompeter' Johann Caspar Altenburg, and thus a grandfather of Johann Ernst Altenburg. Werner made the assumption on the basis of name, occupation, proximity of employment and the fact that Johann Caspar was born at Alach, near Erfurt, where Johann Michael died in 1640. It seems to me that more than three generations would be involved, but if Werner is otherwise correct, then the first German composer to publish music with trumpet parts may have been a great-grandfather of the last author on the Baroque trumpet and one of its last great exponents.

Shortly after the appearance of Altenburg's *Gaudium Christianum*, two publications of Michael Praetorius appeared at Wolfenbüttel. Both must have required a considerable amount of preparation. It is possible, therefore, that the suggestions as to performance in both publications were applicable toward the end of the previous century. The one publication was a collection of vocal-instrumental pieces set in the Venetian polychoral style of Gabrieli; the other was a treatise on the 'new' Italian manner of composition, orchestration and performance. These were the *Polyhymnia caduceatrix et panegyrica* (Wolfenbüttel 1619) and the third volume of the *Syntagma Musicum* (Wolfenbüttel 1619). Both are important in a study of the Baroque trumpet. The first is important because it makes idiomatic use of the natural trumpet; the second is of particular importance because one entire section is devoted to explaining the function and use of the trumpet at the beginning of the seventeenth century.

In his *Revisionsbericht* to the modern edition of Praetorius's *Polyhymnia . . .*, Gurlitt suggests that the collection first appeared in 1617.[7] This is possible, since the collection is discussed at length in volume iii of the *Syntagma . . .*, which, although published in 1619, must have been in preparation for some time before. The composition with trumpets is number 34 in the collection, *In dulci jubilo à 12. 16. & 20 cum Tubis* (p. 566 in vol. xvii (2) of the collected edition). Praetorius prefaces the work with the following information:

Welcher gestalt dieses und andere auf die Trommetten gerichtete 'Concert' anzuordnen / dasselbe ist meistenteils in 'Tomo Tertio' [vol. iii of the 'Syntagma . . .'], am 8. Cap. bei der ersten Art / erinnert worden. (Anweisung für die 'Tubae'; 1. Art. Darinnen der 'Principal', Alter Bass und beide Clarien nach den Noten

[7] Collected works of Praetorius, vol. xvii (2), *Polyhymnia caduceatrix et panegyrica*, Wolfenbüttel-Berlin, 1933, edited by Wilibald Gurlitt.

gesetzt / darzu kann der Volgan und Grob von eim jeden darzu gebraucht und gesunden werden. — II. Art. Noch können die trommetten uff eine andere Art darzu gebraucht werden: Sonderlich wenn man nicht zween Clarien Bläser / so die 'Music' verstehen / haben kann: Alsdann kann derjenige / so den 'Principal' führt / bisweilen den andern Clarien / wie es allhier darbei mit eingezeichnet / führen und halten: Doch dass der 1. Clarien aus der 1. Art / 'sub Numero' 17. von einem andern gemacht werde. Und wenn 'Omnes' und 'Ripieno' darbei gezeichnet / so fallen alle Trommetten und Heer Paucken zugleich mit einander zusammen.) [8]

The tonality of the work is C major and there are only infrequent excursions away from the tonic and dominant. The scoring is in six specifically indicated groups: '1. Chorus, 2. Chorus, 3. Chorus, Chorus pro Capella, Tubae, Bassus Generalis.' The recommended instrumental doublings that Praetorius gives in each part are reproduced with the original clefs in Gurlitt's edition.[9] Each choir is in four parts with the first three doubled by the following instruments: violins, violas and/or viols, violone, cornetto, bassoons, flutes and trombones. The 'Chorus pro Capella' has no indication of doubling instruments. The 'Tubae' are indicated from highest to lowest as follows: '1. Clarien; 2. Clarien; 1. Art: Principal oder Quinta, II. Art: Principal vnd 2. Clarien; [I. Art]: Alter Bass, II. Art: tacet.' As suggested in the previously quoted preface and, as we shall see in a moment, three additional trumpet parts were intended —the 'Volgan', 'Grob' and 'Fladdergrob'.

In the fourth bar of the 'Bassus Generalis' there appears the direction 'Tutti cum Tubis et Tympanis'. The bass notes in all such tuttis that occur throughout the entire piece are C's or an alternation between C and G_1. The timpani would have played some rhythmic figures on these tones, since they would be the only possible notes for a pair of timpani tuned to

---

[8] 'The way in which this concerto [i.e., concerted music or cantata] and others intended for the trumpets are to be arranged, has been called to the reader's attention for the most part in vol. iii, 8th chapter [of the *Syntagma Musicum*], the first part. (Instruction for the brasses: Method I— In this method the *Principal*, *Alter Bass* and both clarinos are set to music, in addition the *Volgan* and *Grob* may be used and sounded by each one [i.e., player] for this purpose. Method II—Moreover, the trumpets may be used in yet another way for this purpose; especially if one cannot have two clarino players who can read music: In this case the one who plays the *Principal* may at times lead and support the other clarinos as it is marked down here in the appropriate places, but with the condition that the first clarino [part] according to Method I under number 17 must be performed by someone else. And if "Omnes" and "Ripieno" are indicated, then all trumpets and kettledrums fall in together simultaneously.)'

[9] *Ibid.*, p. xxxii.

the tonic and dominant. The two 'Clarien' have an inclusive range of a sixth, from c^1 to a^1; the 'Principal oder Quinta' part has only the 4th, 5th, 6th and 8th partials for a trumpet in C, i.e. c, e, g and c^1; the lowest trumpet part in the score, the 'Alter Bass', is in alto clef (the first three parts are in treble clef) and has only the 4th, 5th and 6th partials, i.e. c, e and g.

In dulci jubilo is predominantly in ternary rhythm, but the closing section (a repetition of the text, 'Eya, eya, wären wir da?') is in duple rhythm. The trumpets in the closing section have three similar fugato-like interludes, which imitate the material in the other vocal and instrumental parts. The third statement is played at the end of the piece over a series of sustained longs in the other parts. The direction 'Darauf so bald eine Intrada zum Final' is printed in the trumpet parts and refers to an improvised trumpet statement. Praetorius (1614–19, vol. iii, p. 171) defines an *Intrada* as being the same as a *praeambulum* and *final*, and says that trumpeters will play the *Intrada* (a) before their *Sonaden* (see below), (b) when they play at table, and (c) on holds (fermatas) and *Final*, i.e. the final, usually held chords at the end of a composition, such as the end of *In dulci jubilo*.

Although Praetorius (*ibid.*, p. 172) tells us that his compositions with trumpets are to be found in his '. . . I. II. *Polyhymnia Heroica seu Fusicinia* [sic., i.e. *Tubicinia*] & *Tympanistria* . . . ,' and in the '. . . *Appendice III. Polyhymniae Panegyricae* gesetzet befunden', only the *Polyhymniae* are known.

Some interesting conclusions may be drawn from Praetorius (*ibid.*, p. 169) concerning what he calls 'Die Erste Art' ('the first style'), employed in his '. . . newer zwar geringen *Operibus*' ('new, indeed trifling compositions'), his *Polyhymnia*. In effect he says that if one cannot, will not or must not use trumpets or timpani, the pieces scored as such, e.g. *In dulci jubilo*, will sound just as well in town churches that are lacking such instruments; if other performers are available the trumpet parts may be played on 'Geygen / Zincken und Posaunen'. This sounds like an earlier version of Cazzati's remark, 'When a trumpet is missing play the part on a violin' (*see* Chapter 4).

The inclusion of some trumpet performance practice remarks by Praetorius is most useful. He says (*ibid.*) that because trumpet players usually rush (because they need so much breath and therefore try to get all the notes played before running out), a conductor should speed up the beat when the trumpets enter, or else they always finish their parts ahead of everyone else ('. . . sonsten kommen sie mit ihren *Sonaten* allzeit zu früh zum ende'). He adds that the beat can be slowed down afterwards— until the trumpets play again, that is! He implies that trumpet players were like most other performers at the time and were expected to ornament and improve ('verbesserung') their parts:

Ich hab aber zu einen jedem solchen 'Concert'-Gesange / die Stimmen / wie sie die Trommeter darzu blasen können (doch auff eines jeden verstendigen verbesserung) mit dabey gesetzt.[10]

Praetorius (*ibid.*, p. 172) suggests that many trumpeters could not read music and knew their *Sonaten*,[11] chorales, etc., by memory only. This follows, in light of the secretive and clannish behaviour of most *Kameradschaft* and *Stadtpfeifer* trumpeters. Their repertory, at least until the seventeenth century, was committed to memory. Without recourse to printed tutors and with little or no musical sources, trumpeters learned their art and their repertory in the time-honoured fashion: by an aural, unwritten tradition, with the master passing on his knowledge and repertory to the apprentice.

Concerning the performance of his own music, Praetorius (*ibid.*, p. 171) says:

Und müssen unter den Trommetern vor allen dingen zum wenigsten zween / als einer der die 'Quint' führet / und der ander / der das ander 'Clarin' bläset / die Music verstehen / und es also / wie ich es auffgesetzet und vorgeschrieben / auss den 'Noten' zu wegen bringen können / vorhanden seyn.[12]

But the composer (*ibid.*) goes on to suggest that if musically literate trumpet players are not available, those on hand may perform their 'Sonaden' at the appropriate places and for such duration as the 'Concert-Gesang' requires. Amazing as this may sound, it should be remembered that at a given time and place, during the period we are discussing, musicians would have been familiar with only the current taste and style. The trumpeters would not have inserted just any 'Sonaden'. The musical clichés they used would have been the same ones with which Praetorius was familiar and, in all probability, used himself.

[10] 'But for each one of such concerted arrangements I have written down the parts which the trumpeters can play to harmonize with them (which may be improved [ornamented] by anyone who knows what he is doing).'

[11] He says that a 'Sonada vel Sonata ist / deren sie sich zum Tisch blasen / auch zum Tanz gebrauchen . . .' ('A sonata is something which they [the trumpeters] play during meals and also use for dancing . . .').

[12] 'Above all things there must be at least two trumpeters who understand [i.e. can read] music—such as the one who plays "Quint" [*Principal*] and the other who plays second "Clarin"—and can, therefore, play the notes as I wrote them.'

The rest of Praetorius's 'Erste Art' is mostly a definition of trumpet terminology. His explanation of some terms is, however, of special interest in this study. During the Baroque the usual designation of a third trumpet part was 'Principal'. Praetorius (*ibid.*) explains why a third trumpet part, one that frequently sounds a simple tonic and dominant figure below the more florid and difficult 'Clarino' part, is called the principal part:

Der 'Principal', Quinta, oder wie es etliche nennen 'Sonata', ist der rechte Tenor, der den gantzen Chor der Trommeter unnd Heerpaucker regiert unnd führet.[13]

Earlier, while discussing the general function of each trumpet part to his *Polyhymnia*, Praetorius suggested the importance of the *Principal* in that the trumpet parts called *Volgan*, *Grob* and *Fladdergrob*, as well as the timpani part, follow, i.e. are led by, the *Principal*. The *Volgan*, *Grob*, *Fladdergrob* and timpani are given no music in Praetorius's *In dulci jubilo*, but the composer explains that those being led by the *Principal* can find their parts by themselves and have no need of written music.

The *Volgan* (*Volgano* in Monteverdi's *Orfeo*; see Chapter 4), *Grob* and *Fladdergrob* are the same terms that Speer (1697, p. 209) uses toward the end of the seventeenth century to define the single-note lower parts found in pieces for several trumpets. For a comparison of Girolamo Fantini's trumpet register terminology discussed in Chapter 4 and that of Praetorius and Speer, *see* Westrup, 1940, p. 237.

Praetorius (*Syntagma*, iii, p. 172) makes an interesting point in the penultimate paragraph of 'Die Erste Art'. He explains why some peculiar dissonances exist between the trumpets and other parts in the 'Concert-Gesang', *In dulci jubilo*. Some trumpet notes, usually in the 'Alter Bass' part, actually belong to a different harmony from that given by the other parts or by the figures of the 'Bassus-Generalis' at those places in question. Two such discords are found in the initial trumpet statement on the third beat of bars six and seven (Ex. 11). Praetorius says: 'Wiewol es doch allzeit ohne *Dissonantien* und anderen verbottenen *Speciebus* nicht wol kan gesetzt werden.' In other words, when writing music with trumpet parts, dissonances and other forbidden intervals are sometimes unavoidable.

One point that Praetorius does not mention in the entire discussion of trumpet performance practice is non-harmonic trumpet tones. The fact that none are introduced in his only work with trumpets means very little

[13] 'The *Principal, Quinta*, or as it is sometimes called, the *Sonata*, is the true tenor; it guides and leads the entire choir of trumpets and timpani.'

in itself. But hardly any are found in other sources of early German trumpet music. The implication is that, unlike Fantini and other Italians, the Germans at that time were reluctant to write non-harmonic trumpet tones, even as quick passing notes or neighbouring tones of short duration. Some sources occasionally introduce the *b* natural, but the more exotic non-harmonic tones do not occur in German trumpet music until later in the seventeenth century. Whether this indicates that the Germans had a less developed trumpet technique than the Italians in the early seventeenth century, or that they were dissatisfied with the effect of such false notes, is uncertain. To make matters worse, there is no way of knowing when the *tromba da tirarsi* (i.e. the *Zugtrompete*) was used. Praetorius says nothing about the instrument, and, although it is mentioned in seventeenth-century church inventories, it is not specified in musical sources until the eighteenth century. The intended use of such an instrument would certainly explain the appearance of many non-harmonic natural trumpet tones later on.

Ex. 11. Praetorius: trumpet discords from *In dulci jubilo.*

Some very imaginative trumpet writing is to be found in the music of Heinrich Schütz. His earliest work with trumpets, which, as was mentioned before, might predate Altenburg's *Gaudium Christianum*, is his setting of Psalm cxxxvi, *Danket dem Herrn, denn er ist freundlich (SWV 45).* It belongs to the 1619 publication, *Die Psalmen Davids*, and appears in Philipp Spitta's collected edition of Schütz's music [*SGA*], vol. iii, pp. 182 ff. Werner Bittinger (1960) states that a considerable part of the 1619 collection may be dated between the summer of 1612 and the winter of 1615. If *Danket dem Herrn* belongs to this earlier part, it is then the earliest German work with natural trumpet parts specified, post-dating

Monteverdi's *Orfeo* by only three years. In addition to three choirs of voices and instruments, the scoring of *Danket dem Herrn* also requires 'Trombette e Timpani'. The title of the continuo part reads: '*Psalmus 136. à 13. Mit Trompeten vnd Heerpaucken*'. Only one part is given and there is no timpani part. But this presents little or no difficulty in view of the simple tonic-dominant bass at those places where the trumpet notes occur. If we follow the relevant suggestions of Praetorius, mentioned above, a timpani part, as well as the other trumpet parts (probably two more), may be stylistically reconstructed.

The trumpet part in the British Museum copy, like the one in Spitta's edition, is notated in soprano clef. It uses only partials 4, 5, 6, 8, 9 and 10 of a trumpet in C, and in short, repetitive melodic patterns—often when the 'capella' group is required.

One of the most interesting things concerning the trumpet parts is Schütz's direction at the end of the bass part: '*Darauff wird stracks eine Intrada* zum *Final geblasen*'. This is precisely the same kind of instruction as that printed at the end of the trumpet parts to *In dulci jubilo* by Praetorius (*see* above). The only difference is that Praetorius supplies the 'Intrada' and Schütz does not. Some appropriate short piece, however, like the Praetorius example, will do very nicely in a performance.

The next use that Schütz made of the trumpet was in his *Symphoniae Sacrae . . . à 3. 4. 5. 6. . . . . opus Ecclesiasticum Secundum*, published at Venice in 1629. A complete set of parts is preserved in the library of Christ Church, Oxford (Catalogue No. 881-6). The work with trumpet is number 13 in the collection, with the title *Buccinate in neomenia tuba Prima Pars* (*SWV* 275)—*Iubilate Deo Secunda Pars* (*SWV* 276), a setting of Psalm lxxx in the Vulgate. Both sections require the following: 'Cornetto, Trombetta o Cornetto, Fagotto, Tenori I, II, Basso, Bassus pro Organo'.

The 'Trombetta' part is completely within the compass of the natural trumpet harmonics. Schütz gives the higher dominant fugal entries to the trumpet for at least two reasons: to avoid the lower non-harmonic tones and to keep the scale of notes within the compass of a natural C trumpet. The part has a key signature of one flat in the original print. The range of the trumpet in the *Buccinate* . . . and the *Iubilate Deo* . . . is from g to c^2. There is the occasional f^1 sharp but it is always approached by step from e^1. The upper limit c^2 is usually approached scalewise and through the 15th partial (b^1 natural). There are, however, some difficult moments in the fifteenth and sixteenth bars of the *Iubilate Deo*. The c^2 is twice approached by leap—in bar fifteen from g and in bar sixteen from c^1. The fourteenth partial (b^1 flat) occurs seven times, while the fifteenth partial (b^1 natural) occurs only three times.

In the second set of *Symphoniae Sacrae*, published in 1647, Schütz again uses trumpets. No. 4 in the collection, *Meine Seele erhebt den Herren* (*SWV* 344), a setting in German of the *Magnificat*, does not have the same orchestration throughout, but has various pairs of instruments in different sections. Although where the trumpets are intended the parts read, 'Cornetto o Trombetta I, Cornetto o Trombetta II', the parts were, nevertheless, conceived for a natural trumpet. Later on Schütz requires 'Cornettino o Violino', but the writing is very different and intended for the wide-range chromatic instruments as indicated.

Since the timbres of a cornetto and a real trumpet are not dissimilar, particularly above c^1, it is understandable why there is the frequent alternative choice of instruments during the seventeenth century. There is also the consideration that competent trumpeters may not have always been available. There was probably a surfeit of capable cornetto players.

The range of 'Trombetta I' in *Meine Seele erhebt den Herren* is e to b^1, including four f^1 sharps, and a c^1 sharp, which is approached by leap from an f^1 natural. 'Trombetta II' has a comparable range to 'Trombetta I', but in addition to several f^1 sharps the part has two rare d^1 sharps, the first of which is approached by leap from g^1. Since this is the only instance in Schütz's music where there are so many extraordinary non-harmonic trumpet tones, it is possible that two *Zugtrompeten* were intended.

It is difficult to know exactly in what year Schütz composed his next work with trumpets. His *Historia von der Geburt . . . Jesu Christi*, the so-called 'Christmas Story' (*SWV* 435, 435a, and 435b), has parts for two trumpets, and it is thought that the earliest version was composed prior to 1664.[14] Since there is a set of MS. parts preserved at Upsala, Sweden, there is a possibility that the work was composed or at least performed while Schütz was at the court of Christian IV of Denmark.

On two occasions, once from 1633 to 1635 and again from 1642 to 1644, Schütz was *Kapellmeister* of the royal court at Copenhagen. The royal households of Denmark and Sweden were not without adequate musical resources. The music of the period that is found in both countries would be sufficient evidence of the large performing ensembles that were available to composers in the seventeenth century. But the court records during the reign of Christian IV (1577–1648), for example, also indicate that his court 'band' was no less than seventy-seven strong. In addition

[14] Bittinger, 1960, p. 94.

to the thirty instrumentalists and thirty-one singers, Christian had a corps of sixteen trumpeters.[15] The 'Christmas Story' of Schütz may have been performed under the direction of the composer at some time during the two periods he was in Scandinavia.

In all versions of the 'Christmas Story' trumpets are indicated in the 'Intermedium VI', which has the additional information, 'Herodes Bassus solus cum duobus Clarinis vel Cornettinis. à 3'. The association of a king with trumpets is very traditional. From the earliest biblical times trumpets are a symbol of majesty and authority. The appearance of Herod with two trumpets is, therefore, an obvious image. The 'clarino-cornettino' parts have a key signature of one flat, i.e. the key of F, the principal tonality of the entire work. The parts are for two C trumpets, however. The range of the 'Clarino primo' is g to c^2; the g appears only once, c^1 being the lowest note otherwise. 'Clarino secundo' has an identical range, but the g is encountered with greater frequency. Both parts have occasional f^1 sharps where there is a momentary modulation to the major mediant.

The trumpet-cornetto parts in the Berlin version [16] have the same range as those in the Upsala MS., but they play only in the nine-bar introduction before the entry of Herod. The writing is very different, both thematically and stylistically. The florid sequences of semiquavers in fugal imitation are reminiscent of many mid seventeenth-century Italian opera and sonata parts. Since this version is spurious there is little reason to attach much importance to the disparate trumpet parts. The writing is atypical of Schütz and, by comparison, inferior to his trumpet parts in the Upsala MS.

The last work with trumpets that can be definitely attributed to Schütz is the polychoral piece, *Herr Gott, dich loben wir* (*SWV* 472). It is one of the more bombastic pieces in the Baroque trumpet repertory and is scored for several groups, requiring violins or cornettos, a 'clarino' with the 'Cantus pro organo', SATB chorus, three trombones, two other 'clarino' parts, timpani, two parts each marked 'Trombetta' and the 'Continuus'. The parts were originally in the library of the Michaelis church at Erfurt,[17] but are now in the Deutsche Staatsbibliothek at Berlin (Mus. MS. 20374): *Herr Gott dich loben wir à 12 Voc. Cantus pro Organo, 2 Clarin, 2 Violin/ Corn, 3 Trombon, CATB Chori cum Continuo di H. Schüzzen.*

In the preface to the edition in vol. xviii of the *Heinrich Schütz Sämtliche Werke* (Leipzig, 1927, pp. xiv–xv), Spitta remarks that this piece is pro-

[15] Hammerich & Elling, 1893, p. 89.   [16] *See* Bittinger, 1960, p. 97; Schöneich, 1955.
[17] *See* Noack, 1925, pp. 65–116.

bably one and the same as that described in a printed programme of a 1668 'Dankfest' at Dresden. The Erfurt parts date from a performance on 30th November 1677, having been copied by one Johann Chr. Eppelmus.[18] The text is in German and is that of the *Te Deum laudamus*.

The 'clarino' part that doubles the 'Cantus pro organo' seems to have been notated in the wrong octave. By doubling the vocal part at the unison the 'clarino' would have to play the non-harmonic tones d, f, a and b natural with unusual frequency. If not intended for a *Zugtrompete* but for a natural trumpet playing an octave higher, the range would not be unusual for Schütz: c^1 to d^2, the d^2 being played only once. The part is notated in soprano clef.

The 'Trombetta I, Trombetta II' parts are notated in alto and tenor clefs respectively. They are possibly *Zugtrompeten* parts and are meant to sound an octave higher—especially since both nearly double the 'Cantus pro organo' throughout. The two parts are mostly in unison, but there are some occasional and most interesting flourishes towards the end of the piece where they play separately.

The most unusual thing about this piece is the continuous interruptions by the other two 'clarini', often with the support of the 'Timpano', a rhythmically conceived part on the note C. Example 12 reproduces all the parts from bars 46 and 47 (*SGA*, xviii, page 162). Since the groups marked 'Capella' and 'Chorus' do not perform at the same time, they have been put on the same staves. These two bars give some idea of the extraordinary sound that may be heard at nearly every other bar throughout the entire piece.

Finally, there remains a work thought to be by Schütz which is orchestrated for four choirs of voices and instruments and is set to the often-used and previously mentioned text, *Es erhub sich ein Streit im Himmel* (*SWV Anhang* 11). The fourth choir includes a part for a 'Trombetta', but the principal cornetto writing in the third choir is suspiciously trumpet-like, especially in the opening section where the struggle between good and evil is portrayed in a most descriptive musical setting. In the initial fourteen bars (see *SGA*, vol. xviii, pp. 1 ff.) there are several florid exchanges between the 'Trombetta 1' and the 'Cornetto 1'. As in all of Schütz's trumpet music, a C trumpet is required. The date of composition is not known, and although Heinrich Spitta attributes this piece to Schütz,[19] Bittinger (1960) feels that the authorship is spurious.

[18] See *SGA*, vol. xviii, p. xiv, and *SWV*, p. 122.
[19] *See* the preface to *SGA*, vol. xviii.

Ex. 12. Schütz: bars 46–7 from *Herr Gott, dich loben wir* (*SWV* 472).

For most of his life Schütz worked as *Kapellmeister* at Dresden, the principal city of the electorate of Saxony. At a comparatively short distance to the north-west is the Saxon city of Leipzig, where trumpet playing flourished during the entire Baroque era. Long before J. S. Bach's appearance on the Leipzig musical scene in 1723, a tradition of large musical settings—many with trumpets—had been established. An examination of many pieces written for and performed in the Leipzig *Hauptkirche* of St Thomas during the seventeenth century actually makes Bach's orchestrations appear small by comparison. From 1616 to 1750 the *Thomaskantoren* were as follows:

1616–1630 Johann Hermann Schein aus Grünhain
1631–1657 Tobias Michael aus Dresden
1657–1676 Sebastian Knüpfer aus Asch
1677–1701 Johann Schelle aus Geysing
1701–1722 Johann Kuhnau aus Geysing
1723–1750 Johann Sebastian Bach aus Eisenach.[20]

All of these composers contributed to the repertory of the Baroque trumpet. At the same time, and as regards this study, some of the organists at the three main Leipzig churches (St Thomas, the Nikolaikirche and the Neukirche) are of interest and made sufficient contributions to the Baroque trumpet repertory. They are Vincenzo Albrici, a former assistant of Schütz at Dresden, who worked as an organist under the direction of Schelle at St Thomas from 1681 until 1682; Johann Rosenmüller, who in 1655 was an organist at the Neukirche; Georg Philipp Telemann, who was also an organist at the Neukirche in 1704; and Johann Kuhnau, who served as an organist under Schelle at St Thomas from 1684 until 1701, and then as *Kantor* at the same church.[21]

What Schein composed for the trumpet is not definitely known, but there are several contemporary sources that mention performances of his music in which trumpets participated. While Schein was *Kapellmeister* at Weimar (1613–16), a post that Bach was to hold exactly a hundred years later, he undoubtedly made frequent use of the resident trumpeters who were at his disposal. The church services must have taken on a new splendour with Schein's music, for the records mention the accompaniment of the vocal music in the *Schlosskirche*, '. . . mit Zinken, Drummeten und Heerpaucken, mit Fideln und Lauten gar künstlich musiciert'.[22]

In 1618, two years after assuming his duties as *Kantor* at Leipzig, Schein composed a 'Jubelfest' for the wedding of Jonas Möstel, son of Leipzig's *Bürgermeister*.[23] The accompaniment included parts for trumpets and

[20] *See* Knick, 1963.

[21] See the preface to Arnold Schering's edition of seventeenth-century Leipzig church cantatas in *DdT*, vols. lviii–lix, pp. xiii–xiv.

[22] Pasqué, 1897, p. 134: '. . . with cornetts, trumpets and timpani, with violins and lutes artfully and musically played indeed'.

[23] Wustmann, 1909, p. 80–1.

drums—some apparently played by a few *Stadtpfeifer* engaged from the nearby town of Naumburg.[24]

Schein's successor was Tobias Michael. He wrote a collection of vocal pieces with instrumental accompaniments, entitled *Musikalische Seelenlust*, published at Leipzig in 1637. One piece from the collection, undoubtedly performed at St Thomas's, begins with the text *Lass dich ihre Lebe* and is scored for two trumpets, bassoon, organ and SSATTB chorus. A set of parts is found in the Stadt Bibliothek at Augsburg, and the trumpet writing is not unlike Altenburg's in his *Gaudium Christianum*. Michael requires two C trumpets, which frequently double the two soprano parts. The range of each part is somewhat narrow and neither instrument has to play above a^1.

The next three *Kantoren* to succeed Tobias Michael at St Thomas's are represented in Arnold Schering's edition of seventeenth-century Leipzig church cantatas.[25] The first cantata with trumpets is Sebastian Knüpfer's *Ach Herr, strafe mich nicht*, scored for 'Clarino I, II, Timpani, Traverso I, II, Violino I, II, Violetta I, II, Fagotto', SSATB chorus and organ continuo. It is a rather straightforward verse anthem, beginning with a short instrumental introduction and with intermittent 'ritornelli'. The chorus parts are mostly homophonic and in the solos Knüpfer has given special attention to the pair of trumpets, which are heard throughout most of the composition. What is of particular interest is that the two 'Clarino' parts are notated with two flats, implying C minor, the prevailing tonality of the work. This is one of the rare instances of trumpets being scored in the minor mode. In Handel's *Judas Maccabaeus*, for example, the bass aria 'With honour let desert be crown'd', is in A minor and is scored for a D trumpet; there is a frequent use of the natural seventh harmonic c^1 in order to sound the mediant of A minor. Another use of a Baroque trumpet in the minor mode is to be found in Pavel Vejvanovský's *Sonata à 4* (*see* Chapter 7), where a C trumpet is used in a way comparable to that of the Handel aria, but down one tone in the key of G minor (like the Biber work also mentioned in Chapter 7).

Knüpfer's 'Clarini' are in C and scored with their ancillary pair of timpani—one drum tuned to a C, the other to a G_1. The 'Clarini' are semi-independent of one another, and have therefore comparable ranges: g to b^1 flat. The extraordinary thing is the frequency of the non-harmonic tones b natural, e^1 flat and a^1 flat. In every case the b natural occurs as a lower

---

[24] *Ibid.*, p. 81.
[25] *DdT*, lviii–lix (1918), Leipzig.

neighbour tone of c^1 and usually at cadences; the e^1 flat is used as both a passing tone and is approached several times by leap; the a^1 flat in both trumpet parts is in almost every case a passing tone from g^1 to b^1 flat, but a notable exception is the leap from f^1 to the a^1 flat in the first trumpet part near the beginning of the work and in the second trumpet part in the penultimate bar. Except for a more soloistic treatment in polyphony when used to accompany the vocal solos, the trumpets do little more than punctuate the chorus accompaniment. They do, however, have the last word. As all the other instruments (except continuo) and the voices finish playing and singing in the penultimate bar on the word 'plötzlich', the trumpets continue their short phrase to a complete cadence in C major.

The works with trumpets by the St Thomas *Kantor* Johann Schelle are very much along the lines of the polychoral style of Buxtehude. In *Lobe den Herrn, meine Seele (DdT*, lviii–lix, pp. 122 ff.) Schelle uses a large orchestration with two five-part choirs of voices—not unlike some of Buxtehude's large-scale works for double chorus and orchestra. The four 'Clarini' are in C and are scored in pairs with an orchestra consisting of 2 Vn, 2 Vla, Bsn, 'Cornettino I, II', 3 Tbn, Ti, and Org. As in the case of Buxtehude's orchestrations, Schelle's higher 'Clarino' parts are numbers one and three, while the lower parts are numbers two and four. This is, perhaps, an indication of the physical placement of the instruments. In other words, trumpets I and II played together at one place in the church and trumpets III and IV played together in another. This may well be the explanation of Buxtehude's scoring, as well as the origin of the later pairing of horns in the 'classic' orchestra. In nearly all cases where there are four trumpets scored in a seventeenth-century polychoral setting, their antiphonal use is in pairs: I and II in antiphony with III and IV. Except for the brief moment by themselves in the antiphonal instrumental introduction, the trumpets in Schelle's *Lobe den Herrn* . . . are only an additional colour in the usual *tutti* scoring. The range of all four 'Clarino' parts is nearly the same. 'Clarino I' and 'Clarino III' are scored from g to a^1, while the other two parts, with the exception of a single a^1 in the 'Clarino IV', have c to g^1. There are no passages of any difficulty for the trumpets in this piece and there are no non-harmonic tones.

Schelle's *Vom Himmel kam der Engel Schar (DdT*, lviii–lix, pp. 167 ff.) is also scored for a large number of instruments, but with only one choir of voices and less a third and fourth 'Clarino', a third trombone and a bassoon. The work is a multi-verse cantata based on the chorale *Vom Himmel hoch da komm ich her*. The chorale is used throughout, but variation from one verse to another is achieved by thematic decoration for solo voices, changes from binary to ternary rhythm, and the use of antiphony in the orchestral accompaniment.

The opening statement in the trumpets and timpani is rather unusual:

Ex. 13. Schelle: initial trumpet and timpani statement from *Vom Himmel kam der Engel Schar*.

A series of quick alternating notes in intervals wider than a second is rare in the seventeenth-century trumpet repertory.[26]

As each verse progresses, the trumpet material is varied, but Schelle recapitulates the opening section for the sixth and final verse. The range of the two trumpet parts is the same as the first and second 'Clarino' parts in *Lobe den Herrn* . . . Their thematic material is also fragmentary, serving more as a rhythmic than a melodic element.

Some of Schelle's compositions are to be found in the Bodleian Library at Oxford. They are in MS. parts, bound in a single volume called 'Sacred vocal compositions by Schelle, Rosenmüller . . .', with the shelf number MS. Mus. Sch. C. 31. One work, Schelle's *Salve solis orientis*, is found on leaves 49–67. It is written for the Feast of John the Baptist. What is particularly interesting is the name of the trumpet required and an explanatory note about the instrument—presumably in the composer's own handwriting. The trumpet part is on leaf 50 with the indication 'Clarino piccolo'. On the inside of the wrapper-title page there appears the

[26] Two other notable examples of Baroque trumpet writing in figures of quick alternating notes (mostly in thirds) appear in Cazzati's *Sonata à 5*, 'La Bianchina' (bars 18–19), already discussed in Chapter 4, and Schmelzer's remarkable *Sonata a 5* (bars 19–20 and 46 in the first section and in the trumpet 'Presto' section) found at Kroměříž and now preserved in the 'Liechtenstein' music microfilm archive at Syracuse University (Breitenbacher-Smithers, IV, 106).

following: 'NB Der Clarin bey diesem Stück ist auf einer kleinen Italienischen Trompette gesetzet, welche einen Tohn höher, wovon aber diese Stimme auf einem andren Instrument / soll geblasen werden, muss es einen Tohn höher geschehen, / dann [= als] das Stück ausser d[er] R[egel].' [27]

The instrument held by Gottfried Reiche in his portrait by Elias Gottlob Haussmann may show what is meant by a 'Clarino piccolo'. The Italian *tromba da caccia* is perhaps what Schelle intended when he wrote 'kleine Italienischen Trompette'. The rest of the remarks about the 'Clarino piccolo' refer to its pitch and what is necessary if another instrument is used in its place. Supposedly, the instrument sounded a tone higher, so it was necessary to compensate for the difference of pitch if the part was played on a normal trumpet.

A particularly interesting feature about this piece is the single trumpet part with a large chorus (SSATTB) and a weighty instrumental accompaniment of strings, 'cornettini', three trombones and continuo. This would certainly be one of the earliest instances of a solo trumpet in ensemble with many other instruments and voices. Only two other examples of a solo trumpet part with strings and voices have been noted from the German repertory at the time, and, interestingly, they too are by Schelle. His evident predilection for this particular combination of voices and instruments, which is noted in *Gott sei mir gnädig* and *Schaffe in mir Gott* (for the particulars of each score see Appendix), may have had something to do with the availability of additional but competent trumpet players. The *tromba prima* during most of Schelle's tenure at St Thomas's would have been Johann Pezel. He is the only one who is ever mentioned in approbatory terms in contemporary records. He may well have been the only player, at least for a time or for particular occasions, whom Schelle trusted with a difficult and hardly unobtrusive instrument. One superlative player by himself is worth any number of unskilled journeymen! Predictably, the 'Clarino con sordino' required in *Schaffe in mir Gott* plays from music that is transposed a tone below the other parts, *ergo* performing at correct pitch, since a trumpet when muted sounds a tone higher.

Many of Johann Kuhnau's extant works include trumpet parts. Some display a later style of writing than is evident from his general style of

[27] '*Nota bene:* The clarino part in this piece is scored for a small Italian trumpet which sounds a tone higher. But in case this part should be played on a different instrument it has to be transposed up a tone higher than the piece as regularly.'

composition or his dates (1660–1722). His cantata *Wenn ihr fröhlich seid an euren Festen* (*DdT*, lviii–lix, pp. 244 ff.) has four trumpet parts entitled: 'Clarino I, II, Trombetta, Principale'. All four instruments are in C and the 'Principale' is notated in soprano clef. The introductory 'Sonata' gives the trumpets some very energetic fanfare passages, the 'Clarino I' having to play from *c* to *c²*. The scoring is similar to that in Bach's early Leipzig cantatas, and each part is confined to a particular register. The later solo passages for the first trumpet contain some long and difficult melismas (written for Gottfried Reiche?). Non-harmonic tones are wanting in all four trumpet parts. Although the style of the work is still seventeenth-century, the trumpet writing is clearly in advance of anything we have met so far in the German repertory.

A seventeenth-century cantata with a solo trumpet part, in the Bodleian Library at Oxford, may have been written by Kuhnau. The work is in parts, with the title *Muss nicht der Mensch auf dieser Erde* (B.L. MS. Mus. Sch. C. 43). Both title and scoring agree with a work given in Schering's list of Kuhnau's music.[28] This work is for solo tenor, 'Clarino', violin, bassoon and organ. A set of parts is mentioned as being in the archives of the Nikolai church at Luckau, a small city about forty-five miles south-east of Berlin. Schering notes that the parts are dated 1715. No comparison of the Luckau and Oxford parts has been possible as yet, but those in the Bodleian Library require exactly the same voice and instruments.

The scoring of *Muss nicht der Mensch* . . . is most satisfactory, and the trumpet writing, while interrupted by long stretches of rests, is rather florid and technically more demanding than most late seventeenth- and early eighteenth-century German sources. An edition of the work is in preparation and should it concord with the one at Luckau it will be a welcome addition to the available works of Bach's immediate predecessor at Leipzig.

The last Leipzig composer with whom we shall be dealing was not a *Kantor* but a *Stadtpfeifer*. This was Johann Pezel (sometimes spelled Petzold or Pezelius). He was, as mentioned in the previous chapter, a *Kunstgeiger* before joining the *Stadtpfeifer* as a trumpet player. His output of instrumental music was large, and many of his pieces display a keen imagination and appreciation of specific instrumental technique. A list of his twenty-two known collections and individual compositions is given by Schering (1921, pp. 41–2).

The bulk of Pezel's work is instrumental ensemble music. Six of his

[28] *See* Arnold Schering's preface to *DdT*, lviii–lix, p. xlvi.

collections have not survived, but three interesting vocal-instrumental pieces are in the Deutsche Staatsbibliothek at Berlin. Pezel is not usually associated with choral works, but his *Singet dem Herrn ein neues Lied* (Berlin: D.S.B. MS. 16900, No. 8) appears to be an interesting composition and has the added attraction of two 'Clarino' parts. Johann Philipp Krieger's 'Verzeichnis'[29] of compositions used at Weissenfels mentions three vocal works of 'Pezelius' that have trumpet parts: *Dies ist der Tag, Lobet ihr Knechte des Herrn* and a *Sanctus*. Nothing more is known about these works and they are undoubtedly lost.

Having been both a *Kunstgeiger* and a *Stadtpfeifer* Pezel is understandably well known for his *Turmsonaten*. Most of this type of music was intended as *Ratsmusik*, one collection even bearing the title *Hora Decima Musik*— the 'tenth hour music', which, as we have seen, was usually played just before lunch by the *Stadtpfeifer* from the *Pfeiferstuhl* on the town hall. Most of these pieces are scored for two cornetti and three trombones. To perform them only on modern trumpets and trombones, as is the fashion nowadays, is a mistake. There is no substitute for the timbre of the cornetto, but since there are now very few cornettos and fewer cornettists, the oboe would be a better choice than the modern trumpet. At any rate, most of these pieces by Pezel were originally intended for instruments other than trumpets. One collection, however, contains several pieces the upper two parts of which seem to be natural trumpet music. This collection is in the British Museum (Pr. Mus. C. 31) and each of five part-books has the following title page:

Johannis / PEZELII / Fünff-stimmigte blasende Music, / Bestehend / Intraden, Allemanden, Balleten, Cou- / renten, Sarabanden und Chiquen, / als / Zweyen Cornetten und dreyen / Trombonen. / . . . / Frankfurt am Mayn / Drucks und Verlags Balthasar Christopher Wusts Anno M.DC. XXCV.

The collection containts seventy-six pieces, most of which are 'Intradas'. *Intrada* No. 71 is obviously a trumpet piece. It avoids all non-harmonic tones for a C trumpet in the first part ('Cornetto I'), and both cornetto parts employ the usual characteristic figures of seventeenth-century trumpet music. The second part ('Cornetto II') has only one non-harmonic tone and that is a neighbour *f* at the final cadence. The last four pieces in the collection (*Intrada* Nos. 73–6) are probably trumpet music as well. With the exception of one *b* natural in the first cornetto part to *Intrada* No. 74,

[29] See *DdT*, liii–liv (1916), p. lviii. Leipzig.

which is a cadential neighbour tone before the first double bar, the two upper parts of these four pieces are idiomatic seventeenth-century trumpet writing. The *b* natural does not belie the possibility of this. It has already been pointed out that parts specifically scored for a Baroque trumpet do occasionally use the *b* natural at cadences and as a neighbouring tone in rapid passages. *Intrada* Nos. 50 and 69 exhibit stylistic elements of trumpet writing, but the avoidance of non-harmonic tones occurs in the first part only.

Schering (1926, p. 278) has indicated that *Intrada* No. 41 is for '. . . 2 Trompeten, 3 Posaunen'. This is possible, although the frequency of a *b* natural in both parts is much greater in this piece than in any of those mentioned previously. Inasmuch as the parts include too many non-harmonic tones in the bass register, the lower three parts in Pezel's five-part wind music are in all cases for trombones. Such notes would not only be impossible for a natural Baroque trumpet, but would also be unplayable on a *Zugtrompete*.

Although so much of his work is for cornettos and trombones, Pezel did write trumpet music. In the Nationalbibliothek at Vienna and in the university library at Upsala are complete copies of his *Bicinia*, published at Leipzig in 1675. It is a collection of seventy-five sonatas for various pairs of instruments (violins, cornettos, trumpets and bassoon), all with *basso continuo* accompaniment. Nos. 69 to 74 are 'Sonatinas' for two 'Clarini' and continuo, and No. 75 is a 'Sonata' for 'Clarino', bassoon and continuo. Of these, the first (No. 69), third (No. 71) and last (No. 75) are the most rewarding. In many respects none of the trumpet pieces measures up to the imaginative writing found in the five-part cornetto and trombone pieces. But the first 'Sonatina' for two trumpets does have an almost folk-like robustness, especially in the repeated two quaver, dotted quaver-semiquaver figures in bars five to nine.

Like so many early Baroque trumpet pieces, Pezel's *Bicinia* lack sufficient harmonic interest, there is not enough thematic development, and the *basso continuo* writing is quite static. Yet here, in one of the earliest examples of solo trumpet music, the composer makes the most of the limited possibilities of the natural trumpet. Pezel employs the full range of the trumpet in both 'Clarino' parts in nearly every piece.

In the first of the trumpet sonatinas (No. 69) c^2 occurs twice in both trumpet parts; in the *Sonatina* No. 71 there is a melismatic sequence of semiquavers where the 'Clarino 1' ascends to a d^2; and in the *Sonata à 2. Clarino e Fagotto* (No. 75) c^2 occurs with remarkable frequency in the trumpet part. In all of the trumpet pieces the non-harmonic tone b natural also appears with unusual frequency, most often as a lower neighbour tone of c^1. Where a shift of mode was desired, b flat is used to good effect, especially in the *Sonatina* No. 74. Pezel also uses dynamic contrasts on occasion, repeating a phrase ending with the dynamic marking p. The use of wide leaps and difficult demisemiquaver figures in the *Sonata* for trumpet and bassoon betokens a formidable trumpet technique by 1675.

At about the time that Pezel was publishing his various collections of *Bicinia*, *Turmmusik* and instrumental suites in the French manner, the Bohemian-born Andreas Hammerschmidt was composing works with important trumpet parts. Working at Zittau most of his life, Hammerschmidt represents one of the more important composers of the generation following Praetorius, Schein and Altenburg. His output consists mainly of published collections of vocal and instrumental settings of religious texts. Those with trumpets are listed in the Appendix.

Hammerschmidt is described in his epitaph as the 'Orpheus' of Zittau.[30] He was organist of the Zittau *Johanniskirche* from 1639 until his death in 1675. The vocal and instrumental forces of the town could not have been large, and doubtless the trumpet and trombone parts to his various works were played by the local *Stadtpfeifer*. Most of his compositions with trumpets are noteworthy for their simplicity, straightforwardness and 'chamber' sonority. Only his *Musikalische Andachten*, part iv (1654) and his *Missae* (1663) require comparatively large forces. They were probably modelled upon the polychoral works in the Venetian style by Praetorius and other composers of his generation. Even Hammerschmidt's *Lob und Danck aus dem 84. Psalm* is somewhat conservative in its scoring. The piece was composed for the '. . . Einweihung der wieder erbawten Kirche S. Elizabeth in Breslaw . . .'[31] and was published in 1652.

In much of the seventeenth-century music composed at Breslau the performing forces were extensive. Emil Bohn's two catalogues of the pre-eighteenth-century music that was preserved in various Breslau archives is sufficient testimony of the extent to which large forces were used in that Silesian city during the seventeenth century.[32] Though scored for nine vocal parts doubled by five trumpets, three trombones and five 'Violen', Hammerschmidt's *Lob und Danck Lied* . . . cannot com-

[30] *See* Adrio, 1956, col. 1428.

[31] For the '. . . consecration of the rebuilt church of St. Elizabeth at Breslau [now the Polish city of Wrocław] . . .'

[32] *See* Bohn, 1883 and 1890.

pare with the numerous Breslau works with enormous orchestrations. Working at St Bernhardin at Breslau, the seventeenth-century organist and composer Martin Mayer, for example, scored his *Jubilate Auff mein Psalter und Harfenklang* for as many as forty-four separate parts.[33] The concluding 'Alleluja' requires eight trumpets and timpani, with a host of assorted wind and stringed instruments, and voices. Another work, *Frischauff ietzt ist es Singes Zeit* by the seventeenth-century Breslau composer Johannes Phengius, has thirty-four separate performing parts for voices and instruments divided among five choirs.[34] Even an abbreviated version of the same work has some twenty parts.

Whether by choice or of necessity, the next three seventeenth-century German composers to be mentioned, like Hammerschmidt, used trumpets with a limited number of voices and instruments. The first was the Darmstadt *Kappellmeister* Wolfgang Karl Briegel.

In his *Musikalischer Lebens-Brunn*, published at 'Darmstatt' in 1680, Briegel scored three pieces for two trumpets, two trombones, voices and continuo; the trumpets and trombones are occasionally doubled by violins and violas. There are nearly eighty pieces in the collection, but only Nos. 5, 75 and 77 include trumpets. Like many mid-seventeenth-century composers who wrote in a similar style, Briegel seems to have modelled the greater proportion of the collection on works by Schütz.

The most interesting of the three pieces with trumpets is No. 5, *Ich will singen von der Gnade*. It begins with a seven-bar 'Intrada' for only trumpets, trombones and continuo—one of the rare appearances of Baroque trumpets with trombones without other groups of instruments. The instruction 'senza violin' appears in the trumpet parts and 'senza viola' in the trombone parts. Following the 'Intrada' are eighteen bars of vocal solo statements for an alto, a tenor and a bass before the vocal and instrumental 'tutti'. The part-writing tends to be parallel for much of the time; modulations are usually to the dominant, and chromatic alterations are infrequent. The trumpet parts toward the end of the piece, if they are actually for trumpets, are unusual considering the number of non-harmonic tones, especially in the 'Trombetta II' part. Since the parts are also for violins, it is suspected that they were indeed written as string parts. If trumpets were included in the section 'Lob, Preis und Dank, Herr Jesu Christ', the trumpeters probably inserted notes more agreeable to their instruments.

Briegel's other pieces are written in the same style, and, excepting the

[33] *See* Schneider, 1918, pp. 225 ff.
[34] *See* Appendix, and Bohn, 1890, p. 165.

missing 'Intrada' which does not prelude those pieces, there is little differ-ence in the trumpet writing.

A departure, for the moment, from the vocal-instrumental ecclesiastical medium are the two *Capriccen* for two 'Clarini' and continuo by Johann Jacob Löwe. Both are in a style comparable with Pezel's *Sonatinas* for two trumpets and continuo, and were included in Löwe's *Sonaten, Canzonen und Capriccen*, published at Jena in 1664. They are both short and somewhat uninteresting harmonically, but are rhythmically exuberant and success-fully employ a wide range in both trumpet parts, some repeated note fan-fare figures, and a pleasant mixture of note values in a contrapuntal texture.

Löwe was a Saxon musician who served as *Kapellmeister* at various Ger-man courts between 1650 and 1703. He was for a time at Dresden, working within the sphere of Schütz's influence in 1652. From there he went to Wolfenbüttel and served for nearly ten years as *Kapellmeister* in the court of Duke August the Younger. In 1663 he went to Zeitz, and while he was still the director of Moritz of Saxony's *Hofkapelle* the collection of *Sonaten* were published at Jena. The trumpet pieces may have originally been used as *Tafelmusik*.

One of the last composers to be mentioned who employed trumpets with small ensembles was Johann Krieger. Not to be confused with his famous older brother Johann Philipp Krieger who worked at Weissenfels, Johann was for a time *Director Chori Musici* at the *Johanniskirche* at Zittau, a post formerly held by Hammerschmidt. Some examples of Krieger's trumpet music are to be found in his *Neue musicalische Ergetzligkeit . . .* , published at Frankfurt and Leipzig in 1684.

The first piece with trumpet parts in Krieger's collection is No. 4, *Der Herr ist mein Panier*. Like most of the other pieces, the setting is for a solo voice (a bass in this case), continuo 'con violon' and other concerted instruments—here two trumpets. Some of the pieces with trumpets also include a pair of timpani, and there are separate timpani parts for Nos. 13, 14 and 20. The index to the entire collection states, however, that *Der Herr ist mein Panier* includes timpani as well. This is either a mistake or, more likely, the timpani parts somehow were omitted from the edition. Nevertheless, using the other pieces as models, it is not difficult to recon-struct a timpani part that will be musically and stylistically as the composer might have intended.

Krieger's part-writing and scoring are by far the most inventive of all the music of this *genre* that has been mentioned so far. The ranges of both trumpet parts are wide, and there is sufficient mixture of note values and variety of harmony to keep the listener's interest. Each piece begins with a short *ritornello*, usually called a 'Sinfonia'. In No. 4 the 'Sinfonia' is twelve bars long and in a contrasting rhythm from the rest of the piece; it is in binary while the vocal-instrumental section is in ternary rhythm. The 'Sinfonia', although motivically unrelated to the rest of the piece, serves as a joyful introduction, and, in keeping with the Baroque 'doctrine of affections', sets the prevailing mood or affect for the entire piece.

The vocal sections in every 'Andacht', as they are called on the title page, consist of monothematic settings in several verses. In *Der Herr ist mein Panier* the bass begins the ternary section and is answered by the trumpets, playing the same material two octaves higher. There follows a middle section for bass alone, which, before a restatement of the initial line, modulates to the dominant, G major. There is an exact restatement of the opening material concluding with a complete cadence in the tonic, C major, for bass and trumpets together.

The tenth piece from the same Krieger collection, *Der Heiland hat gesiegt*, is for solo soprano, two trumpets and continuo, and is also in C major. No indication of timpani is given, but their use may have been intended. The 'Sinfonia' here is most interesting. It is one of the rare instances where trumpets are scored in the sub-dominant. By the use of a held over b^1 flat in the sixth to the seventh bars, Krieger effects a temporary modulation to F major, with a quick shift to its sub-dominant (B flat) at bar thirteen. The feeling of F major is sustained until the penultimate bar when there is a sudden modulation back to C major. This is most exceptional and has not been encountered in any other works of the period.

Krieger's scoring becomes more imaginative in his *Neue musicalische Ergetzligkeit*. No. 13, *Der Drache bläset Lermen*, is called a 'Michaelis-Andacht' and is scored for bass solo, three trumpets, timpani and continuo. No. 14, the largest orchestration in the collection, is a New Year's 'Andacht' and requires a soprano, two trumpets, timpani, two cornettos, three trombones, two violins, two violas, a bassoon and continuo. The last two pieces with trumpet(s), Nos. 16 and 20, are both for a solo soprano: No. 16 with a trumpet, cornetto, violin and continuo; No. 20 with two trumpets, timpani and continuo. The pieces without trumpets are scored variously and include cornettos, violins, trombones and 'Schalmeyen', i.e. seventeenth-century shawms, precursors of the Baroque oboe.

From 1684 until the end of the century a year-to-year inventory of Johann Philipp Krieger's music was kept at Weissenfels. The first entry reads as follows:

Kirchen-Sachen / So von 'Advent' 1684 biss wieder dahin 1685 / welche in der Schloss Kirchen zu Weissenfels / 'Musiciret' worden / von / 'Joh:' Philip Krieger / Capellmeister.[35]

Space does not allow a complete discussion of Johann Philipp Krieger's music. Many of his masses, cantatas and operas include important trumpet parts. The inventory of Krieger's music given by Seiffert [36] shows that he was a prolific composer and frequently scored for trumpets. The trumpet writing in his *Magnificat à 13* (*DdT*, liii–liv, p. 1) and his cantata *Preis, Jerusalem, den Herren* (*DdT*, liii–liv, p. 221) approaches the brilliance found in contemporary Italian operas, sinfonias and concertos. There is one florid outburst for the trumpet in the *Magnificat à 13* where the 'Clarino 1' part ascends by leap to a d^2 and then continues downward in a flurry of semiquavers.

It should be mentioned that many of Johann Philipp Krieger's works (several with trumpet parts) are erroneously attributed to his younger brother in Eitner's *Quellen-Lexikon*. A correct inventory of both composers will be found in *MGG*, vol. vii (1958), cols. 1794–6 and 1800–2.

One of Krieger's contemporaries was the *Hof- und Stadt-Organist* at Eisenach, Johann Christoph Bach. First cousin once removed of Johann Sebastian Bach, Johann Christoph wrote a Michaelmas cantata with trumpets and timpani. The text is from Revelation xii. 7–12, which, as mentioned earlier, deals with the allegorical struggle between the archangel Michael and the Devil. Like the Altenburg, Hammerschmidt and Schütz works, as well as J. S. Bach's cantata *BWV* 19, Christoph Bach's cantata is also entitled *Es erhub sich ein Streit im Himmel*. Forkel (1802, pp. 17–18) says that the Bach family knew the cantata, and he mentions that information about it was given him by Carl Philipp Emanuel Bach. The image may seem obvious today, but for those who, in the seventeenth century, could remember the turmoil of the Thirty Years War, the vivid descriptiveness of the trumpets and drums suggesting the conflict of good and evil must have evoked from the listener more than a casual response.

---

[35] *DdT*, vols. liii–liv (ed. Max Seiffert, 1916), p. xxiii. Leipzig. 'Church pieces which have been played in the castle church at Weissenfels from Advent 1684 to the same time 1685, by Johann Philip Krieger, *Kapellmeister*.'

[36] *DdT*, liii–liv (1916). Leipzig.

A modern edition of the work was prepared by Geiringer (1955, p. 31). After the introductory 'Sonata' for two violins, four violas, bassoon and continuo, there follows a ternary section of sixty-two bars in which the battle gradually commences. The two 'concertae' bass voices with continuo introduce the text in canonic imitation, and the character of their melodic material is fanfare-like, suggesting the sound of the trumpets soon to be heard. After sixteen bars of reiterating the text, 'Es erhub sich ein Streit im Himmel, Michael und seine Engel stritten mit dem Drachen'; there begins the entry of the timpani; four bars later the four 'trombetti' enter one by one and start a clamour that lasts for thirty-nine bars. The trumpets are in C and play only from G to c^1 in this section.

The relief of voices and strings alone follows; the trumpets and drums are not heard again until the section 'Der die Ganze Welt verführet'. At the point where the text reads '. . . und ward geworfen auf die Erden', all the instruments and voices descend to their lowest registers. The first trumpet has G, while the others descend to the rarely scored C—the note Praetorius (1614–19, vol. iii, p. 171) calls 'Grob'. The timpani continue to hammer out their relentless C, C, G_1, and the section closes with the first and third trumpets playing a unison G while the second and fourth trumpets play their resonant and robust second partial-C.

The cantata continues with a 'Sinfonia' in which the trumpets and timpani are repeatedly echoed by the strings. The trumpet writing from this point, through the next chorus and to the end of the work, is more florid and has a wider range. Like the pairing of trumpets in Buxtehude's large-scale works and the later pairing of horns in the 'classic' orchestra, Johann Christoph Bach gives the higher, more florid parts to the first and third trumpets and the simpler tonic-dominant writing to the second and fourth trumpet parts.[37]

The work closes with a burst of semiquavers in the trumpet parts, with the timpani in the penultimate bar beating out eight semiquavers on a C. Christoph Bach's only known work with trumpets is certainly one of the most exciting in the seventeenth-century Baroque trumpet repertory.

In this chapter we have so far been talking about trumpet music mostly

---

[37] The not unusual alternation of high and low in the distribution of music for four trumpets (in the second half of the eighteenth century, for four horns) may derive from an originally intended antiphonal use of pairs of instruments—trumpets 1 and 2 having been placed in a different location from trumpets 3 and 4. Consequently, by virtue of the frequently employed 17th-century statement-answer formula, the first and third, as well as the second and fourth, trumpet parts would have had comparable ranges.

by Saxon composers, or composers who worked in South Germany. North Germany was also an important area for trumpet playing and the composing of music with significant trumpet parts. Weckmann, Lübeck and Buxtehude worked in and around the city of Hamburg, the most important of the *Hansastädte*, and each wrote music with trumpet parts of special interest. A few comments on their work will suffice.

Weckmann was an organist and composer at St Jacobi at Hamburg. His style of composition probably follows that of his mentor, Thomas Selle. One of his larger works uses the same text as the Michaelmas cantatas of Johann Christoph Bach, Altenburg, Hammerschmidt and Schütz. Weckmann's *Es erhub sich ein Streit im Himmel* is scored for two violins, three trumpets, a five-part *ripieno* chorus and a four-part choir of soloists. A copy of the work was found in the *St Michaelisschule* at Lüneburg; it is now preserved in the Deutsche Staatsbibliothek at Berlin (D.S.B. MS. 22.220).[38] Performances of this work and other Weckmann pieces, many of which were directed by Selle, took place in St Jacobi and at meetings of the Hamburg *collegium musicum*. The musicales, begun in 1668, were held at the cathedral of Hamburg and at the adjoining monastery, in a dining-hall made available to the *collegium musicum*.[39]

Vincent Lübeck's cantata, *Gott wie dein Name*, is one of only three known surviving vocal works by the seventeenth-century North German organist. A modern edition of Lübeck's extant works, ten keyboard pieces and three cantatas, was published in Gottlieb Harms's one-volume edition (Klecken, 1921). *Gott wie dein Name* is the only work in the edition that includes trumpets. It is a charming piece and requires the rare combination of simply three trumpets, three (solo?) voices (alto, tenor and bass) and continuo. Lübeck was organist of the St Nicolai church in Hamburg from 1702 until his death in 1740, but his cantata with trumpets was probably written in the last decade of the seventeenth century while he was at Stade.

An interesting point about Lübeck's trumpet writing and of much other North German trumpet music is the relative freedom and independence of each part. In large works, where there are often four trumpet parts, there is a high-low pairing of the first and third and second and fourth parts. In works requiring two or three trumpets, however, contrapuntal considerations are often foremost, so that each trumpet part is an independent element within the musical structure. This is an exemplary

[38] *See* Seiffert, 1908, p. 620.
[39] Seiffert, 1900, p. 112: '. . . der Speisesaal des ehemaligen Klosters eingeräumt.'

feature in the trumpet writing of Henry Purcell and, to some extent, in that of his English contemporaries.

Gott wie dein Name begins with a twenty-eight bar sinfonia-like introduction, where only the trumpets and continuo are heard; the cantata proceeds for several bars with the three voices and continuo alone. The trumpets then interject with melodically related 'ritornelli'—the fourth time as an exact echo of the vocal material and the fifth time as a note-for-note accompaniment.

The range of each trumpet part is nearly the same. Except for two b^2 naturals in the first trumpet part, all three parts have a range from c to a^2. The non-harmonic tone b natural occurs as a cadential neighbour tone only once in the second and third trumpet parts; it does not appear in the first trumpet part at all.

Little needs to be said here about Buxtehude's musical importance. But since his method of scoring for the trumpet is not generally known, some comment here seems appropriate. Six of his many church cantatas, motets, etc., have trumpet parts. Nearly all his surviving works were published in a collected edition (referred to as *Works*). The cantata *Ihr lieben Christen, freut euch nun* was published in vol. xiv of the *DdT* (Leipzig, 1913), edited by Max Seiffert, and does not appear in the collected edition. Most of the original sources of Buxtehude's music are preserved in the university library at Upsala and most are in MS. German organ tablature.[40] The six works with trumpets are listed in the Appendix.

Since Buxtehude spent most of his time in the city of Lübeck, it is supposed that his trumpet parts were played by the Lübeck *Stadtpfeifer*. His trumpet writing ranges from the simple triadic fanfare figures in the cantata *Mein Gemüt erfreuet sich*,[41] to the florid clarino style most evident in the above mentioned work, *Ihr lieben Christen, freut euch nun à 13*. The original tablature MS. of this work is found in the Stadtbibliothek at Lübeck—one of the few sources not at Upsala and, possibly, the reason why it was overlooked in the preparation of the complete edition. The latter is the only instance of trumpets being scored by Buxtehude in the key of D major, and, because of some interesting aspects with regard to the trumpet parts, this work can serve as the focal point in the discussion of Buxtehude's contributions to the Baroque trumpet repertory.

Ihr lieben Christen . . . requires two 'Clarini in sordino' (later two 'Trombette in sordino'), along with three parts for violins (doubled by cor-

[40] *See* Stiehl, 1889, pp. 2 ff.
[41] *Works*, vol. vii, 1937. Hamburg. Edited by Gottlieb Harms and Hilmar Trede.

nettos), three parts for trombones (the first two for violas as well), SSATB chorus and continuo. The trumpets would have been pitched in C, but, as mentioned in Chapter 4, a muted Baroque trumpet sounded a tone higher. Therefore the two 'Clarini in sordino' sounded in D, the tonality of *Ihr lieben Christen*. . . .

The use of muted trumpets in German Baroque music is rare, but Buxtehude uses them on one other occasion. One of his few published pieces, the wedding aria *Auf! stimmet die Saiten*, has an 'Aufzug' and a 'Ritornello' which are scored not only for two 'Trombetti in Sordino', but also for two 'Trombone in Sordino'.[42] This is certainly one of the earliest uses of muted trombones before the nineteenth century.

Seiffert's edition of *Ihr lieben Christen* . . . probably has a misprint in the second trumpet part at bar eighteen. The *f* natural on the second beat is spurious. A written *g* (*a* at sounding pitch) was probably intended. Seiffert's edition has the *f* approached by leap from a written *c*¹. A leap to a non-harmonic tone, particularly a leap as wide as the interval of a fifth, has not been encountered before.

Non-harmonic trumpet tones in Buxtehude's music are infrequent, which makes the first four bars of trumpet music in the final chorus of *Ihr lieben Christen* . . . ('Ei lieber Herr . . .') rather enigmatic. The appellation of the trumpets is changed from 'Clarino' to 'Trombetta', and there are seven non-harmonic tones in two of the four bars in the first trumpet part and six non-harmonic tones for the same bars in the second. The change in the name of the trumpets and the appearance of so many non-harmonic tones raises two questions: (1) Are the 'Trombette in sordino' supposed to be variable-pitch, single-slide trumpets, i.e. *Zugtrompeten*, and, therefore, capable of playing the non-harmonic series notes? Or (2) are the first four bars of trumpet music notated in the wrong octave and the name changed only because the terms 'Trombetta' and 'Clarino' were possibly interchangeable? It is the present writer's opinion that the parts are not for slide trumpets and that the omission of an extra stroke over some of the letters in the original MS. German organ tablature score accounts for the parts being indicated an octave too low. The change in the name of the trumpets should not evoke much comment. Throughout the seventeenth century trumpet parts were frequently referred to by both terms and given exactly the same kind of music, particularly in German church music.

It makes musical sense if the two 'Trombetta' parts are an octave higher until bar six of the last chorus. The altitudinous cornetto 1—violin 1 part

[42] *Ibid.*

remains high, with the cornetto II—violin II part generally about a third lower. For the normally soprano-register trumpets to sound far below the soprano and alto voices, as well as the cornetto III—violin III part, is unstylistic and not to be found in any other similar seventeenth-century musical setting. The range of both trumpet parts in the rest of the movement is from e to a^2 and there are no other non-harmonic tones. Buxtehude does not score for timpani in any of his compositions, but that fact does not preclude their having been intended. Timpani were probably used in his larger settings with trumpets.

A great deal of space has been allotted to a discussion of seventeenth-century German musical sources for the Baroque trumpet. The amount of space may seem disproportionate when compared with that given to other repertories. But the German sources are the most numerous and, with respect to the use of trumpets in ecclesiastical music, are the most important. Unfortunately, much of this material is not discussed elsewhere, and information about the use of trumpets in Germany during the seventeenth century is scanty. It should be obvious from the magnitude of the musical repertory that trumpets were an important adjunct of German court and community life from the first decade of the seventeenth century and for more than a hundred years thereafter. No other area of Europe had as many trumpets, players, and composers writing for the instrument.

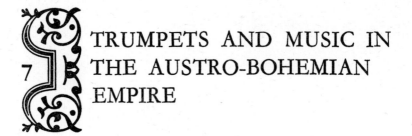

7

TRUMPETS AND MUSIC IN THE AUSTRO-BOHEMIAN EMPIRE

A crossroad tends to be a busy place. Within the south-eastern reaches of the Holy Roman Empire lay the geographic centre of the European continent, and what we now call Austria and Czechoslovakia was the cultural and commercial crossroad of East and West, North and South. The kingdoms of Bohemia, Moravia, and the Habsburg lands of Austria, Styria and the Tyrol were destined to play an important part in the cultural evolution of Europe. It is difficult to estimate to what extent political and economic forces contributed to the development of music in those areas. Nevertheless, as benefits in trade and commerce were reaped as a result of the fortuitous geographical and political positions of the Austro-Bohemian territories, music also prospered. Not even the religious and political upheaval throughout the entire area during the first half of the seventeenth century seems to have thwarted the development of music.

Despite the fame and reputation acquired by many seventeenth-century composers and performers from those areas north of the Alps and west of the Elbe, musicians from the Germanic territories to the south and east display a comparable talent and productivity. The modern reputation of most Baroque composers has depended upon the availability of and the knowledge about their works. Those composers from the north and west have been fortunate in this respect; those from Austria, Bohemia and Moravia have been less fortunate. The bulk of surviving music by many of these composers was never published. Single MS. copies of their works still lie in church, castle and municipal archives, where they were deposited nearly three hundred years ago, and some of these archives are as yet uncatalogued. With respect to our study of seventeenth-century trumpet music, court and ecclesiastical records of the time present enough evidence to show that the Austro-Bohemian areas were amply supplied with trumpets, trumpeters and trumpet music. But what music has survived, particularly from the east, was written after 1650, and much of it is still inaccessible.

In the Southern Empire, Austria was the most important region for the development of the trumpet before 1700. As early as the fifteenth century the courts of the Austrian province of the Tyrol incorporated many trumpeters for ceremonial as well as musical purposes. As a count of the Tyrol, the Habsburg Holy Roman Emperor Maximilian I established his court at the Tyrolean capital of Innsbruck. In the Innsbruck records, where mention is made of court musicians, chaplains and organ makers, the following 'Trumetter' are listed (the year is that in which the individual's name was entered on the court records): [1]

Arnold von Metzol	1506
Asmus	1506
Dietrich 'Claretter'	1498, 1500 [2]
Frank, Hans	1491
Frech, Caspar	1492–5, 1500–2, 1505
Gross, Hans 'aus dem Hegau'	1500
Hess, Georg 'Claretter'	1510, 1512
Hübl, Georg 'Claretter'	1509
Kugelmann, Hans	1519
Mair, Christof	1511, 1512, 1514, 1519
Mair, Georg	1519
Mair, Ludwig	1490–5, 1498, 1500
Maurer, Matheus 'von Voburg'	1506–14, 1516, 1519
Marx, Perner or Werner	1513, 1519
Musikabiter [sic], Friedrich	1519
Panzer, Michael	1492
Pfandler, Sebastian	1492–5
Pfandler, Ulrich	1506–11, 1514, 1519
Philipp, 'Claretter'	1500 [3]
Rieder, Christoff	1509, 1511, 1512, 1514, 1519
Riedt, Hans	1491

[1] From Waldner, 1897.
[2] From Wessely, 1956, p. 93.
[3] In 1500 he was paid 10 gulden for expenses. From Wessely, *ibid.*, p. 88.

Rosenzwykh, Hans	1519
Schmalzer, Wolfgang	1500 [4]
Seger, Hieronymus	1490–5, 1499–1507
Seydenmann, Balthazar	1507, 1509–12, 1514
Stelzer, Christian	1492, 1494, 1495, 1502
Tollenstein (Doldenstein), Conrad [5]	1490–5, 1498, 1502–12, 1514, 1516–19
Tollenstein, Urban	1506–10, 1512–14
Tubinger, Georg	1490–5
Tuttenkofer, Georg	1491–5, 1498, 1500–3, 1506–1514, 1516–19
Tynzlinger, Vinzenz	1507, 1509

Her Paugger (Timpanists)

Aichperger, Heinz 'der Paugger von Salzburg'	1507, 1509
Neuner, Sigmund	1510–12, 1514, 1519
Talran, Wernher	1492–4
Undernutsch, Martin	1490–2, 1494
Weinhardus 'trummelschlacher'	1518
Zott, Christian	1506

Among the rest of the names are the organists and organmakers, lutenists, singers, trombone players (in 1503 Hans Neuschel is mentioned as playing trombone [6]), the chaplains (who, in some cases, are also mentioned as singers), 'pfeiffer' (probably shawm or krumhorn players) and, of particular interest, the names Ludwig Senfl, 'Sänger und Komponist' (1515, 1519); Heinrich Ysaac, 'Hofkomponist und Sänger' (1496, 1497, 1500, 1515); and Paul Hofhaimer, 'Hoforganist, Einleitung und Jahrgang' (1490–8, 1502, 1504, 1506, 1513, 1515). Hofhaimer's brother Wilhelm is also mentioned as an organist in 1517.

All the musicians listed from 1490 to 1519 are in the following numerical distribution:

trumpeters	27
Clareta players	4

[4] *See* Wessely, 1956, p. 114: paid '25 Rheinisch gulden' for his 'Kranckhait'.
[5] In the records he is often referred to as 'Conrad Trumetter von haidlberg'.
[6] Wessely, 1956, p. 111.

timpanists	5
drummer	1
organists	5
organ makers	3
trombonists	4
lutenists	2
Pfeifer	2
singers	5

The relatively few singers mentioned does not mean that the choir was small. Neither the 'Knaben' (choir boys) nor the clerks-in-ordinary would have been listed. Waldner (1897, p. 45) is of the opinion that the Innsbruck choir was from forty to fifty strong. Mention of 'Kleidung' (vestments) for forty-nine 'Gsellen und Knaben' would substantiate this.[7]

The Innsbruck court records suggest that trumpets were used not only in processions, at table ('zur Tafel') and during feasts, but also in the chapel and in the 'Pfarrkirche'. The same records frequently mention more of a particular instrument than is accounted for by the personnel listed in the payment books. For example, the payment books mention only one 'Pfeipffer', Jörg Rennick (1519), but in 1500 there is mention of '3 pfeiffer'.[8] An entry dated 1491 refers to '4 Pfeiffer' and '2 Trommel-schläger'. From this evidence it may be assumed that there were even more trumpeters at Innsbruck than officially accounted for in the payment records.

In 1521 the emperor Charles v appointed his brother Ferdinand to govern Germany. The German governor, 'Majesty of Hungary and Bohemia' and elected Emperor Ferdinand 1 in 1558, maintained a *Kapelle* at both Munich and Vienna. The 1527 list of Ferdinand's 'Cappeln' mentions 'Hainrich Füngkh' (Heinrich Finck) as the Munich *Kapellmeister* and 'Arnoldt von Prigkh' (Arnold von Brück) as *Kapellmeister* at Vienna.[9] The 'Cappel Ordnung' lists several posts for each city. Among the various titles and positions that are mentioned (chaplains, *Kapellmeister*, trumpeters, singers, etc.) some merited the use of a horse as well as being given a substantial salary. Following the list of 'Trumetter' is the direction 'Yedem ain Pferdt' ('a horse for each'). The position of 'Hörpaughker' (timpanist) also merited a horse.

[7] Waldner, 1897, p. 46.
[8] *Ibid*, p. 33.
[9] Hirzel, 1909, p. 151 ff.

The use of a horse was not simply for the personal convenience of the player and as a symbol of prestige. The trumpeters and timpanist needed horses to accompany their sovereign on various journeys and during military campaigns. Hirzel mentions a journey of Friedrich IV von der Pfalz in 1600 during which he was escorted by seven mounted trumpeters.[10]

Ferdinand's trumpeters, both at Munich and at Vienna, were required, in addition to their quasi-military duties, to play *Tischmusik* ('Die sollen ordenlich all mal zu tisch plasen'). At least four of the Munich trumpeters and a timpanist appear on the Vienna list as well. Undoubtedly they made the journey from Munich to Vienna with their sovereign on more than one occasion; hence the necessity of horses.

After the election of Maximilian II (emperor from 1564 until 1576), son of and successor to Ferdinand I, the activities of the Habsburg dynasty were centred at Prague, the capital of Bohemia. The Austro-Bohemian court remained there until the death of King Matthias in 1619. The Prague records from this period contain many references to trumpeters. The terms 'Musikalische' and 'Nicht Musikalische' are introduced at this time and appear next to the names of specific trumpet players. In 1566, for example, while the 'Obrister Capellmeister' Philipp de Monte was in the service of Maximilian II, the list of court musicians mentions four 'Musikalische' and eleven 'Nicht Musikalische' trumpeters.[11] The list of musicians in 1598, while Philipp de Monte was in the service of Rudolf II, mentions between sixteen and twenty 'Trompeter und Musici, darunter 12 musikalische'.[12] A 'musical' trumpeter, as opposed to a 'non-musical' one, may have been equivalent to a *Kammertrompeter*. The trumpeters who were incapable of playing anything more complicated than a *Feldstück* or *Signal*, and who may not have been able to read music, were probably the 'Nicht Musikalische', or 'non-musical' players.

One trumpeter in the *Kapelle* of Rudolf II seems to have had an unprecedented career. This was Alexander Orlogio (or Horlogio). In 1583 he was paid thirty guiders for his diligent service as a musician and trumpeter.[13] In 1587 he is again mentioned as a 'trummeter und musico', but in the same year he was paid sixty guilders for a madrigal that he composed and

[10] *Ibid.*

[11] Köchel, 1869, p. 49.

[12] *Ibid.*, p. 52.

[13] Smijers, 1921, p. 185: 'Alexander Orlogio . . . musicus und trometter, in ansehung seiner vleissigen dienst willen . . . dreissig gulden. . . .'

dedicated to Rudolf II.[14] His ability as a composer must have been exceptional, for in 1603 he acquired the title of *Vice-Kapellmeister*, and only three years later the Prague and Vienna records designate him as 'Capellmaister', a position rarely attained and, perhaps, rarely sought by trumpeters.

The so-called 'italienische Zeit' of Austrian music,[15] which lasted for more than a hundred years, began with the cultivation of music at Graz towards the end of the sixteenth century. The Archduke Charles, brother of the Emperor Maximilian II, engaged the composer, theorist and singer Lodovico Zacconi, as well as hiring some Italian trumpeters for his Graz court orchestra.[16] Many of the other instrumentalists and singers who were not Italian had been sent to study in Italy with some of the finest composers and performers of the time. In 1611 the Archduke Ferdinand (elected Emperor Ferdinand II in 1619) journeyed from Graz to Vienna to attend the marriage of King Matthias. With the archduke travelled his Graz court *Kapelle*. Many of the Graz 'Instrumentisten vnnd Trumetter' mentioned in Codex 165 (folio 420) in the National Museum at Budapest [17] appear in the 1619 list of 'Instrumentisten und Hoftrompeter', when, as emperor, Ferdinand established his court at Vienna.[18] It is interesting to note the large number of Italian and Spanish musicians employed by Ferdinand, both at Graz and at Vienna. The lists of *Hofmusiker* in the Prague courts of Rudolf II and King Matthias include many more German and Slavic names.

After 1619 the capital of the Habsburg empire was Vienna. It is there that much of the seventeenth-century trumpet music from the region is to be found. Preserved in the Nationalbibliothek at Vienna are hundreds of seventeenth-century works with trumpet parts—masses, motets, operas, ballet music, instrumental suites, etc. There was never any shortage of trumpeters to perform the vast number of compositions with specific trumpet parts. From the time of Ferdinand II until the death of the Emperor Leopold I in 1705, the Viennese court records abound with the names of trumpeters and timpanists.

Nettl's survey of seventeenth-century Viennese court musicians pro-

[14] *Ibid.*: 'Alexander Orlogio . . . trummeter und musico . . . wegen seiner . . . dedicierten madrigal . . . sechzig gulden. . . .'
[15] *See* Orel, 1953, p. 343.
[16] Wellesz, 1940, p. 105.
[17] *See* Federhofer, 1952, p. 131.
[18] *See* Köchel, 1869, pp. 57–8.

vides several interesting items specifically related to the Baroque trumpet.[19] In 1636 the 'khays.[erlich] Hoff und Velttrompettern' Heinrich Kholben was reimbursed for the purchase of trumpets and trombones for the emperor's musicians.[20] The name and location of the instrument maker are not mentioned, but an entry from 1658 does provide such specific information:

'*Auf bezahlte Wahrn. Michaeln Nagl Posaun und Trompeter machern zur Nuernberg wegen für die Khays. Trompeter gelieferten 12 Silbern und vergolten Trompeten 1169 fl. 22 kr.*'[21]

Michael Nagel was one of the first-rank Nuremberg trumpet makers (Pl. 5). The description of his twelve trumpets (silver with gilding) would seem to indicate that each instrument was similar to the Haas ceremonial trumpets described in Chapter 3 and in the *Galpin Society Journal*.[22] The payment to Nagel and the number of Nuremberg trumpets and trombones that survive in Austrian collections suggest that Nuremberg provided most of the brass instruments used in the Austro-Bohemian courts during the sixteenth and seventeenth centuries.

The remaining entries concerned with trumpets and trumpeters are records of payment to trumpeters for teaching their art to apprentices, remuneration for travelling expenses, and payment for the kind of services and activities quoted by Cart de Lafontaine (1909). But one item from the Vienna *Hof* payment books is unique. In 1655 there is an entry for the payment of twenty florins to a female trumpeter for playing before the Emperor Leopold I.[23] With the possible exception of some individual female members of itinerant theatrical troupes, few women would have possessed the art of playing the Baroque trumpet. Under most circumstances it is unlikely that the trumpeter *Kameradschaft* would have tolerated the playing of trumpets by women. Johanna v[on] Hoff must have been a very exceptional female.

Unlike the social structure of Protestant German towns and cities, with their own municipal music and musicians, the Catholic areas of the Austro-

---

[19] Nettl, 1929 [part I], pp. 70 ff.   [20] *Ibid.*, p. 17.

[21] Nettl, 1931 [part III], p. 34: 'For wares paid. To Michael Nagl, trombone and trumpet maker from Nuremberg, 1,169 florins, 22 crowns for the imperial trumpets: 12 silver and gilded trumpets delivered.'

[22] *See* Smithers, 1965, pp. 23 ff.

[23] Nettl, 1931 [part III], p. 25: '1655 Johanna v. Hoff Trompeterin, die vor Ihrer Khays. May. geblasen zur verehrung 20 fl.'

Bohemian territories were provided with music mostly by official court composers and instrumentalists, as well as by ecclesiastical court musicians. Municipal music of the kind associated with the German *Stadtpfeifer* seems to have had less importance in Austria and Bohemia. The Viennese seventeenth-century trumpet repertory was principally court music. Ecclesiastical music in the city was provided by the various court composers and the respective church, chapel and cathedral organists. A significant feature of the trumpet repertory, not only at Vienna but also at most other Austro-Bohemian secular and ecclesiastical courts, was the many sonatas and *balletti* composed for the often sumptuous court entertainments during the reign of Leopold I. The most extravagant of the *balletti* was the *Rossballett* (literally, 'horse ballet').

There has been a long association of equestrian expertise with the city of Vienna. Today the so-called 'Spanish riding school' of Vienna is the result of a tradition of horsemanship and trained cavalry that goes back to the Middle Ages. As the capital of an empire whose military strength and well-being depended upon disciplined horses and riders, there is little wonder that Vienna became an important centre for the cultivation of equestrian activities. What was first and foremost a cavalry exercise became a splendid form of circus-like entertainment. Actually, the term *carrousel*, which during the time of Louis XIV was applied generally to such 'horse ballets', is defined as 'a tournament in which cavalrymen divided into troops execute evolutions, often with scenic shows, etc., added'.[24]

Where and when these choreographic cavalry manœuvres became shows of strength and impressive entertainments is debatable. Evidence points to Italy some time in the fifteenth century. In the sixteenth and early seventeenth centuries Italian nobles often included 'horse ballets' at weddings and celebrations of special significance. At Florence, for the wedding of Cosimo di Medici and Maria Magdalena of Austria in October 1608, there was a 'ballo di persone a cavallo'.[25] We can suppose that military music, i.e. music for trumpets and drums, accompanied this spectacle. Callot's engravings of the 'guerra d'amore' at Florence in 1615 show a carrousel with many mounted trumpeters and drummers accompanying the spectacle.[26] Of special interest are Callot's engravings of the choreographies,

[24] *Webster's New Collegiate Dictionary*, 1956, p. 127, 'carrousel'.

[25] Wellesz, 1914, p. 55–6.

[26] Callot's engravings are included in *Mostra della guerra d'amore festa del serenissimo gran duca Cosimo secondo di Toscana fatta in Firenze il Carneuale del 1615*. In Firenze . . . Zanobi Pignoni . . . MDC. XV. There is a copy in the Spencer Collection of the New York Public Library.

which give some idea of how complicated and difficult the various evolutions were. In 1616 there was a 'Guerra die bellezza, festa a cavallo' for a prince of the house of Urbino; the musical accompaniments and instrumental interludes were composed by Jacopo Peri and Paolo Francesino.[27] In Chapter 10 there is a discussion of the spectacular French carrousels during the reign of Louis XIV, all of which relied on the sound of trumpets and timpani for the musical accompaniment.

At Vienna in 1631 there were many allegorical-musical festivities for the marriage of Ferdinand III and Maria Anna, daughter of Philip III of Spain. A *Rossballett* took place, during which the names of the emperor and his bride were spelled out by vast numbers of cavalry.[28] There are no specific details about the musical accompaniment, but the accounts and surviving documents concerned with the *Rossballett* for the marriage of the Emperor Leopold I and Princess Margareta Theresa of Spain give us some idea of the importance of trumpets and trumpet music on such occasions.

In 1667 the wedding festivities of Leopold and Margareta included the 'Balletturnier' *La contessa dell'aria e dell'aqua festa a cavallo*. It was probably the most spectacular event of its kind. It required enormous forces of cavalry, dancers, mounted trumpeters and timpanists, and it included many floats, theatrical designs and a full-scale model of a ship. Rehearsals for this august and magnificent spectacle were begun on 30th August 1666; there were rehearsals on 20th and 23rd December in the same year; and on 3rd January 1667 the final dress rehearsal was held on the *Burgplatz* within the Vienna *Hof*, where the first performance was given on 24th January 1667. A repeat performance was given at the same place exactly one week later, and the total cost of the production was estimated at 60,000 Reichsthaler.[29]

The musical accompaniment to *La contessa* . . . was provided by Antonio Bertali and Johann Schmelzer. The five pieces by Schmelzer, four of which are scored with trumpets, were included in the descriptive account also published in 1667. Besides an edition printed in Italian, another appeared in German. Copies of both are kept in the New York Public Library and the one in German has the following title:

'Sieg-Streit dess Lufft und Wassers Freuden-Fest zu Pferd zu dem Glorwürdigisten Beyläger Beeder Kayserlichen Majestäten Leopoldi dess Ersten Römischen

[27] Wellesz, 1914, p. 56.
[28] Liess, 1946, p. 63.
[29] Wellesz, 1914, p. 52.

Kayser / auch zu Hungarn und Böhaim König / Ertz-Hertzogens zu Oesterreich / und Margarita / Geboren Königlichen Infantin auss Hispanien dargestellet in vero Kayserlichen Residentz Statt Wienn Gedr. zu Wienn in Oesterreich bey Mattheo Cosmerovio / der Röm: Kayserl: Majest: Hoff-Buchdrucker / Anno 1667.'

Following the thirty-eight pages of descriptive commentary are the *Arie per il Baletto a Cavallo. Composte dall Gioanne Enrico Schmeltzer, Musico di Camera di S.M.C.*[30] *Vienna, M. Cosmerovio, 1667.* The music is in score and is followed by several large engravings by Van Hoye and Ossenbeeck. Many of these illustrations show mounted corps of trumpeters and timpanists. Similar illustrations of the same event appear in the *Diarium Europaeum* xv, 1667, *Appendix I*, copies of which are found in the Nationalbibliothek at Vienna and the British Museum.

Schmelzer's five pieces are entitled and scored as follows:

1 'Corrente per l'Intrata di S.M.C. et di tutti i Cavaglieri.'
   Six parts 'Con Trombe et Timpani'.
2 'Giga per Entrata de i Saltatori, e per molte altre figure.'
   Seven parts 'Con viol. et Clarini'; Clar., 1, 2; Vn 1, 2; Vla 1, 2; Bass.
3 'Follia per nuovo ingresso de i Saltatori, et altre operazioni de Cavalli.'
   Six parts 'Con Trombe et Timpani'.
4 'Allemanda per gl'intrecci e figure di passegio grave introdotto d. S.M.C. e Cavaglieri.'
   Five parts 'Con Viol.': Vn 1, 2; Vla 1, 2; Bass.
5 'Sarabanda per termine del Balletto.'
   Six parts 'Con Trombe et Timpani'.

The first, third and fifth pieces have composed echoes, where only the first two 'Trombe' play the two-bar repeated phrase endings. Each piece with trumpets is about twenty-four bars long—in two sections of six bars each with repeats. The longest piece is the 'Allemanda', but for strings alone. Since the duration of the entire 'ballet' would have been considerably longer than Schmelzer's five published pieces, the mounted corps of trumpets and drums shown in the various contemporary illustrations must have supplied additional pieces (fanfares, *Feldstücke*, etc.). It should be assumed that each of the trumpet parts in these pieces required several players, probably three or four trumpeters to a part, with several pairs of timpani mounted on horseback. The first two trumpet parts are indepen-

[30] 'Sua Maestà Cesare', or, 'His Majesty the Emperor'.

dent of one another, with the second trumpet frequently ending above the first. The range of the first two trumpet parts is nearly the same: trumpet one plays from g to a^1; trumpet two from e to a^1. The four lower parts are comparable with those named lower-register trumpet parts ('Vulgano', 'Grob', etc.) mentioned by Monteverdi, Praetorius, Fantini and Speer (*see* Chapters 4 and 6). The third trumpet part, notated in soprano clef, has only the notes c, e and g; the fourth trumpet part (in alto clef) consists of one tone, the note G; and the lowest part, the tonic and dominant notes C and G, is obviously the timpani part, but probably intended to be doubled by trumpets with large, deep-cupped mouthpieces.

During the performance of the 'ballet', there would have been very little relationship of the music to the equestrian gyrations. The illustration 'Decima quarta' (fourteenth) from the *Diarium Europaeum* shows several mounted but stationary trumpeters and timpanists in the foreground and several leading the large groups of 'Ritter' and 'Cavalliere'.[31] The clamour of all those trumpets and drums probably had the same function as the din provided by a brass band at a twentieth-century three-ring circus. But no modern ensemble could ever equal the excitement and splendour of mounted trumpets and drums making a most splendid noise. Only the Versailles carrousels at the court of Louis XIV (*see* Chapter 10) would have been as exciting. Perhaps more so, considering the number of oboes that were used with trumpets, timpani and, possibly, bass reinforcing trombones.

Besides the instrumental requirements of the less spectacular 'horse ballets' that were given at Vienna in 1662, 1663, 1666, 1674, 1697, and the 'Karusell in der Favorita' of 1699,[32] trumpets were employed at the Viennese *Hofbälle* and *Kammerbälle*. These court and chamber balls, usually as masquerades, required suites of dances played by a variety of wind and stringed instruments. Even such events as the 1677 'Feuerwerk vor dem Burgtor' would have required many orchestral suites and dances, each employing large numbers of instruments with as many as eight trumpets and two pairs of timpani. A 'Balletto di Centauri . . . per la festa a Schonbrün', in 1674, called for three choirs of instruments, including three 'piffari' (shawms), two 'cornetti mutti' and three trombones.[33] Schmelzer's 'Balletto zu dem Geburts-Dag ihre Mt. der regierenden Keisserin' on 12th July 1670 specifies two choirs of instruments. Although the

[31] A reproduction of this illustration will be found in *EDM*, vol. xiv, p. ix.
[32] Nettl, 1921, p. 50.
[33] *See* Breitenbacher, 1928, pp. 127–8, No. 29.

second choir is scored with only one trumpet and three trombones, the composer's own title page directions explain why there are two 'Clarin' parts: 'Choro 2do hat 1 clarin, 3 tromboni undt 1 fagotto; kennen entlich ausgelassen werden; das Clarin sollen ihe [sic, probably *ihr*] zwen alternatim blassen, einen kem es zu schwer.' [34] There are a number of other 'Balletti' dedicated to the empress and various dignitaries, or written for particular celebrations, masquerades, etc. Many were composed by Schmelzer, Bertali and Biber, and are preserved in the archives at Kroměříž, Moravia, which belonged at one time to the Prince-Bishop Karl Liechtenstein-Kastelkorn. More will be said about these pieces and the Kroměříž collection in the discussion of trumpet music in Bohemia and Moravia.

In the Nationalbibliothek at Vienna are the manuscript 'Particells' of music by Johann Heinrich Schmelzer and his son Anton Andreas. Both manuscript collections are bass and treble reductions of *balletti*. Since many of the pieces concord with the fully orchestrated *balletti* at Kroměříž and elsewhere, the two collections may have been prepared as conducting scores or as possible keyboard arrangements. The title of Vienna, Nationalbibliothek Mus. MS. 16583, the Johann Schmelzer collection, is

'*Arien zu den Balletten, welche an der röm. Keyserl. Meyestät Leopoldi des Ersten von Johann Hainrich Schmelzer Keyserl. Camer Musico.*'

This 'Particell' contains several pieces which are scored for trumpets in the orchestrated versions. No. 8, for example, is entitled a 'Ross Ballett'. It consists of the treble and bass parts from Schmelzer's 1667 carrousel music, with the same number of movements and the same title for each. At Kroměříž there are at least thirty-two sonatas and some forty-two *balletti* by Schmelzer, with as many as sixteen separate instrumental parts.

Johann Schmelzer enjoyed the special favour of Leopold 1. But inasmuch as he was native born and lacked the prestige invariably accorded to Italian musicians, Schmelzer was only made a *Vice-Kapellmeister* in 1671, after waiting some time for the appointment. With the death of the Italian *Kapellmeister* Giovanni Sances in 1679, the only logical choice of a successor was Schmelzer. He received the appointment from Leopold, but he was not to hold the position for long. In the following year Schmelzer died of the bubonic plague that had been devastating south-eastern

[34] *Ibid.*, p. 132, No. 130: 'The second choir has one clarino, three trombones and one bassoon; a few can be left out; the clarino [part] should be played by two of them [i.e. two players] alternately, since it would be too difficult for one.'

Europe since 1675, claiming some 76,000 Viennese in 1679 and about 81,000 inhabitants of Prague in 1681.

Schmelzer is usually mentioned as a violin virtuoso, but few authors note that he was also a cornetto player. In Viennese records of 1643 there is an item concerning a nine-florin wedding present given to Schmelzer. The record entry mentions that he was a cornettist in the cathedral of St Stephen at Vienna: 'den 27. dito [June] zalte Ich dem Johann Hainrichen Schmölzer *Cornetisten* zu St. Stephan . . . 9 fl. . . .' [35] Schmelzer's ability to play the cornetto may have some relation to the number of pieces by him that are scored for the instrument. One published collection contains not only sonatas with cornettos, but also two sonatas with trumpets. This is Schmelzer's *Sacro-Profanus Concentus Musicus*, published at Nuremberg in 1662.

Dedicated 'Leopoldo Givlielmo Archduci Austriae', the Schmelzer collection contains twelve sonatas with various combinations of instruments. The *Sonata prima à 8*—in C—is scored for two trumpets, two violins, four 'viole' and continuo; the *Sonata duodecima à 7*—also in C— is scored for the unusual combination of two trumpets, two 'cornettini', three trombones and continuo. The collection was published in eight separate parts with the continuo marked 'Organo'. The *Sonata secunda à 8* is marked 'Duobus Choris' and is scored for one violin, three 'viole' in the first choir and one 'cornettino', three trombones in the second choir.

Schmelzer's trumpet sonatas from his *Concentus Musicus* are both in three distinct sections, which, by alternations of metre and changes of tempo, outline a basic movement structure. The first sonata alternates from ternary to binary to ternary rhythm; the twelfth is in the opposite arrangement, i.e. binary, ternary, binary. Both trumpet pieces are contrapuntally imitative, and the composer treats each group of instruments in antiphony.

The *Sonata prima*, with its scoring for two trumpets and six-part strings, contains the most inventive thematic ideas of the two trumpet pieces. What is meant by 'viole' is uncertain.[36] Four violas may have been intended, but the fourth part, written in bass clef, descends to C_1 and its highest note is only G. The other three parts, however, may be played on violas. A violoncello is the only possible alternative for the fourth part, unless four viols were intended and not violas. But even if the scoring was very conservative, the year 1660 is rather late for viols, especially in

---

[35] Koczirz, 1964, p. 53.

[36] The use of 'viole' in seventeenth-century scores was probably as a generic term for all *viola da braccio* instruments, which included not only the violin and viola but also violoncello.

Central Europe. The range of the trumpet parts is fairly wide: the first trumpet plays from e to c^2, the second from e to a^1. The second 'movement', marked 'Adagio-Allegro', is scored for the strings alone.

The *Sonata duodecima* is straightforward in most respects. Its thematic ideas are not as well conceived as those of the *Sonata prima*, but there are some interesting features. Besides the attractive combination of instruments (if cornettos are not available for a modern performance little injustice will be done to the composer's intentions if oboes are used), one unusual aspect of this piece is the disregard of traditional prerogative of an instrument's entry by order of number and register. Invariably, the second trumpet plays before the first in most entrances; the second and third trombones often play before the first trombone has been heard. Schmelzer was more concerned with a particular contrapuntal texture and voice-leading than with prerogatives. Another unusual aspect of this sonata is the trumpet writing in the third section. This is the only Baroque trumpet piece to be noted where both the first and second trumpets play in the 'Grob' register for the specific effect that Schmelzer requires. Alternately, the second trumpet part and then the first trumpet part are notated in tenor clef and each plays

The two instruments echo one another, the first trumpet answering the second. After this extraordinary digression the writing in all parts again becomes contrapuntal. There are fewer chromatic alterations for the trumpets in this sonata than in the first, and the range of each instrument is the same, C to a^1. Since the modern trumpet is only about one half as long as the Baroque trumpet, the rare descent to C can only be remedied by giving those bars to a pair of trombones or playing the out-of-range C's an octave higher when today's B flat or C trumpets are used. Such instances, however, serve to remind us of some of the advantages in using original instruments (or properly made reproductions). There is no substitute for the robust and magnificent tone of an eight-foot natural trumpet playing in the lower register, especially down to C.

Many of Schmelzer's trumpet compositions (sonatas, *balletti*, etc.) were written as incidental interludes, or as ballet music to various Italian operas that were produced at the Vienna *Hof*. As was the custom in Schmelzer's day, the native born composers of lesser rank than the imported Italians were frequently required to supply such music at the request of the

Italian *Kapellmeister* or a visiting Italian composer of 'great distinction'. Antonio Draghi's opera *Il fuoco eterno* had, for example, inserted ballet pieces by Johann Schmelzer.

With few exceptions, the trumpeters employed in Central and Northern European opera performances until the end of the eighteenth century would have been the first-rank *Kammertrompeter*. The many trumpet parts in the operas of Bertali, Ziani, Draghi and others that were produced at Vienna were, in all likelihood, played by many of the same trumpeters who performed in the 'horse ballets' and in the *balletti*, serenades, etc., composed by Schmelzer, Biber, Poglietti and others.

Church music is another important source of seventeenth-century Austrian trumpet music. Much of it was composed and performed at Vienna, but some of the most interesting compositions were presented at Salzburg. The use of trumpets at Salzburg was given a flying start with the consecration of the cathedral in 1628. Orazio Benevoli's C major *Missa* and *Hymnus*, both in fifty-three parts, were written for that occasion. Included with the vast orchestration of two eight-part choirs of voices, choirs of strings, trombones and cornettos, are two 'clarini' and two separate choirs of four trumpets, each with a pair of timpani. A modern edition of Benevoli's manuscript score was prepared by Guido Adler and includes a facsimile of a page from the original.[37]

An engraving dating from some time between 1668 and 1687 gives an idea of the magnificence and splendour of the consecration.[38] The four transept balconies of the cathedral are filled to capacity with musicians, and there are singers on either side of the altar. Although not visible in the engraving, the nave gallery would have been filled with musicians. The left side of the picture shows one balcony with trumpeters (one player is holding his trumpet over the balcony railing) and another, nearer the altar, with several trombonists and apparently singers.

Considering they were written in 1628, or earlier, the trumpet parts of Benevoli's consecration mass are quite elaborate and technically demanding. The short, fragmentary material often given to the two 'clarini' shows an unusual anticipation of the later classical rhythmic punctuation of the harmony with pairs of trumpets and/or horns. There are two florid outbursts for the 'clarini' in the 'Christe eleison'—once at bars 67–68, and

---

[37] In *DTÖ*, xx, Vienna, 1903. The original MS., which had barely escaped the fate of so many MSS. as butcher paper in the nineteenth century, was destroyed in the bombing of Salzburg in the Second World War. We must be for ever grateful to the scholarship of Guido Adler.

[38] See *MGG*, vol. iv, *Tafel* 5 (facing cols. 95–6).

an exact repetition at bars 84–87. But on the words '. . . et vitam venturi saeculi, amen' (bars 218–232) at the conclusion of the 'Credo', and during both statements of the 'Osanna', the two 'clarini' and the highest parts in each choir of four trumpets contain the most florid passages in the work.

On the whole, the range of all ten trumpet parts is narrow and usually no higher than a^1. However, the two 'clarini' during the 'Christe eleison' ascend to c^2 and, similarly, at the conclusion of the 'Credo' both the 'clarini' and the first part in each choir of trumpets ascend to c^2. During the 'Osanna' 'clarino 1' plays b^1 flat as the highest note in a pattern of florid semiquavers. The trumpet parts rarely double one another, antiphony being used nearly throughout. There is, however, one noticeable exception. At the conclusion of the 'Benedictus-Osanna' the two 'clarini' and two 'trombe' double one another in the last three bars, beginning with a short pattern of semiquavers in parallel thirds.

The concluding *Hymnus*, 'Plaudite tympanu', also in the same scoring of fifty-three parts, is a short anthem written in the same style as the mass. There is a greater use of antiphony between the two choirs of sixteen voices, but the trumpet writing is rather unexceptional.

Generally, the overall style of the *Missa* and *Hymnus* are, in their grandiosity, related to the Venetian polychoral tradition. But having been written only fourteen years after the death of Giovanni Gabrieli (1612), Benevoli's style, use of harmony and certainly his orchestration are well in advance of anything written at Venice, or anywhere else, for large groups of voices and instruments.

Trumpets continued to be an important part of the music at Salzburg Cathedral well into the eighteenth century. For special religious feasts trumpeters from the archbishop's private band were called upon to perform there. Music for these occasions was provided by the cathedral organist or the *Hofkomponist* in the employ of the *Erzbischof*. The Salzburg Cathedral organist and composer Andreas Hofer was one of many to maintain the custom of festive, elaborately scored pieces. His C major *Missa Archi-Episcopalis* ('Erzbischöfliche Messe') [39] *à 19 Parti* is scored for '8 voci concert. col Coro, 2 Violini, 2 Viole, 2 Clarini, 2 Cornetti, 3 Tromboni Organo con Violone'. A set of parts of the work is found at Kremsmünster, where it may have been performed after its initial presentation at Salzburg.

Hofer was succeeded at Salzburg by one of the most important of

[39] *See* Weinmann, 1918, p. 81.

seventeenth-century Austro-Bohemian musicians, Heinrich Ignatz Franz Biber.[40] More will be said about his activities and his trumpet music preserved at Kroměříž in the following discussion of Moravia and the *Fürstbischof* Karl Liechtenstein-Kastelkorn, for whom Biber worked before assuming his duties at Salzburg. A violin virtuoso and composer, Biber produced many works with trumpets while in the service of the Salzburg *Erzbischof* Maximilian 1 Gandolf von Kuenburg; he also continued the Salzburg tradition of large-scale vocal compositions with substantial trumpet parts. One of these vocal works is a *Litania de S. Josepho à 20*, which includes eight voices, ' 2 Violini, 5 Viole, 2 Trompette', and ' 3 Tromboni'.[41] Some similar pieces also require two 'Piffari' (seventeenth-century shawms). His *Requiem à 15 v Concert* includes parts for 2 trumpets, 3 trombones and 2 'Piffari'.[42]

As late as 1757 works in the Baroque polychoral style were still being written and performed at Salzburg. Assuming that performance practices changed very gradually before the last quarter of the eighteenth century— indeed were almost static in ecclesiastical music from 1690 until 1750— Marpurg's mid-eighteenth-century remarks about Salzburg music would have been applicable toward the end of the seventeenth century.[43] His interesting information about the trumpet players at the court of the Archbishop of Salzburg would certainly have been relevant at the end of the previous century.[44]

Most of the ten trumpet players from Marpurg's list (entitled ' Chöre Trompeten und Paukken . . .') who played at Salzburg Cathedral are mentioned as 'Hof- und Feldtrompeter'. The 'Obertrompeter aus Bayern' Johann Baptist Gesenberger is praised for his good and famous trills. He and the last trumpeter on the list are the only ones not specifically mentioned as being able to double on a stringed instrument. All the other trumpeters are said to have played violin, viola or violoncello. The 'Hof- und Feldtrompeter' Andreas Schachtner (third on the list) and Ignatius Finck (fifth on the list) are mentioned as playing both violin and violoncello; Schachtner is said to have played the violin especially well. It is said

[40] Biber's musical ability and his association with Leopold 1 won him a title of nobility. With the granting of an official diploma in 1690, the illustrious composer was known as Heinrich Ignatz Franz von Biber.

[41] *See* Rosenthal, 1930, p. 86.

[42] See *DTÖ*, xxx.

[43] Marpurg, 1757, pp. 183–98.

[44] *Ibid*, p. 196.

that Caspar Köstler, the second trumpeter-violinist on Marpurg's list, gave the trumpet a very 'pleasing and singing tone', and that 'one hears from him with great delight fine concertos and solos'. Even the two timpanists ('Hof- und Feldpaucker') are mentioned as playing violin; the second of the two, Florian Vogt, 'spielt sehr gut die Violin'.[45] Marpurg concludes this section as follows: 'Es wird kein Trompeter noch Paucker in die Hochfürstl. Dienste genommen, der nicht eine gute Violin spielet: wie sie denn bey starken Musiker bey Hofe alle erscheinen, und die zweyte Violin oder die Viola mit spielen müssen; wo sie nämlich von dem, der die wöchenliche Direction hat, hin beordert werden.' [46]

Marpurg's description of the actual placement of musicians in the Cathedral of Salzburg is indicative of the point that performance practices changed very gradually. The description, which follows in the original German, agrees in many respects with the illustration of the 1628 consecration ceremony mentioned earlier.

Die Hochfürstl. Domkirche hat hinten beym Eingang der Kirche die grosse Orgel, vorn beym Chor 4 Seitenorgeln [positive organs], und unten im Chor eine kleine Chororgel, wobey die Chorsänger sind. Die grosse Orgel wird bey einer grossen Musik nur zum Präludiren gebraucht: bey der Musik selbst aber wird eine der 4 Seitenorgeln, beständig gespielet, nämlich die nächste am Altar rechten Hand, wo die Solosänger und Bässe sind. Gegenüber auf der linken Seitenorgel sind die Violinisten und auf den beyden andern Seitenorgeln sind die 2. Chöre Trompeten und Paukken. Die untere Chororgel und Violon spielen, wenn es völlig gehet, mit. Die Oboe und Querflöte wird selten, das Waldhorn aber niemals in der Domkirche gehöret. Alle diese Herren spielen demnach in der Kirche bey der Violine mit.[47]

[45] *Ibid.*, p. 197.

[46] *Ibid.*: 'No trumpeter or drummer shall be employed in princely services who does not play the violin well, since they all have to appear at court for large-scale musical performances and have to join in playing second violin or viola; to which [parts] they will be ordered by him who is supervising for that week.'

[47] *Ibid.* p. 195: 'The most illustrious cathedral has the great organ at the rear of the church, by the [nave] entrance, four positive organs in front of the choir, and a small choir organ [portative] down by the choir next to the choristers. The great organ is used only for improvisations during a large-scale musical performance, but for this musical performance itself one of the four positive organs is played constantly, namely the one next to the altar on the right-hand side, where the soloists and basses are. Opposite by the left positive organ are the violinists, and by the other two positive organs are the second choir, trumpets and drums. The lower choir organ and the violone join in during the *tutti* passages. The oboe and the transverse flute are heard rarely, but the waldhorn is never heard in the cathedral. All these gentlemen, therefore, join in playing the violins in the church.'

Conservative considerations of performance practice at Salzburg Cathedral may have been related to the protection of prerogatives by the *Stadtpfeifer*, especially with respect to the *Waldhörner*, which seem never to have been heard in the cathedral. As Marpurg says, the trombonists, 'namely the [ones who play] alto, tenor, and bass trombones', were the 'Stadtthürmermeister' and two of his subordinates.[48] That they in particular may have resented the 'new fangled' horns and obstructed their being heard in the cathedral is suggested by the scoring of musical compositions for the cathedral until the end of the eighteenth century. Even Mozart's Salzburg masses and anthems retain the traditional use of trombones doubling the vocal parts. That horns were used as early as 1723 in Leipzig church music[49] may have had something to do with different local *Stadtpfeifer* regulations, and also that the playing of horns—at least at Leipzig—was the prerogative of the *Stadtpfeifer* trumpet players. The trumpet players at Salzburg seem to have been *Kameradschaft* members and were attached to the archbishop's court.

Seventeenth-century trumpet music in Moravia and Bohemia

In 1921 Paul Nettl, then at Prague, published an article[50] in which he presented a number of interesting documents, letters and inventories, all dealing with the musical activities at the court of a seventeenth-century prince-bishop at the small but historically important Moravian towns of Olomouc (Ger. Olmütz) and Kroměříž (Ger. Kremsier). Nettl devoted very little space to an actual discussion of the music that had been written and performed at those places; nevertheless, the facts and details presented in his article made it obvious that during the seventeenth century the two Moravian towns were musically important and that much of the still surviving music was equally important. Nettl made various references to the same Moravian cities and music in his important study of seventeenth-

---

[48] Marpurg, *op. cit.*

[49] *See* J. S. Bach's cantatas *BWV* 40, 105, 136, and 179, which all require horns and may be dated as early as 1723. Of course, Bach was not the first to use horns in church music, particularly at St Thomas's. Kuhnau requires pairs of horns in F in at least two settings: one, as might be expected, a Christmas 'cantata' based on the chorale 'Wie schön leuchtet der Morgenstern', a text which Bach was also to set with horns in 1725, the other, a similar work, 'Welt ade, ich bin dein müde', for the 24th Sunday after Trinity—the same Sunday in the Lutheran church year for which Bach in two other cantatas (*BWV* 26, 60) once again scored for horn.

[50] Nettl, 1921–2a, pp. 485–96.

century Viennese dance music.[51] Oddly, thirty-five years elapsed before any additional musical information was available. In 1956 Ernst Hermann Meyer published his comprehensive article in which he discusses at some length the musical repertory alluded to in Nettl's earlier surveys.[52]

In view of the composers represented and the significance of their work, it is odd that thirty-five years should have passed with little or nothing being done about Moravian music. For example, some musical histories and dictionaries of musicians would have us believe that Heinrich Ignatz Franz Biber was little more than an outstanding violinist and only composed some violin pieces using scordatura. Few writers on music and its history mention his many motets, masses, sonatas and *balletti*; and mention is rarely made of the other seventeenth-century Moravian and Bohemian composers and their still surviving compositions preserved in the Liechtenstein archives at Kroměříž. A catalogue of the Kroměříž music was prepared some time after Eitner's *Quellen-Lexikon* by Antonín Breitenbacher (1928). It was published in the Czech language and, unfortunately, in a limited edition, which makes it very difficult to obtain. At any rate, an opportunity to examine at first hand the musical repository at Kroměříž has brought to light a vast collection of seventeenth-century compositions, many of them Baroque trumpet pieces or large works with attractive trumpet parts.[53]

In order to understand the *raison d'être* of the Liechtenstein archives, it is necessary to say a few words about Bohemia and Moravia and their social and musical situation at the beginning of the seventeenth century. Bohemia was the principal province of the Austrian empire. It is situated at about the geographic centre of the European continent, and though surrounded by mountains it has always been accessible through Moravia. For no other reason than their geographic location Bohemia and Moravia were destined to play an important role in the cultural development of Europe. Both areas were and still are the border between the German-speaking and the Slavic peoples.

At the beginning of the seventeenth century the forces of Maximilian of

---

[51] Nettl, 1921.

[52] Meyer, 1956, pp. 388–411.

[53] *See* Smithers, 1970, pp. 24 ff., the first published account of the seventeenth-century music at Kroměříž to appear in English. All of the seventeenth-century musical manuscripts at Kroměříž are now preserved in the 'Liechtenstein' music microfilm archive in the library of Syracuse University at Syracuse, N.Y. A revised edition in English of Breitenbacher's catalogue for this collection is in preparation.

Bavaria, Duke Ferdinand of Styria (later elected Emperor Ferdinand II) and their Polish, Spanish and Italian allies crushed the Protestant movement of Bohemia. After 1621 there was a wholesale confiscation of Bohemian and Moravian territory; the ancient indigenous aristocracy was driven into exile and Catholicism was completely reinstated. These were the events that constituted the first phase of the Thirty Years War, which had erupted at Prague, the capital of Bohemia, in 1618. What began as primarily a religious conflict developed into a violent political conflagration. Accompanied by a catastrophic shock-wave of pillaging, burning and plundering, the Thirty Years War nearly destroyed every aspect of cultural life in Bohemia and Moravia.

In 1627 a token representative Bohemian government was allowed to exist, but the Emperor Ferdinand II created an overruling body which consisted of the Catholic Archbishop of Prague and certain other ecclesiastics who had been granted lands and titles. As a consequence of the imposing authority of the Viennese Habsburgs, and with so much confiscated Bohemian and Moravian territory in the hands of Austrians and Germans, the national language was supplanted by German. From that time until the twentieth century the cultural history of the area is inseparable from that of Austria.

Before the Thirty Years War the most important musical centre of Bohemia and Moravia was Prague. In 1612 the number of instrumentalists in the Prague *Hofkapelle* was six violinists, one cornetto player, one lutenist, a harpsichordist, twenty trumpeters, a timpanist, and between five and twelve apprentices studying trumpet and organ.[54] With the removal of the court from Prague to Vienna upon the election of Ferdinand II as emperor in 1619, and as a result of the calamities of the Thirty Years War, music went into a state of decline at Prague and throughout Bohemia and Moravia. It was not until the middle of the seventeenth century that music and art began to take on new life at those courts and residences that had been parcelled out to Austrians and Germans after the territorial confiscations earlier in the century. In Bohemia, music increased in the households of Clam-Gallas, Czernin, Lobkowitz, Mannsfeld, Morzin, Pachta, Sachsen-Lauenburg, Schwarzenberg, Sporck, Thun, and at the residence of the Archbishop of Bohemia. In Moravia-Silesia, music was cultivated by the families of Althau, Dietrichstein, Haugwitz, Hoditz, Liechtenstein-Kastelkorn, Magnis, Podstatzky, Questenberg, Rottal, Salm and Cardinal Schrattenholz. The places of residence of these and

[54] Quoika, 1956, p. 52.

several other important musically inclined nobles are given by Quoika (1956, pp. 68–9). For the cultivation of trumpet music one name is of paramount importance: Liechtenstein-Kastelkorn.

From 1664 until his death in 1695 Karl Liechtenstein-Kastelkorn was the *Fürstbischof* of Olomouc,[55] the ecclesiastical metropolis of Moravia and for a number of centuries the capital of that Slavonic kingdom. Toward the end of the Thirty Years War the capital was moved to Brno (Ger. Brünn), but Olomouc remained the episcopal seat of Moravia. Liechtenstein was often at Olomouc, but he spent most of his time at his residence in Kroměříž. It was at Olomouc, in Northern Moravia, that Liechtenstein carried out most of his official ecclesiastical duties. The most imposing of the city's churches is the Gothic cathedral, where some of the works with trumpets by Biber, Schmelzer, Vejvanovský and others were performed.

South of Olomouc, on the River Morava, is the city of Kroměříž (about ninety miles north-east of Vienna). In 1643 it was sacked, burned and then occupied by the Swedes. Upon assuming his duties in Moravia nearly twenty years later, Liechtenstein had the palatial bishop's residence rebuilt and surrounded by classically landscaped gardens complete with statuary in the Greek and Roman tradition. Both religious and secular forms of music were extensively cultivated at the Kroměříž residence, as well as music for the Roman Rite in the nearby Collegiate Church of St Mauritius. Liechtenstein was a count of the Austrian family of Liechten-stein-Kastelkorn; he was educated at Innsbruck and Ingolstadt, and was appointed bishop while at Salzburg.[56]

Another member of this important family had a residence near Warten-berg (today, Straž pod Ralskem) in Northern Bohemia. It was there that Heinrich Ignatz Franz Biber was born in 1644, his father being at that time in the employ of Liechtenstein's uncle, Christoph Paul, the *Landes-hauptman* of Moravia. Little is known about Biber's youth and musical training, but at the age of twenty-two he was already a musician in the service of the *Fürstbischof* Liechtenstein at Kroměříž. Biber was a virtuoso violinist, composer, and *Kapellmeister*, both at the bishop's palace at Olomouc and at the Kroměříž residence. The bishop required almost as much secular music for his many serenades, divertimentos and other

[55] *Fürstbischof* means literally in German, 'prince bishop'. From 1588 all the bishops of Olo-mouc (after 1777 archbishops) were created princes of the empire, giving them both temporal as well as spiritual power.

[56] *See* Nettl, 1921–2 b, p. 486.

entertainments at Kroměříž as he did religious music for both cities. Biber's large output during his period of service with Liechtenstein is represented by both the sacred and secular, as well as many instrumental pieces. One of his trumpet works, the *Sonata S. Polycarpi à 9: 8 trombe tympanu* [and *violone*],[57] was probably written for the religious celebrations in the Collegiate Church of St Mauritius on 26th January, the feast day of the second-century Christian martyr Saint Polycarp. It is a noisy piece, scored for eight trumpets in two antiphonal choirs. The bass is supplied by the 'Tumpanu' and the 'Violone e bassi'. It would not be incorrect to assume that one or two keyboard continuo instruments would have been included, especially in view of the composer's own directions:

NB . . . Der Violon aber der Bass Continuus, so vil es sein kan, müssen strarck [sic] besetzt werden, die quartuba kan wohl braucht werden.[58]

A florid 'clarino' style of writing is generally restricted to the first trumpet part in each choir, the other parts having simpler triad figures and repeated notes. That the two groups of trumpets are separated for the sake of antiphony is suggested not only by the music but also by the composer's *nota bene*:

Das Tromba 1. et 2. auch 5. und 6. alle vier müssen beysamen stehen. Undt Tromba 3., 4., 7., 8. auch beysammen, dann sie gehen in tripla ad duos choros.[59]

Among the nearly twenty-five sonatas and *balletti* by Biber preserved in the castle archives at Kroměříž, some with trumpets were intended as *Tafelmusik* for the Prince-Bishop. The title of the *balletto* No. 173 in Breitenbacher's enumeration adds 'Trombet undt musicalischer Taffeldienst'.[60] The *Sonata pro tabula à 10*, although not scored with trumpets, was nevertheless performed at table.[61] Instead of trumpets Biber scores for five recorders and strings. A number of his other instrumental pieces were

[57] Breitenbacher, 1928, p. 115, No. 187.

[58] '*Nota bene:* But the violone, the basso continuo, as many as there can be, must be played energetically; the *quartuba* [bass trombone?] may well be used.' A 'quartuba' was either a bass trombone and used to double the 'violone' part, or a trumpet played in the 'Fladdergrob' register, i.e. a trumpet played with a deep-cupped mouthpiece and capable of doubling the timpani part.

[59] 'Trumpets 1 and 2, as well as 5 and 6—all four must stand together. Trumpets 3, 4, 7, 8 also together, because in the triple time they split up into two choirs.'

[60] Breitenbacher, 1928, p. 134, No. 173.

[61] *Ibid.*, p. 135, No. 206.

probably written for the various festive open-air celebrations among the trees and classical statuary in the grounds of the bishop's residence.

Biber wrote several sonatas for one and two trumpets with strings and continuo. The *Sonata à 6 Vom Hainrich J. F. Biber* is scored for '2 violin, tromba sola, 2 viole et violone con organo', and is in C major.[62] In the preface to the edition published by Musica Rara of London in 1958, the editor, Kurt Janetsky, says that there are '. . . two existing versions (C and B flat). . .'. Since he says nothing about either version and includes no critical notes, the existence of a B-flat version is viewed with suspicion. If a B-flat source is authentic, it is the only significant Baroque trumpet piece in that key.

Biber's *Sonata X à 5* from his published collection for one and two trumpets with strings and continuo, the *Sonatae tam aris . . .* of 1676 (mod. ed. DTÖ 106–7), is scored for trumpet, violin, three violas [the third viola part is ostensibly for a cello, since the part descends to C_1] and basso continuo. It is unusual in that a natural trumpet is scored in the minor mode. Like the examples mentioned in the previous chapter, as well as the Vejvanovský sonata discussed below, Biber builds his themes in the minor mode around the available notes of the Baroque trumpet, taking particular advantage of the flat seventh harmonic. Another unusual feature of this piece is the striking similarity of the theme from the second section to the opening bars of Vejvanovský's *Sonata à 4*. Since both composers were at the Kroměříž residence of Karl Liechtenstein-Kastelkorn, Biber may have followed Vejvanovský's example, considering the latter was an expert trumpeter and doubtless knew better than most what was possible on the natural instrument. Another piece in Biber's 1676 collection, No. 11 of the twelve duets for two trumpets, is of interest not only because here again we have minor tonality, but also because the short *bicinium* in G minor turns up with only the slightest changes in Altenburg's *Versuch . . .*[63] over a century later, where it has no attribution other than one previously thought to be for Altenburg himself.

For unexplained reasons, Biber left the service of Liechtenstein rather unexpectedly in the late summer of 1670. Before taking up his duties at Salzburg, by 1673 at the latest, he is reputed to have sought refuge in an attempt to elude agents of the *Fürstbischof*. His notable successor at Kroměříž was the Slavic 'Tubicine Campestri' (*Feldtrompeter*) Pavel Josef Vejvanovský (1639 or 1640–1693; his name is spelled variously, e.g. 'Weiwan-

[62] *Ibid.*, p. 111, No. 110.
[63] Altenburg, 1795, p. 104.

owski', 'Weywanowsky' or 'Weiuanouski'). Mentioned, like Alexander Orlogio, in connection with the court of Rudolf II at Prague, Vejvanovský was one of the few Baroque trumpeters to attain the position of *Kapell-meister*. His output of musical compositions was large: numerous masses, motets, etc., and at least thirty-four sonatas, *balletti*, intradas and sere-nades. Most of his instrumental pieces are scored with trumpet(s)—many with the specification 'solo clarino', a part which Vejvanovský un-doubtedly played himself.[64]

In addition to being prolific in his output, Vejvanovský was more imaginative than many of his contemporaries from the standpoint of orchestration. The *Sonata à 8 SS Petri et Pauli*,[65] for example, is scored for two choirs of instruments, a solo trumpet with three trombones in the first choir and a solo violin with three violas in the second. The strings and brass do not play together until the last twenty bars (they answer one another in antiphony from the beginning until bar 169), but the contrast of instrumental colours is most gratifying. The composer successfully uses the same orchestration again in the *Sonata ab. 8 Solo clarino con 3^{bus} trom-bonis, solo violino con 3^{bus} violis*.[66]

One of the most interesting of Vejvanovský's trumpet pieces is the *Sonata à 4, Be mollis*,[67] *solo clarino, solo violino, con 2^{bus} violis, Domine Deus noster, quam. Ab authore Paulo Weywanowsky*.[68] It is in G minor with a fre-quent use of e^1 flat and c^1 sharp in the trumpet part. As in the rare examples cited earlier, Vejvanovský employs the technique of scoring for a natural trumpet in the minor mode. As in the case of Handel's 'With honour let desert be crown'd', from *Judas Maccabaeus*, and the previously mentioned sonata by Biber, Vejvanovský's *Sonata à 4* is written in a key that is the minor dominant of the required trumpet's tonality. He can therefore use the seventh harmonic as the mediant tone in G minor. Since the non-harmonic tones e^1 flat and c^1 sharp are not hastily approached from the adjacent harmonic series notes, we can assume that the player (probably Vejvanovský) had little difficulty in 'lipping' these notes into correct pitch.

[64] Much of Vejvanovský's trumpet music appears in the modern series, *Musica Antiqua Bo-hemica* (abbr. *MAB*), vols. 36, 47, 48 and 49, published at Prague in 1958 and afterwards.

[65] Breitenbacher, 1928, p. 107, No. 10 (*MAB*, vol. 49, p. 67).

[66] *Ibid.*, No. 13 (no modern publication).

[67] The term 'Be mollis', which refers to the minor mode of this sonata, is written in a different ink and appears to be in a different hand from the rest of the title page and parts.

[68] Breitenbacher, 1928, p. 108, No. 43 (*MAB*, vol. 36, p. 12).

Some of the MS. title-page instructions found with Vejvanovský's trumpet pieces suggest that the coiled variety of Baroque trumpet, i.e. the *tromba da caccia*, was used at Kroměříž. On several occasions Vejvanovský refers to the trumpets as 'trombae breves'. The trumpet parts in most Kroměříž compositions are usually specified as 'clarini', 'trombae', or, in several cases, 'tubae campestres', i.e. *Feldtrompeten*—'field trumpets'. Vejvanovský seems to be the only composer of all those represented to imply that a different kind of trumpet may have been required on occasion. In two cases he is quite specific. The title of the *Sonata Venatoria* refers to the trumpets as '. . . 2 clarini seu trombae breves . . .', and the title of the *Sonata à 5* as '. . . 2 clarini, trombae breves. . .'. [69]

The titles of some pieces do make a distinction between 'clarino' and 'tromba'. Rittler's *Sonata S. Caroli à 17* refers to the six required trumpets as '2 clarini' and '4 trombae'.[70] Bertali's *Sonata Sublationis, Scriptum Viennae, anno 1665 28. April* specifically mentions '2 clarini con.[certino]' and '2 trombae ad libitum'.[71] These, however, are distinctions of register, not an implication that different kinds of trumpets were intended. Some Baroque composers even use the terms 'clarino' and 'tromba' interchangeably, with no reference to a higher or lower register. It is unlikely that horns were denoted by either of these terms, especially since the pieces with horns are explicit in their titles about the intended instruments. The title of an anonymous *Sonata da caccia con un cornu*,[72] for example, specifies '2 violini, 2 violae, cornu di caccia con violone o cimbalo'. Thus, the term 'tromba breve' most probably implies the use of the small, coiled-up variety of trumpet. That Vejvanovský is the only one to make the distinction may be due to the fact that, having been a trumpeter, he was more aware than others of the different kinds of trumpets and the use to be made of each.

Some of the other composers represented by trumpet music at Kroměříž are Johann Heinrich Schmelzer, Alessandro de Poglietti, Antonio Bertali, the Jesuit Fr. Johann Tollar (sometimes spelled Dolar or Thollary), Ferdinand Tobias Richter, August Kertzinger and Philipp Jacob Rittler. The archives even include pieces by the Emperor Leopold I, who, like

[69] *Ibid.*, p. 116, Nos. 199 and 200.

[70] *Ibid.*, p. 112, No. 123.

[71] *Ibid.*, No. 119.

[72] *Ibid.*, p. 110, No. 81, one of the earliest sources of music specifically for the horn, then newly introduced into Bohemia from France, presumably by the Northern Bohemian Count Anton von Sporck.

many of the Habsburg emperors before and after him, had a profound interest in music and was an able composer. But not all of these composers worked either at Kroměříž or at Olomouc. The title pages of many compositions include the name of the city where the composer actually wrote. Mention has already been made of Bertali's *Sonata Sublationis*, which included the information 'Scriptum Viennae'; there is also a sonata by 'G.[eorg] Muffat', composed at 'Pragae 1677'.[73] Most of the Schmelzer pieces preserved at Kroměříž were composed at Vienna for one occasion or another and then sent some time later to the *Fürstbischof*. Many of these pieces were subsequently performed during the outdoor entertainments at the palace or, as we may gather from some of their title pages, were intended 'per Kiesa e per camera'.[74] In letters exchanged between the *Fürstbischof* and Schmelzer thanks are often expressed by the former for compositions received, or some other comment is made about the music sent by Schmelzer to Kroměříž from Vienna. Some of this correspondence is quoted by Nettl, from whom the following two excerpts are taken.

The *Fürstbischof* writing to Johann Schmelzer:

'*Dessen angenehmes habe ich jüngsthin wol erhalten und bedanke mich wegen der überschickten compositionen . . . Kremsier, 9. März 1673.*'[75]

—and again from the *Fürstbischof* to Schmelzer, but in a less grateful tone:

'*Die überschickte Sonata ist sambt dessen schreiben wol eingeloffen; es wird die iberbrachte specification über ausgeworfene noten zeigen, dasz ich soliche allerbereith bei hunderten habe . . . Wischau, 9. April 1673.*'[76]

Similarly, most of Poglietti's music at Kroměříž was written while the composer was at Vienna. Next to Biber and Vejvanovský, Poglietti and Schmelzer are represented by the second largest number of instrumental pieces found at Kroměříž. It is extraordinary that neither composer has as yet had much of a share in the modern revival of Baroque trumpet music; and no less extraordinary that almost none of their many trumpet works is included in any of the present-day monumental editions of early music. To know their music is to have a better understanding of Baroque music and the musical life of Central Europe.

[73] *Ibid.*, p. 112, No. 118.

[74] *Ibid.*, p. 111, No. 105: *Sonata à 8, 2 trombe, 6 viol . . . Dal Smelzer. Anno 1679 praesentirt.*

[75] Nettl, 1921, pp. 166 ff.: 'I thank you for the enclosed pleasant compositions which I recently received in good order . . . Kroměříž, 9th March 1673.'

[76] 'The sonata sent has arrived together with your letter; the enclosed list of rejected pieces will show that I already have hundreds of similar ones . . . Vyškov, 9th April 1673.'

In Bohemia, music for the Baroque trumpet continued to be cultivated in the larger cities after the Thirty Years War. Trumpets were much used at Prague in the second half of the seventeenth century, and church music seems to have provided the greatest opportunity for trumpet playing in the Bohemian capital before 1700. But one of the most surprising places in Bohemia to cultivate trumpet music on a grand scale was the small town of Osek (Ger. Osseg).

Not far from the German border, in Northern Bohemia, Osek lies nearly at the intersection of lines drawn from Chemnitz (Karl Marx Stadt) to Prague and from Dresden to Pilsen. The Cistercian monastery in the town would seem to have provided opportunities for the development of instrumental music similar to those afforded by Olomouc and Kroměříž. Two early eighteenth-century inventories of the monastery's music and musical instruments supply the evidence for this assumption. The first inventory was taken in 1706 with the title:

Inventarium sive Catalogus Musicalium cum annexa Specificatione Instrumentorum Musicorum Ecclesiae B. V. Mariae de Ossecco Combinatum et hoc ordine digestum Anno 1706.[77]

The title of the second inventory reads as follows:

Catalogus Musicalium anno 1720 in ordinem digestus ab eodem a quo et Anno 1733 est renovatus.[78]

Among the compositions of both inventories the largest category is instrumental music, i.e. 'Sonatae, Balletae, Sinfoniae', etc. The important seventeenth-century composers who were at Vienna—Schmelzer, Fux, Caldara and others—are credited with most of these pieces, while the remainder was composed by Moravian and Bohemian musicians. Among the names of the latter will be found that of Finger. This was probably Gottfried (Godfrey) Finger, who was from Olomouc and worked in England at the end of the seventeenth century.[79] More will be said about Finger in the next chapter, where we shall discuss some of his trumpet music now in the British Museum.

The orchestration of the instrumental pieces mentioned in the Osek inventories is not given; but, judging from the similarity of the titles

[77] From Nettl, 1921–2a, p. 351 ff.; also included in Nettl, 1927.

[78] *Ibid.*

[79] There was a mid-seventeenth-century Olomouc *Stadtpfeifer* by the name of Johann Finger who may have been the father of Godfrey.

found at Kroměříž and the number of composers whose names are associated with the same archives, we must assume that many of the sonatas, *balletti*, etc., had important trumpet parts. This conclusion is further justified by an examination of the 'Specificatio Instrumentorum Musicalium' from the 1706 inventory.[80] Besides the violins, regal, harpsichords, gamba, etc., found on the list, there are 'Tubae campestres ex Clavi C quinque ex Clavi D duae cum dependentiis'.[81] Also listed are several 'Tubae ductiles' (trombones), a single kettle drum, two large trumpet mouthpieces, one large and two small trombone mouthpieces, two 'Cornus vulgo Zinckhen' (cornettos) and two 'Litui vulgo Waldhörner' in G.[82]

Like most European courts and many churches, the monastery at Osek owned several trumpets. Who the players were and where they came from is not known, but their availability is suggested by the inventories of 1706 and 1733. Further proof of the availability of trumpeters and other instrumentalists in similar circumstances are the surviving musical materials and comparable inventories of many German and Austrian monasteries. Even as late as the second half of the eighteenth century Baroque trumpet music continued to be associated with monastic musical activities. Thus, a copy of Johann Michael Haydn's 'Concerto' in D major with a part for a 'Clarino solo' is preserved in the Benedictine monastery at Lambach,[83] a small town in Upper Austria, midway between Salzburg and Linz; another work by Michael Haydn for Baroque trumpet is found in the Benedictine monastery at Göttweig in Lower Austria.[84] Most of the instrumentalists who took part in musical performances at Austrian and Bohemian monasteries were probably members of the community, especially among the austere Cistercian and Benedictine Orders.

At the beginning of this chapter it was said that a crossroad tends to be a busy place. Musically, there was hardly a more active and busy area than the Austro-Bohemian territories during the seventeenth century. The degree of social intercourse between Austria, Moravia and Bohemia and

---

[80] Nettl, 1921–2a, pp. 39–40.

[81] 'Field trumpets—five in C, two in D with dependents', i.e. appurtenances, such as tuning bits, crooks, etc.

[82] This is one of the few seventeenth-eighteenth-century references to the *lituus*. Two 'litui' in B flat are required in J. S. Bach's cantata *O Jesu Christ, mein's Lebens Licht* (*BWV* 118). Bach obviously meant the same thing by the term *lituus* as that given in the 1706 Osek inventory, i.e. a *Waldhorn*.

[83] Stift Lambach, MS. No. 329.

[84] Stift Göttweig, MS. *Sinfonia* for 'Clarino Conc[erta]to'.

the rest of Europe is evidenced not only by the amount of surviving music in various national styles, but also by the number of composers of different nationalities who worked in such places as Innsbruck, Kroměříž, Olomouc, Salzburg and Vienna. The trumpet music by those composers represents a significant part of their output. That so much of their music is for the Baroque trumpet is indicative of the role played by the instrument in nearly every aspect of musical life, from the church to the court, from the field to the palatial gardens of kings, emperors and prince-bishops.

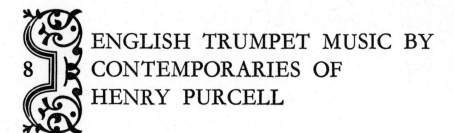

ENGLISH TRUMPET MUSIC BY CONTEMPORARIES OF HENRY PURCELL

8

In the various libraries and archives at such places as Darmstadt, Kroměříž, Ljubljana, London, Oxford, Upsala and Vienna an astonishing number of trumpet pieces by seventeenth-century non-Italian composers has been discovered; or pieces by Italians whose music had been imported, or who had themselves worked in those areas. At London, Oxford and Cambridge, for example, there are several Italian trumpet sonatas, or sonatas modelled upon those of Italian origin, with relatively few differences from sonatas of the Bolognese school. There are manuscripts and printed concordances in Britain of works of Italian origin that clearly represent the Bologna and Modena schools of trumpet writing. In the Bodleian Library at Oxford there is one of two known sources of a Torelli sonata for trumpet and strings, and another trumpet sonata with strings by Alessandro Melani; also at Oxford, in the library of Christ Church, is a manuscript score of a *sonata con tromba* by Pietro Ziani, the only known concordance of a copy found at Upsala, Sweden. In the college library of St Michael's, Tenbury, there is a set of manuscript parts for the Corelli trumpet sonata in D major, as well as several other vocal and instrumental works by the Bolognese composers Cazzati, Colonna, Nenna and Perti. English composers in the seventeenth century saw and heard much of this music and emulated the Italian style in many pieces for occasional entertainments, including overtures and incidental music to masques, odes and operas.

In my article 'Seventeenth-century English trumpet music',[1] which reproduces some of the material given here, I describe one important repertory of English trumpet pieces by Daniel Purcell, John Barratt,

[1] Smithers, 1967, pp. 358–65.

Godfrey Finger, James Paisible and John Eccles, a comparatively recent acquisition of the British Museum (B.M. Add. MS. 49599). This repertory and the trumpet pieces found in the Magdalene College, Cambridge, part-books (now Cambridge Fw. MS. 23E 13–17), as well as those in B.M. Add. MSS. 30839, 39565–7, are the earliest and practically the only surviving sources of English trumpet music by contemporaries of Henry Purcell. Although many of the pieces in these repertories are called sonatas, much of this music could have been adapted from the incidental overtures and act tunes used in contemporary English operas, odes and masques, which themselves often follow the basic lines of the Bolognese trumpet sonata. The Henry Purcell trumpet sonata in D major (Z 850) lends support to this idea. This three-movement sonata is thought to be the overture to the lost 1694 ode *Light of the World*.[2] The libretto by Matthew Prior suggests that it contained a trumpet sonata. Many other examples of Henry Purcell's instrumental pieces from his larger dramatic works, when isolated and performed as separate compositions, fall easily into the category of a sonata.[3] But this is not to say that the above-mentioned pieces by Daniel Purcell, Godfrey Finger, James Paisible and John Eccles are all abstractions from their many larger dramatic compositions. Investigation into this possibility, judging from an examination of their extant operas and other sources from which these works might have been taken, has in all but four cases proved negative.[4]

It is possible that many of these pieces were composed for particular entertainments or concerts of non-programmatic works. We know, for example, that Parliament's closing of English theatres in 1642 actually

[2] A 'Hymn to the Sun Set by Dr. Purcell and sung before Their Majesties on New-'Years Day, 1693/4'. See Zimmerman, 1963; Tilmouth, 1959, p. 109.

[3] One example of such a piece is the third act overture in *The Indian Queen*, Purcell Society edition, vol. xix, pp. 60–6.

[4] After a careful survey of the surviving odes and dramatic music of Eccles, Finger, Paisible and Daniel Purcell, only four pieces—three by Purcell and one by Eccles—were found to concord with the sonatas in B.M. Add. MS. 49599. All four were found in the most likely place, the settings of Congreve's masque, *The Judgement of Paris* (see p. 197). The Eccles sonata No. 16 is identical with the 'Symphony for Mercury', the opening movement in his *Judgement of Paris*, I. Walsh (n.d.) (B. M.: Hirsch II. 22b.); all three of the Daniel Purcell sonatas were found in his entry in the competition based on the Congreve masque, *The Judgement of Paris*, I. Walsh (n.d.) (B. M.: Hirsch II. 749.) Sonata No. 12 is the same as the 'Trumpet Sonata for Pallas', p. 26; the sonata No. 14 equals a nameless three-movement interlude on p. 51; and the sonata No. 18 is identical with the 'Overture' on p. 1, which includes a timpani part in the outer movements. *See also* Appendix, John Weldon.

gave impetus to the rise of such concerted chamber music. The creation of music houses on the premises of taverns and public houses during the Commonwealth saw the development of the earliest public concerts in Europe.[5] Although Parliament again in 1657 enacted punitive measures forbidding the performing of music in taverns, alehouses and similar public meeting places, it could not thwart the desires of the relatively large number of interested listeners or the designs of the many musicians and composers whose lot was a sad one with their loss of livelihood from the closing of the theatres.

The Restoration of the Monarchy in 1660 brought about a reopening of the theatres and enabled musicians once again to find employment. At first the number and quality of music-house concerts declined, but the phenomenon persisted. Concerts organized by the composer-violinist John Banister (1630–79), one-time 'Chief of His Majesty's [Charles II] violins', began in December 1672. An advertisement in the *London Gazette*, No. 742, '. . . From Thursday December 26 to Sunday December 30 1672 . . .', gives some idea of this early form of public music making: 'Advertisements. These are to give Notice, that at Mr. *John Banisters* House, now called the Musick School, over against the *George* Tavern in *White Fryers* this present Monday, will be Musick performed by Excellent Masters, beginning precisely at four of the Clock in the afternoon, and every afternoon for the future, precisely at the same hour.' In the following year Banister advertised in No. 834 of the *London Gazette*, 'Thursday November 13 to Monday November 17 1673', that there would be '. . . new Musick, Vocal and Instrumental, beginning and ending at the same hours as formerly. . .'.

Banister's friend and early associate in organized public concerts, the knowledgeable and learned coalmonger Thomas Britton, began in 1678 a regular and established programme of weekly concerts. These wining-and-dining musical affairs were attended by such notables and social luminaries as the earls of Oxford and Pembroke. In the early part of the next century composer-performers such as Handel, Pepusch and a host of others graced the upstairs 'concert room' above Britton's shop. Britton's keen interest and intelligent appreciation of books and learning, coupled with the quality and high breeding of his audiences, led many to suspect that his coal business and musical enterprises were a façade for sinister and treasonable activities. He was suspected of being a 'magician, an atheist, a Presbyterian, and a Jesuit'.[6] Notwithstanding, his concerts were of high

---

[5] Scott, 1936, pp. 446–57.   [6] Hawkins, 1853, vol. ii, p. 791.

quality and offered the best music of the time played by first-rate musicians and composers.[7]

It may be noted that some of the previously mentioned composers in England of trumpet works contemporaneous with those being written at Bologna and elsewhere were in close association with one another. Lafontaine's extremely valuable compilation of records relating to the royal music and the activities of musicians in the royal employ from 1460 to 1700 [8] gives an accurate picture of the close contact, both musically and socially, these composers had with one another. An extract from the Lord Chamberlain's records of 1674 (vol. 745, pp. 547–8) given in Lafontaine (pp. 280–1) lists all who took part in the opulent and famed masque at Whitehall in 1674–5. Of the nearly eighty performers listed we find James Paisible playing recorder, John Banister and Henry Eagles (Eccles) among the violins. In a subsequent entry of 19th December 1687 we find that 'Mr Peasable' (Paisible) and 'Mr Finger' are included among the instrumentalists who '. . . attended his Majesty at Windsor Castle last summer for 113 days. . .'. [9] At the end of the century John Eccles, composer of the sonata for trumpet, and nephew of the above, gained second prize for his entry in a competition for the best music to Congreve's masque *The Judgement of Paris*. The third and fourth prizes were awarded to Daniel Purcell and Godfrey Finger respectively.

Since most of the English post-Restoration composers were at one time or another employed at the courts of Charles II, James II or William

---

[7] An extensive list of Britton's music and musical instruments appeared in a printed catalogue after his death in 1714. It is described as '. . . being the entire collection of Mr. Thomas Britton of Clerkenwell, small-coal man, lately deceased, who at his own charge kept up so excellent a consort forty odd years at his dwelling-house, that the best masters were at all times proud to exert themselves therein. . . .' Included in the 200 odd collections of instrumental and vocal music are the following with trumpet(s): '. . . 25. Mr. H. Purcell's musick in Dioclesian with trumpets, Mr. Finger. 9 books with ditto (trumpets). 26. Trumpet pieces in 4 and 5 parts by Dr. Pepusch, etc. 93. 6 Concertos for trumpets, hautboys, and Mr. Eccles's Coronation of Q. Anne. 107. Mr. Keller's Sonatas for Trumpets, Flutes, Hautboys, etc. Dutch print. 139. 8 Concertos, Italian writing, for Trumpets, etc. divers authors. 157. 6 books of Trumpet Sonatas and Tunes for 2 flutes and 2 hautboys. . . .' Although giving no specific instrumentation, many other collections would seem to have included trumpets. One item of particular interest is '. . . 65. Overtures and tunes, 4 parts. By Mr. Paisible. . . .' This may well have been the four part-books in Paisible's hand described below and now in the British Museum (Add. MSS. 39565–7, 30839).

[8] Cart de Lafontaine, 1909.

[9] *Ibid.*, p. 384–5.

and Mary, it is quite possible that some of the trumpet pieces mentioned above and those discussed below were intended for royal entertainment. This is suggested, in one instance at any rate, by the carefully tooled leather portfolio of B.M. Add. MS. 49599, the high quality of the copyist's manuscript and the gilded edges of the parts themselves. Someone of means and perhaps of nobility had the parts elegantly prepared and made up as a single collection compiled from various sources.

Unlike the historical and musical position of the Bologna school at the Basilica of San Petronio, however, no English composer in the seventeenth century enjoyed the same opportunity for composing such specific music nor did any composer have at his disposal such large orchestral forces. The overwhelming number of performers available to the Bolognese composers, as cited by Vatielli (1927, pp. 208–9) from the archives of San Petronio, never existed for a composer in seventeenth- or early eighteenth-century Protestant England. While Torelli, Perti or Domenico Gabrielli had as large an orchestra as 123 'ripienists', [10] the greatest total of performers found in an established court orchestra of a seventeenth-century English monarch is the band of twenty-four strings plus twenty-five other instrumentalists during the reign of Charles II.[11] Of the eighty performers mentioned in connection with the spectacular masque at Whitehall in 1674, only fifty-two were instrumentalists.

The Chapel Royal, the only institution in England regularly to employ instruments in a liturgical capacity, used the twenty-four 'violins' with occasional additions of wind instruments supplementary to the normal ensemble. Outside the sphere of court activities, the theatre orchestras were not large, and the number of performers in any of the tavern or music-house concerts was always small. Even the scope of English sonatas is narrower than most of the Bologna pieces. Few would have required more than twenty performers. The largest scoring in any of the works with trumpets is Godfrey Finger's C major sonata (No. 5 in the original enumeration of B.M. Add. MS. 49599), which is scored for two trumpets, three oboes, strings, bassoon and continuo. Most of the English trumpet works, including movements from stage works by Purcell and others, are by their very nature undemanding in size of performing forces. Many follow the lines of the earlier Italian canzona-like sonata, with independent contrapuntal parts over a *basso continuo*.

[10] Giegling, 1949, p. 29.
[11] Cart de Lafontaine, 1909, p. 345.

Rarely do we find the block orchestral effects so often encountered in the sonatas and *sinfonie* of the late seventeenth-century Bolognese. When scoring for a pair of trumpets, the English composers generally treat each part separately rather than, as Torelli and Perti so often do, as a single 'instrument' scored in thirds. The homogeneous effect of strings and winds sharing the same material in the orchestral tuttis is an infrequent device in later seventeenth-century English pieces. Antiphony for the sake of orchestral variety and effects of loud and soft are more often found in English trumpet pieces during a slow introductory section, especially if there are two trumpets in juxtaposition with strings.

The range and technical difficulty of English trumpet parts are on the whole conservative when compared with parts of Italian and German origin. Throughout the entire Baroque era English trumpet parts rarely venture above a^1 and avoid difficult non-harmonic tones; generally, too, they avoid difficult intervals and make greater use of the less difficult lower harmonics. The strong and resonant 4th to 8th partials—the lower register of the trumpet—are more easily played and account for the triadic character of most trumpet music. The opening slow movement of the Daniel Purcell sonata No. 18 in B.M. Add. MS. 49599, with its characteristically trumpet-like intervals, is indicative of the opening statement of much English trumpet music in the seventeenth and eighteenth centuries. (Compare the opening figures of this sonata with the first movement of the overture to Henry Purcell's St Cecilia ode of 1692, *Hail, Bright Cecilia*.) Henry Purcell, whose trumpet pieces compare more favourably with the North Italian compositions than with those written by any other English composer, was one of the few musicians in England to extend the capabilities of the trumpet from the normal *principale* register to the upper harmonics of the *clarino* tessitura. Perhaps English composers disliked the basically out-of-tune upper partials; more probably, they were handicapped by the limitations of the performers and a lack of virtuosos. Even Handel usually avoids high d^2, c^1 sharp and b^1 when scoring for a trumpet in D. There are, for example, only two d^2's in the entire first trumpet part of *Messiah*. Compare this with any of the Bologna concertos or *sinfonie con tromba*, or with the many first-trumpet parts in the works of J. S. Bach. When any unusual non-harmonic tones do occur in the middle register of English trumpet parts, it usually turns out that the part is doubled by an oboe or violin, in which case the trumpet player would have made some harmonically agreeable alternative. The only possible way of making such physically non-existent tones playable would have been to use a 'flatt' trumpet, described by the seventeenth-century English writer James Talbot.[12] This was the instrument pre-scribed by Henry Purcell in the *Queen Mary Funeral Music*, now in the library of Oriel College, Oxford.[13] But here is a clear case of many middle-register, non-harmonic tones being intended for a special trumpet capable of shifting its harmonic series by quickly altering the length of bore, very much in the same way as a trombone. It is very unlikely that any other trumpet but the normal one of between seven to eight feet in length was used in the performance of most English music before the second half of the eighteenth century. If there was any reluctance on the part of English composers to extend the trumpet into the *Clarino* register and include occasional non-harmonic tones, it was probably due to the players themselves.[14]

Of the many trumpet players listed in the Lord Chamberlain's records at the courts of Charles II, James II and William and Mary, only a few are mentioned in other sources as being particularly outstanding and of virtuosity comparable with continental players. These are William Bull and Mathias, William and John Shore (frequently spelled Shaw, Show, Showers, or Shoar). Bull was also a trumpet maker of great repute, and his work has been discussed in Chapter 3. It was the Shores who played many of the demanding parts in Henry Purcell's odes and operas; it may have been one or more of the Shores and Bull who performed the pieces described above, as well as the Clarke, Paisible and Corelli pieces in B.M. Add. MSS. 30839, 39565–7. These four manuscript part-books contain many instrumental pieces (suites, sonatas and short dances) probably in Paisible's own hand, many having been composed by him. This collection contains not only the 'Suite de Clarke', which is for trumpet, two oboes, strings and continuo (the fourth movement, 'Rondeau', is the famed 'voluntary' formerly attributed to Henry Purcell), but also a complete version of the Corelli sonata in D major for trumpet, two violins and

[12] The Talbot manuscript, a collection of notes on musical instruments located in the Christ Church Library, Oxford (MS. 1187), is reprinted in sections in the *Galpin Society Journal*, vol. i (1948) onwards and has been discussed earlier.

[13] Modern edition, Purcell Society edition, vol. xxxi, p. 92, edited by Thurston Dart.

[14] Burney (1789, Book IV; 1957, p. 801), in remarking on the trumpet part to Handel's over-ture in *Atalanta*, which had been played by Valentine Snow at Covent Garden in 1736, says bluntly, 'The fourth of the key is, however, too much used even for vulgar ears to bear patiently. . . . Indeed, whenever the fourth or sixth of the key is otherwise used than as a passing-note, the ear is offended.'

continuo, entitled 'Corelli con duo discando Tromba'. A discussion of the Corelli work will be found in Chapter 4.

One of the most interesting discoveries in B.M. Add. MS. 49599 concerns the Bononcini sonata 'For 3 Violins a Tenor [viola] Viol [violone] Basse'—the second of two pieces with a number 5 in the set. Having transcribed the trumpet pieces from Giovanni Bononcini's opus 3, the *Sinfonie à 5. 6. 7. e 8. Instromenti, con alcune à una e due Trombe...*, published by Monti at Bologna in 1685, I recognized the sonata for three violins to be one and the same as the *Sinfonia Settima à 6.* in the above. There is only one known printed source of this splendid collection by a rather precocious fifteen-year-old Bononcini. It is listed in Sartori (1952) as 1685f and lacks the first violin part (*see* Chapter 4).

One theory as to how this *Sinfonia-Sonata* comes to be included in a collection of English pieces may also throw some light on another point: the obvious but unsubstantiated relation of certain stylistic considerations of apparent seventeenth-century Bolognese origin and the instrumental music of Henry Purcell, which '. . . have more in common than is easily explained by contemporaneity'. [15] Purcell and his younger brother Daniel, as well as many other English composers at the courts of James II and William and Mary, in all probability had a chance to see pieces of Italian origin, especially from Modena and Bologna. Maria d'Este, daughter of Laura d'Este, the guardian of Giovanni Bononcini after his father's death in 1678, was the wife of James II. The famed Estes of Modena were great patrons of art and music, making Modena at that time one of the important centres of music-making; and, because of their close approximation to one another, Bologna and Modena often shared their musical resources of performers and composers. It is highly likely that Queen Mary brought some of the Este music and books with her to London upon the accession of her husband James II in 1685. Certainly the opus 3 *Sinfonie* of Bononcini were known. How the four trumpet pieces were regarded can only be conjectured.

The trumpet itself was a great determinant of the thematic and motivic structure of many seventeenth- and eighteenth-century compositions. The usual natural trumpet in D was limited to a single overtone series, which is shown and explained in Chapter 1. In rare instances and only in the hands of a relatively few virtuoso performers could the Baroque trumpet reliably produce any notes beyond the natural harmonics. Certain idiomatic figures, arising from the instrument's own capabilities and

[15] Hutchings, 1961, p. 70, note 1.

limitations, were soon applied to other instruments and became the characteristic short motivic, often thematically repetitive style of the Italian *Sinfonia* and concerto. In much the same way a large number of Baroque motivic figures grew out of the technical considerations of limited position fingering in string playing. Long melodic stretches, except on rare occasions when written for such virtuosos as Bach knew at Köthen and Leipzig, were, by virtue of the player's endurance, almost a physical impossibility. The English composers, like the Bolognese, wrote very idiomatically for the trumpet, exhibiting an appreciation of the performer's capacities with the inclusion of frequent rests. This also accounts for the often fragmentary and brief motivic statements encountered in this kind of music.

In fast passages the natural trumpet performs at its best in diatonic figures in the upper range of the instrument, or in the *clarino* register. Recurrent sequential passages indicate one other subtle point the composers understood about the instrument's capabilities, namely that a player could best perform a given figure if it was repetitive and centred about a recurring tone. The performer could focus his attention on a given pitch and slur ('lip') or articulate ('tongue') a particular group of notes around it.

Because the natural trumpet is restricted to the available tones of the harmonic series shown on p. 24, or some transposition depending upon the fundamental pitch of the instrument, much Baroque trumpet music was relatively simple in its key structure. Modulations except to the dominant or subdominant normally excluded trumpets, as well as any sections with excursions through various keys. The sonatas of Daniel Purcell, Eccles, Paisible, Finger and Barratt in B.M. Add. MS. 49599 are quite simple and straightforward in their key scheme in the trumpet movements. Only in the slow movements, usually in the relative minor and without trumpets, do we find any attempt at modulatory and chromatic changes. Interest in the trumpet sections—which, as regards tonality, rarely move any further away from the tonic than the dominant —is maintained through the use of antiphony, rhythmic vitality and counterpoint. There are frequent cadential hemiolas that add much character and charm to these pieces. In the sonatas scored for a pair of trumpets, the second trumpet part has a much more independent character than is found in many of the Bolognese and German compositions. The Daniel Purcell and Paisible sonatas compare quite favourably with the Darmstadt trumpet pieces of Telemann in the use of the second trumpet.

Excepting the five- and six-movement sonatas of Godfrey Finger, almost all the English trumpet pieces described previously are in the same form as most of the Bologna trumpet sonatas, i.e. in the fast, slow, fast triptych of the Italian overture. The Eccles four-movement sonata in D (No. 16) seems to be unique with the inclusion of a fugal allegro second movement in 3/4 following a fugal allegro first movement in 4. The usual movement scheme, however, is as follows: Fast ₵, Slow C or 3/4 (3/2), Fast 3/8 or 6/8; or, Introduction (slow) C, Fast ₵, Slow C or 3/4 (3/2), Fast 3/8 or 6/8.

The English composers generally avoid overworking the Italian echo formula of statement (trumpet) and answer (strings), encountered in many continental solo trumpet pieces. The interdependence of trumpet and strings is more apparent in the English sonatas of the period, following more closely the lines of the Corelli sonata and the sonatas of Bononcini, and comparable to the later compositions of Telemann. Even the Henry Purcell sonata for trumpet, which uses the Italian statement-answer device, particularly in the first movement, avoids the tedium of its being used too often by overlapping the instruments at cadential points. Thus, each sonority is given a more interdependent quality, rather than the frequent impression of two isolated entities constantly stating and restating thematic material in antiphony. Actually, only the Finger sonata for trumpet, oboe and basso continuo (No. 2) uses re-iterated antiphony to any extent. But here is a case of a 'contest' between two solo instruments rather than a single instrument scored with string accompaniment. This six-movement sonata is unusual, too, in that its one and only minor movement (the fifth) is not in the relative minor, but in the tonic minor, i.e. C minor.

In concluding our discussion of English trumpet music by Henry Purcell's contemporaries, there are two other points to be mentioned. The ancillary role of a pair of timpani, a normal adjunct in the German scoring for trumpets, and to a lesser extent in the Italian trumpet *Sinfonia*, is often wanting in English trumpet music. None of the previously mentioned MS. collections includes timpani. Henry Purcell uses timpani only occasionally and in music of a kind very different from the sonata-like compositions. In pieces from B.M. Add. MS. 49599, like the Finger sonata in C (No. 5) and the sonata in D (No. 3), as well as the Paisible sonata in D (No. 6), timpani might have been expected to accompany the wind 'band'. But there are no parts and no indications, either in the titles or in any of the lists of instrumentalists mentioned previously. In English seventeenth-century brass music, timpani seem to have been relegated to accompaniments only on festive occasions, and with trumpets in music of a ceremonial or fanfare character. With respect to the tonality of these sonatas (including the Finger sonata in C for violin and oboe (No. 8) which, as far as the oboe part is concerned, could have been played on a natural trumpet), there is an almost even division of sonatas in C and those in D. There are five sonatas in C major and six in D major. An explanation of this might have been found in a consideration of the kind of continuo instrument [16] intended and the standard of pitch at the time. But since the English adopted the Italian concert pitch method of notating trumpet parts, and since all the parts of a particular piece agree on key, transpositions due to lower tuned continuo instruments cannot be the answer. The standard trumpet was in D and sometimes E flat, but was capable of 'crooking' down to C. The choice of one key or another seems almost arbitrary, and perhaps an explanation is to be found in considering the keys of other music that might have been played with these pieces. Most of Henry Purcell's trumpet music is in D major, as are most continental pieces in the latter part of the seventeenth century. The C major pieces are exceptional only with respect to key. Thematically, they do not differ from the D major works, nor is there any difference in their inter-movement tonality relationships. The particular key, then, seems to be an unexplained choice on the part of the composers.

[16] Many printed and manuscript sources of seventeenth-century trumpet music specify *organo* as the continuo instrument intended for performance. B.M. Add. MS. 49599 merely states 'basso continuo'. Since both the organ and the harpsichord were used with equal frequency in the performance of English instrumental music, it is impossible to say which of the two would have been preferred.

THE TRUMPET MUSIC OF
HENRY PURCELL

9

Without exception, the most important and imaginative trumpet writing in seventeenth-century England (and in most other countries at that time) is to be found in the music of Henry Purcell. Almost all of his larger, dramatic compositions include trumpet parts, and his scoring displays a keen appreciation of the trumpet's musical and dramatic possibilities. Not only did he use the trumpet idiomatically as a fanfare and martial instrument of pomp and ceremony, but he also treated it melodically—extending its range and employing all of the continental idiosyncratic figures and techniques usually associated with later Central European composers such as Bach, Telemann and Stölzel. He gave further musical impetus to the trumpet and his trumpet parts by creating melodic material not only suitable for but also characteristic of the instrument. In composing a movement, aria or sonata with trumpet he displays a remarkable talent for and appreciation of the Italian technique of building the thematic structure and motives of the entire piece around the melodic possibilities of the natural trumpet. The principal themes of any piece with an important trumpet part are constructed so as to fit within the instrument's abilities and powers of execution. This somewhat predetermined method of thematic invention was mentioned earlier, but above all other compositions of English origin, Henry Purcell's music epitomizes the art of writing for the Baroque trumpet and shows great understanding on the part of the composer for the instrument's capabilities as well as its limitations.

The instrument required in most of Purcell's trumpet music is a trumpet in D. Conley (1959, pp. 3–11) makes the erroneous statement that Purcell wrote more often for a trumpet in C than in D. A closer look at the music shows that the actual number of pieces and movements with trumpet(s) favour the standard 8-foot diapason instrument in D described earlier. The table on pp. 207–11 is a comprehensive list of all Purcell's indicated scoring for the Baroque trumpet. The list includes the title of each work, the Zimmerman (Z) number,[1] and is arranged in chronological order according to the actual or probable date of composition given by Zimmerman; the volume reference in the Purcell Society edition is given, as well as the key.

As nearly as can be ascertained, Purcell is one of the earliest English composers to score for the Baroque trumpet. At any rate, there seem to be no earlier surviving manuscript or printed sources of seventeenth-century English trumpet music before his 'Birthday Song' (1690) for Queen Mary, *Arise my Muse* (Z 320). Purcell's older contemporaries, Locke, Child, Humphrey and Blow, may have scored for the trumpet before 1690, but no music by these composers written before that date and indicating the use of trumpets appears to have survived.

There is, however, a substantial corpus of iconographic as well as documentary and literary evidence showing that trumpets were frequently employed in England before the last decade of the seventeenth century. Francis Sandford's *History of the Coronation of James II*, for example, gives sufficient pictorial evidence of the function and use of the natural trumpet in English music before any scoring attributions that survive. But was the role of the instrument again merely that of a ceremonial-musical effervescence? And if not employed for fanfares alone, in what concerted music was it used? None of the nine anthems composed by Purcell, Blow, Turner, Lawes and Child for the coronation of James II in 1685 includes trumpet parts. Had the trumpeters shown in Sandford (1687) been playing only fanfare music during the festivities of James II's coronation, it is unlikely that any music would have been written down, since most martial-like trumpet music belonged to an unwritten, aural tradition.

The only other English composer at the time who shows any inclination in scoring for the trumpet is John Blow. His 'Marriage Ode' in D major is the only one of his works that might antecede the Purcell ode of 1690 in the use of trumpets. That work, however, is undated, and in their preface to its only modern edition Walter Bergman and

[*continued on page 211*]

[1] Zimmerman, 1963.

TABLE 2. INVENTORY OF PURCELL'S TRUMPET MUSIC

1690 *Arise my Muse* (Birthday song for Queen Mary) Z 320 XI, 36
  1 Symphony 2 Tr, 2 Vn, 2 Va, Bc
      a (Grave) D maj.
      b (Canzona) D maj. Sym. = Ov. Z 628
  3 b Ritornello D maj. 2 Tr, 2 Vn, 2 Va, Bc
  4 b 'Then sound your instruments' D maj. SATB, 2 Tr, 2 Vn, Va, Bc
  6 c Ritornello D maj. 2 Tr, 2 Ob, Bc

1690 *Of old when heroes thought it base* (Yorkshire Feast Song) Z 333 I, 1.
  1 Symphony 2 Tr, Str
      a (Grave) D maj.
      b (Canzona) D maj.
  3 a Ritornello D maj. 2 Tr, Str
  9 a 'And now when the renown'd Nassau' D maj. aa, 2 Tr
      b Ritornello D maj. 2 Tr
 13 b Ritornello D maj. 2 Tr, Str
 13 b 'Long flourish the city and county of York' D maj. SATB, 2 Tr, Str

1690 *The Prophetess, or the History of Dioclesian* Z 627 IX
  2 a Second music C maj. 2 Tr, Str, 3 Ob, Bsn
      b [Trumpet tune] C maj.
  7 b Symphony C maj. 2 Tr, Str
      c (Canzona) C maj.
  8 c Flourish ('With all instruments in C fa ut key')
      d 'Let all mankind the pleasures share' C maj. SATB, 2 Tr, 2 Ob, Str
 10 Ritornello C maj. 2 Tr, 2 Ob
 12 = 10
 21 Trumpet tune D maj. 2 Tr = Z(T) 697
 22 'Sound, Fame, thy brazen trumpet' D maj. a, Tr
 23 a 'Let all rehearse' D maj. SATB, 2 Tr, Str
      b 'All sing his glory' D maj. SATB, 2 Tr, Str
 24 Fourth Act Tune = 21 with addition of Str
 29 Paspe C maj. 2 Tr, Str
 38 a 'Triumph, victorious Love' C maj. atb, SATB, 2 Tr, 2 Ob, Str
      b Ritornello C maj. 2 Tr, 3 Ob, Str
      c = a
      f Prelude C maj. 2 Tr, Str
      g = a
      h Ritornello C maj. 2 Tr, 3 Ob, Str
 39 'Then all rehearse in lofty verse' C maj. SATB, 2 Tr, 3 Ob, Str

1691 *Welcome, glorious morn* (Birthday song for Queen Mary) Z 338 XI, 72
  1 Symphony 2 Tr, 2 Ob, Str
 13 a 'Sound all ye spheres' C maj. t, 2 Tr
      b   ,,   C maj. SATB, 2 Tr, Str

1691 *King Arthur, or the British Worthy*   Z 628   XXVI
    4 a Overture D maj. 2 Tr, 2 Vn, 2 Va
       b Canzona D maj. 2 Tr, Str
                     Ov. = Sym. Z 320/1a, b
  10 a Symphony C maj. 2 Tr, 2 Ob, Str
       f Ritornello C maj. 2 Tr, 2 Ob
  31 Fourth Act tune, 'Trumpet tune' C maj. Str only, but 1st Vn part is
          playable on a Baroque Tr
  33 Symphony C maj. Tr, Str and possibly Ob
  39 b 'Our natives not alone appear' C maj. SATB, 2 Tr, 2 Ob, Str
  40 Fifth Act tune, 'Trumpet tune' C maj. Str only, but as per No. 31
  (Appendix 4) 'St George the patron' C maj. s, 2 Tr

1692 *Hail, bright Cecilia* (A song for St Cecilia's Day)   Z 328   VIII, 1
   1 Overture 2 Tr, 2 Ob, Str
      a (Grave) D maj.
      b (Canzona) D maj.
      d Allegro D maj.
  11 a Prelude D maj. 2 Tr, Ti
      b 'The fife and all the harmony of war' D maj. a, 2 Tr, Ti
  13 'Hail, bright Cecilia' D maj. SATB, 2 Tr, 2 Ob, Bsn, Ti, Str

1692?*The Libertine, or the Libertine Destroyed*   Z 600   XX, 45
   2 a Prelude C min. 4 Flatt trumpets = Z 860/1
   3 a Prelude C maj. Tr
      b 'To arms, heroic prince' s, Tr
      c 'But battles' s, Tr

1692 *The Fairy Queen*   Z 629   XII
   3 Overture (Act 1) 2 Tr, Str
      a (Grave) D maj.
      b (Canzona) D maj. Ov. = Z(T) 692
   8 c 'Echo' C maj. 2 Tr, 2 Ob, Bc (the Tr and Ob are in unison)
  27 'Sonata while the sun rises' (Act IV) 2 Tr, Ti, Str
      a (Grave) D maj.
      b (Canzona) D maj.
      d (Allegro) D maj.
      f = d
  30 Entry of Phoebus D maj. 2 Tr, Ti, Str
  32 a 'Hail, great parent' D maj. SATB, 2 Tr, Ti, 2 Ob, Str
      b 'Light and comfort' D maj. SATB, 2 Tr, Ti, 2 Ob, Str
      c = a
      d 'Thou who giv'st all' D maj. SATB, 2 Tr, Ti, 2 Ob, Str
  37 = 32?
  42 a Symphony C maj. 2 Tr, 2 Ob, Str
      b (Symphony)
      c = a
  43 'Thus the gloomy world' C maj. a, Tr, 2 Vn
  48 a Prelude C maj. Tr
  50 e 'They shall be as happy'

1693 *Celebrate this festival* (Birthday song for Queen Mary)   Z 321 XXIV,
   1 Symphony 2 Tr, 2 Ob, Str   36
      a (Grave) C maj.
      b (Canzona) C maj.
   2 b 'Celebrate this festival' C maj. SATB, Tr, 2 Ob, Str
   4 b = 2b
   5 ''Tis sacred, bid the trumpet' C maj. s, Tr, (SATB)
  12 a 'While for a righteous cause' C maj. b, Tr
      b 'Let guilty monarchs shun' C maj. b, Tr
  14 b 'Kindly treat Maria's day' C maj. SATB, Tr, 2 Ob, Str

1693/4 *Light of the world*   (missing)   Z 330
    See pages 195 and 220 f.

  ? *Trumpet Sonata* in D maj. Tr, Str   Z 850 XXXI, 80

1694 *Te Deum and Jubilate* (in **D** maj.)   Z 232 XXIII, 90
   1 a Prelude D maj. 2 Tr, Str
      b 'All the earth doth worship Thee' D maj. SATB, 2 Tr, Str
      f 'Thou art the King of Glory' D maj. SSATB, 2 Tr, 2 Vn
      l 'O Lord, in Thee have I trusted' D maj. SATB, 2 Tr, Str
   2 a Prelude D maj. Tr
      b 'O be joyful in the Lord' D maj. a. Tr
      c   „   D maj. SATB, 2 Tr, Str
      g 'Glory be to the Father' D maj. SATB, 2 Tr, Str
    (h) 'Amen' D maj. SATB, 2 Tr, Str

1694 *Come ye sons of art* (Birthday song for Queen Mary)   Z 323 XXIV, 87
   1 Symphony Tr, Ob, Str
      a (Grave) D maj.
      b (Canzona) D maj. Sym. = Z 630/5a, b
   2 c 'Come ye sons of art' D maj. SATB, 2 Tr, 2 Ob, Str
   9 b 'See Nature' D maj. SATB, 2 Tr, 2 Ob, Ti, Str

1694 *Don Quixote*, Part II   Z 578 XVI

   7 a Prelude C maj. Tr
      b 'Genius of England' C maj. t, Tr
      c 'Then follow' C maj. t, Tr

1694? *Timon of Athens* ('The Masque')   Z 632 II

   1 Overture Tr, Str
      a (Grave) D maj.
      b (Canzona) D maj. Ov. = Z 342/1a, b (in C maj.); Z(T) 691
      d = b

1695 *Queen Mary Funeral Music*   Z 860   XXXI, 92

    1 March 4 Flatt Trumpets = Z 600/2a
    2 Canzona   ,,

1695 *Thou knowest, Lord, the secrets of our hearts*   Z 58C.   XXXII, 88
        SATB [4 Flatt Tr], [2] Bc

1695 *Who can from joy refrain?*
    (Birthday song for the Duke of Gloucester, July 24, 1695)   Z 342 IV, 1

    1 Symphony Tr, 2 Ob, Str
        a (Grave) C maj.
        b (Canzona) C maj. Sym. = Ov. (D maj.) Z 632/1a, b; Z(T) 691
    2 c 'Wond'rous day' C maj. atb, SATB, Tr, 2 Ob, Str
    6 'Sound the trumpet' C maj. a Tr
    7 'Chaconne' C maj. 3 Ob, Tr, Str
    8 d Ritornello C maj. Tr, 2 Ob, Str
        e 'Then Thames shall be Queen' C maj. SATB, Tr, 2 Ob, Str

1695 *Bonduca, or the British Heroine*   Z 574   XVI, 45

    15 a Symphony C maj. Tr, Bc
    16 a Prelude C maj. Tr, 2 Ob
        b 'Britons strike home' C maj. a, SATB, Tr, 2 Ob

1695 ?*The Indian Queen*   Z 630   XIX, 1

    4 a Trumpet tune C maj. Tr, Str = Z(T) 698
        i = a
        j = a
    5 Symphony Tr, 2 Ob, Str, Bsn
        a (Grave) C maj.
        b (Canzona) C maj. = Z 323/ 1a, b (D maj.)
    6 b 'We come to sing' C maj. SATB, Tr, 2 Ob, Str, Ti
    8 = 4a
    9 a Symphony C maj. Tr, Ti, Str
        c = 6b
    11 Second Act Tune: Trumpet tune C maj. Tr, Str
    16 Trumpet Overture D maj. Tr, Str

    Additional Act by Daniel Purcell

        Symphony C maj. Tr
        'Sound the trumpet' C maj.
        Trumpet air C maj.
        'Let loud Renown' C maj.

[2] See Zimmerman, 1963, p. 56; Westrup, 1937, p. 82–3.

Keyboard transcriptions of trumpet music, or keyboard music (with or without trumpet mentioned in the title) suitable for performance on a natural trumpet; arranged in chronological order by date of first publication and/or the Zimmerman (Z) number.

1689 *Musick's Handmaid*, Part II

Z 647
Z 648
Z(T) 678 'Cibell' This tune was used by D'Urfey in *Songs Compleat*, II, p. 70 with the text, 'Crown your Bowles, Loyal Souls'. It is also found in the Magdalen part-books (Cambridge, Fw. MS. 23E 13–17), '53rd Sett', No. 5 scored for trumpet and strings.
Z(T) 687
Z(T) 694
Z(T) 695

1690 Z(T) 697 = Z 627/21

1692 Z(T) 692 = Z 629/3a, b

1694?,
1695 Z(T) 691 = Z 632/1a, b; = Z 342/1a, b (C maj.)

1696 *A Choice Collection of Lessons for the Harpsichord or Spinet*
Z(T) 698 = 630/4a

The following pieces are listed in Zimmerman as spurious instrumental compositions. An examination of the sources cited by Zimmerman still leaves the question of attribution open for further investigation.

Z (S) 120 This 'air' ('Prince Eugene's March') is cited in Zimmerman as being written by Jeremiah Clarke and attributed to Purcell in Bodleian MS. Mus. Sch. E 397. It is found on page 45 of the manuscript without any attribution.

Z (S) 124 This is the well known 'Trumpet Tune' or 'March' in D maj. thought to be by Purcell (VI, 37). Zimmerman attributes this piece to Clarke. Bodleian MS. Mus. Sch. E 397, which is a late seventeenth-, early eighteenth-century manuscript keyboard book containing pieces by Henry Purcell, Clarke and 'Du Pairs' (Du Par or Dieupart), has this piece on page 32 with the following attribution: 'Trumpet tune by Mr Purcell.'

Watkins Shaw indicate that it was probably written after 1690.[3] The scoring—for alto and bass soli, solo trumpet and strings in the first movement, and for two trumpets, strings and chorus in the last—shows a generally more sophisticated understanding of the trumpet than does

[3] John Blow, *Marriage Ode*, Schott, London, 1954.

his only dated work with trumpets known to this writer: the verse anthem *I was glad*,[4] written for the opening of Christopher Wren's choir of St Paul's Cathedral in December 1697. In neither work does the composer take the first trumpet to the 16th partial. The highest trumpet tone in the 'Marriage Ode' is a b^1 natural (13th partial) for a trumpet in D, while the first trumpet (in C) in the verse anthem has a single b^1 natural (15th partial). But apart from range and technical considerations, the trumpet writing in the first movement of the 'Marriage Ode' displays a much smoother and melodically inventive use of the instrument. An unusual feature, too, is the integral part the solo trumpet plays with the strings in the overall contrapuntal texture. It is definitely treated as a melodic instrument, sharing almost equally the musical material with the violins, violas and bass instruments. If the work is post-1690, it is very difficult to imagine why Blow waited until he was over forty years of age to write a work not only with trumpets but also with a trumpet part of rather exceptional character. Perhaps he learned only from Purcell's example.

Irrespective of the earliest date that may be assigned to the first appearance of the trumpet in English music, it is obvious that the heaviest demands made upon the instrument were in the scores of Purcell. In the last two years of his life, 1694 and 1695, Purcell attached greater importance to the instrument than in any of his previous years as a composer. But it would be a mistake to regard his later efforts as superior to those of 1690 or 1691. Only in the frequency of its appearance, not in the style and quality of its musical material, does the instrument become more important. There are, for example, some very substantial trumpet parts in the 'Yorkshire Feast Song' of 1690 (Z 333); and the trumpet writing in *Dioclesian*, composed in the same year, is most exemplary. Certainly the third-act 'Sonata' in *The Indian Queen*, composed five years later, has some of the most beautiful and brilliant trumpet writing in the entire Baroque era and can only be compared with the *Sonata* in D major (Z 850), found by Richard Newton in the library of York Minster. But Purcell's genius for comprehending the use and function of a difficult and unique orchestral instrument can be seen in his trumpet writing from the first instance to the very last. In some cases, such as the scoring of his 1694 St Cecilia Day *Te Deum and Jubilate Deo* (Z 232), his treatment of the trumpet is hardly matched by anyone but Bach in its use as a melodic instrument and as an integral part of the orchestral texture. What never ceases to amaze

4 Oxford: Bodleian Library MS. Mus. Sch. C. 40, pp. 176–206. Score: aatb, SAATTBB, 2 Tr, Str, Org, C maj.

the performer in this composition is the ease and subtlety with which Purcell has combined the two trumpet parts. The second trumpet is often completely independent of the first and will often pass through and above the first trumpet, or else begin and end a thematic declamation well above the first. This rarely happens in either German or Italian seventeenth-century music. Not only were the dictates of the continental trumpet guilds severely critical of the second or third trumpets ever domineering or challenging the 'inalienable' rights and 'supremacy' of the first trumpet, but most composers—either by virtue of guild mandates or because of musical considerations—rarely allowed the second part to venture above the first, or be given the degree of independence encountered in Purcell's scores. In the next few pages we shall discuss Purcell's trumpet music as it occurs in various representative works written between 1690 and 1695.

For Queen Mary's birthday celebrations in 1690 Purcell composed *Arise my Muse* (Z 320); it is presumably his earliest work for trumpet, but the scoring is not unlike that in works composed some five years later. The trumpet parts in this work follow his usual scoring procedure of independence, i.e. separate treatment rather than frequent scoring in thirds. The ode begins with a 'Symphony' that is not mentioned in Zimmerman (1963) as being identical with the 'Overture' in *King Arthur* (Z 628). The scoring is somewhat unusual in that there are two viola parts. As in the case of the 'Sunrise Symphony' from the *Fairy Queen*, it is also unusual for a trumpet overture to begin with a one-bar bass introduction.

In the first section of eight bars strings answer trumpets in antiphony, except that the second viola is coupled with the trumpets. Zimmerman has labelled the two sections of this 'Symphony' '(Grave)' and '(Canzona)' respectively.[5] Actually the '(Grave)' section has a seven-bar introduction with the bass reiterating in an ostinato-like fashion the first bar motive. At bar eight this figure is then stated in the first trumpet and is answered on the third beat by the first violin, thereafter restated fugally in all the other parts. The opening motive given to the upper parts is incorporated into the countersubject of the second section fugal treatment of the initial bass subject. Both the '(Grave)' and '(Canzona)' sections are predominantly tonic oriented with the occurrence of two *g* sharps as the only accidentals in the entire 6/8 '(Canzona)' section. The highest note in either trumpet part is a single b^1 natural (13th partial) for the first trumpet in bar 18 of the '(Grave)'. The 'Ritornello', following the chorus

[5] Zimmerman, 1963, No. 320.

'All hail, Gloriana', is scored for two trumpets, two oboes and continuo. The oboe parts, with the exception of an occasional c^1 sharp, are treated in exactly the same way as the trumpets. The work is unusual for its type in that it does not close with trumpets, though it does end in D major and on a very encouraging and quasi-triumphant note in the text: '. . . go on, great Prince, go on.'

An especially interesting discovery was made while examining a most valuable source of the above ode—a manuscript score thought to be in Purcell's own hand. The score, which includes names of original performers, is bound with Purcell's MS. of his 1692 St Cecilia ode, *Hail, bright Cecilia*, as well as some of his anthems and those of Blow and Bishop. The manuscript is in the Bodleian Library at Oxford and is catalogued as MS. Mus. C. 26. Of particular interest is the cover or wrapper of the 1690 birthday ode, which, being bound in the collection as it was originally found enveloping Purcell's MS., has had the folio numbers 70 and 95 added to it. It first appeared to be a violin part from a collection of sonatas. On leaf 70, written in black ink and in a very bold hand, are the words, 'La bovil aqua Sonata Undecima'; on leaf 95, following the Purcell ode, appears, 'La Strozza Sonata Duodecima'. In a sepia coloured ink and in a different hand, possibly Purcell's own, are written the words 'Queens Birthday Ode Ap 30 1690', just below the sonata title on folio 70. A careful look at the contents of Italian instrumental music collections quoted in Sartori (1952, p. 424) indicates that two sonatas of the same name and numbers are to be found in the *Tavola* of the *Opera Decima Ottava* sonatas for two violins and continuo by Mauritio Cazzati. The music in the first violin part of these Cazzati sonatas, first published in Venice in 1656 and reprinted in Bologna in 1659, agrees with that on folios 70 and 95 in the Bodleian MS. Here is once again strong evidence that Purcell and his contemporaries were familiar with works of Bolognese origin.

Another work to appear in 1690 that makes important use of trumpets is Purcell's 'Yorkshire Feast Song' (Z 333). What a splendid, jubilant beginning! The 'Symphony', scored for two trumpets, strings and continuo, begins with an eleven-bar, fanfare-like section in D major. The first violins enter on the first beat with the theme, while the second trumpet, entering on the second beat, sounds the bold, repeated note triad figure of the counter subject. This is answered on the fourth beat by the first trumpet playing an inversion of the second trumpet entry, beginning on an a^1. The principal and secondary thematic material in this opening section is very close, and the use of trumpets is quite brilliant;

it is followed by a fugal section in 3/8, also in D major, forty-eight bars long, with the trumpets sharing the thematic material equally with the violins. The trumpet scoring is once again typical of Purcell: independent parts, each instrument treated as an individual contrapuntal voice with hardly any scoring in parallel thirds. The only non-harmonic tones in the trumpet parts are two g^1 sharps in the first and one in the second; with the exception of two b^1 naturals, the highest note in either part is a^1.

The short ritornello immediately preceding the alto and bass duet, 'Brigantium, honour'd', has the two trumpets doubled by violins, but it ends with another of Purcell's scoring devices—that of having the second trumpet above the first at the cadence. Although there is some writing in parallel thirds in the alto duet, 'And now when the renown'd Nassau', the two trumpets are frequently independent of one another. There is also one of Purcell's rare uses of the non-harmonic tone c^1 sharp, which occurs as a neighbouring tone of d^1 on two occasions in the second trumpet.

The close of this work, the chorus 'Long flourish the city and county of York', is interesting from the standpoint of the use of repeated notes in the trumpets. The four semiquaver d^2 occurs twice in each trumpet part, which are independent not only of one another but of the string parts as well. As a matter of fact, the violins never play as high as d^2. The use of repeated notes in the extreme upper register of the trumpet is very rare in the entire Baroque era. It is unlikely that such a figure would have been relished by the performer any more in Purcell's day than in our own!

The third work to be written in 1690, employing trumpets to good effect, is *The Prophetess, or the History of Dioclesian* (Z 627). The score requires larger orchestral forces than are encountered in any of Purcell's earlier compositions. In addition to the required strings, two trumpets and continuo, the score includes parts for bassoon and three oboes—treble oboes and a larger, tenor oboe, similar in size to a modern *cor anglais*. The movements with trumpets, from the 'Second Music' and 'Trumpet Tune' to a chorus and 'Ritornello', proceed unexceptionally. Playing in five of the first twelve numbers, the two trumpets in C have the occasional non-harmonic tone b natural and a single f^1 sharp in each part in the 'Symphony'. But there is nothing in the writing that is exceptional to those parts in the preceding works written in the same year. What is extraordinary is the sudden, unexplainable shift to D major in numbers 21 to 24. After the 'Butterfly Dance' at the beginning of Act IV, a movement for strings and continuo which begins and ends in C major, the predominant tonality of the entire work, there at once follows a 'Trumpet Tune' for two trumpets and continuo which is in D major. The rest of the act, consisting of an air and chorus and a reprise of the 'Trumpet Tune' with the addition of strings, is also in D major. The work then continues with Act v and the 'Masque,' which are in G major and back to C major respectively. Concluding the chorus 'Hear, mighty Love!' there is a shift again to D major after a cadence in A minor. But the scoring is without trumpets. A momentary change to D major following a cadence in A minor is quite plausible, but not so sudden a change from C major to D major. What is particularly difficult to explain is this most exceptional shift of tonality as regards the usual Baroque practice of keeping the trumpets in one key throughout an entire work. It occurs also in *The Indian Queen* and *The Fairy Queen*, and conversely, from D major to C major, in *King Arthur*. No other Baroque works observed, either sacred, secular or purely instrumental, ever change the pitch of the trumpets from that of their first appearance.

Following the various tonal excursions through arias, duets and choruses after the last appearance of trumpets, which were heard in the 'Paspe' and back in C, the work closes with the brilliant chorus 'Triumph, victorious Love'. Here, as separate choirs, the trumpets, the oboes and bassoon, and the strings answer one another antiphonally in the instrumental ritornelli. The first ritornello is an inverted anticipation of the first 'Trumpet Tune' in *The Indian Queen* (Z 630/4a):

Ex. 14. Purcell: *Dioclesian* (Z 627), 'Triumph, victorious Love' (first ritornello).

Ex. 15. Purcell: *The Indian Queen* (Z 630), first 'Trumpet Tune'.

After the chorus section in the tonic minor, which excludes the oboes and trumpets, there is a very unusual non-harmonic tone in the second trumpet in the second bar of the return to C major:

Ex. 16. Purcell: *Dioclesian* (Z 627), 2nd trumpet non-harmonic tone in 'Triumph, victorious Love'.

etc. The use of a passing *f* natural is very rare, not only in Purcell but in nearly all Baroque trumpet parts. It is the only non-harmonic tone for either trumpet in the entire chorus and is either a mistake or the sort of note Fantini says can be used if it passes quickly (*see* p. 84).

In the 'Birthday Song' of 1691, *Welcome, glorious morn. . . .* , the opening statement of the 'Symphony' is very similar to the closing ritornelli in the 1692 ode, *Hail, bright Cecilia.* The use of repeated notes, first in the trumpets, then in the strings, and finally in the oboes, with the entire orchestra playing a fourth and concluding statement, is a most grand and noble way in which to open such a work. Each choir has its turn at the ritornello but between the statements and at the very beginning are *tutti* chords which give this symphony a weight and majesty rarely encountered in any of the instrumental preludes of the other odes and birthday songs. The trumpets play a comparatively minor role in this work and exhibit a greater pairing in thirds than is normally found in Purcell's scores.

Although the trumpet writing in *King Arthur* is not exceptional, and the use of the instrument slight, there are some points of interest worth mentioning. The 'Overture' is identical with the 'Symphony' of the 1690 birthday song for Queen Mary, *Arise my muse.* It is the only section in D major in the entire work that is scored for trumpets, the other trumpet movements being in C major. As was mentioned in connection with the change of trumpet tonality in *Dioclesian,* it is atypical for a Baroque composition to require a trumpet of more than one pitch. In trying to explain Purcell's reasons, if any, for asking his trumpet players to change the 'crooking' of their instruments during a performance of these enigmatic works, one or more of the following is a possible answer: (1) that a preconceived tonal scheme was the overriding consideration; (2) that because of vocal ranges or the technical considerations of some instrumental parts, especially the strings, a choice of C or D major was to be preferred; (3) that a shift of tonality was chosen for its dramatic effect; or (4) because the composer wished to avoid the necessity of re-copying previously composed inserted music.

Like many 'Curtain Tunes' and act overtures, the Act iv 'Trumpet Tune' in *King Arthur,* scored for strings only, does indicate by its avoidance of non-harmonic trumpet tones that a trumpet may have been included. Such pieces may have actually been conceived for strings alone and carefully written so as to imitate a part otherwise thought to be for trumpet. It is the opinion of this writer, however, that in many such cases a specific scoring indication, i.e. 'Trumpet', 'Strings', etc. has been inadvertently omitted.

The solo in 'Appendix 4' of the Purcell Society edition of *King Arthur* (vol. xxvi), 'Saint George the patron of our Isle!', has one of the longest melismas for trumpet in the Baroque: the last sixteen bars are without a single rest.

In 1692 Purcell produced three works of notable interest for the Baroque trumpet: the great St Cecilia ode, *Hail, bright Cecilia* (the only one of four St Cecilia odes to require trumpets); *The Libertine*, a stage work based on Shadwell's libretto that requires not only a natural trumpet but also four 'Flatt' trumpets in the first prelude;[6] and an opera, *The Fairy Queen*, adapted from Shakespeare's *Midsummer Night's Dream* and written for one of the many Dorset Gardens Theatre productions in London. Although the trumpets do not appear with the same frequency as in many other works, Purcell's trumpet writing in *Hail, bright Cecilia* demands great virtuosity of the player and offers the listener some incomparable moments of beauty and excitement.

In the 'Overture' to Purcell's 1692 St Cecilia ode the opening section (Grave) begins with the often used dotted quaver-semiquaver figure which may be found in many trumpet 'Symphonies' and Italian-French overtures of the time.[7] In the canzona-like section that immediately follows, Purcell once again displays his technique of creating two trumpet parts of almost complete independence. Neither part has any more weight or importance than the other; nor do they have any more importance than the string parts, which are doubled in the overture by two oboes. Following a contrasting antiphonal section, Purcell concludes the 'Canzona' with a return of the initial statement in the first trumpet, which, without the appearance of the countersubject, serves as a recapitulation as well as a close to this movement. The next allegro in 3/8 is a brilliant piece of trumpet writing. A repeated note figure is used to good effect with the first trumpet being extended to the limit of its range in executing the motive on a high d^2. As was the case in the closing movement of the Yorkshire Feast Song (Z 333), only the trumpet is given this high, climactic note. The violins play almost throughout the entire overture in their

---

[6] The 'March' from the Queen Mary Funeral Music of 5th March 1695 is a less ornamented version of this prelude. Both the 'March' and the 'Canzona' for Queen Mary's funeral are scored for flat trumpets.

[7] Compare the opening section with Daniel Purcell's 'Sonata' in D major for two trumpets, strings and continuo—the first movement—in B.M. Add. MS. 49599, No. 18.

middle register. The composer has utilized the entire compass of the Baroque trumpet in this movement, from a to d^2. With the exception of a single g^1 sharp occurring in both trumpet parts in the 'Canzona', neither instrument is required to play any non-harmonic tones or difficult accidentals.

The two trumpets are not heard again until the countertenor solo 'The Fife and all the Harmony of War'. Here their appearance is marked by the first noted use of timpani in any of Purcell's music. This is somewhat extraordinary, particularly in view of the number of English literary and iconographic sources that depict trumpets with their ancillary pair of kettledrums. There are few examples of French or German seventeenth-century trumpet music that do not include timpani, and the Italians, though not disposed to score for timpani with the same frequency as the French or Germans, require a pair of drums more often than not in works with more than two trumpets. In 'The Fife and all the Harmony of War', the trumpets are given to more military-like fanfare figures with many repeated notes; if the trumpets are playing music more associated with the field and the military, it is understandable that timpani are required. The short bursts of trumpets constantly answering the voice part in this solo are stylistically similar to the Italian *Sinfonia* conception of trumpet-string writing. There is a greater use of parallel thirds and sixths in this movement with continuous *forte-piano* contrasts of dynamics. A very rare non-harmonic tone is found in the penultimate bar in the first trumpet part. The exceptional use of an f^1 natural in D major (a lowered tenth harmonic) in Baroque trumpet writing [8] is here necessitated by an exact imitation of the final countertenor cadence in the tonic minor. The basso continuo throughout this aria is associated with the voice part only; the timpani serve as the only bass whenever the trumpets play.

The ode is brought to an exciting close with the final chorus, 'Hail! bright Cecilia'. The momentary shift to the dominant, A major, five bars from the *fine*, is beautifully effected by the first trumpet having the chromatic alteration of g^1 sharp along with the oboes and violins. This somewhat out-of-tune eleventh harmonic is rarely used by Purcell, but always to good effect when he does so. He almost never introduces it unprepared, i.e. to be played by leap or as an isolated tone preceded by a long rest.

[8] The use of a flatted tenth (or sharpened ninth) harmonic in seventeenth-century trumpet music has been noted by this writer in the following rare instances: Mayr: *Regina Coeli* from his *Sacri Concentur*, 1681; Kerll: *Missa a tre cori*, 1687 (DTÖ, xxv, 1, 162); Kusser: *Erindo*, 1693, Act II, Scene 1; and Vejvanovský: *Sonata à 4 Be Mollis*.

Purcell usually allows the player the necessary moment to 'lip' the note so as to bring it to correct pitch.

The one trumpet work of Purcell to have thoroughly established itself in the present day repertory is the Sonata in D major. There are at least four recorded versions of this work, and more seem to be on the way. Discovered by Richard Newton in the library of York Minster, it exists in a manuscript score with the title: *Sonata by Hen: Purcell*. The parts are entitled, 'Trumpet, 1st Treble, 2nd Treble, Tenor, Bass'; the handwriting and other calligraphic elements would seem to indicate that it was copied in the late seventeenth century. It is catalogued as York Minster MS. M. 15. S., and it has already been suggested that it may be the overture to the lost ode *Light of the World* (*see* Chapter 8, p. 195).

The first movement, in three contrasted sections, begins with trumpet and continuo for the first three bars, with the strings answering in the dominant from bars 4 to 6. With a short-lived modulation to A major at bar 7, the trumpet and strings begin an antiphonal section returning to the tonic with the cadence at bar 11. This antiphonal section is a brief question-answer exchange between the trumpet and the other instruments (when the trumpet plays, the continuo is omitted, resting with the violins and viola), based on the succinct initial motive. At bar 11 the trumpet and continuo begin a contrasting motive in quavers, anacrusic, as in the beginning.

The strings again answer antiphonally with their last statement making the cadence on the super tonic. The trumpet interjects with a descending anacrusic figure rhythmically akin to the opening motive. This figure is treated antiphonally in rapid succession between the trumpet and strings with continuo. The momentum is slowed down at bar 16 with a crotchet movement in all parts and on a cadence in E moving to the dominant in the next bar. At this point the trumpet sustains an a^1 while the strings move through a typical Purcellian modulatory section in the minor dominant. At the cadence in the major dominant at bar 19 the pace quickens, with the violins introducing a semiquaver motive. Again, followed by an antiphonal treatment between the trumpet and the other instruments, the new motive begins to be compressed and shortened until all that remains before the cadence at bar 26 is a fragment of the original. Once more, the pace is slowed with an elongated contrasting movement in quavers, similar to the figure beginning at bar 11. There is a further slowing down at the final D major cadence from bars 28 to 29.

The whole character of the movement is based on an anacrusis rhythm, which gives it drive and vigour by avoiding the tedious accentuation of strong beats. Even the bass part is made to avoid strong down-beats by an almost continuous use of an up-beat impulse.

The only movement with an indication of tempo in the original MS. is the slow middle movement, 'Trumpet rest all ye adagio'. [9] The movement has little motivic character but is one of Purcell's exemplary pieces of harmonic writing. The first eight bars are nearly all in crotchet motion, with the first bar a B minor reminiscence of the opening statement in the overture to *Come ye sons of Art*. The extended modulatory progression beginning at bar 9 is a frequently-heard technique used by Purcell to add length '. . . by adroitly postponing cadences with suspensions and sequential devices'. [10] Following these tonal excursions, the movement closes with a cadence in D major.

The essence of the third and last movement in D major is found in the opening motive, first stated in fugal imitation by the strings. The trumpet enters at bar 13 with an exact statement of the subject, and nicely overlaps the strings before the element of antiphony is introduced at bar 17. This exchange between the trumpet and strings is based on two ideas: a triad figure in the trumpet and a semiquaver figure in the strings that is rhythmically related to the opening motive.

Following a semiquaver extension in the trumpet from bars 27 to 30, accompanied only by the continuo, there is a hemiola cadence in the tonic. The strings then continue with another fugal section, this time based on an inversion of the initial subject. The trumpet returns at bar 47 with the same material. The next antiphonal section is an inversion of the material from bar 17, but the strings answer with the triad figure, not the derivative semiquavers.

After a short *tutti* restatement of the initial subject, which makes a hemiola cadence at bar 62, the remainder of the movement is based on the antiphonal semiquaver string motive from bar 17. With all the instruments now playing the semiquavers, the strings and trumpet, answering in antiphony, ascend and descend on a tonic triad. The movement is brought to a close with the final outburst of the trumpet doubled by the first violin at bar 76.

With the exception of 3 g^1 sharps in the first movements, there are no non-harmonic tones for the trumpet in the entire sonata. The range is normal for Purcell's trumpet parts, not going below d or above b^1. There

[9] The Purcell Society edition gives only 'adagio' (vol. xxxi, pp. 88).
[10] Bukofzer, 1947, p. 214.

are frequent rests for the trumpet; it never plays more than three con-secutive bars in the first movement or more than six in the last. The longest statement for the instrument is in the opening three bars of the first movement.

This sonata is unlike most of Purcell's trumpet overtures and preludes, and is very much along the lines of the many seventeenth-century Bolog-nese archetypal concertos. Had Bukofzer [11] known of this piece when writing his comments about the relation of Purcell's overtures to the church sonata, he would have undoubtedly chosen it as the most out-standing seventeenth-century English example.

As an effective theatrical gesture, Purcell's use of the trumpet in *The Fairy Queen* and *The Indian Queen* is noteworthy. He underscores the mood and heightens the dramatic content of these two works with a judicious interposition of trumpet tone. Occurring less frequently than in *Dioclesian*, for example, the instrument has all the more impact in these two works. The writing itself is not unlike Purcell's other trumpet parts mentioned previously, but the theatrical implications are more evident.

In *The Fairy Queen* a pair of trumpets enhance the scoring texture with sparkle and dash, lending an appropriate tone colour to the overall mirth and light-heartedness of the work. In movements such as the overture, the 'Sonata while the sun rises' and the 'Entry of Phoebus' the trumpets are indispensable in helping to communicate the magic and delight of both plot and poetry.

Technically the parts offer few difficulties, and the appearance of trum-pets doubled with oboes in the fourth act 'Symphony' in C major has, by virtue of preceding tonalities, a more reasonable explanation as to the change of trumpet pitch with respect to the choice of key. But the trumpet part in the following 'song', also in C major, was thought by many to be an enigma, however erroneous that conclusion. In 'Thus the gloomy world' the solo trumpet is treated in as melodical a fashion as one of the preceding doubling oboes. The problem is concerned with what was assumed to be Purcell's use of a passing *a* and *b* natural on two occasions. Neither of these tones is in the required instrument's harmonic series, and both are very difficult to produce by 'lipping', if at all. The use of a *b* natural by the composer is rare, but the *a* occurs nowhere else in Purcell's trumpet music and almost never in the entire Baroque trumpet repertory.

It is possible that an oboe could have been used, or at least could have doubled the part for trumpet. But this is to be discounted after a careful

[11] Bukofzer, 1947, p. 214.

examination of the rest of the part: all the other notes, except the occasional but playable f^1 sharp, lie easily within the compass of a Baroque trumpet. One might say, by way of a rationalization, that Purcell frequently wrote 'trumpet parts' for oboes, at least by virtue of the absence of non-harmonic tones in some oboe parts which seem to have been written in an attempt to imitate the sound of trumpets. But this is specious reasoning. Another explanation, one that makes much better sense, is that some players, perhaps Mathias or John Shore, who are known to have performed Purcell's trumpet parts, could have produced some semblance of tone for such notes, and since they are passing could at least have created the impression that they were played.

Without venturing an opinion as to the method of performing these non-harmonic tones, Philip Conley (1959, p. 4) mentions Purcell's supposed use of '. . . a single appearance of A between the sixth and seventh partials, and B between the seventh and eighth partials . . .' at bars 11 and 108 in 'Thus the gloomy world' from Act v of the *Fairy Queen*; he also (*ibid.*, p. 7, Ex. 10) supplies a musical example of the particular passage. Maurice Peress (1961, pp. 124–5), in claiming to be able to produce non-harmonic tones on a severely restored and undated Wilhelm Haas trumpet, also mentions the same passage from Purcell's *Fairy Queen*: 'The availability of the lipped notes explains a number of otherwise baffling trumpet passages such as those found in Purcell's "Thus the gloomy world" . . .'. He too (*ibid.*, p. 126, Ex. 4) supplies a musical example of the passages in question. Neither author, however, seems to have consulted an original MS. source of the *Fairy Queen* in the Royal Academy of Music at London, which is the principal source used in the preparation of J. Shedlock's edition, revised by Anthony Lewis.[12] The Royal Academy source does not have the questionable notes; only the edition of 1903 has them, and in both cases they were misprints a minor third too low; the revised edition is correct in both cases.

Irrespective of supposed dilemmas and fictitious notes, the writing is delightful and with its musical cheer does dispel gloom and make the world '. . . begin to shine'.

Purcell's last full-scale work to employ the Baroque trumpet is *The Indian Queen*. Referring to the chronological list of his compositions with trumpets (Table 2) it is curious to note that in the last year and a half of his composing activities Purcell required only one trumpet. With the excep-

[12] *The Works of Henry Purcell*, vol. xii, *The Fairy Queen*. Edited by J. S. Shedlock, 1903; revised edition by Anthony Lewis, 1968, London.

tion of his St Cecilia Day *Te Deum and Jubilate,* his only service not composed for a liturgical use in the usual sense, Purcell does not score for more than one natural trumpet after *Come ye sons of art.* Whatever his reasons were for omitting a second trumpet, it is obvious that none of his odes and theatrical compositions of 1694 and 1695, except two choruses in the 1694 Queen Mary birthday song (*Come ye sons of art*), require more than a solo trumpet. So too in his scoring of the music to the libretto adapted from Dryden and Howard's tragedy, *The Indian Queen.*

Composed for a Drury Lane Theatre production in 1695, *The Indian Queen* is scored for a trumpet in C until the D major overture in Act III, which, as expected, is scored for a D trumpet. The first appearance of the trumpet is in the lively fanfare-like movement immediately preceding the prologue, 'Wake, Quivera'. This catchy little piece is identical with the 'Trumpet Tune' in the 1696 publication, *A Choice Collection of Lessons for the Harpsichord or Spinet* (Z (T) 698). The trumpet is next used in Act II, in the 'Symphony' in C major. The first two movements are the same as the D major 'Symphony' which begins the 1694 ode *Come ye sons of art.* In the former the trumpet is by itself, scored with a single oboe, violins and continuo. In the later 'Symphony' in C it is doubled by the first oboe throughout with the second oboe alone on the second part. The rest of the scoring is identical with that of the 1694 ode, except for a bassoon doubling the bass part. Unlike the earlier version, the second act overture is in three movements, a third contrapuntal movement in triplets having been added to the earlier material. The trumpet writing is not particularly difficult, although it is required to ascend to a high c^2 (a d^2 in the 1694 version) at the end of the first movement. With the exception of a single f^1 sharp in the 'Canzona', there are no other difficult notes for the trumpet.

Purcell doubles the first violin and first oboe with a trumpet in the following chorus, 'We come to sing great Zempoala's story'. Here a pair of timpani make their first of only two appearances in the opera. The next use of trumpet and drums is in the short and lively 'Symphony' at the end of the second act.

The trumpet is not heard again until the significant 'Trumpet Overture' in Act III. Following the G minor ending of the foreboding and portentous words of the God of Dreams ('All must submit to their appointed doom; fate and misfortune will too quickly come. Let me no more with powerful charms be press'd, I am forbid by Fate to tell the rest.'), the trumpet and strings pronounce the noble and stirring opening bars of the D major 'Trumpet Overture.'

With an ease and skill hardly met before, Purcell gives the impression of being completely unhindered by the inherent musical limitations of the natural trumpet. Working with only eight different notes he indeed makes '. . . a virtue of necessity.' [13] In the fourteen-bar introduction we hear a sweep, a gesture, carefully worked out in an overlapping contrapuntal treatment of all parts. The next section, a 'Canzona,' is longer than most of Purcell's similarly conceived movements. It gives the trumpet some sparkling passages against the background of a contrapuntal fabric. A remarkable piece of composition are the trumpetless nine bars of the concluding slow section.[14] Here are the implications of the misfortune and doom forbidden by Fate to be revealed by the God of Dreams. How ironic it is that this sonata-like overture with its intended implications is probably Purcell's last composition with trumpet. The additional fifth act by Daniel Purcell includes a trumpet, but the use of the instrument is almost trite in comparison with the example set before.

Late in December 1694 Queen Mary II succumbed to an epidemic of smallpox. It was only fitting that the composer who had written and dedicated to his queen nearly half a dozen birthday odes should have composed for her funeral early in the following March '. . . a plain, Naturall Composition; which shows the pow'r of Music, when 'tis rightly fitted and Adapted to devotional purposes.' [15]

The music composed by Purcell for the funeral procession was a *March* and *Canzona*; the former is an almost exact transcription of the fifth-act prelude in *The Libertine*. The pieces were used to accompany the bier on its way to Westminster Abbey, and were later sounded in the Abbey. The utter simplicity of these pieces is astonishing. How ironic, too, that the same music should have sounded for the composer's own obsequies in the Abbey the following November. As he knew the value of trumpets to quicken the spirit, so too did he realize their effect in a time of awful solemnity.

[13] Westrup, 1937, p. 140.

[14] Some performances have lately included the trumpet in the last nine bars. Any edition that alters the original scoring in this way does little justice to Purcell's intentions.

[15] From Thomas Tudway's remarks on Purcell's anthem composed for the funeral of Queen Mary, *Thou knowest, Lord, the secrets of our hearts*; in his compilation of church music for the Earl of Oxford (B.M.: Harley MS. 7340, fol. 3; music on fol. 264b). Quoted from Westrup, 1937, p. 83.

Purcell scores the *March* and *Canzona* for a quartet of 'flatt' trumpets and is said to have used the same instruments to accompany the anthem *Thou knowest, Lord.* . . . This is the instrument which, as described in Chapter 2, was the immediate predecessor of the English slide trumpet. All parts of the above compositions are easily played on an instrument with only four extended positions, i.e. the ability to lower the basic harmonic series by four semitones. Not even the number of positions Talbot [16] says are possible would be necessary. Assuming that the first or closed position produces an overtone series built on *C*, the upper three instruments would never have needed more than two extended positions, or a total of three positions (the second position produces a *d* sharp, or *e* flat). With a larger, deeper cupped mouthpiece, the lowest instrument could easily play the fourth part—the instrument requiring a total of five positions, however. Example 17 reproduces in a keyboard score the whole of the *March* with the position numbers for a flat trumpet in C

Ex. 17. Purcell: *March* for 'flatt' trumpets (Z 860).

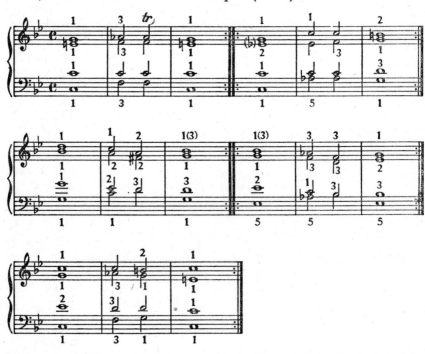

[16] Talbot, James: MS. on musical instruments in the library of Christ Church, Oxford (*see* Chapter 1, pp. 25, 28).

given above the first and third parts and below the second and fourth parts.

The *Canzona* presents no difficulties, especially if performed at a speed commensurate with the spirit of the occasion for which it was written.

Our purpose has not been to extol the virtues of Purcell's art. Others have done so more eloquently and his music speaks for itself. That some of his best compositions should have been scored with trumpets is indeed fortunate for our study. An attempt has been made to show in detail how an imaginative composer could write articulately and idiomatically for a difficult instrument with a highly specialized performance technique. Janus-like, Purcell faced two musical media: the service of worship in the church and the milieu of the restoration theatre. As the bulk of his stage works falls into the last six years of his life, so does his output of works with trumpets. The odes and welcome songs which are found in almost all phases of his career do not employ trumpets until his activities as a stage composer begin. That he was aware of the trumpet's dramatic possibilities is seen in its every use.

10 · THE BAROQUE TRUMPET IN FRANCE

In France the Baroque trumpet was nearly the exclusive property of great noblemen. For most of the seventeenth century little was written for the instrument outside the court and military establishment of the *Roi Soleil*. Because of its principally military function, the French repertory of the Baroque trumpet tends to be limited, and virtuoso music of the kind associated with seventeenth- and eighteenth-century German courts and towns is almost unknown. Nevertheless, there are a few instrumental as well as choral compositions from this period that have noteworthy trumpet parts. Before discussing these pieces, however, let us briefly examine the function and use of the trumpet in France before the reign of Louis XIV.

Little is known about French trumpet music before the seventeenth century, but it is certain that trumpets were used in France prior to 1600. Mention has already been made of two medieval French trumpet-makers (see Chapter 3, p. 54), and French iconography presents sufficient evidence to assume that, during the Middle Ages, trumpets were as much a part of court and military life in the Gallic territories as elsewhere in Europe. Before the centralization of the French government during the sixteenth century, with most court, military and cultural activities being carried on at Paris, there are a number of references to trumpets and trumpet playing in other French cities. References to musical activities in south-west France in the fifteenth century mention payment to trumpeters and other musicians on occasions of public rejoicing.[1] At Bordeaux, on 13th April 1407, payment was made by the town treasurer for repair of

---

[1] Artières, 1930, pp. 328–9 and *passim*.

'the silver trumpets, . . . so that the town can make use of them.' [2] Another reference relates to the surrender of the town's silver trumpets by the outgoing treasurer on 27th July 1407.[3] The 'Three Estates' of Bordelais and the commune of Bordeaux were summoned by these trumpets on important occasions.[4]

From the MS. records the accounts of the constables of Bordeaux (the chief financial officials of the English administration in Gascony) provide many valuable references about the function of trumpets and trumpeters in France during the first half of the fifteenth century. Between 29th September 1423 and 23rd March 1424 payment was made to two trumpeters for two proclamations made by them at Bordeaux, by order of the royal council there; payment was also made to 'Cook, trumpet' for taking letters to various captains of frontier garrisons.[5] On 10th May 1431 3s. sterling was paid to a trumpeter to proclaim a certain matter.[6]

In time of war, or when a city was threatened by invading armies, trumpeters seem to have been an important means of communicating information. On 7th July 1428 1s. sterling was paid to 'the trumpeter of the captal de Buch [a local nobleman] for trumpeting in the city of Bordeaux so that aid might be sent to Marmande,' which was apparently under siege at the time; later in the same year 'the trumpeter of Bordeaux' was paid to proclaim that assistance should be sent to another besieged castle.[7] In September 1436 the 'trumpeter of the lord of Montferrand' was paid for 'crying through the city of Bordeaux' in order that aid be sent to the frontier.[8] At Easter 1438 payment was made to the 'trumpeter of Domme,' for proclaiming that none of the king's subjects were to undertake pilgrimages to rebel areas.[9]

There are numerous other accounts of trumpeters being employed by French courts and cities during the fifteenth and sixteenth centuries, but nowhere else in France are the number of trumpet players as large as in

---

[2] *Archives Municipales de Bordeaux, Registres de la Jurade*, vols. iii and iv, Bordeaux, 1873–4: 'E plus, orderen que las trompas del argent, lo tresaurey fassa reparar, en tau partit que la bila s'en pusqua serbir.'

[3] *Ibid.*, vol. iii, p. 239.

[4] *Ibid.*, vol. iv, p. 288.

[5] City of Bordeaux, Public Record Office, E. 101/189/2, No. 14.

[6] *Ibid.*, E. 101/190/2, No. 7.

[7] *Ibid.*, E. 101/190/4, No. 23.

[8] *Ibid.*, E. 101/192/9, No. 27.

[9] *Ibid.*, No. 24.

Paris after the first quarter of the sixteenth century. At that time, during the reign of Francis I, the *Grande Écurie* was established. This was the select group of instrumentalists in the direct service of French monarchs from about 1530 until the end of the eighteenth century. Under the command of a *Grand Écuyer* the *Grande Écurie* was responsible for the performance of music in the king's private chambers and in his chapel; they were also required for various occasions and ceremonies, such as balls and masquerades, religious and state celebrations, special military events, and at any other times when music was desired by the king. During the two hundred and fifty years of its existence the *Grande Écurie* consisted of twelve trumpeters, four fife players, four drummers and timpanists, twelve musicians who were 'joueurs de violons, hautbois, saqueboutes et cornets . . . ,' as well as five krumhorn and *tromba marina* players, and six players of the musette and *hautbois du poitou*.[10] Nearly all the trumpet players of the *Grande Écurie*, as well as most of the other instrumentalists in the service of French kings from Francis I until Louis XVI, are mentioned by Brossard (1965).

The trumpeters in the *Grande Écurie* were exempt from various taxes, tolls and rates exacted from the French citizenry. Like the Central European *Kameradschaft* trumpeters mentioned in Chapter 5 (page 110 ff.), the trumpet players of the *Grande Écurie* were guaranteed various privileges by the king; but these were in effect more of a financial nature than were the privileges of the Holy Roman Empire.[11]

During the reign of Louis XIV the twelve trumpeters of the *Grande Écurie* were divided into two groups: 'quatre trompettes ordinaires ou de la chambre,' and 'huit trompettes non servants.' [12] The function and duties of each group, cited by Rhodes from the *Archives Nationales de France (carton O¹ 878)*, make it clear that trumpeters in France were required more often as ceremonial ornaments than as performers serving in a real musical capacity.[13] The comparatively few French Baroque works with trumpet parts of any consequence is a further indication of the importance placed in France upon trumpets as military-ceremonial instruments, at a time when the Baroque trumpet was enjoying enormous success as a concerted musical instrument in other European countries. It was not until the latter half of the seventeenth century that French composers

[10] Ecorcheville, 1901, p. 625.
[11] *See* Rhodes, 1909, pp. 25–6.
[12] Ecorcheville, 1901, p. 610.
[13] Rhodes, 1909, pp. 19–20.

began to score for the trumpet in any way commensurate with scoring procedures in Germany, Austria, Italy and Bohemia.

The most reliable indications of how the natural trumpet was used in France before the last quarter of the seventeenth century are the accounts of Pierre Trichet and Marin Mersenne. Both writers describe the trumpet in their respective treatises on musical instruments, compiled at almost the same time that Fantini published his *Modo* (described in Chapter 4). The earlier account is that of Trichet, the *Traité des instruments de Musique par Pierre Trichet, Bourdelois*. The author's original MS. is preserved in the Bibliothèque Sainte-Geneviève (MS. 1070); a modern French edition has been prepared by Lesure,[14] from which was made the English translation, given below, of the information concerning the Baroque trumpet.

Trichet was an 'Avocat au Parlement de Bordeaux.' Some of his literary works were published, including two tragedies, and he seems to have taken an interest in collecting musical instruments. An autograph inventory of some of his instruments is found in the Bibliothèque Nationale at Paris (B.N. MS. Yc 12590), and among the instruments listed are harpsichords, double reed instruments, four lutes, cornettos and a 'trompette de bois alpinoise'. His *Traité des instruments* is supposed to date from about 1631, four years before the earliest publication of Mersenne's *Harmonicorum*.[15] Trichet corresponded with Mersenne before 1635, and in the preface to the first part of his *Traité* he mentions Mersenne, as well as the *Syntagma Musicum* of Michael Praetorius. He claims to have had difficulty in obtaining the publications of Praetorius, especially the third volume of the *Syntagma* (*see* Chapter 6, pp. 135 ff.); Mersenne seems to have had the same difficulty.[16] Trichet's remarks on the trumpet are as follows:

In France and in many other countries trumpets are at present in use only among the cavalry and in warships intended for sea battles, leaving the drum and the fife for the infantry. The great lords also have trumpets played after meals. At Bordeaux our public administrators, known as jurats or aldermen, have two officers each of whom carries before them a long, straight silver trumpet with a banner attached bearing the arms of the city. But this takes place only on the occasion of city processions, bonfires and other public ceremonies. The same officers are employed with their trumpets to make public proclamations and are obliged to be present at executions of criminals condemned to undergo some punishment for their crimes as an example to their fellow men. . . .

[14] Lesure, 1955, pp. 283–390 ('Des Trompettes', pp. 384–6).   [15] *Ibid.*, p. 287.

[16] *See* Tannery & de Waard, 1946, p. 117; also Lesure, 1955, p. 291.

Before reaching the end of this account it is most fitting and relevant that I should say a word about the mute: a piece of wood fashioned by a turner which is inserted into the bell of the trumpet and blocks it so effectively that its sound is weakened and muted. In order that the mute may be pushed into the bell with ease it has a handle attached to it, made all of a piece with it, but very much narrower than the rest, although broadening slightly at the end. This mute must be bored and hollowed out completely from one end to the other, leaving the walls very thin so that it is slightly flexible and can adapt to the bell; indeed, this concavity is so necessary that without it the trumpet would not sound at all, as the air could find no way out. Thus it can clearly be recognized that the function of the mute is to narrow the opening of the bell and to weaken and muffle the sound, which, as it passes through a very narrow wooden passage, becomes less strident as if it encountered an obstruction. For this reason the mute is used when there is a risk of being discovered by the enemy or when it is wished to surprise them, as also when it is desired to decamp or secretly withdraw: an example which I must follow, lest I should bore those who have had the courage to follow me this far.[17]

Father Mersenne's remarks about the trumpet corroborate those of Trichet, especially those that suggest that a 'clarino' technique, i.e. skill in successfully producing the high and more melodic harmonics, was relatively unknown to French trumpeters in the first half of the seventeenth century. While suggesting this, Mersenne also mentions Girolamo Fantini, who is reputed to have mastered the art of 'clarino' playing:

I imagine that the most skilful trumpeters can control their breath in such a way that they can produce one by one all the notes from the third, or from the fifth, upwards; that is, they can go upwards step by step. This belief of mine is supported very strongly by a letter which the learned master Bourdelorius Medicus sent to me from Rome; in this he says that he has heard from Girolamo Fantini, the most excellent trumpet player in all Italy, that he is able to play all the notes on his trumpet, and that he has played them with the organ of Cardinal Borghese, on which Girolamo Frescobaldi, organist of the Duke of Etruria and of the church of St Peter in Rome, played very skilfully. But the Duke of Créqui was at that time performing an extraordinary diplomatic mission in Rome on behalf of our most Christian King Louis XIII, and Bourdelorius Medicus tells me that the Duke's trumpeters said that the notes produced by the trumpet player in question were false, confused and utterly disordered. Whatever the truth of the matter may be, whether these notes can be produced or whether they resist all efforts to play them, it is

[17] Trichet, *op. cit.*, folio 62; Lesure, 1955, pp. 385–6.

worth considering why these notes, and the intervals mentioned above, are not easy to obtain, so that someone may at length arrive at the true reasons for this phenomenon.[18]

In both his *Harmonicorum* and his *Harmonie universelle* (Paris, 1636) Mersenne also corroborates Trichet's remarks about the design and function of the trumpet mute and how it was used in France:

Now this mute is used when it is not wished for it [the trumpet] to be heard in the place where the enemy is, as happens in besieged towns and when one wishes to decamp. . . . Now it must be noted that this mute is pierced throughout from its mouth . . . to the end . . .; and that the edges . . . are very thin and slender so that they bend a little when they are pushed into the end of the bell. For if they were not hollow and pierced . . . the trumpet would not be able to sound, because the wind would not be able to come out. Thus it serves simply to make the opening of the [trumpet's] bell narrow, and to stifle the sound by the interpolation of the [narrow and hollow] handle. . . .[19]

Lastly, Mersenne again makes the point of the trumpet's less musical role in France, at least until 1636:

As to the use of the trumpets, they serve in time of peace and war for all sorts of public celebrations and solemnities, as is seen in marriages, banquets, tragedies and carrousels. But its principal use is destined for war, the greatest part of the actions of which is signified by its different tones. . . .[20]

Mersenne mentions the use of trumpets in carrousels. This was the most splendid use made of the Baroque trumpet in France during the seventeenth century. The earliest surviving music for these gargantuan 'horse ballets' is found in the Bibliothèque de Versailles, and in the Conservatoire de Paris collection of music now in the music division of the Bibliothèque Nationale at Paris. Both are exact copies, in score, of music used for various royal occasions during the reign of Louis XIV, and both contain pieces used for the carrousels of 1683 and 1686. The contents of both collections were compiled in 1705 by André Danican Philidor l'aîné, one of the most famous members of the *Grande Écurie*, a timpanist, krumhorn player and performer on the *tromba marina*. Although he was a famous instrumentalist in the *Grande Écurie* and a composer, particularly of

[18] Mersenne, 1635, p. 109.
[19] Mersenne (trans. Chapman, 1957), pp. 329–30.
[20] *Ibid.*, p. 331.

military marches, fanfares and trumpet calls, '. . . his chief claim to a place in musical history rests upon his work as a copyist'. [21]

As librarian of Louis XIV, André Philidor compiled volume upon volume of music for ballets and operas, as well as military music, carrousel accompaniments, and a host of other musical items. Copies of seventeenth-century pieces in his own hand, pieces that survive nowhere else, are preserved at Paris, Versailles and Tenbury. In the library of St Michael's College, Tenbury, for example, there are about 300 volumes in Philidor's hand, containing hundreds of works by Lully, Lalande, Campra and many other composers associated with the court of Louis XIV. The Philidor collections containing carrousel music are entitled:

Partition de plusieurs marches et batteries de tambour . . . fifre . . . hautbois . . . timballes et trompettes à cheval . . . fanfares de trompe . . . Recueilly par Philidor l'aîné . . . 1705.

The copy in the Conservatoire de Paris collection, now in the Bibliothèque Nationale, is a large MS. volume in 8° containing fifty-seven pages.

Exactly how many of the pieces written down by Philidor in 1705 were intended as carrousel music is not known; the name of the composer and the instrumentation are not always given. There are, however, several compositions included in the contents which indicate the composer and specifically mention either the 1683 or 1686 carrousels. The most interesting from our point of view is the suite by Lully for the 1686 carrousel, entitled:

'*Les Airs de Trompettes, timballes et hautbois faits pour Mr de Luly par l'ordre du Roy pour le Carousel de Monseigneur de l'an 1686.*'

There are four movements ('Prélude, Menuet, Gigue, Gavotte'), the first scored for four trumpets, four oboes and timpani; the last movement, the 'Gavotte', evidently lacks the third and fourth trumpet parts and second and third oboe parts as well. The fourth trumpet part in the other movements doubles the timpani part most of the time; it seems to have been notated an octave too low. Since it has only the notes C_1 and G_1, the usual practice, as explained earlier, would have been to use a trumpet with a large mouthpiece, but playing C and G. It is possible, however, that trombones were used, in which case the part would have been played as written. The fourth oboe part is obviously a bassoon part, having been written in the bass clef with a two-octave range from C_1 to c. All the trumpets would

[21] Fellowes, 1931, p. 116.

have been C trumpets, the usual pitch of the Baroque trumpet in seven-teenth-century France. Trumpets one and two are notated in the French violin clef—the normal method of notating French trumpet parts—and the third trumpet part in soprano C clef. The first oboe part is in French violin clef, the second oboe in soprano C clef, and the third oboe part is notated in mezzo-soprano C clef, but the part never goes below *b* natural, so it could have been played on the Hotteterre model two-key oboe.

The 'Prélude' is very noisy, with all the instruments hammering away in C major, the tonality of all four movements, for the first five bars. At the sixth bar there is a cadence on G, which was not prepared by its leading note. The next four bars are in the dominant and the oboes play by themselves, with *f* sharp occurring in the second and third parts. The movement continues with all instruments, again in the tonic, and there is a great deal of doubling of the first two trumpet parts with the first and second oboe parts. At the penultimate bar the trumpets and timpani con-clude on a minim, while the oboes proceed by themselves to the last bar.

Both the 'Menuet' and 'Gigue' are scored for all instruments; the latter is marked 6/4, but the note values show that 6/8 was intended. The missing parts of the 'Gavotte' are easily filled in, especially since the same parts have little more than tonic and dominant figures in the first three movements, which is, presumably, what they would have had in the last movement also.

One of the items in Philidor's 1705 collection does not have trumpet parts but it is, nonetheless, a most interesting piece. It is a duet for two players on four timpani. The piece was written either by André Philidor or by his younger brother Jacques (who was also a timpanist), or by both. It was written for the carrousel of 1683 and, most likely, played by André and Jacques—one playing a pair of drums tuned to G_1 and C, the other a pair tuned to E and G. Both parts are rhythmically interesting and together form a thematically well conceived, if not unique, composition.

Another work with trumpet parts in the Philidor MS. is the essentially three-part composition entitled *La marche royalle*. The instrumentation is not specified, but three trumpets and timpani were obviously intended. The piece is in only three parts, since what would appear to be the timpani part is doubled by what must be a part for bass-register trumpet. With the exception of six non-harmonic *b* naturals in the second part, all the notes in the other parts belong to the harmonic series of a C trumpet. As in most Baroque trumpet writing, the use of the non-harmonic tone *b* natural in *La marche royalle* is in a rhythmically weak position and as a lower neighbour tone of c^1. The second part is considerably more florid than the first and ascends to a^1, one note higher than the first part.

Since nearly all trumpet playing in France before 1700 was the province of military trumpeters, it is not surprising that trumpet parts in opera, ballet and vocal compositions by most French composers of the time are in the same style as military trumpet parts. The stylistic similarity is most evident in the works of Lully, particularly his *Te Deum* in C major and his operas *Cadmus et Hermione*, *Alceste* and *Amadis*. The trumpet parts of these works are almost lacking even the most basic 'clarino' writing. Often there is only one trumpet part, which is repetitious, narrow in range and devoid of any noteworthy chromatic alterations or non-harmonic tones. What can be exciting, however, is the frequent rhythmic vitality. What would be even more exciting is a performance employing the number of players per part originally intended. This is one of the distinctive features of Baroque trumpet playing in France—at least before the eighteenth century. Whereas most German, Italian and Austro-Bohemian trumpet parts were usually performed by only one trumpeter per part,[22] the French made an enormous noise, with sometimes as many as four players on a part. This, again, was a military tradition. Evidence of this is the large folio engravings known as the *Cabinet du Roi*, engraved in the seventeenth century by François Chauveau, Israel Silvestre and others, and showing vast numbers of trumpets and timpanists taking part in the famed carrousel of 1662[23]. Further evidence is the account of two timpanists playing on four drums and nine trumpeters performing in Lully's *Ballet des ballets* of 1670, with all nine trumpet players sometimes on a single part! [24] The descriptions and iconography of the sumptuous 'horse ballets' at Vienna under Leopold 1 make it clear that large numbers of trumpeters were engaged on those splendid occasions. But, if for no other reason than that competent trumpeters were not in such generous supply in most European courts and municipalities, it is unlikely that such wholesale doubling of trumpet parts was practised in chamber and

---

[22] For an indication that some non-French Baroque trumpet parts were performed by more than one player, at least in the Austro-Bohemian areas, *see* Chapter 7, pp. 174–5.

[23] *See* the *Cabinet du Roi*, vol. x, *Courses de Testes et de Bague, faites par le Roy, et par les princes et seignevrs de sa cour en l'année M.DC. LXII.*, leaves 9–16: 'Marche des Maréchaux de Camp & des cinq Quadrilles, depuis la grande Place qui étoit derrière l'Hotel de Vendome, jusqu'à l'entrée de l'Amphithéatre. . . .'

[24] Laurencie, 1906, p. 254.

sacred vocal music, or in most theatrical productions outside the court of Louis XIV.

A significant use of the Baroque trumpet is found in the works of Michel-Richard de Lalande and Marc-Antoine Charpentier. Both composers score for the trumpet more extensively and, perhaps, more imaginatively than Lully. Nevertheless, their style of trumpet writing is still closely associated with the military and the clichés employed by the trumpeters of the *Grande Écurie*. Seldom are there any melismatic and extended passages in the 'clarino' tessitura, as found in the works of Purcell, of most German composers and of the Italians writing in the last quarter of the seventeenth century. Like Purcell and most of the continental composers, however, Lalande and Charpentier more often than not score for trumpets in D. An explanation of this may be found in the purpose for which much of their music was composed and the places where it was performed. Unlike Lully's music with trumpet parts, which is, by and large, theatre music, most of the trumpet music of Lalande and Charpentier is chamber and church music, and is probably in D major because of the pitch of continuo instruments used during performance.

There is one possible explanation regarding the choice of tonality of Baroque compositions, especially those with trumpets, which has not been mentioned: a preconceived association of tonality with mood or *Affekt*. If we subscribe to the statements of Baroque composers and theorists alike, that the key or tonality of a musical composition is to be related to a particular feeling or emotion, then there is nothing haphazard in the choice of tonality and the use of trumpets. In Charpentier's *Règles de composition*, supposedly prepared for the Duke of Chartres in about 1690, the composer expresses the following views concerning the relationship of key with a specific mood:

Why [use] different keys ?

The principal reason is for the expression of the different passions for which the different feelings of the several keys are appropriate.

The key-feelings [abridged]

C major	Gay and warlike
D major	Joyous and very warlike
D minor	Grave and pious
E flat major	Cruel and harsh

F major	*Furious and quick-tempered*
A minor	*Tender and plaintive*
B minor	*Solitary and melancholy* [25]

It may be questioned whether or not the composer's theory was, in fact, practice. 'Assuming that Charpentier's table refers to the keys considered as predominant tonalities—what Rameau would later call *tons regnants*—and not as temporary tonal levels visited in the course of modulations, we find that the oratorios are in general responsive to the composer's theories on keys.' [26] This may, then, be one reason why Charpentier chose the key of D major when scoring for trumpets in such works as his *Te Deum* (Paris: B.N. Vm¹ 1138, No. 8754), his *Marche de Triomphe pour les violons, trompettes, timbales, flutes, hautbois* (B.N. Vm¹ 1138, No. 8748) and the *Epithalamio In Lode dell' Altezza Serenissima elettorale di Massimiliano Emmanuel Duca di Baviera. Concerto a cinque voci con stromenti* [1698] (B.N. Vm¹ 1138, No. 8715). The last work, in particular, would seem to substantiate the composer's theory about the relationship of key with a specific affection or mood, irrespective of the word 'Epithalamio' (a nuptial or wedding poem) having been added to the title by a different hand and, supposedly, at a later date. [27]

Charpentier's '. . . In praise of his most serene electoral highness Maximilian Emmanuel Duke of Bavaria' probably contains the most exemplary trumpet writing in the entire seventeenth-century French Baroque trumpet repertory. Composed in honour of the elector of Bavaria, the work is thought to have been written in 1698. [28] Since Charpentier was for a time in the service of the Dauphin, it was perhaps a combination of such circumstances as the marriage of the dauphin to Marie Anne of Bavaria (sister of Maximilian Emmanuel) and the favourable relations between Louis XIV and Maximilian after the Treaty of Rijswijk (1697) that provided the opportunity for the composition of . . . *In Lode* . . . *Massimiliano Emmanuel Duca di Baviera*. Maximilian's court and *Kapelle* moved to Brussels in 1692, and it is therefore most likely that Charpentier's cantata was performed in that city during the 1697–8 festivities celebrating Maximilian's peace with France. It is a glorious piece, and

[25] From Hitchcock, 1955, p. 58.

[26] *Ibid.*

[27] *See* Quittard, 1905, p. 324: 'Une main postérieure d'écriture très différente a ajouté, avant les premier mots, cette indication "*Epithalamio*".'

[28] Crussard, 1945, p. 79.

much of its impressiveness is a direct result of the way in which the composer scores for the pair of trumpets. The MS. score requires 'due soprani,
contralto, tenore, basso'. The 'stromenti' are 'Prima e seconda tromba;
taballi [sic, i.e. timballi]; primo violino, piva e flauto; secundo violino,
piva e flauto; cembalo, violone e fagotto'. The term 'piva' is most likely
synonymous with piffaro, which, in France at the end of the seventeenth
century, would probably have meant a type of oboe.

Settings of the Te Deum laudamus provided many opportinities for the
use of the Baroque trumpet in France toward the end of the seventeenth
century. Lully's requires two C trumpets; Lalande's superb Te Deum in
D major, although it has only one part for trumpet, would have required
several players in the many brilliant sections scored for the instrument.[29]
Charpentier's Te Deum in D major (B.N. Vm¹ 1138, No. 8754), like that
of Lalande, seems to have only one part for trumpet, but the score also
requires oboes, bassoon, timpani, strings and chorus; the trumpet part
would probably have required several players.

The Te Deum was usually performed at Paris in celebration of a French
victory on the battlefield, or upon the conclusion of peace terms with some
adversary of the French crown. On 16th November 1697, for example, a
Te Deum was performed in the Sainte-Chapelle '. . . pour la paix faite avec
l'Espagne'.[30] On 8th January 1698 the Te Deum in the Sainte-Chapelle
'. . . pour la paix faite avec l'empire' was probably performed to commemorate the treaty of Rijswijk and the peace made with Leopold I and
other members of the Grand Alliance.[31]

The records do not mention the names of composers or the orchestral
forces that may have been required. But toward the end of the seventeenth
century the operatic style of the French court had invaded the domain of
sacred music, and orchestral instruments were used to accompany the
voices in the Te Deum in the Sainte-Chapelle and in the Chapelle du
Louvre.[32] That trumpets were used in these performances may be inferred

[29] A score of Lalande's Te Deum will be found in the '6e Livre' of the 'Motets de feu M. de
Lalande . . . Livre 1 à 20', Paris, 1729, preserved in the Bibliothèque Nationale at Paris (B.N.
Vm⁷ 1117); another copy is in the Fitzwilliam Museum at Cambridge (No. 331, shelf No. 23 H
2 book 6). Several of the trumpet movements from the Te Deum will also be found in the MS.
collections of Lalande's music in copies by Philidor and others entitled Symphonies pour les
soupers du Roi (Conservatoire de Paris Rés. 581 vols. i, ii—now in the B.N.).

[30] Brenet, 1910, p. 259.

[31] Ibid.

[32] Brenet, 1909, pp. 285-6.

from the surviving choral works set to the text of the *Te Deum laudamus* that do have trumpet parts. It seems to have been a favourite musical form with many French composers at the time, and most required trumpets with the usual complement of strings and organ continuo.

With respect to the actual French Baroque trumpet parts themselves, in sacred as well as in secular and instrumental forms of music, there is one interesting, if not unique, possibility that has not been encountered in the trumpet music of any other European country: that trumpets of different pitch may have been used alternately in the same composition. In the Bibliothèque Nationale at Paris there is a small oblong MS. volume of music in score that was at one time in the collection of the Conservatoire. The shelf number is MS. Mus. Rés. 921 and its title would seem to indicate that it is another of the many Philidor collections compiled from various musical sources:

Pièces de trompettes/ de Mrs de la Lande, Rebelle et Philidor/ L'aisné . . . et enrichy des Pièces de Mr huguenet l'aisné compositeur des triots de trompette plus antien ordinaire de la Musique du Roy.

The volume consists of 283 pages, with some pieces by Lalande bearing the following titles: 'La fugue de M. de La Lande (2 dessus et basse de trompettes entrant en canon)' [p. 164], 'Grande pièce de M. de La Lande' [p. 166] and 'Menuet de M. de La Lande' [p. 181]. But the most interesting title in the collection is the 'Pièce a double trompette et le different ton et le gros basson de Philidor'. To account for the unusual number of non-harmonic tones in this piece it has been suggested that the title implies the use of two instruments, a trumpet in C and one in G.[33] It is unlikely that one player used two instruments of different pitch. With the number of players available in the *Grande Écurie* the most likely answer is that two players performed this piece, one using a C trumpet and the other a G trumpet. The work is undated, but it is not improbable that such a piece was performed at one of the previously mentioned carrousels and with several players to each part. That such a piece suggests the use of trumpets of different pitch in the operas of Lully, whose trumpet parts occasionally have unusual non-harmonic tones, is too bold an assumption. The difficulty with some trumpet parts found in the opera scores of Lully is that they were often intended also for violins. When such was the case, the trumpeters, who were probably playing from their own and corrected parts anyway—or, more than likely, from memory, since the

[33] Rasmussen, 1962, p. 9.

scenarios of many operas require the trumpeters on stage—would have played a harmonic series note that agreed with the other parts. Since non-harmonic trumpet tones are rare in French Baroque trumpet music, there is little reason to assume that the relatively few encountered in the works of Lully and others were not dealt with in the most obvious and simple way: by a competent player producing a note on his instrument that was harmonically agreeable.

With almost no tradition of 'clarino' playing having existed in France, and with trumpet parts being written in a simpler style than elsewhere in Europe, there was a far less dramatic stylistic change in French trumpet parts as the art of Baroque trumpet playing began to decline in the eighteenth century. Because of this and related reasons the French style of trumpet playing was readily adaptable to the new instrumental forms with their brass parts scored so as to punctuate the harmony and intensify particular rhythmic elements. Assimilation of the trumpet into the 'classic' symphony and opera orchestra was rapid in France once it had transcended its almost singular and restrictive role as a military instrument. The development of its younger rival, the horn, with its then simpler repertory and less difficult technique, was partially responsible for the diminished role of the trumpet in French music after the beginning of the eighteenth century. This shift from trumpets to horns following the reign of Louis xiv is also partially explained by the horn's more popular and pastoral associations toward the end of the seventeenth century. On the other hand, neither instrument ever had the demands made on it in France as were made elsewhere, certainly not until the era of Hector Berlioz.

 POST SCRIPTUM

Ten years is not a long time to write a book. Perhaps it is longer than the subject here deserves; then again, perhaps it is not nearly long enough. More than likely there are more studies needed to do the subject real justice. Whatever the case may be in this respect, it must be noted that the issues implied here have much more significance than could have been anticipated ten years ago. To say that this work is simply about an instrument and its music is to describe All Saints' Day as merely the 1st of November. To speak of the history of a musical instrument, a highly important and difficult instrument, is to speak of the history of a people, of their culture and peculiar customs. The trumpet is one of the oldest and relatively unchanged musical instruments since antiquity. From whatever prehistoric and natural ancestors it evolved—conch or *corno*, cupped hands or birch bark—the still primal trumpet, that 'harbinger of blood and death' (as Macduff vociferates in *Macbeth*), presents far too strong a profile to be disposed of in one short study, seen from so brief a chronological span and so particular a point of view.

Looking back over the last decade in which this work took shape and finally saw the light of day, the author now sees larger and more important social implications emerging out of what was first thought to be a rather narrow context. Regarding this as a first and rather tentative assault on merely the tip of a large, however proverbial, iceberg, it is my thesis that there is far more to a trumpet than meets either eye or ear. 'The trumpet shall sound' has more than superficial sensual significance; it takes in an entire world of associations. It has no less significance for us today than it had when first addressed to the people of Corinthia. For the trumpet is more than a musical instrument: it is an idea, a concept, with deeper allegorical associations. It is from this point of view that I now see so much more could have been said in a work that purports to treat the subject 'in fitting manner'. More, much more needs to be said, not only about a musical instrument but an ethos inextricably bound up with it and its history. The task remains for others and self to realize the host of relationships only touched upon here. It also remains to discover and, if possible, explain the *raison d'être* of a musical instrument with a gamut of social relationships as long as, if not longer than, most other acoustical systems, evolving with man and sharing his own long destiny from forest and savannah to court and choir gallery.

# APPENDIX

AN INVENTORY OF MUSICAL SOURCES FOR
BAROQUE TRUMPET arranged by composer in
alphabetical order beginning with the anonymous pieces

The following inventory of Baroque trumpet music was compiled with
the assistance of several persons over a period of ten years and represents
the most complete catalogue of its kind made to date. No doubt many
trumpet pieces will come to light in future, especially as some now
inaccessible libraries in countries like Spain and the Soviet Union make
their holdings known, but it is felt that the works accounted for here comprise by far the most substantial body of existing trumpet music composed
before the era of mechanization at the turn of the eighteenth century.
It has not been possible to examine every source given here. Some
important music libraries were destroyed as recently as 1945. The importance of these collections is verified by the published catalogues that
survive elsewhere. Some of these catalogues are highly descriptive of
specific musical works now lost, so descriptive in fact that it is often
possible to draw conclusions about a variety of musical and historical
considerations. While the number of these sources is rather small in
comparison with the number of compositions actually scrutinized, they
are nevertheless specified by an appropriate catalogue reference or some
other indication that will explain the origin of the particular entry. Most
entries of this sort are associated with the libraries of Wrocław (formerly
the city of Breslau), which were largely destroyed after the state of siege
was declared by the belligerents in the winter of 1945. When possible,
modern scholarly editions are noted with the particular sources.

For his special contribution of knowledge about many musical sources,
without which the following inventory would have been severely limited
in scope, the author would like to express his gratitude to Mr Robert
Minter, whose unselfish interest in Baroque trumpet music is in itself a
great tribute to the lasting fame and heritage of the once princely *Kameradschaft* trumpeters.

Anonymous

MS. (c. 1720) *Concinat pleba* (motet)   A, 2 Tr, Str, Org
　　　Bologna: S.P. Lib. A. 10.

MS. *Motteto à 4: ad melos cithare*   2 Tr, Str, Trb, Org, SATB
　　　Bologna: S.P. Lib. A. 8.

MS. *Concertino con 4 Violini soli . . . con Tromba*   4 Vn, Vc, Org (Tr missing)
　　　Bologna: S.P. Lib. A. 14.

MS. *Sonata a due Trombe*   2 Tr, Str, Org
　　　Bologna: S.P. Lib. A. 14.

MS. *Sinfonia*   2 Tr, 2 Ob, Str, Org
MS. *Sinfonia*   2 Tr, 2 Ob, Str, 'Tiorba'
MS. *Sinfonia a 6*   2 Tr, Str, Org
　　　Bologna: S.P. Lib. A. 15.

MS. *Sonata a quattro Trombe*   4 Tr, Str, Bc
MS. *Sonata con Trombe e Violini*   4 Tr, Str, Org
MS. *Sonata*   Tr, Str, Bc
　　　Bologna: S.P. Lib. A. 16.

MS. *Cantata a 4* 'Frode, Onore, Gloria, Otio 1687'   Tr, Str, 'Tiorba'
　　　Bologna: S.P. Lib. A. 13.

MS. *Sonata a 3:* Tr, Vn, Bass
　　　BQ III, 1959, p. 51

MS. *Sonata a 3: Violino, Clarino, Trombone* [and continuo] in C maj.
　　　Kroměříž: B IV 64 (by Schmelzer?)

MS. *Sonata* in C maj.   2 Tr, 2 Vn, Bc
　　　Kroměříž: B IV 121

　　　(There are several other anonymous works with trumpet parts
　　preserved at Kroměříž, with microfilm copies in the university library
　　at Syracuse, N.Y.)

MS. *Sonata* in D maj.   Tr, 2 Vn, Bass
　　　London: B.M. Add. MSS. 39565–7, 30839.

Anonymous (German)

MS. *7 Suonatine a due Clarini*   2 Tr (no accompaniment)
　　　Modena: Bib. Estense G 332

MS. *[24] Sonate da [due] Trombe Tedesche*
　　　Modena: Bib. Estense F 1529

Anonymous

MS. Suite in D maj. for Tr, 2 Ob, Str, Bc
　　　Paderborn: Erzbischof. Bib. (Mistakenly attrib. to Handel in
　　　the Hinnenthal ed. pub. at Bielefeld)

MS. *Sonata a 2 Tr* (col basso)
    2 Tr, violone, Bc.
    Vienna (Haas)

MS. *Sonata à 8 Istrumenti con tromba*
    Tr ò Crn, 2 Crn ò Vn, 2 Vn, A Vla, T Vla, Vc, violone, tiorba,
    bsn, org. Adag. C, Alleg. C, Adag. C, Alleg. 3/4, Largo (Tr solo)
    C, Alleg. C.
    Vienna (Haas)

MS. *Sonata à 6 con tromba*
    2 Vn, A violetto, Va, Tr, Basso, Org. Adag. C, Alleg. C, Grave
    3/2, Presto C.
    Vienna (Haas)

MS. *Sinfonia a due trombe*
    2 Tr, violone, Org. D maj. Grave C, Alleg. 3/4, Grave C, Alleg. C.
    Vienna (Haas)

MS. *Concerto Clarino Concertato*   Tr, Str, Bc
    Washington: Lib. of Congress

MS. *Geistliche Lieder*, No. 36 in C maj. s, b, Clar, Vn (Tr, Vn missing)
    Wolfenbüttel: Herzog August Bib. MS. Saml. 294.

MS. *Laudate Dominum omnes gentes*
    19 parts in 4°: S12 A T B conc.; SATB cap. (Voc, Vn), 2 Vn, Tr,
    Trb, Trb gr, 'trombetto e cornettino' 1, 2, Clar 1, 2, Bc pro org.
    Wrocław (Bohn, 1890)

MS. *Hallelujah. Es steht Gott auf*
    18 parts in fol., nr 2 in 4°: Chorus 1: 2 Vn; Chorus 2 & 3: SATB;
    Chorus 4: Clar, Crn ò Tr 1, 2, Tr, Trb, Trb gr; Crn 1, 2; sop cap
    chor 3; bc pro org; bc pro vlo
    Wrocław . . .

MS. *Hallelujah. Lobet den Herren in seinem Heiligthum*
    à 8 and 16 voc. 9 parts in fol: Chorus tubicinius: Clar, 'trada,'
    'ducata,' B and Vox vulgar; Cap. ch 2: SATB; Bc
    Wrocław . . .

MS. *Herr Gott Israel, es ist kein Gott*
    8 v 12 parts in fol.: Chorus superius: S 1, 2, 3 (Voc and Vn) B
    (Voc, Vn, 'trombetto'); Chorus inferius: SAT (Voc, Trb, 'trom-
    betto') B (Voc and Trb) A (Trb and 'trombetto'); 2 Bc
    Wrocław . . .

MS. *Hörett an die Aufferstehung unsers Herren*
    26 parts in fol.: T (Evangelista) S 1, 2, A T 1, 2; Cap.: S 1, 2, A T

1, 2 B, Va d gam 1, 2, Clar 1, 2, Trb 1, 2, Trb 1, 2, 3, Tymp; B cap.
pro org, bc
Wrocław . . .

MS. *Lobet den Herren alle Heyden.*

8 and 12 voc. 12 parts in fol., and 2 in 4°: Chorus 1, 2: SATB;
Cap. ch 2: SATB instr, Clar 1, 2
Wrocław . . .

MS. *Magnificat a 16 voc.*

28 parts in fol.: Chorus 1: S 1, 2 TB; Ch 2: SATB; Ch 3 instr:
Trb gr; Cap 1: SATB; Cap 2: SAB, Clar 1, 2, Bc pro Vlo, 2 tab 2 v
Wrocław . . .

MS. *Singet dem Herrn ein Neues Lied*

15 parts in fol. and 2 in 8°: Ch sup: Voc and Crn 1, 2 T B ; ch inf:
S A T (Voc and Trb) B and Trb gr; ch vn: S 1, 2 A B, Clar 1, 2,
Bc pro Vlo, tab 2 v
Wrocław . . .

(The eight entries above have been missing from Wrocław since
1945.)

Ahle, Johann Rudolf (1625–1693)

MS. Cantata

Marburg (Kassel: *Microfilm Cat.* Vol. 5, p. 135)

PR. *Neu-gepflantzter Thüringischer Lustgarten. Theil I. Mühlhausen, Joh.
Hüter . . . in Erfurt,* 1657. 2°

Nr 25 à 8: Wie ein lieber Buhle, per choros (Ius: 2 SATB; IIus:
A2TB), cum 2 trombetti ò crn ad placitum.
Upsala: Un Bib. 9 bks in fol.
Sig.: 700–708.
London: B.M. G. 74., G. 74. d. (1.).
ditto *Theil 2 . . . 1658.*
Nr 12 à 5: Ich will den Herren loben . . . 2 tr
Nr 28: Fürchtet euch nicht
Upsala: Un Bib. ditto 700–8.
London: B.M. G. 74. a. G 74 d. (2.)
ditto *Nebengang . . . 1663.*
Nr 8 à 7 & 12: Sie ist fest gegründet, Psalm 87 . . . 2 SATB 2 viol ò
trombetti. . . .
Upsala: Un Bib. Sig.: 700–1, 3–5, 8.
ditto *dritter u. letzter Theil 1665*
London B.M. G. 74. b.

d'Albergati, Pirro (1663–1735)
>   MS. *Sonata à stromenti con tromba*, with 2 cantatas 'à voc sola senza strum.'
>   Bologna: S. P.

Alberti, Giuseppe Matteo (1685–1751)
>   MS. Sonata for Tr, Str, Bc (missing?)
>   MS. Two sonatas for 2 Tr, Str, Bc
>   (One includes parts for two oboes.)
>   MS. *Sinfonia Teatrale* in D maj. 4 Tr, Str, Bc
>   Bologna: S. P.

Albinoni, Tomaso (1671–1750)
>   MS. *Sonata à 6 con tromba*
>   2 Vn Vla Ten Vla Tr Org. Allegro C, Grave C, Allergo 3/4.
>   Vienna (Haas)
>   MS. Concerto in C maj. Tr, 3 Ob, Bsn, Bc
>   Paderborn: Erzbischof. Bib. (mod. ed. Sikorski)

Albrechtsberger, Johann Georg (1736–1809)
>   *Concertino* . . . 1771 in E♭ [Tr], Str*
>   Budapest: N. B. 'Széchényi' MS. Mus. 2556.

Albrici, Vincenzo (1631–1696)
>   MS. *Sonata à 5*. 2 Tr 2 Vn Bsn Bc
>   Upsala: U. B.
>   (Mod. ed. in Schering, 1931, p. 278)

Aldrovandini, Giuseppe (1665–1707)
>   MS. Two *sinfonie* (score) in D major for Tr, Str, Bc
>   MS. Sonata in D maj. Tr, Str (parts)
>   MS. Two sonatas for 2 Tr, Str, Bc
>   MS. *Sinfonia* for 2 Tr, Str, Bc
>   Bologna: S. P.

Altenburg, Johann Ernst (1734–1801)
>   PR. *Concerto* for 7 'Clarini' and timpani in:
>   Altenburg (1795). Other works for two or more trumpets, at least one
>   of which is by Heinrich Biber, are included in this treatise.

---

* This is one of 4 concertos composed between 1769 and 1771, the others in D, F, and E respectively. Like the other three, it is probably for a *Trombula*, an Austro-Hungarian folk instrument not unlike the traditional Jews' harp.

Altenburg, Johann Michael (1584–1640)
>PR. *Gaudium Christianum* (with Tr and Ti) . . . *Jena, 1617*
>>Berlin: D. S. B.
>PR. *Hochzeitliche musicialische Freude* . . . *Erfurt, 1620.* 'Darein zugleich
>>ein Choral Stimme beneben 2. Clareten und 1. Trombet, gerichtet
>>ist. . . .'
>>London: B. M. [8 parts] C. 29a.

Anfossi, Pasquale (1727–1797)
>MS. Sinfonie   Ob Tr Vn Vla Bass
>>Dresden: (*QL*)

Arnold, Georg (fl. c. 1660)
>PR. *Missae, Psalmi et Magnificat. Op. 2*, Innsbruck, Michael Wagner, 1656
>>Nr. 2: Missa II à 9 vel 14 applicari potesti (2 SATB '2 viol e 2
>>clarinis vel cornetis necessariis sine reliquis instrumentis e vocibus')
>>Upsala: U. B. 12 bks in 4°. Sig.: 4–15.

Bach, Carl Philipp Emanuel (1714–1788)
>>A 'March' for 3 Tr and Ti, and various cantatas with trumpet(s),
>>some listed as 'Clarino,' in the Bibliothèque du Conservatoire
>>at Brussels. Noteworthy trumpet parts are also to be found in his
>>setting of the *Magnificat* and some of his oratorios.
>>*See* Wotquenne, 1905.

Bach, Johann Christian (1735–1782)
>MS. *Concerto/A Piu Stromenti con Oboè' e/ Corni da Caccia Obligati/del Sig.
>>Gio. Bach.*
>>Concerto in E flat maj. *Tromba Prima Obligata, Tromba Secunda
>>Obligata, Oboè Secundo Obligato* (first Oboe missing?), *Violino
>>Primo, Violino Secundo, Viola e Basso.*
>>Milan: Bib. d. Cons. B/36-21

Bach, Johann Sebastian (1685–1750)
>>Excepting Bach's F Major *Brandenburg Concerto* (No. 2) and both
>>D major orchestral suites (Nos. 3 and 4), all of his trumpet
>>writing will be found in his sacred and secular vocal compositions.
>>The various cantatas, Latin works, etc. with trumpet(s) are listed
>>in Neumann, 1947 (1967).

Baer (Beer) Johann (1655–1700): *see* pp. 115ff.
>MS. *Concerto* in B flat maj. for *Corne de Casse ed Posthorn*, 2 Vn, *Bassus
>>Continuo.*
>>Schwerin: Landesbib.

Banister, John (1630–1679)
 MS. Ten sets of Brawles, Dances, etc.—one for trpts. (?)
   Oxford: ChCh 1183
  The title of one piece in the above MS. collection of viol parts is
  'Trumpett.' It is a viol piece with one part missing. It is definitely
  not a trumpet piece—even for a flat trumpet, but rather the title of a
  piece for viols. (Similarly, see Robert Parson's *Fantasia* for viols in
  B.M. Add. MS. 31390 entitled 'Trumpett', which concords with
  another source in Christ Church, MS. 779–83, entitled 'The Songe
  called Trumpetts.')

Barratt (or Barrett) John (c. 1674–c. 1735)
 MS. *Sonata* Ob, Tr, Str, Bc
   London: B.M. Add. MS. 49599, No. 1.

Barsanti, Francesco (c. 1690–before 1776)
 PR. *Concerti grossi, Parte 2.* Tr, 2 Ob, 2 Vn. *Op. 3, Edinburgh 1743 (1800?)*
  Vla Bass Ti
   London: B.M. g. 261.

Beer (see Baer)

Bendinelli, Cesare (fl. 1600)
 Various 'suonate' in his *Tutta l'arte della Trombetta* (*see* Chapter 4).

Benevoli, Orazio (1605–1672)
 MS. 'Festmesse' and 'Hymnus' à 53 (includes parts for ten trumpets)
   Salzburg: Museum Carolino-Augusteum (see *DTÖ* x/1, Vol.
   20). (Original destroyed in World War I.)

Bernkopf, Anton (*fl.* last quarter of 17th century)
 MS. *Sonata* in D maj. 2 Tr, Vn solo, 2 Vla, Org.
   Kroměřiž: Liechtenstein Archive

Berthali (Bertali), Antonio (1605–1669)
 Many of his compositions which feature trumpets are preserved both
 at Vienna and Kroměříž.

Biber, Heinrich Ignatz Franz (1644–1704)
 MS. *Requiem à 15 in Concerto*
   SSATBB, 4 'Viole da brazzio,' 2 Tr, 3 Trb, 2 'Piffar: ad lib.', 6
   'voci à capella,' Bc
   Salzburg: Cathedral Archives
 PR. [12] *Sonatae/Tam Aris, quam Aulis servientes, ab Authore/Henrico J. F.
  Biber/Musico et Cubiculario/Salisburg: J. B. Mayr Anno M.DC.LXXVI.*
   2 Tr, 2 Vn, 4 Vla, Bc
   Kroměříž (Breitenbacher)
  (There are numerous other works by Biber with significant trumpet

parts, i.e. masses, motets, sonatas, and *balletti*. Most of these will be found in MS. copies in the Liechtenstein Archive at Kroměříž, with microfilm copies in the university library at Syracuse, N.Y.)

Biber, Karl Heinrich (son of Heinrich Ignatz) (*fl.* 1730)
    MS. Mass in C
        (Chor, 2 Vn, 2 Tr, Ti, Bc—1st Kyrie has some very jubilant fanfare passages for the trumpets)
    MS. Various sonatas 'con clarino', some dated 1729, including one for Clar, Vn, 4 Tr, Str
        Salzburg: Cathedral Archives

Biscogli, Francesco (*fl.* mid 18th century)
    MS. Concerto in D maj.   Tr, Ob, Bsn, Str, Bc
        Paris: B.N. (Conservatoire collection); also noted in Schwann Cat. 1959; *BQ* III, 1959, p. 51.
        (Only one other work by this composer has been noted to date, which is a string composition preserved at Lucca.)

Blow, John (1648–1708)
    MS. Verse anthem, *I was glad.* aatb, SAATTBB, 2 Tr, Str, Bc
        Oxford: B.L. MS. Mus. Sch. C. 40.
    MS. 'Marriage Ode'. ab, SATB, Tr, Str, Bc
        London: B.M. Add. MS. 31452 (MS. of Wm Croft)
        London: B.M. Add. MS. 31405 (omits concluding chorus)
        London: Gresham College V. 3.35 (also MS. of Wm Croft)
        (Mod. ed. Schott, London, 1954)

Böhm, Georg (1661–1733)
    Cantatas
        See *Gesamtausgabe*, Wiesbaden, B & H

Bond, Capel (before 1768–1790)
    PR. Concerto in D, in *Six Concertos in Seven parts*, 1766.
        London: B.M. g. 538.

Bononcini, Giovanni (1670–1747)
    PR. *Sinfonie à 5.6.7. e 8. Istromenti, con alcune à una e due Tromb* . . . G. Monti, Bologna 1685. *Opera Terza.* (Sartori (1952): 1685f)
        Sinfonia Quinta à 6. Tr, 2Vn, 2 Vla, Vc, Bc
        Sinfonia Ottava à 6.
            Tr, 2 Vn, 2 Vla, Vc/'con il terzo violino se piace'.
        Sinfonia Nona à 7. 2 Tr, 2 Vn, 2 Vla, Vc, Bc

Sinfonia Decima à 7. 2 Tr, 2 Vn, 2 Vla, Vc, Bc
>   Bologna: B.C. x 124 (Vn I missing). This is the only known printed source.
MS. Symphonies, op. III (ditto the above). Score in MS., copied by Brossard. One vol. in 12° obl.
>   Paris: B.N. Vm⁷ 1476 (last three sections of the *Sinfonia Quinta* not included)
MS. Two 'Cantatas' (really just arias) for Soprano and/or Tenor, Trumpet and Strings.
>   London: B.M. Add. MS. 31487

Boyce, William (1710–1779)
PR. 8 Symphonies. London, c. 1750; No. 5 in D major.
>   2 Tr, Ti, Str
>   London: B.M.
>   London: R.C.M.
>   Cambridge: Fw
MS. Various Birthday and New Year Odes, for George III, some with distinguished trumpet parts.
>   Oxford: B.L.

Briegel, Wolfgang Karl (1626–1712)
PR. *Musikalischer Lebens-Brunn. Darmstatt . . . 1680*, in 4°.
>   No. 5: Auff das H. Christ-Fest: 'Ich will singen von der Gnade' (Intrada: 2 'trombetti' and 2 'tromboni').
>   No. 75: 'Wol dem der ein Tugentsam Weib hat'
>   2 Tr, 2 Trb
>   No. 77 'Ich bin eine Blume zu Saron' 2 Tr, o Crn, 2 Trb
>   Upsala: U.B. 9 bks in 4°.
>   Sig.: 59–67.
>   Also complete or partial copies in Frankfurt, Berlin, London, Vienna, Königsberg (Kaliningrad), Kamenz.

Bruhns, Nicolaus (1665–1697)
MS. Cantatas, some with Trumpets
>   Berlin: D.S.B.
MS. *Canzon Spirituale*
>   Berlin: D.S.B.

Büchner, J. M. (*fl.* around 1600)
PR. 'Villanelli, Täntze, Galliarde, Courante', Nuremberg, 1614. This collection is mentioned by Menke (1934, p. 40) in connection with early trumpet music and is mentioned by Eitner (1900–4) as being in Paris (B.N.), but its whereabouts has not been traced to date.

Buxtehude, Dietrich (1637–1707)

> The following works with trumpets are to be found in the collected edition of Buxtehude's music (ed. by Gottlieb Harms and others, published at Klecken from 1925 to 1937 in seven volumes):
> *Ich bin die Auferstehung*
>> Bass solo, Str, Bsn, 2 'Trombetti,' 2 Crn, Bc
>> *Works*, vol. ii, p. 60 ff.
> *Benedicam Dominum*
>> 2 Chor (SSATB conc., SATB), Str, 4 Tr, 2 Crn, 5 Trb, Bsn, Bc
>> *Works*, vol. iv, p. 23 ff.
> *Aria sopra le nozze di Sua Maesta il Re di Svecia*   SSB, Str, 2 Tr, Bc
>> *Works*, vol. v, p. 96 ff.
> *Gott fähret auf mit Jauchzen*
>> SSB, 2 'Trombetti,' 2 Crn, 2 Trb/Vla, Bsn, Bc
>> *Works*, vol. v, p. 44 ff.
> *Auf! stimmet die Saiten*
>> AAB, 2 'Trombetti in sordino,' 2 Trb 'in sordino,' Bsn, Bc
>> *Works*, vol. vii, p. 116–17.
> *Mein Gemüt erfreuet sich*
>> 4 Vn, 2 'Trombetti,' 3 Trb, 3 Bsn, 2 'Flauti,' 4 Crn, SAB, Bc
>> *Works*, vol. vii, p. 10 ff.
> Cantata: *Ihr lieben Christen, freut euch nun* (includes 2 'Trombetti/ clarini in sordino')
>> *DdT*, xiv

Cafaro, Pasquale (1706–1787)

> MS. *Salve Regina*
>> sop., Ob ('Oboe ò clarino'), Tr, Vn, Vla, Bass, Bc
>> Milan: Bib. d. Cons.

Caldara, Antonio (1670–1736)

> MS. *Sonata* in C maj.   4 Tr, Ti, Str, Org
>> Vienna: N.B. Sm. 3617
> MS. *Sonata* in C maj. 3 Tr, Ti, 2 Vn, Bc
>> Vienna: N.B. Sm. 3616
> MS. 'Sinfonia' to *Adriano in Siria*, 1732, has f^2 in Clar 1.
>> Berlin-Dahlem: MS. 2770
> MS. 'Aria' in *Lucio Papirio Dittatore* 8 Tr, Ti, a, Bc
>> Berlin-Dahlem: MS. 2771
> (There are numerous works by Caldara with significant trumpet parts preserved at Vienna that were associated with the chapel or theatre of the Imperial Habsburgs.)

Capricornus (Bockshorn), Samuel (1629–1665)
>PR. *Opus Musicum*, Nürnberg . . . 1655.
>>Nr 1: *Kyrie* (complete mass: KGCSA)
>>>*à 5 in concerto.* SA 2 TB
>>>*à 5 in rip.* SA 2 TB, 2 Vn, 2 Clar, 3 Trb
>>Nr 7: *Te Deum Laudamus à 8 in conc.* 2S2A2T2B
>>>*à 8 in rip.* 2S2A2T2B, 2 Vn, 4 Clar, 20 bks in fol.
>>>Upsala: UB. Sig.: 723
>>>Breslau (Wrocław): UB
>>>Vienna: N.B.
>PR. *Geistlicher Harmonien mit zwey u. drei stimmen. Stuttgart, Rösslin, 1659.*
>>Frankfurt (Israel)—2 Vn, Bsn, Tr, Crn
>>Halle: 2nd & 7th part books
>>Breslau (Wrocław): MS. (missing since 1945)

Carcasio, Giuseppe (*fl.* 1700)
>MS. *Sonata d'Organo con Trombe, ed Oboe Del Sig: Giuseppe Carcasio.*
>>Two-stave keyboard score, no extra parts, with Tr and Ob entries indicated above the music.
>>Formerly Osek, now Prague XXXIV C. 221.

Cazzati, Mauritio (c. 1620–1677)
>PR. *Sonate à due, tre, quattro, e cinque, con alcune per tromba . . . G. Monti, Bologna, 1665.*
>>(Sartori (1952): 1665a)
>>Sonata à 5, 'La Caprara' tr, vn, 2 vla, vc, bc (with trombone)
>>Sonata à 5, 'La Bianchina' tr, vn, 2 vla, vc, bc (with trombone)
>>Sonata à 5, 'La Zâbeccari' tr, vn, 2 vla, vc, bc (with trombone)
>>Bologna: B.C. y 29.

Cesare, Giovanni Martino
>>(*QL*: Caesar(ius), Johann Martin. In 1612 he was a cornettist in the Bavarian *Hofkapelle*.)
>PR. *Musicali melodie per voci et instrumenti. Monaco, N. Hanrico, 1621.*
>>Regensburg: Proske Bibl.
>PR. *Beata es Virgo Maria.* Tenor, 3 Tr, Bc
>>Regensburg: P.B.

Cesti, Marc' Antonio (1623–1669)
>>*Il Pomo d'Oro* (produced at Vienna in 1667): 'Coro' 2 Tr, Str, Chorus; 'Sonatina' I & II 2 Tr, Str, Bc
>>>Mod. ed. *DTÖ* iii, 2 and iv, 2

Charpentier, Marc-Antoine (1634–1704)
> Various works with trumpet(s), i.e. a *Te Deum*, an *Aire de Trompette*, etc., in:
>> Paris: B.N. Vm¹ 1138.
> Various sections from his opera *Medée* have significant trumpet parts.

Clarke, Jeremiah (1670–1707)
> MS. 'Suite de Clarke,' transcribed or copied by Paisible   Tr, Ob, Str
>> Sections: ₵ (no title), 3-'Mourir,' ₵ 'Sibelle,' 2-'Rondeau,' 3-'Escosoisse,' ₵ 'Bourée,' ₵ 'Escosoisse,' 2/3-'Hornepipe,' 6/4-'Gigue.'
>> London: B.M. Add. MSS. 39565–7 (1st treb., tenor, bass), and Add. MS. 30839 (2nd treb.).

Colonna, G. P. (1637–1695)
> MS. *Sonata à 5 Tromba e Cornetto con Violini e B.C.*
>> Bologna: S.P.
> Opinion is divided as to the authorship of this work. The two wind parts are marked 'Tromba Pᵃ' and 'Tromba I'; there is no part marked cornetto, despite the title page indication.
> MS. (score) *Laudate pueri à 8 con stromenti e tromba 1676.*
>> Vienna: N.B. 15543
> MS. (score) *Beatus vir* [qui timet dominum]/*A cinque concertato/ Con Violini, Viola e Tromba/ Del Sig: Gio: Pauolo Colonna.*
>> Münster: Santini MS. 1164
>> Tenbury: S.M. 1217
> MS. (autograph score)
> *Domine ad adjuvandum. A 5* [voci] *concertato con tromba ed instrumenti. 1686.*
>> Vienna: N.B. 16771
> MS. (autograph score)
> *Laetatus* [sum] *à 5* [voci] *con istromenti e tromba. 1677.*
>> Vienna: N.B. 16780
> MS. (autograph score)
> *Motetto* [Lyrae, plectra, plaudite, canite] *à 5 voci concertato con stromenti e tromba per ogni tempo. 1688.*
>> Vienna: N.B. 16781
> MS. (score) *Confitebor* [tibi Domine in toto corde] *à 4* [voci] *con violini e tromba.*
>> Vienna: N.B. 18824
> MS. *Messa a 5 voci*
>> Vienna: N.B. 18940
> (This has significant trumpet parts; an opening 'Sinfonia' is for solo Tr with Str and Org.)

Corbett, William (c. 166°–1748)
    PR. 6 sonatas. Roger, Amsterdam (n.d.)
        2 Ob/Tr, 2 Vn, Bc
        Fétis-Bib.; Cobbett-Ch. Mus.
    PR. *6 sonatas with an overture and aires in 4 parts for a trumpet, violins, and
hautboys flute de allmain bassoons or harpsichord . . . Op. 3* (parts) *Walsh
and Hare, London* (c. 1708).
        London: B.M. (imperfect)

Corelli, Archangelo (1653–1713)
    MS. Sonata in D   Tr, 2 Vn, Bc
        (see: *MMR* 90, p. 217; *BQ* iv, pp. 103, 156).
            London: B.M. Add. MSS. 39565–7, 30839.
            Vienna: N.B. (Haas p. 169b, 'Sonata con aboe . . .')
    PR. Sonata in D (=above)
        London: Trinity Coll. of Music
        Naples: Cons. S.P.M.
    MS. 'Sinfonia' (=above)
        Tenbury: S.M. 1312
    MS. Concerto in D (authorship doubtful)
        2 Tr ò Vn, Vn 'primo principale,' Vc, Bc. Alleg. C, Grave (parts
missing), Presto ₵.
        Vienna: N.B. (Haas)
    MS. Sonata con oboe (possibly for tr) e violini
        (not the same as Haas, p. 169b).
        Ob, 2 Vn, violone (missing). Alleg. C, Alleg. 6/8, Largo (Vn solo)
C, presto C, Grave C, Alleg. 12/8.
        Vienna: N.B. (Haas, p. 168a).

Croft, William (1678–1727)
    PR. *Musicus Apparatus Accademicus*, 1713.
        Oxford: B.L. Fol. Bs. 49 and Mus. 20b.

Damian, P. S. P. (c. 1665–1729)
    MS. *Concerto, Veni consolator* Soprano, Tr, Org
        Warsaw: Modern ed.: *Monuments of Early Polish Music*, vol. 13.

Degli Antonii, Pietro (*fl.* last quarter of 17th century)
    PR. Motet, *Date Lilia date Rosas* b, *Tromba overo Violino primo*, Vn II, Vc,
Org
        Bologna: Museo Civico
        Zürich: Zentral Bib.

Draghi, Giovanni Battistia (*fl.* in London 1667–1706)
> MS. St. Cecilia ode of 1687, *From Harmony*, has parts for trumpets, which may be the first surviving source for their use in England before Purcell and Blow.
>> London: B.M. Add. MS. 33287

Eberlin, Johann Ernst (1702–1762)
> MS. *Te Deum, Dixit Dominus, Magnificat* in D   2 Clar, Ti, Str, SATB, Org
>> Salzburg: Cathedral Archives

Eccles, John (1668–1735)
> MS. *Sonata**   Ob/Tr, Str, Bc
>> London: B.M. Add. MS. 49599, No. 16.
> PR. *Third Book of Theater Musick . . . with trumpet tunes . . . I. Walsh, London, 1700.*
>> Durham: Cathedral Lib.
>> London: B.M. Hirsch II. 22b.

Endler, J. S. (before 1720–1729)
> MS. *Sinfonia* in F maj. '16 April 1748'
>> 2 Clar, 5(!) Ti ('à 5 F.G.A.B.C.'), 2 Fl, Str, Bc
> MS. *Sinfonia* in F maj. 25th August 1749
>> Clar, 2 Hn, Ti, 2 Vn, Cemb
> MS. *Sinfonia* in D maj. 1st Jan. 1750
>> 3 Tr, Ti, 2 Hn, Ob, 2 Vn, Bc
> MS. *Sinfonia* in D maj. 1st Jan. 1751
>> 3 Tr ('Clarino' I, II, 'Principale'), Ti, 2 Hn, Ob, 2 Vn, Bsn, Bc
> MS. *Sinfonia* in D maj. 25th August 1756
>> 2 Clar, Ti, 2 Fl, 2 Vn, Bc
> MS. *Sinfonia* in D maj.   2 Clar, Str, Bc
> MS. *Sinfonia* in E flat
>> 3 Clar, Ti, 'Violino Concertato' (in scordatura), Ob, Str, Bc
> MS. *Sinfonia* in E flat   2 Clar, Str, Bc
>> Darmstadt: Hessische Landes- und Hochschulbib. Nos. 1231/
>>> 2, 5, 13, 14, 15, 18, 12, 28.
> MS. *Ouverture a 6* in D maj.   2 Tr, Str, Bc
>> Darmstadt: H. L. u. Hb, 261/9.

Esterhàzy, Pàl (Paul) (1635–1713, grandfather of Haydn's patron, Nikolaus)
> PR. *Harmonia Caelestis seu Moelodiae Musicae Per Decursum totius Anni*

---

* From Eccles's *Judgement of Paris*, I. Walsh (n.d), No. 16, 'Symphony for Mercury.' This ode also contains an aria for s, 4Tr, Ti, Bc.

*adhibendae ad Vsum Musicorum AVTHORE PAVLO SACRIRO-
MANI IMPERŸ PRINCIPE ESTORAS DE GALANTA
REGNI HVNGARIAE PALATINO ANNO DOMINI
M: DC. CXI.*

(A collection of 55 Latin hymns, each set in strophic verse-ritornello
form, not unlike Krieger's *Neue Musikalische Ergetzligkeit* of 1684.)
Nos. 2, 22, 26, 29, and 53 with trumpets.

> Budapest: N.B. 'Széchenyi'
> Vienna: Gesellschaft d. Musikfreunde

Faber, Johann Christoph (*fl.* 1725)

MS. *Neu erfundene obligate Composition von diesem Numeralisch-Lateinischen
Alphabet . . . aus einem Zu Rovan in Frankreich par Barthelmy Fermier
1584 gedruckten Buch, titulirt: Les Bigarrures du Seygneurs des Accors.*
Clarino, 2 Vn, Vla, Vc, Cemb
Wolfenbüttel: Herz. B. (*QL*).

Fantini, Girolamo   Various sonatas, *passagii*, etc. in his *Modo* . . . (see Chap. 4).

Fasch, Carl Friedrich Christian (son of Johann) (1736–1800)

MS. *Concerto* in E maj. 'Clarino Concertato, Violino Concertato, Oboe
d'Amore Concertato'
2 Vn, Vla, Bc
Brussels: B.d.C. W.7308.

Fasch, Johann Friedrich (1688–1758)

MS. *Concerto* in D maj. for Tr, 2 Ob, Str, Bc
Darmstadt: Hessische Landesbibliothek (mod. ed. Sikorski)
MS. *Ouverture à 10* in D maj.   2 Clar, 3 Ob, Bsn, Str, Bc
Darmstadt: Hessische Landes- u. Hochschulbib. 1184/13
MS. Overture in D maj. 2 Ob, Bsn, Str
Darmstadt: Hessische Landes- u. Hochschulbib.

Feckler, J. P. (18th century)

MS. Opera *Applauso Poetico* includes an aria in D maj. for 'Tromba', alto
solo ('Fama') and continuo.
Vienna: N.B.

Finger, Godfrey (c. 1660–after 1723)

MS. Four sonatas with trumpet(s) and a sonata for 'A Violin/Hautboy
and Basse', which, excepting a single non-harmonic trumpet tone in
the oboe part, is playable on a Baroque trumpet.
London: B.M. Add. MS. 49599, Nos. 2, 3, 4, 8, 10

259

Fischer, Johann Kaspar (c. 1665–1746)
  PR. *Le Journal du Printemps.* Op. 1. Augsburg, 1695.
    2 tr, str, bc
      Upsala: U.B. (*DdT*, x)

F[oggia], Francesco? (?–1688)
  MS. *Sonata à 6 con Tromba di A. F.* in D maj.
    Bologna: S. P.

Förster, Christoph (1693–1745)
  MS. *Sinfonia a 8* 2 Tr, 2 Ob (2 Fl in the 2nd movement), Str, Bc
      Upsala: U.B. Caps. 15:14 (see Breitkopf, *Thematic Catalogue*, 1762, p. 7).

Franceschini, Petronio (c. 1650–1680)
  MS. *Sonata à 7 1680* in D Maj. 2 Tr, Str, Ob, Theorbo, Bc
  MS. *Domine à 5* (motet)
    Bologna: S.P.
  MS. Aria in D from *Arsinoe* s, Tr, Str
    Venice: Bib. Marciana

Fromm, Andreas (1621–1683)
  PR. *Actus Musicus de Divite et Lazaro. Das ist Musikalischer Abbildung der Parabel vom Reichen Manne und Lazaro. Lucae 16. . . . mit . . . bc und allerley instrumenten, als Orgel Clavicymbel, Laut, Violdigam, Trompeten, Paucken, Dulcian, Corneten, Posaunen, Geigen und Flöten. In 14 Stimmen auff 2 Chöre . . . Stettin, Gedr. Georg Götzken, 1649.*
      Breslau (Wrocław): U. B. (Bohn, 1883). Königsberg (MS.?)

Fux, Johann Joseph (1660–1741)
  PR. *Serenada à 8.* In: *Concentus Musico-Instrumentalis . . . Op. 1. Nürnberg, Felseckers Erben, 1701.*
    2 Tr, 2 Ob, 2 Vn, Vla, bass
    (Giessen?) (see *DTÖ* xlvii)
  (Various operas, masses, motets, and sonatas by Fux with notable trumpet parts are to be found in the Nationalbibliothek at Vienna. A rather extraordinary aria (in C) for trumpet, Ob, Bsn, Str, Bc and the character 'Bacco' (probably originally sung by a castrato) is found in the opera *La Corona d'Arianna*, preserved at Vienna, during which the trumpet ascends to e^2 and trills stepwise down to g^1. Another interesting piece of vocal-trumpet writing by Fux is *Plaudite, sonat Tuba,* for solo tenor, Tr, Str, Bc, pub. in *DTÖ*. His opera *Costanza e Fortezza* (composed for the coronation of Emperor

Charles VI at Prague in 1723) includes various ballet music, *sinfonie*, instrumental interludes and choruses with significant trumpet parts (mod. ed. *DTÖ* xvii).)

Gabrielli, Domenico (1659–1690)
MS. Six sonatas in D maj. for Tr, Str, Bc
MS. Sonata in D maj. for 2 Tr, Str, Bc
    Bologna: S. P.

Gilles, Bonaventura (*fl.* c. 1720)
MS. *Concerto à 9 strumenti.*
    2 Ob, 2 Tr, Ti, 2 Vn, Va, Bass
        Vienna: N.B. MS. 15940 (score) (*QL*)

Gillier, Mr le jeune
    (son of Jean-Claude, lived at the end of the seventeenth century. His Op. 3 was published for him in London—*QL*)
PR. *L'Hymnée royal. Divertissement présenté à la reine des romains. Les paroles de Mr S. J. Pellegrin. Paris, C. Ballard, 1699.*
    Duos and trios with arias for Tr, Ob, Fl, Vn, Bsn, Ti
    Paris: B.N.
    Vienna: N.B.

Gletle, Johann Melchior (1626–before 1684)
PR. *Musica Genialis Latino-Germanico.* Augsburg, 1675.
    contains duets for 2 Tr (orig. says '. . . Trombe Marine . . .'!)
    2 sonatas 2 tr, bc, 36 *stückeln*, 2 Tr
        London: B.M. c. 196. 7 parts (Vn II, which contains Tr II, is missing).
        Zürich: Zentral Bib. (complete)

Graupner, Christoph (1687–1760)
MS. 5 sonatas. Tr, Fl, Va d'am, Bc
MS. 114 Sinf.: 3 sinf. à 2 Clarin, 2 Fl, 2 Vn, Vla, Cemb, score.
    2 concertos in D maj. Tr, Str, Bc. (No. 1 pub. by Sikorski)
        Darmstadt: Hessische Landes- und Hochschulbibliothek (scores)

Grimm, Heinrich (1593–1637)
PR. *Wie schön leuchtet der Morgenstern*, 16 parts—
    3 chor. C I, II (Crn ò Tr)
        Breslau (Wrocław): U.B. (Bohn, 1883)
        Dresden: 8 parts in MS. (*QL*)

Gros, S[igismund?] (18th century)
>   *Concerto à Clarino Solo* in D maj.
>> Tr, Str, Bc
>>> Washington: Lib. of Congress.

Grossi, Andrea (*fl.* 1690)
>   He is possibly a grandson of Lodovico Grossi da Viadana.
> PR. *Sonate à 2. 3. 4. e 5. Instromenti . . . op. 3. G. Monti, Bologna, 1682.*
>   (Sartori (1952): 1682)
>>> Sonatas 10, 11, 12—Tr, 2 Vn, Vla, Bassetto, Org
>>> Bologna: B.C.

Guzinger, Johann Peter (*fl.* c. 1726)
> MS. *Concerto gr. à Vn:* 2 Tr, 2 Vn, Bc
> MS. *Concerto à Vn, I, II:*
>>> 2 Tr, 2 Vn, Bc (*QL*: inc.—Vn I, Tr II missing)
> MS. *Concerto Grosso* in C maj. Vn solo, 4 Tr, Ti, Str
>>> Wolfenbüttel.

Hainlein, Paul (1626–1686) Nuremberg trumpet maker (*see* p. 65)
> MS. Sonata 'Batallia.' 'Trommet', 2 Vn, 2 Va, Violon, Org
>> Upsala: U.B.

Hammerschmidt, Andreas (Brüx, Bohemia 1612–Zittau 1675)
> PR. *Kirchen und Tafelmusik* . . . Zittau 1662.
>>> Nr 2 'Sonata super Nun lob mein Seel, à 7'
>>> S solo, 2 Clar, 4 Trb, Bc
>>> Nr 20 'Sonata, Herr haddere mit mir meinen Hadderen, à 7'
>>> A solo, 2 Clar, 4 Trb, Bc
>>> Nr 21
>>>> Upsala: U.B. Sig.: 4–8, 15.
>>>> London: B.M.
>>> Breslau (Wrocław): U.B. (Bohn, 1883)
> PR. *Musikalische Andachten.* Theil IV. Freiberg u. Meissen (1654).
>>> Nr 37 'Veni sancte spiritus, à 3 Favoriti [ATB], capella à 5' (2
>>> SATB, 2 Vn/2 Tr *ad plac., cum & sine fundamento*).
>>> Nr 39 'Singet dem Herrn ein neues Lied, à 8 per choros' (SATB,
>>> 2 Tr, 2 Trb *ad plac.*).
>>> (Nr 11, 13?)
>>>> Upsala: U.B. Sig.: 700–709
>>>> London: R.C.M. I.A. 10.

PR. *Missae 5–12 et plurium vocum*. Dresden . . . 1663.

    Nr 15: Pro organo à 12: 2 SATB, 2 vn, 2 crn, 3 trb, 2 tubis e ti, cum Sanctus ad Praefationem (preceded by a sym. à 7).

    Upsala: U.B.

PR. *Lob und Danck Lied aus dem 84. Psalm, v. 1.2.3.4. mit 9 Vocal Stimmen, darrinen mit begriffen 3 Posaunen, 5 violen und 5 Trombeten. Auff die rühmliche Einweihung der wieder erbawten Kirche S. Elisabeth in Breslaw . . Gedr. zu Freybergk bey Georg Beuthern Im Jahr 1652.*

    Breslau (Wrocław): U.B. (Bohn, 1883)

Handel, George Frideric (1685–1759)

    Many vocal and instrumental works with important trumpet parts. *See* the various volumes of the *Handel Gesellschaft Ausgabe*, ed. by Friedrich Chrysander. A work by Handel not included in the collected edition is another overture to his oratorio *Resurrezione*: MS. Overture in D maj. to *Resurrezione posto in Musica Dall Sig Hendel detto il Sassone* (produced at Rome in 1708), 2 Tr, 2 Ob, 3 Vn, Vla, 'Viola da gamba', Bc.

    Münster: Santini collection MS. 1873 I. (Score)

Hart, Philip (before 1700–1749)

    MS. *Ode to Harmony* aria for b, 2 Tr, Bc

    London: B.M.

Haydn, Michael (1737–1806)

    MS. *Sinfonia* for 'clarino conc[erta]to' in C maj.

    Tr, Str, Fl

    Stift Göttweig

    MS. 'Concerto' for 'clarino solo' in D maj. (part of a larger serenade)

    Tr, Str, 2 Hn

    Stift Lambach

Hertel, Johann Wilhelm (1727–1789)

    MS. 4 concertos Nos. 1, 2 E♭ maj., No. 3 D maj. Tr, Str, Bc

    No. 4 E♭ maj., Tr, Ob, Str

    Sinfonia D maj. Tr, 2 Ob, 2 Bsn

    Brussels: B.C.

Hoefer, Anton (also Höffner, Antonius) (*fl.* 1670)

    MS. *Sonata à 8 ex C.*

    2 Tr, Bsn, 2 Vn, 'violetta,' 2 'braccie'

    Upsala: U.B.

    MS. *Missa Archi-Episcopalis à 19 Parti*

    Kremsmünster

Horn, Johann Kaspar (c. 1630–1685)
  PR. *Geistliche Harmonien. Sommer Theil. Dresden . . . 1681.* (At the end of
    the alto book is the following: 'Dass auch vor Schalmeyen die
    Flöten, und vor Trompeten die Cornetten usw. in Ermanglung zu
    gebrauchen solches und übriges alles stellet man zu des Hrn. Direc-
    toris gefälliger Anordnung . . .'*)
    Upsala: U.B.

Humphries, John (1707–1730)
  PR. Concerto for Tr, Str, Bc, Op. 2
    Oxford: B.L.
    Concertos in 7 parts, Op. 3:
      No. 1 2 Tr, Ti, Str
      No. xii Tr, Str
      London: B.M.
      Brussels: B.C.

Iacchini (or Jacchini), Giuseppe Maria (?–1727)
  MS. *Sinfonia con Tromba 1690* in D maj.
  MS. Two sonatas *con Tromba*, one dated 1695, in D maj. both with Str, Bc
  MS. *Sonata con Tromba . . .* 1695, in D maj. 2 Tr, Str, Trb, Org
  MS. *Sinfonia con due Trombe in D maj.* (with Str, Org)
    Bologna: S.P.
  PR. *Trattenimenti per camera à 3.4.5. e 6. . . . à 1. e 2. tr . . . Bologna, 1703.*
    Bologna: B.C.

Jan, Martin (*fl.* 1650)
  MS. *Ich frewe mich im Herren.* à 10 voc., 13 parts in fol. and 4 in 4°.
    Ch. voc.: 2 SATB; Ch. instr.: 2 Tr (Fl, Vn, ò Crn), Trb, Trb gr;
    2 Vn; Cap.: S (Voce e Crn) ATB; Bc pro org . . .
  MS. *Nun Dancket alle Gott,* à 7, 10, 15, 20, 22, o 25 v. (Musikalische Jubel
    Frewde . . . Herrn M. Valentino Thilone . . . gesetzet.) 7 parts in fol.
    2S (Crn, Tr, Fl, Vn) S 3, 4 Voc., AT (Voc, Trb, Vn, Fl) B (voc.,
    Trb, Vlo, Bsn), Bc
      Breslau (Wrocław): U.B. (Bohn, 1890)

Keiser, Reinhard (1674–1739)
    'Sinfonia avanti l'opera Croesus' 3 Clar, Ti, 'Zuffolo', Ob, Str, Bsn,
    Bc
    Modern ed. *DdT* 37–38.

---

* If shawms are not available use flutes, and if there are no trumpets use cornetti, etc., letting the
musical director make the most agreeable arrangements.

Keller, Godfrey (?–1704)
>PR. *Six sonatas. The first three for a Trumpett, Haubois, or violins, with Double Basses. The other three for two Flutes and two Haubois: or two violins with Double Basses . . . Amsterdam . . . Stephen Roger.*
>>Tr, Fl, 2 Ob, Vn 1, 2, tenorVn, Vc, Org
>>London: B.M. R. M15 i. 2.

>PR. *6 sonates . . . dédiés à la Princesse de Danemarc, les 3 premiers à 2 violons, un alte, une trompette et 1 basse. Amsterdam, E.* (?) *Roger* (c. 1699/ 1700). (the same as the above?)
>>(Fétis lists this as: *6 sonate a 5 cio e 3 a* . . . [2 Vn, Tr, O, Ob, Va, Bc]. *London, 1710; Amsterdam, Roger.*)
>>Upsala: U.B.

Kerll, Johann Caspar (1627–1693)
>Various sacred and secular works with important trumpet parts. For unusual non-harmonic tones see his *Missa a tre cori* (*DTÖ* xxv, 1, 162); see also p. 219.

Kern, Johann
>MS. *Sonata* in C maj.   Clar, 3 Trb, Str, Bc
>>Kroměříž: Liechtenstein Archive

Kerzinger, Pater Augustin (*fl.* mid 17th cent.)
>MS. *See* Breitenbacher, 1928.

Knüpfer, Sebastian (1633–1676)
>MS. A collected volume of cantatas in score, 22 pieces with German text à 3, 4, 5, 6 and 8 parts with Vn, Hn, Tr, Bsn, Trb, Crn, Bc—dated 1677.
>>Berlin: D.S.B.
>MS. *Victoria! Die Fürsten sind geschlagen*, à 13 to 18
>>5 Voc, 2 Vn, 2 'braccie' Bsn, 3 'Trombette'
>>Upsala: U.B.
>>See also *DdT* 58–9

Kopp, Georg (c. 1600–1666)
>MS. *Sonata à 6*   2 Tr, 2 Vn, 2 'braccie', Org
>>Kroměříž (Breitenbacher)

Krieger, Johann Philipp (1649–1725)
>MS. *Heut singt die wertha Christenheit*
>>SB, Tr, 2 Vn, Bc
>>Berlin: D.S.B. MS. 12152 (No. 6)

MS. *Cantate Domino canticum novum*
    4 Voc, Tr, 2 Vn, 2 Va, Bsn, Bc
        Berlin: D.S.B. MS. 12151 (No. 2)
MS. *Preise, Jerusalem, den Herren*
    SATB, 2 Tr, Ti, 2 Crn, 3 Trb, 2 Vn, 2 Vla, Bsn, Bc
MS. *Gloria in excelsis à 4 voci*
    (with Tr, Vn, 2 'Violette,' Bsn, Bc)
        Berlin: D.S.B. (*DdT* 53–4)
    See inventory in *DdT* 53–4, preface

Krieger, Johann (1652–1735)
    MS. *Arie 3. Also preisen wir die Zeiten*
        2 Vn, 2 Clar, B solo, Bc
    Vor der Oration: Frolocket Gott in allen Landen
        SATB, 2 Vn, 2 Clar, Bc
    Nach der Oration: Geht also geht ihr matten Seelen
        2 Tr, 2 Vn, SATB, Bc
    Arie 1. Das Jubelfest geht nun zu Ende
        SATB, 2 Vn, 2 Clar, Bc
        Zittau: S.B. MS. B.22
    MS. 33 parts bound together:
    Hallelujah, Lobet den Herren, à 32: 8v 4 rip
        2 Tr, Ti, 2 Crn, 3 Trb, 2 'Flauti', 2 Vln, Bsn, 2 Org, Cemb 1, 2, 3
        Upsala: U.B.
    PR. *Neue Musikalische Ergetzligkeit. Theil 1. Geistliche Andachten.* Frankfurt-
    Leipzig, 1684.
        No. 4: Über das Churfürstl. Symbolum: 'Der Herr ist mein
            Panier' b, 2 Tr, [Ti]*
        No. 10: Oster-Andacht: 'Der Heyland hat gesiegt' s, 2 Tr
        No. 13: Michaelis-Andacht: 'Der Drache bläset Lermen' b, 3
            Tr, Ti
        No. 14: Zu ende des kirchen-Jahrs: 'Gott lob, die Kirche blüht'.
            s, 2 Tr, Ti, 2 Crn, 3 Trb, 2 Vn, 2 Vln, Bsn
        No. 16: Auff ein Frieden-Fest: 'Ach zu hohen Frieden-Fürst'
            s, Tr, Crntini, Vn, Vlo
        No. 20: Nach der Trauung: 'Wol dir, der hast es gut' 2s, 2 Tr,
            Ti
            Upsala: U.B. Sig.: 827

Krieger (Johann or Johann Philipp?)
    See cat. of Royal Music coll. in B.M.

* There is mention of Ti, but no part.

Kuhnau, Johann (1660–1722)

    MS. Cantata *Muss nicht der Mensch*

      t, Tr, Vn, Bsn, Bc

        Oxford: B.L. MS. Mus. Sch. C.43. (Although no author is given, the title and instrumentation agree with those given in *DdT* 58–9, p. xlvi. See Chap. 6.)

      See inventory of works and some music in *DdT* 58–9.

Kusser, Johann (1626–1696) (Father of Johann Sigismund—*QL*)

    MS. 28 sacred songs for chorus, soloists, and instruments; 2 *Magnificats*; other pieces with instr. (Tr?)

      See: *QL*

Kusser, Johann Sigismund (1657–1727)

    MS.(?) *Arie, duette und Chöre aus 'Erindo.'* (1693)

    (See: *EDM* III)

Lalande, Michel-Richard de (1657–1726).

    Various sacred works with significant trumpet parts in Paris: B.N. Vm⁷ 1117. *Symphonies pour les soupers du Roi*

      Paris: Conservatoire Rés. 581.

Laz(z)ari, Fra. Ferdinando Antonio (1678–1754)

    MS. *Sonata à 6 con 2 Trombe e Stromenti*, in D maj.

      Bologna: S.P.

Legrenzi, Giovanni (c. 1625–1690)

    PR.(?) *Suonate da chiesa e da camera a 2.3.4.5.6. e 7. stromenti, con trombe e senza overo flauti, libro sesto, op. 17. Venice, 1693.*

      This collection is mentioned by Fétis (1877–80), but there is no known source to date.

    MS. *Laudate Pueri, à 5v* Tr, 2 Vn, 2 Vla, Bsn, Bc

      Berlin: D.S.B. MS. (old number 12720)

      Dr Karl-Heinz Köhler of the Deutsche Staatsbibliothek in Berlin has stated in correspondence that this MS. was one of the hundreds that were moved prior to the Second World War to various libraries throughout Germany. He was of the opinion that this particular MS. had been moved to Marburg. Herr Ramge of the music division of the Stiftung Preussischer Kulturbesitz, Staatsbibliothek, Marburg, first stated that this work was not in their collection; a subsequent letter stated that the work had been located and is now in the D.S.B. with the new MS. number, MS. Mus. P. 30229.

Lemaire, Louis (c. 1694–c. 1750)
    PR. *Fanfares ou concerts de chambre. Paris, 1743.*
        Vn, Fl, Ob, Bsn, Tr, Ti, 'musette,' 'vielle'
        Paris: B.N.

Leopold I, Holy Roman Emperor (1640–1705)
    MS. *Serenata: Psiche Cercando Amore* aria for a, Clar, Bc
    MS. *Sonata* 2 Tr, 2 Trb, Str from 'Hymnus' for church dedication
    MS. *Gloria* in C maj. Voc, Tr, Bsn, Bc
        Vienna: N.B. (mod. ed. in Guido Adler's ed. of music by
        Habsburg emperors, 2 Vols., 1892–3)
    MS. *Laudate Dominum* Clar, 'Canto solo', '4 Voci di Cap.', Org
        Upsala: U.B.
        Some works by Emperor Leopold with Tr parts are to be found
        at Kroměříž (Liechtenstein Archive).

Libertino (*see* Breitenbacher, 1928)

Linek (Linka), Jiří Ignác (1725–1791)
    MS. *Sinfonia Pastorale*, 1743. C maj. Clar. Fl, Ob, Str
        Various intradas and fanfares composed for the Coronation of Maria
        Theresa in Prague.
        Prague: Národiní Muzeum (*see* Schwann recording)

Linike, Johann Georg (*fl.* c. 1720)
    MS. *Mortorium à 5, 1737 Tromba con Sordini Hautbois con Sord* [sic] *Fl*[ute]
        Traversiere Violine con Sordini et Basso con Sordini
        Schwerin: Landesbibliothek

Lotti, Antonio (1667–1740)
    MS. *Missa à 3 cori*, Tr, Ob, 2 Vn, Vla, 3 Trb, Bc
        Berlin: S.B. MS. 13160 (*QL*)
    MS. *Missa Sapientiae*
        (K., Gl.) à 5, 6 Voc, 2 Vn, 2 Vla, 2 Ob, Tr solo, Bc
        Dresden: MS. A217c (*QL*)
    MS. *Requiem à 4 v.*, 2 Vn, Va, Tr, Org
    MS. *Dixit Dominus à 5 Voc*, 2 Vn, Va, Tr, Org.
        Dresden: Archiv der katholischen Kirche Schrank 2 (*QL*)

Louis Ferdinand, Prince of Prussia (1772–1806)
    MS. March, Tr, 2 Ob, Bass
        Upsala: U.B.

Löwe, Johann Jacob (1628–1703)
　PR. *Sonaten, Canzonen und Capriccen* . . . Jena, 1664.
　　(17 pieces in all comprise the contents of this collection.)
　　Vn, Vla, Clar, Bc
　　No. 16: *Capriccio à 2 clarini*, Bc
　　No. 17: *Capriccio Secunda à 2 clarini*, Bc
　　Upsala: U.B.

Löwenstern, Matthaeus Apelles von (1594–1648)
　MS. *Singet dem Herrn ein neues Lied*, à 8 v.
　　8 parts in fol. Ch. sup.: SAT (Voc, Crn, Tr) B; Ch. inf.: S (Crn,
　　Vn, Tr, Voc) A (Trb, Vn, Tr, Voc) B (Trb, Vlo grandi, Tr, Voc);
　　Cap.: S (Crn).
　　Breslau (Wrocław): U.B. (Bohn, 1890)

Lully, Jean Baptiste (1633–1687)
　MS. Carrousel music (1686)　4 Tr, 4 Ob, [bsn], Ti
　　Versailles: B.V. MS. 168
　　See various ballets, operas, etc., and *Te Deum*, in *Works*.

Mancini, Francesco (1672–1737)
　MS. *Missa a due Chori*　2 Tr, 4 Vn, Vla, Vc, Vlo, Org
　　Formerly Osek, now Prague XXXII-E-58.
　MS. Overture to *Hydaspes*　Tr, Str, Bc
　　London: B.M.
　MS. *Turno Aricino*, Act III: 2 arias with solo Tr, one in E flat for 'Tromba
　con sordino' in D
　　Münster: Santini MS. 2458

Manfredini, Francesco (1688–1748)
　MS. *Concerto con una o due Trombe*, in D maj.
　　Bologna: S.P.

Matteis, Nicola (*fl.* 1680)
　PR. *Ayres for the violin . . . a concert of 3 trumpetts*. . . . T. *Greenhill Scul, by
　Nicola Matteis of Naples* (n.d.) (Sartori (1952): 1685?)
　　London: B.M. Hirsch IV 1632 T-2
　　(NB: On page 76 in the second part of the volume ('other ayres and
　　pieces. . . .') may be found the following: 'Concerto di Trombe a tre
　　Trombette con violini e flauti. Trombetta Prima.' On the opposite
　　page (77) is the 'Basso della Trombetta. A. 3. Trombe.' The music for
　　trumpets continues through pages 80–81.)
　MS. 'Segnior Nichola's Trumpett' (see entry under *Nicola*).

Mayer, Martin (1643–1709)

> MS. *Hr. Martin Mayers seel: ehmahligen Organistens und Schuel-Collegens, bey der Kirchen zu St Bernhardin in der Neustadt.* . . .
> Nr 1 (1674): *Dom. I. Adv.* 'Hosiana dem Sohne David. 13 o 18 v.' 25 parts: 2 SATB nec., cap.; Vn 1, 2, 2 Clar or Crn, 3 Trb, 2 Pr, 2 Crn, trb 3; 2 Vlo, basso pro org
> Nr 5 (19th of Dec., 1676): *Weihnachten.* 'Es wird dass Scepter von Juda, à 12, 20 ò 23 v.' 22 parts: 2 SATB conc. and cap. (S 1, cap., missing); 2 Clar, 2 Crn, 2 Vn nec.; 2 'principal,' 3 Trb, Ti ad lib.; Bc (Vlo missing).
>
>> Breslau (Wrocław): U.B.(?) (There are some 80 other pieces by Mayer listed in Bohn, 1890.)

Meder, Johann Valentin (1649–1719)

> MS. *Jubilate Deo*   B, Clar, Vn, Bc
>> Upsala: U.B. (Kassel, Microfilm Cat. vol. 4)
> MS. Motet
>> (Kassel, Microfilm Cat. vol. 4)

Melani, Alessandro (1672–c. 1730)

> MS. Sinfonia a 5   Tr, 2 Vn, 'Leuto' (probably theorbo), Bc
>> Oxford: B.L. MS. Mus. Sch. D.260.
> MS. *Sonata a 5: 2 Violini, 2 Hautboies con Basson ed Organo del Sig‍r Alessandro Melani.* This is basically the same piece as the above *Sinfonia con Tromba,* but with an additional wind part and two added movements (a 'Grave' and a quick 3/8). This source has the designations 'Tromba 1.' and 'Tromba 2.' crossed out and the French designation for oboes added. The two extra movements may not be by Melani.
>> Upsala: ihs. 5:56.
> MS. *Cantata a voce sola* [soprano] *con Tromba* [and continuo].
>> London: B.M. Add. MS. 31487

Molter, Johann Melchior (*fl.* 1733)

> MS. 61 concerti a 5—some for Ob, Fl, Clarinet, Tr, St
> QL.
> There are five concertos for 2 Tr, Str; one *Sonata Grossa* with 3 Tr, Ti; and two *Sinfonie* for Clar, solo winds and Str preserved at Karlsruhe. The trumpet parts in these pieces, usually specified as 'Clarino', are often extremely high, particularly in the first movements, with passages demanding the greatest virtuosity.

Mouret, Jean Joseph (1682–1738)
    PR. *Suites de Symphonies . . . Fanfares pour des Trompettes, Timbales, Violons et Hautbois, avec une Suitte de Simphonies mêlées de Cors de Chasse, par M. Mouret, Musicien de la Chambre du Roy.* Paris [1729].
        Paris: B.N. 2 copies, H. 807 and D. 8493.

Mozart, Leopold (1719–1787)
    MS. *Concerto* in D (1762), Clarino, Str, 2 Hn
        Munich: B.S.B. MS. 1275
    MS. *Musikalische Schliffenfahrt* 3 Tr, Ti, Str, Ob, Hn
        Munich: B.S.B. MS. 5306

Mozart, Wolfgang Amadeus (1756–1791)
    Trumpet concerto, K. 47 (lost), mentioned in a letter of his father, Leopold.

Mudge, Richard (1718–1763)
    PR. Concerto in D major
        No. 1 in '*6 concertos in seven parts . . .*' *London* [1760]
        London: B.M. G. 254.

Nicola(?) (Probably Nicola Matteis. See separate author entry.)
    MS. Piece for trumpet solo (or Vn in imitation of a Tr?)
        Oxford: Christ Church MS. 731
        (Scored on two staves, possibly for Tr and Bc, but only the treble part is given, the lower stave being blank. It is the same as 'Segnior Nichola's Trumpett' in B.M. Add. MS. 34695—for organ—and B.M. Add. MS. 22099—for harpsichord.)

Niedt, Nicolaus (?–1700)
    PR. *Musikalische Sonn- und Fest-Tags Lust.* Sondershausen, Schönermarck, *1698.* 2°
        (NB: 'Avec les parties de violon I et II sont indiquées des clarini et avec celles de viola I et II des tromboni.') 11 books in fol.
        Upsala: U.B. Sig.: 858–868.

Orefici, Antonio (*fl.* c. 1690)
    MS. Sinfonia to the opera *L'Engelberta* (Vienna 1709?) in D maj.
        2 Tr, Str, Bc
        Vienna: N.B. MS. 18057
        (It has an unusual 3rd movement, Allegro, where the two trumpets have several passages with no accompaniment whatsoever.)

Orlandini, Giuseppe Maria (1688–c. 1750)
    MS. Overture to *Antigona* (1708), in D maj. 4 Tr, Str, Bc
        London: B.M. score
    MS. Sinfonia from *L'Adelaida* (1729) in D maj. 2 Tr, Str, Org

Paisible, James (1650–1721)
    MS. A Second English Partita. Tr, 2 Vn, Vla, Bass
    MS. A Third English Partita. Tr, 2 Vn, Vla, Bass
        Schwerin (see Kade, O. cat. under 'Bessibel')
    MS. Sonata 2 Tr/Ob, Str, Bc
        London: B.M. Add. MS. 49599, No. 10[a]

Pallavicino, Carlo (1630–1688)
    Sinfonia to the Opera *Il Diocletiano*, Venice 1675.
        Tr, 2 Vn, Bc. Mod. ed. Schering, 1931, p. 293.
    Sinfonia to *Gerusaleme liberata* (mod. ed. *DdT*)

Pepusch, Johann Christian (1667–1752)
    PR. *6 English Cantatas for one voice*—2 with Tr (1720)
        Oxford: B.L. Mus. 2 c.38.
    PR. *6 English Cantatas* (1710)
        London: B.M.
    PR. *6 English Cantatas* (1731)
        London: B.M.
    PR. *6 English Cantatas* (c. 1715), *2nd book. London, Walsh and Hare.*
        London: B.M. G 222/2: *Six English Cantatas for one voice four*
        for a flute and two with a trumpet and other instruments. Compos'd by
        J. C. Pepusch Book ye Second. London printed for J. Walsh . . . (Dedi-
        cated to the Duke of Chandos), n.d.
        Cantatas v and vi (pp. 28–46): Both scored for a treble (or tenor?)
        voice, strings, bc, with a solo tr added in the final section of each.
        Cantata v (p. 28–36): 'Kindly fate at length release me . . .' The words
        by Mr L. Theobold. Sections: Affetuoso, Adagio, Affetuoso,
        Recitative, Allegro. Trumpet in D notated at concert pitch (two
        sh.).
        Cantata vi (p. 37–46): 'While pale Britannia pensive sate . . .' The
        words by Mr Cibber. Sections: Recitative, Largo, Rec., Allegro.
        Tr in C.
        In both pieces the Tr rarely goes above a^1 or below *d*.
    MS. Concerto Grosso in D maj. Tr, 2 Ob, Str, Bc
        Rostock
    MS. Concerto in D maj. Tr, 2 Vn, Bc
        Zürich: Zentral Bib.

Perti, Giacomo Antonio (1661–1756)
    MS. Motets with Tr
    MS. *Sinfonia con Tromba*, in D maj.   Str, Ob, Org—Tr missing
    MS. *Sinfonia avanti la Serenata*, in D maj.   Tr, Str, Bc
    MS. *Sonata con Tromba*, in D maj.   Str, Tr, Org (missing)
    MS. *Sinfonia con due Trombe e Stromenti*, in D maj.
        Str, 2 Tr, Tbn, Org, Theorbo
          Bologna: S.P.
    MS. *Sonata à 4 Trombe Obuè e Violini*, in D maj.
        Str [with Ob?], 4 Tr, Org I, II
          Bologna: S.P.
          Dresden: Sächsische Landesbib., attrib. to Torelli.

Peter, Christoph (1626–1669)
    PR. *Geistliche Arien*. Guben, Gruber, 1667. 4°
        No. 4: 'Lobt Gott ihr Christen allerzugleich,' von Nicolaus
        Herrmann.
        A 2 'trombetti,' 3 Trb
        No. 10: Vom Heiligen Geist: 'Komm Gott Schöpfer Heiliger
        Geist,' von D. Martin Luther.
        S or T 2 'trombetti,' 3 Trb
        No. 16: 'Ich wil den Herren loben,' von Johann Rist.
        A 2 'trombetti,' 3 Trb
          Upsala: U.B. Sig.: 342–48. 7 books in 4°, cartoned.

Pezel, Johann (1639–1694)
    PR. *Bicinium* . . . (Bicinia for various insts. and bc). Leipzig, 1675.
        Nos. 69–74: Sonatinas à 2 'clarini,' Bc
        No. 75: Sonata-'clarino,' Bsn, Bc
          Upsala: U.B. Sig.: Utl. insts. mus. tr. 22:1–3.
          Vienna: N.B.
          Kassel, Microfilm Cat. vol. 3, No. 1/1047.
    MS. *Singet dem Herrn ein neues Lied. Cantata à 5 Voc.*
        2 Vn, 2 Vla, Bsn, 2 Clar, Ti, Org
          Berlin: D.S.B. MS. (score) 16900, No. 8.

Phengius, Johannes (*fl.* c. 1640)
    MS. *Frischauff ietzt ist es Singes Zeit.* 26 v. (34 parts in fol.:
        Ch. i di Viole (No. 1)—Vn 1, 2; Vla; Vlo; 'theorba' (on 2 staves);
        Bc—à 9 v., 2 tab. 2 v.
        Ch. ii di voci (No. 3) . . .
        Ch. iv di voc. conc. (No. 1) . . .
        Ch. v di trombi (No. 2)—Tr 1, 2; Trb piccolo; Trb 1, 2, 3; Trb
        majore; Bc tab. 2 v.

Basso continuo a 26 v., with the indication: Per Pian, Medio e Forte . . .) No date.

Performance notes on a folio sheet with the above indicates that there is a bc with each chor. Further material adds that instead of the clarini, cornetti may be used.

MS. Ditto above *à 20* (shorter version of the above).

Breslau (Wrocław): U.B. (Bohn, 1890)

Pignata, Pietro Romolo (c. 1660–after 1700)

MS. *Sonata con oboe* (Tr?) 2 Vn e basso

2 Vn, Ob (tr?), Org, Basso C maj.

This is identical to Torelli's *Suonata à Cinque 1693* in D maj. (G. 1).

Vienna: N.B. (Haas)

Poglietti, Alessandro (?–1683)

Various sonatas and *balletti* with trumpets may be found in the Liechtenstein Archive at Kroměříž, with microfilm copies in the university library at Syracuse, N.Y.

See Breitenbacher, 1928.

(Poglietti's *Sonata a 3: Cornetto: Flautto: Fagotto: con Organo* preserved at Kroměříž has the cornetto part written within the harmonic series of a natural trumpet. The part may therefore be played on a Baroque trumpet, in keeping with the 17th-century direction, 'per tromba overo cornetto'.)

Praetorius, Michael (1571–1621)

PR. *Polyhymnia caduceatrix et panegyrica. Wolfenbüttel, 1618–19.*

'. . . 1–21 und mehr Stimmen . . . auch Trommetten und Heer-Paucken . . .'

Västerås: all parts.

Stockholm: Royal Academy of Music lib.: 2 dus, 6 tus Decimus-quartus.

Comp. works vol. 17, p. 566 (ed. by Gurlitt): *In dulci jubilo, à 20* —4 Tr, Ti, Chor 1, 2, 3 and other insts.

Preluze, ? (possibly a corruption of Jean Prelleur, a French composer who worked in London in the 2nd half of the 18th century)

MS. *Sinfonia con Violini Ob: Tromb: Viola e Basso*

Dresden: Sächsische Landesbib. 2790/o/1

Prentzl, D(?) (*fl.* c. 1675)

MS. *Sonata* (in C) *à 2. instromenti.* Tr, Bsn, Bc. (before 1690).

Upsala: U.B. Sig.: Instr. mus. i hs 5:11.

Purcell, Daniel (c. 1660–1717)
> PR. *Judgement of Paris*, I. Walsh (n.d.)
>> London: B.M. Hirsch II. 749.
> PR. Additional act in Henry Purcell's *Indian Queen*
>> See Purcell Society edition, XIX.
> MS. Three sonatas: one for 2 Tr, Str, Bc and two for Tr (or Ob), Str, Bc
>> London: B.M. Add. MS. 49599, Nos. 9, 12, 14.

Purcell, Henry (c. 1659–1695)
>> See Table 2 (Chapter 9).

Querfurth, Franz (*fl.* 1750)
> *Concerto: Trompette, Violino Primo, Secundo a Basso* (with bassoon), *Ex Dis* (in E flat). Formerly Osek, now Prague MS. Mus. XXXII—A—505.

Rameau, Jean-Philippe (1683–1764)
> Various operas (*Les Indes Galantes, Les Fêtes de Hebé*, etc.) with notable trumpet parts preserved at Paris (B.N.), many pub. in mod. ed. in Rameau *Works*.

Rathgeber, Pater Valentin (1682–1750)
> MS. Aria No. 4, *Trackt des Ohren-vergnügen*, . . .: 'Die frohe Compagnie.'
>> Tr, Ob, Hn 1, 2, S, Vn, Bc
>> In *EDM* XIX, p. 170.

Rauch, Andreas (*fl.* c. 1630)
> PR. *Concentus Votivus sub serenissimi ac potentissimi Romano-* . . . *Anno 1634. Die 18. Decembris* . . . *Viennae, Gregorium Gelbhaar, 1635.*
>> (NB: 18 parts in fol. à 2 resp. one side of notation: Voce, 2 cornetti ò viol., due Capelle-I Chori V. 1. viola e V., Due Cap. II Chori, V. trb e V. (T. u. B.) Due Capelle III Chori, 2 Clarini, bassis pro Regente u. pro organo.)
>> Breslau (Wrocław): U.B. (Bohn, 1883)

Reinhart, Franz (?–1726)
> MS. *Sonata del Sigr: Francesco Reinhart S[ua] M[aesta] C[esare] Viol[inista]*
>> Tr, 2 Vn, Vc, Org
>> Vienna: Gesellschaft der Musikfreunde MS. XI 23450.

Reutter, Georg von [the younger] (1708–1772)
> MS. *Servizio di Tavola* [1], C maj.
>> 2 Tr, 2 Clar, Ti, 2 Ob, Str, Cembalo (clarino solo in Larghetto)
>> Vienna: Gesellschaft d. Musikfreunde (mod. ed. *DTÖ* xxxi).

MS. *Servizio di Tavola* [11] C maj.
    2 Tr, 4 Clar, Ti, 2 Ob, Str, Cembalo
MS. *Sinfonia* in C maj. 8 Tr (in 2 choirs), Str, Bc
    Vienna: Gesellschaft d. Musikfreunde.
MS. *Sinfonia* C maj.
    2 Clar, Tr, Ti, *Violino I. Obligato*, 2 Vn, Vla, Org
    Vienna: Gesellschaft d. Musikfreunde
MS. *Concerto* D maj. *Clarino solo*, Str, Bc
MS. *Concerto* C maj. *Clarino solo*, Str, Bc
    Heiligenkreutz (near Vienna): Stift Heiligenkr.
MS. *Missa* has very high Tr part in 'Quoniam' for s, Clar, Bc (f^2 for a Tr
    in C)
    Berlin-Dahlem: MS. 18390 (score), 18390/1 (parts)

Ricci, Pasquale (*fl.* c. 1733)
    MS. *Concerto per violoncello con sinfonia e trombe obl.*
    QL.

Richter, Ferdinand Tobias (1649–1711)
    MS. *Sonata à 7 stromenti*, '1685'.
        2 Tr, Ti, 2 Vn, 2 Vla da braccio, Cemb
    MS. *Balletti à Cinque: Sonata, Allemande, Menuet, Sarabande, Ballo, Aria.*
        2 Tr, Vn, Vla, Viola con Violone
        Vienna: N.B. MS. Mus. 18968 (score)

Richter, Franz Xaver (1709–1789)
    MS. *Concerto ex D à 5 voc. Clarino Principale*, Str, Bc, *Per la Capella Principale.*
        Washington: Library of Congress

Riepel, Joseph (*fl.* mid 18th century)
    MS. *Concerto in D Clarino Principale*, 2 Fl, 2 Hn, Str, Bc, *Per le capella*
        Principale Del Sig: Riepel
        Washington: Library of Congress

Rist, Johann (1607–1667)
    PR. *Das Friedhauchzende Deutschland, welches vermittelst eines neuen Schauspiels,*
        theils in ungebundener, . . . Nürnberg, Joh. Andrea Endtern, 1653.
    (NB: The last piece is for SATB, 2 Tr, Bc)
        Breslau (Wrocław): U.B.
        London: B.M.
        Brussels: B.C.

Rittler, Pater Philipp Jacob (*fl.* in Moravia, 2nd half 17th cent.)
    See Breitenbacher 1928.

Roman, Johann Hellmich (*fl. c.* 1725)
    MS. Suite in 25 movements (not unlike Handel's *Water Music*), composed
    for the royal wedding at Drottningholm, Sweden; six movements for
    2 Tr, 2 Hn, 2 Ob, Str in D maj.
        Upsala: U.B.

Romanino, Giuseppe (*fl.* mid 18th century)
    MS. *Concerto di Tromba* in D maj. Tr, Str, Bc
        Schwerin: Landesbib. 4736/6

Rosenmüller, Johann (*c.* 1620–1684)
    Various pieces 'con trombe', some for 'tromba sola' at London
    (B.M. Royal Music coll.) and among the large collection of his MSS.
    now at Berlin-Dahlem.

Rosier(s), Charles (Carl) (*fl.* end of 17th century)
    PR. *Quatorze Sonates pour les Violons et le Hautbois à 6 Parties.* Amsterdam.
    [n.d.].
        Tr, 2 dessus, haute-contre, bassus, bc
        Upsala: U.B.
        Darmstadt: Hessische Landes- und Hochschulbib. (missing).
    (Sonata No. xii for tr/ob, st, bc (mod. ed.) in: *Ausgewählte instru-
    mental-werke.* Herausgegeben von Ursela Niemöller. Düsseldorf, 1957.
    Denkm. reinischer Musik, vol. vii.)

Sartorio, M. Antonio (c. 1620–1685)
    Sinfonia and aria from the opera *L'Adelaide* (Venice 1672) in D maj.
        2 Tr, Str, Bc
        Venice: Bib. Marciana

Scarlatti, Alessandro (1659–1725)
    MS. *Alla Battaglia, Pensieri* (serenade), solo voices, Tr, Str, Bc
        Vienna: Gesellschaft der Musikfreunde
    MS. Cantata, 'Su le sponde del Tebro.'
        s, Tr, Str, Bc
        London: B.M. Add. MS. 31487
        Florence: Cons. Luigi Cherubini, MS. D.2364
        Vienna: Gesellschaft der Musikfreunde
    (mod. ed. B. Paumgartner, Willy Müller-Süddeutscher Musikverlag,
    Heidelberg, 1956.)

MS. 7 'Arie con tromba sola.' sop, Tr, Bc
    Oxford: B.L. MS. Mus. Sch. E.394

MS. Serenata, 'Venere, Adone, Amore.' 3 Voc, Str, 2 Tr (score)
    Oxford: Chr. Ch. 992.
    Münster: Santini MS. 39456, dated '1706'

MS. Oratorio, 'La Colpa, il pertimento, la grazia . . . per La Passione di Nostro Sig.'
    2 Vn, Violetta, 2 Tr, Bc (score)
    Dresden: S.B.

MS. Serenata, 'Il Giardino d'Amore.' s s, Str, Tr, flautino
    Brussels: B.R. 2528. MS. 19646.

MS. *Giardino di Rose: Oratorio La Santissima Vergine del'Rosario A Cinque Voci Con Stromenti: Trombe, Flauti, Oubué, Fagotti, et altri Del Sign: Alessandro Scarlatti.*
    Münster: MS. 3861

MS. 'The introduction to a serenade . . . upon the birth of the late King of the Romans . . .'
    2 Tr, 2 Ob, Bsn, 2 Vn, Vla, Bc
    Berlin: D.S.B. MS. 24(1).

MS. Oratorio, 'San Filippo Neri.' (score)
    Brussels: B.R. 2170.

MS. *Il Giardino d'Amore Serenata a 2:* C[anto] A[lto] *con Violini, Flautino, e Tromba Venere et Adone Del Sig: Alessandro Scarlatti.*
    Münster: MS. 3937
    Berlin-Dahlem.
    (A thematic catalogue of cantatas—some with Tr.)
    Vienna: N.B. MS. 17530.
    Various operas and other serenades have important trumpet parts.

MS. Opera *Mitridite* has several *sinfonie* for 2 Tr, Str—one for 2 Tr, 2 'tromba marine', Ti, Str
    Berlin-Dahlem: MS. 19641

Schelle, Johann (1648–1701)
    Gott sei mir gnädig
        Clarino, 2 Viol., 2 Viole, Fag, C A Bc
        Berlin: D.S.B. MS. (score) 19780
    Lobe den Herrn, meine Seele
        2 Chor (SSATB conc., SSATB), Str, 4 'clarini,' Ti, 2 Crn, 3 Trb, Bsn, Org
        Mod. ed. in *DdT*, LVIII–LIX

Salve solis orientis
> SSATTB, Str, 'Clarino piccolo,' 2 Crn, 3 Trb, Org
>> Oxford: B.L. MS. Mus. Sch. C. 31.

Schaffe in mir Gott
> Clarino con sordino, Viol. piccolo 1, 11 (Cornettino 1 in defect.
> Viol. picc. 1; Cornettino 11 in defect. Viol. picc. 11), 2 Viol., 2
> Violette, Violoncino, SATB, Org
>> Berlin: D.S.B. MS. (score) 19781, No. 11.

Von Himmel kam der Engel Schar
> SSATB, Str, 2 Clar, Ti, 2 Crn, 2 Trb, Org
> Mod. ed. in *DdT*, LVIII–LIX.

Schmelzer, Johann Heinrich (1630–1680)

PR. *Arie per il Baletto a Cavallo. Composte dall Gioanne Enrico Schmeltzer,
Musico di Camera di S.M.C. Vienna, M. Cosmerovio, 1667.*

Orig. in score: 'Corrente con trombe e timp. à 6';* 'Giga con viol.
3 clarini à 7'; 'Follia con trombe e timp. à 6';* 'Allemanda con viol.
à 5'; 'Sarabanda con trombe e timp. à 6'.*

> Breslau (Wrocław): U.B. (Bohn, 1883).

> London: B.M. 9930 i4.—Bound with:

*Sieg-Streit dess Lufft und Wassers Freuden-Fest zu Pferd zu dem (G)lor-
würdigisten Beyläger Beeder Kayserlichen Majestaten Leopoldi dess Ersten
Römischen Kaysers/auch zu Hungarn und Böhaim König/ Ertz-Hertzogens
zu Oesterreich/ und Margarita/ Geboren Königlichen Infantin auss Hispanien
dargestellet In vero Kayserlichen Residentz Statt Wienn. Gedr. zu Wienn in
Oesterreich bey Mattheo Cosmerovio/der Röm: Kayserl: Majest: Hoff
Buchdrucker/ Anno 1667.*

This is an account of the fantastic horse ballet (actually a tremendous
organized circus-like carnival of floats, horses, mounted corps of
trumpets, kettledrums, etc.) shown in the large plates at the back
(after the *Arie*). 38 pages of descriptive commentary, followed by the
Schmelzer pieces.

Both the German and Italian language editions are in the New York
Public Library (Spencer 1667).

PR. *Sacro-profanus concentus musicus fidium aliorumque instrumentorum . . .*
Nürnberg, 1662, Mich. Endter. 9 part books, 13 sonatas.
> Kroměříž: Liechtenstein Archive.
> Paris: B.N.
> Upsala: U.B.
> Washington: Library of Congress

* in *EDM*, XIV.

MS. *Sonata duodecima* (in C) *à* 7 (2 Crn, 2 Clar, 3 Trb)
    (a) keyboard tablature: 2f.
    (b) 8 fasc.: 'cornettino' I, II; 'clarino' I, II; Trb I, II, III; Bc
(=sonata XII of the *Sacro-profanus conc.* . . . . 1662)
    Upsala: U.B. Sig.: Instr. mus. i hs 8:16.
(There are numerous other works by Schmelzer with significant
trumpet parts at Kroměříž and Vienna)

Schneider, Martin (*fl.* 1670)
    PR. *Neue Geistliche Lieder. Theil I. Liegnitz, Z. Schneider 1667.* 4°
        Contains '40 Arien à 5: Canto solo mit 4 instr.: 2 viol. vel Clarinis
        vel Cornetti, Alto viola vel Alto Trombon, Tenor viola vel Tenor
        Trombon, Violon et vere Trombon, Basso Continuo.'
        Upsala: U.B.

Schütz, Heinrich (1585–1672)
    PR. *Symphoniae Sacrae . . . à 3, 4, 5, 6 . . . opus Ecclesiasticum Secundum,*
        Gardano in Venetia, 1629. (Schütz Werke Verzeichnis 249)
        No. 13 à 5, 'Buccinate . . . prima pars'
        No. 13 à 5, 'Iubilate Deo. Secunda Pars'
        'Doi Tenori e Basso con' Vn/Crn, Trombetta, Bsn, Bc
            Oxford: Chr. Ch. 881–6
            Breslau (Wrocław): U.B. (Bohn, 1883)
    PR. *Historia von der Geburt Jesu Christi* . . . (*SWV* 435)
        Upsala: U.B.
        Berlin: D.S.B.
    (For the other known works by Schütz with trumpets, see Chapter 6.)

Schwartzkopf, Theodor (1659–1732)
    MS. *Overture*   Clar, Vn, 2 Vn, Vlo, Cemb
    MS. *Concerto da Camera*   Clar ad lib., 2 Ob, Bsn, Str
    MS. *Concerto da Camera*   2 Clar, 2 Ob, Bsn, Str
        Rostock

Speer, Daniel (1636–1707)
    PR. *Neugebachene Taffel-Schnitz . . . Frankfurt/Main, 1685.*   7 part books
        Paris: B.N. Vm 7, 36 (mod. ed. of several pieces in *EDM* XIV
    PR. *Grund-richtiger, Kurtz-Leicht-u. Nöthiger, jetzt Wol-vermehrter Unter-*
        richt der Musicalischen Kunst. . . . Ulm, 1697.
        London: B.M. B. 822, contains 'aufzüge' for 6 Tr, and *sonatine*
        for 2 Tr.

PR. *Musikalisch Türkischer Eulen-Spiegel*, 1688
   Contains six sonatas for wind instruments: 3 for 2 Clar, 3 Trb, Bc and
   3 for 2 Crn, 3 Trb, Bc. This collection is probably the source for the
   so-called 'Bänkelsänger Lieder', of which one sonata was published
   by Robert King.
   Wolfenbüttel

Sperger, Giovanni [Johann]
   MS. 2 *Concertos per il Clarino* in D maj. *Clarino Principale*,
      2 Hn, 2 Ob, Bsn, Str, Bc, 1778 and 'Occtobr. 1779'.
      Schwerin: Landesbib. MS. 5174 score

Stanley, John (1713–1786)
   MS. Overture to *The Choice of Hercules*   2 Tr, 2 Ob, 2 Vn, Bsn, Org
      London: B.M.

Steffani, Agostino (1654–1728)
   Aria and dance mvts from *Alarico* (1687) with parts for Tr
   Overture to *Niobe* (1688), 4 Tr, Ti, Str
   Aria from *Tassilone* (1709) in D maj., a, Tr, Str
      Mod. ed. in *Denkmäler der Tonkunst in Bayern*, XI, 2 and XII, 2.

Stöltzel, Gottfried Heinrich (1690–1749)
   MS. *Concerto a Quatto Cori* in D.
      6 Tr, 4 Ti, 3 Ob, Fl, Bsn, Str, Bc I, II
      Gotha: Landesbib. (mod. ed. *DdT* 29–30)

Stradella, Alessandro (1642–1682)
   MS. *Sinfonia auanti il Barcheggio a Quattro: Tromba ò Cornetto, due Violini, e
      Basso Del Sig^r Stradella 1681*
      Modena: Bib. Estense (score)
   MS. *Seconda Parte* [to *Il Barcheggio*] *Sinfonia auanti—Violini: Cornetto ò
      Tromba Tutti i V[iolini] all Vnissono Bassi con Tromboni Suonandi* (the
      trumpet or cornetto part ascends to e^2!)
      Modena: Bib. Estense (score)
   MS. *Sonata à otto viole con una tromba e basso continuo.*
      Torino: B.N. Foà 11.

Tartini, Giuseppe (1692–1770)
   MS. Concerto (D?)   2 (?) Tr, Ti, Str, Bc
      Padua: Archive of the Basilica of St Anthony MS. C. 79.

Telemann, Georg Philipp (1681–1767)

MS. *Concerto a 4: 1. Clarino: 2. Violini: e Cembalo di Melante*, in D maj.
    Darmstadt: Hessische Landes- und Hochschulbibliothek MS.
        Mus. 1033/104.

MS. *Concerto* in D maj. Solo Vn, Vc 'obbligato', Tr, Str, Bc
    Darmstadt: .... 1033/79 (parts in the hand of Johann Graupner).

MS. *Concerto* in D maj. 3 Clar, 2 Ob, Str, Bc
    Darmstadt: . . . 1033/28 (mod. *EDM* xi).

MS. *Concerto* in D maj. 3 Clar, 2 Ob, Str, Bc
    Darmstadt: . . . 1033/62 (parts in the hand of Johann Graupner).

MS. *Concerto* in D maj. Tr, 2 Ob, Str, Bc
    Darmstadt: . . . 1033/22 (score)

MS. *Concerto* in D maj. 3 Clar, Ti, 2 Vn ('e oboe'), Vla, Cemb
    Darmstadt
    Magdeburg (mod. ed. C. F. Peters, Leipzig).

MS. *Concerto* in E flat 2 'Trombe Selvatica', Str, Bc
    Darmstadt: . . . 1033/74 (parts in the hand of Johann Graupner).
    (Mod. ed. *DdT* 61/62)

MS. Suite in D maj. Clar, 2 Vn, Vla, Bc
    Darmstadt: . . . (score)

MS. *Concerto da me Telemann*, in F maj. 2 *Tr di caccia ò Tromba ordinaria piccola* (both parts in French violin clef!), 2 Fl, 2 Ob, Vn *concertino*, 2 Vn, Vla, *Fondamento*, Ti in the last two movements.
    Dresden: Sächsische Landesbib. 2392/0/9. (mod. ed. *DdT*
        29–30, pp. 103–95. In the 'Scherzo' the first Tr has g^2 in bars
        12 and 150.)

MS. *Concerto* in D maj. 2 Violino solo, 2 Tr, 2 Vn, Bc
    Rostock: U.B. Mus. saec. XVII. 45[9].

PR. *Getreuer Musikmeister* (several 'instalments' of this prolonged series include parts for trumpet).
    Upsala: U.B.

MS. Cantata, *Die Tageszeiten*, has an aria for 'Kurzer Trompet' in F, s, Str
    Berlin-Dahlem
There are over 900 cantatas by Telemann preserved in the conservatory library at Frankfurt am Main. A large number of these works have parts for trumpets. Telemann's various oratorios and operas also have significant trumpet parts.

Theil(e) (or Thiel), Johann (1646–1724)

MS. *Die Geburt unsers Herrn J. Christ*
    Upsala: U.B.

Thieme, Clement (1631–1668)
>   MS. *Sonata à 8*
>> 2 Tr, 2 Vn, 4 'viole di braccie,' Bc
>> Upsala: U.B.
>
>   MS. *Meine Seele erhebt den Herren*
>> 6 Voc, 2 Clar, 'Tamburini,' 2 Vn, 4 Vla, Bc
>> Berlin: D.S.B.

Tiehl, (?) (*fl.* early eighteenth century)
>   MS. (score) *Concerto a Violini, Trombe,* [Vla, Bc]
>> Dresden: *QL*

Tolar (Dolar), Jan Křtitel (*fl.* 1675)
>   MS. *Balletti e sonata.* Includes a *Sonata à 10.*
>> Clar, 3 Trb, 2 Vn, 4 Vla, Org
>> Kroměříž (Breitenbacher) (mod. ed. in *MAB*, vol. 40, Prague, 1959)

Torelli, Giuseppe (1658–1709)
>   PR. 'Concerto vi' in D. Tr/ob str bc in: *Concerts à 5 6 7 instruments . . . E. Roger, 1713.*
>> Oxford: B.L. Mus. 183 c. 39(1–7)
>> London: B.M.
>
>   PR. *VI Sonates ou Concerts/à 4, 5 & 6 Parties/Composées par/Mrs Bernardi, Torelli & autres fameaux Auteurs . . .* [c. 1715]: No. 1 in D maj. for Tr, Str, Bc; No. 6 in D maj. for Tr, Str, Bc
>> (No. 1 is thematically similar to the *Sinfonia a 4 con Tromba e Violini unisson: 1693*, see S.P. MS. Lib. T. 1, No. 7; No. 6=*Sinfonia con Tromba Torelli* in S.P. MS. T.1.)
>> London: B.M. G. 914.
>
>   MS. music in San Petronio, Bologna: *Works with one Tr, Str, Bc*
>   *Sinfonia con Tromba in D* (score)   Tr, Str, Org (add. in.?)
>> Lib. T. 2 #1
>
>   *Sinf. con Tr* in D (parts)   1 Tr? (see #'s 2, 3 in Lib. T.2), Str, Org
>> Lib. T. 1 #2
>
>   *Sinf. con Tr* in D (parts)   Tr, Str
>> Lib. T. 1 #4
>
>   *Sinf. con Tr* in D (parts)   Tr, Str, Org
>> Lib. T. 1 #6
>
>   *Sinf. a 4 con Tr e violini unissoni* in D, 1693 (parts)   Tr, Str, Org
>> Lib. T. 1 #7
>
>   *Sinf. con Tr* in D (parts)   Tr, Str, Org
>> Lib. T. 1 #8

Sinf. con Tr in D (score & parts)   Tr (part missing) Str, Org
  Lib. T. 1 #11
Sonata a 5 con Tr in D [1690] (parts)   Tr, Vn 1, 2, Vc, Vlo, Org
  Lib. T. 3¹ #1
Sonata a 5 con Tr in D (parts)   Tr (missing), Str, Org
  Lib. T. 3¹ #2
Sonata a 5 con Tr in D (parts)   Tr, Vn, I, II, III, IV, Vla, Vc, Vlo, Org
  Lib. T. 3¹ #3
Sonata a 5 con Tr in D (parts)   Tr, Str, Org
  Lib. T. 3¹ #4
Sonata a 5 con Tr in D (parts)   Tr, Str, Org
  Lib. T. 3¹ #5
Sonata con Stromenti e Tr, 1690 in D (parts)   Tr, Str, Org
  Lib. T. 3¹ #8
Sonata a 5 con Tr in D (parts)   Tr, Str, Org
  Lib. T. 3¹ #9
Sonata a 5 con Tr in D (score)   Tr, Str, Org?
  Lib. T. 3¹ #12
Sonata a 5 con Tr in D (parts)   Tr, 2 Vn, Violetta, Vc, Vlo, Org.
  Lib. T. 3¹ #14
Sonata a 5 con Tr in D (parts)   Tr, Str, Org
  Lib. T. 3¹ #15

Works with 2 Tr, Str, and the noted additional instruments
  Concerto con Trombe ò Oboè in D (parts)   2 Tr, Str (Org?)
    Lib. T. 3 #2
  Concerto con Trombe in D (score)   2 Tr?
    Lib. T. 3 #6
  Concerto a 2 Trombe e stromenti in D (parts)   2 Tr, Str, Org
    Lib. T. 3 #11
  Concerto con Trombe, Oboi, Violini in D (score)
    Lib. T. 3 #13
  Concerto a due Chori con Trombe in D (score & parts)
    Chor. I: 2 Tr, Str, Org
    Chor. II: 2 Ob, Str, Org
    Lib. T. 3 #14
  Sinfonia con Tromba[e?] in D (parts)   2 Tr, Str, Org
    Lib. T. 2 #2
  Sinfonia con Tromba[e?] in D (parts)   2 Tr, Str, Org
    Lib. T. 2 #3
  Sinfonia con Trombe e violini Unissoni in D (parts)
    Tr (other part missing?), Str, Org
    Lib. T. 2 #4

Sinfonia con 2 Trombe in D (score & parts)   2 Tr, Str, Org
  Lib. T. 2 #5
Sinfonia con 2 Trombe in D (score & parts)
  2 Tr, Str (Vc 1–11, Vlo 1–11), Tiorba
  Lib. T. 2 #6
Sinfonia con Oboi, Trombe e violini in D (parts)
  2 Tr, 2 Ob, Str, (Vc 1–11), Org
  Lib. T. 2 #7
Sinfonia in D (parts)   2 Tr, 2 Ob, Str, *Trombone*, Org
  Lib. T. 2 #8
Sonata a 5, due Trombe e violini unissoni 1692 in D (parts)
  2 Tr, Str, Basso Continuo, Org
  Lib. T. 2 #17
Sinfonia con Tromba[e?] in D (parts)   2 Tr, Str, Org
  Lib. T. 1 #1
Sinfonia con 2 Trombe in D (parts)   2 Tr, Str, Org
  Lib. T. 1 #3
Sinfonia con 2 Trombe in D (parts)
  2 Tr, Str, *violone tutti di Ripieno e senza org*
  Lib. T. 1 #5
Sinfonia con 2 Trombe in D (parts)
  2 Tr, Str (viola 1–11, Vc 1–11), Org 1–11
  Lib. T. 1 #9
Sinfonia a 2 Trombe e violini in D (score)
  Lib. T. 1 #10
Sinfonia a 2 Trombe in D (score & parts)   2 Tr, Str, Org
  Lib. T. 1 #12
Sinfonia in D (score & parts)
  2 Tr, 2 Ob, Str (Vn 1–IV, Vla 1–11), *Trombone, Tiorba*, Org
  Lib. T. 1 #13
Sonata con Trombe e Obue in D (parts)   2 Tr, 2 Ob, Str, Org
  Lib. T. 1 #14
Sinfonia con Trombe, Obue et altri Stromenti in D (score) (for the *Accademia*
in 1707)
  Lib. T. 3^1 #17
Sonata a 5 con Trombe in D (parts)   No Tr parts, Str, 2 Trb, Org
  Lib. T. 3^1 #13

Works with 4 Tr, Str, and the noted additional instruments
  Sonata a 4 Trombe in E flat (parts)
    4 Tr, 2 Ob, Str (Vn 1 only, no violone), no Org or continuo
    Lib. T. 2 #15 (missing)

Sinfonia a 4 in C (parts)
4 Tr, 2 Ob (*concertino* & *rip.*), Str (Vns I–II *conc.* & *rip.*) Bsn (*conc.* & *rip.*), Timp, Trombone—no Org (perhaps intended for the *Accademia*).
See Giegling, 1949.

MS. *Sonata con 2. Trombe, 2. Violini, e Viola. Parti. 13. Del Sig: Giuseppe Torelli.*
Vienna: N.B. Sm. 3740.

Tudela (?) (17th century)
MS. 3 books of *Seguidillas con Violini y Trompas* and soprano.
Berlin: D.S.B. MS. 22070 (*QL*).

Tuma, Franz (1704–1774)
MS. *Sonata* in C maj. 4 Tr, Ti, Str
Dresden: Sächsische Landesbib.

Uccellini, Marco (c. 1610–1680)
PR. *Sonate over canzoni da farsi . . . op. 5. Venice, A. Vincenti, 1649.*
Includes a piece for 'Tromba sordina per sonare con violino solo', Bc
(Not for a trumpet but rather a violin in imitation of a trumpet. See Chapter 4.)
Oxford: B.L. Mus. Sch.
Kassel: (in MS.—a 19th cent. copy)
Breslau (Wrocław): U.B. (Bohn, 1890)

Umstatt, Joseph (*fl.* c. 1760)
MS. 2 Parthie—2 Tr, 2 Vn, Bass
Karlsruhe: S.B. MS. 986–7

Vejvanovský (Weywanowsky or Weiwanowski), Pavel Josef (1639 or 40–1693)
MS. *Sonata à 4* Tr, 2 Vn, Vla, Bc
MS. *Serenada* 2 Tr, 2 Vn, Vla, Bc
MS. *Sonata Venatoria* 2 Tr, 2 Vn, Vla, Bc
Kroměříž (Breitenbacher). (mod. ed. of the above in *MAB*, 36, Prague, 1958)
See other works with Tr or 'Clarino' in: Breitenbacher and in *MAB* vols. 47–9, Prague, 1960. All of Vejvanovský's surviving works are preserved on microfilm in the University library at Syracuse, N.Y.

Vitali, Tommaso (c. 1670–1742)
Sinfonia 2 Tr, 2 Ob, Str, Bc
Bologna: S.P.

Vivaldi, Antonio (1669?–1741)
MS. *Concerto in C*   2 Tr, Str, Bc
(=Foà ɪx, No. 1; Pincherle No. 75)
> Torino: B.N., collection Renzo Giordano vɪɪɪ, No. 16. (mod.
> ed. Ricordi)

Several other works, e.g. the *Gloria* in D maj., etc., include trumpet
parts. Most will be found in Torino: B.N.

Viviani, Giovanni (*fl.* 1680)
PR. *Sonata Prima* and *Sonata Seconda per Trombetta sola* (and Bc) in:
Capricci Armonici, Da Chiesa, e da Camera à Violino Solo cioè
Sinfonie, Toccate, Sonate . . . et Sonate per Tromba Sola . . . op. 4.
In Venetia, 1678. (Sartori: 1678c)
> Bologna: B.C.
> Oxford: B.L. Mus. Sch. MS. Mus. Sch. C. 164a–b (Pub. in
> Rome, but it is ident. to the Venice print found at Bologna)

Volckmar, Tobias (1678–after 1724)
PR. *Gott gefällige Music-Freude, welche nicht nur an denen vornehmsten Fest-
Tagen des Jahres, sondern auch grössten Theils zu aller Zeit . . . Denn Drey-
Einigen Gott zu Ehren Und Musicliebenden Hertzen . . . gebraucht werden
kan. Hirschberg*, [the author].
> Voice, 2 Vn, Va, Bc, 1 wind (Hn, Tr, Ob, Fl, etc.)
> Löbau (*QL*)

G.W. (early 18th century)
MS. *Concerto a due Clarini.*   2 Clar, 2 Vn, Bc
Upsala: U.B.

Weichlein, Pater Romanus (*fl.* 1700)
PR. *Encaenia Musices, seu opus musicale . . .*, 1695. Nos. ɪ, v, xɪɪ
> 2 Vn, 2 Vla, 2 'Clarini,' Violon, Org (includes 24 duets for 2 Tr)
> Paris: B.N. Vm.[7] 1490. (mod. ed. Hofmeister, Leipzig, of duets)

Weichmann, Johann (1620–1652)
PR. *Der cxxxiii Psalm. Königsberg, J. Reusner, 1649.* 2°.
> . . . in concert à 5, 10, 14 stimmen. Chor ɪ: 2 CATB; Chor ɪɪ Ripieni:
> CATB 2 viol. 2 clar ò cornetti, 5 trb ò bsn (preceded by a Symphony
> à 5: Trb ò bsn *se piace*)
> Upsala: U.B.

Weise, Christian (1642–1708)

PR. *Bäurischen Machiavellus in einen Lust-Spiele Vorgestellet* den 15. Febr.
1679. Leipzig, Gallus Niemann, 1681.
(Bohn, 1883. NB: In 8°. 5 Seiten Musik zum Schlusschore, . . . halb
gesungen, halb mit Trompeten u. Pauken gespielt.) Includes 2 tr, 4
Trb, Ti
Breslau (Wrocław): U.B. (Bohn, 1883)

PR. *Das Ebenbild eines Gehorsamen Glaubens welches Abraham . . . seines
Isaacs beständig erwiesen . . .* den 4. März 1680 auf der Zittauischen
Schaubühne vorgestellet worden. Im Zittau, Michael Hartmann
1682.
Breslau (Wrocław): U.B. (Bohn, 1883)

PR. *Zittauisches THEATRUM wie solches Anno 1682 praesentiret worden . . .*
Zittau, Hartmann, 1683.
Breslau (Wrocław): U.B. (Bohn, 1883)

Weldon, John (1676–1736)

MS. Anthem, 'O Praise the Lord.'
SATB, 2 Vn, Tr, Bc—score
Tenbury: St Michaels 991.

MS. Score. Long-lost setting of *The Judgement of Paris*, discovered in the
Folger Shakespeare Library, Washington D.C., contains several sinfonias with trumpet. (I am indebted to Charles Cudworth for this
information.)

Zechner, ? (*fl.* 1st half of 18th century)

MS. *Sinfonia* in D maj.   2 Clar, Ti, Str, Bc
Eisenstadt

Zelenka, Jan Dismas (1679–1745)

MS. *Melodrama*, 1723 and *Serenata* for the coronation of Charles VI in 1723.
Overture   Tr, Fl, Ob, Str, Bc
Dresden: Sächsische Landesbib.
MS. A. 427a, MS. B. 875a

Zeutschner, Tobias (1615–1675)

PR. *Musikalische Kirchen- und Haus-Freude.*
Some pieces with clar, etc., but most parts missing.
Upsala: U.B.
Breslau (Wrocław): U.B. (Bohn, 1883)

MS. *Tobias Zeutschner . . . Notar Publ. Caesar undt Organisten zu St Mar.*
Magdalen- mann propria.
'Hallelujah. Höret an die Geburt. 18v. (Die Geburt unsers Herren und
Heylandes Jesu Christi. Nach dem Hl. Evang.: Mathe:)'
Breslau (Wrocław): U.B. (Bohn, 1890), 'NB: 24 St in fol.—
S¹ (Angelus) S₂ 2A 2T (Evangelista), 2T 2B (Pastores)—
2 Vn, 2 Clar, Crn, 2 Fl, 3 Trb, Vla da gamb, Bc pro org Org
cappella.'

Ziani, Pietro Andrea (1620–1634)
MS. *Sonata* in D.   Tr, Str, Org
Oxford: Chr. Ch. 771. (score)
Upsala: U.B. Instr. mus. i hs. 66:4. (includes a part for Bsn)
Warsaw: U.B. (attrib. to Albinoni)
Zürich: Zentral Bib. (attrib. to Bononcini)
Various operas, etc., also have notable trumpet parts.

BIBLIOGRAPHY

For abbreviations see pages 13–16

ADRIO, ADAM, 1956. Hammerschmidt, *MGG*, vol. v. Kassel.

AGRICOLA, MARTIN, 1529. *Musica instrumentalis deudsch*. Wittemberg.

ALDIS, ELIJAH, 1873. *Worcester Cathedral, carving and sculpture*. London.

ALESSI, G. D', 1929. *Organo e organista della cattedrale di Treviso*. Vedelago.

ALTENBURG, JOHANN ERNST, 1795 (facs. repr. 1911, 1967). *Versuch einer Anleitung zur heroisch-musikalischen Trompeter- und Pauker-Kunst*. Halle (facs. repr. Dresden, New York).

ANGLÉS, HIGINIO, and SUBIRÁ, JOSÉ, 1946–51. *Catalogo musical de la Biblioteca Nacional de Madrid*, 3 vols. Barcelona.

(ANONYMOUS), 1715. *The rules and orders establish'd . . . in . . . Hamburgh and Amsterdam for suppressing the rage of fire. Translated from the original*. London.

——, 1927. *Le chiese di Bologna*. Bologna.

——, 1951. *Bayerische Nationalmuseum. Ausstellung alter Musik, Instrumente . . . Katalog*. Munich.

ANTHON, C. G., 1943. *Music and musicians in Northern Italy during the 16th century*, thesis, Harvard University. Cambridge, Mass.

APEL, WILLI, 1946. *Harvard Dictionary of Music*. Cambridge, Mass.

ARKWRIGHT, G. E. P., 1915–23. *Catalogue of [MS.] music in the library of Christ Church, Oxford*, 2 vols. London.

ARNHEIM, AMALIE, 1911. Aus dem Bremer Musikleben im 17. Jahrhundert, *SIMG*, xii, pp. 369–416. Leipzig.

ARNOLD, DENIS, 1955–6. Ceremonial Music in Venice at the time of the Gabrielis, *PRMA*. London.

——, 1957. Brass instruments in Italian church music of the sixteenth and early seventeenth centuries, *BQ*, vol. i, pp. 81–92. Durham, New Hampshire.

ARNOLD, DENIS, 1959. Con ogni sorte di stromenti: some practical suggestions, *BQ*, ii, No. 3. Durham, New Hampshire.

ARNOLD, G., CAIN, A. M., HUMPHRIES, C., NEIGHBOR, O. W., and SIMONI, ANNA, 1959. *Catalogue of printed books in the British Museum, accessions third series: part 291 B, books in the Hirsch Library with supplementary list of music.* London.

ARTIÈRES, J. (ed.), 1930. *Documents historiques sur la ville de Millau.* Millau.

AUBRY, PIERRE, 1907. Iter Hispanicum . . . II. Deux chansonniers français à la Bibliothèque de l'Escorial, *SIMG*, viii. Leipzig.

AURIVILLIUS, P. F. (ed.), 1814. *Catalogus librorum impressorum Bibliotecae Regiae Academiae Upsaliensis*, 2 parts. Upsala.

BACHMANN, S., 1954. Über die Stadtpfeifer bei Alt-St.-Martin, *Fränkische Blätter für Geschichtsforschung und Heimatpflege*, vi, No. 25. Bamberg.

BARBOUR, J. MURRAY, 1940 (Sept.). The use of brass instruments in early scores, *Bulletin of the American Musicological Society.* New York.

BEER (or BAER), JOHANN, 1719. *Musicalischer Diskurse durch die Principia der Philosophie deduciert . . .* Nuremberg.

BENVENUTI, G., 1932. *La musica strumentale in S. Marco.* Milan.

BERGER, JEAN, 1951. Notes on some seventeenth-century compositions for trumpets and strings in Bologna, *MQ*, xxxvii. New York.

BESSARABOFF, NICHOLAS, 1941. *Ancient European musical instruments.* Boston.

BESSELER, HEINRICH, 1950. Die Entstehung der Posaune, *AcM*, xxii. Leipzig.

BIERDIMPFL, K. A., 1883. *Die Sammlung der Musikinstrumente des Bayerischen Nationalmuseums.* Munich.

BITTINGER, WERNER, 1960. *Schütz Werke Verzeichnis [SWV].* Kassel.

BLANDFORD, WILLIAM F. H., 1940. Clarino and Trumpet, *Musical Times*, No. 81. London.

BOHN, EMIL, 1883. *Bibliographie der Musik-Druckwerke bis 1700 welche in der Stadtbibliothek . . . zu Breslau aufbewahrt werden.* Berlin.

——, 1890. *Die musikalischen Handschriften des XVI. und XVII. Jahrhunderts in der Stadtbibliothek zu Breslau.* Breslau.

BONTA, STEPHEN, 1967. Liturgical problems in Monteverdi's Vespers, *JAMS*, xx, No. 1. Boston, etc.

——, 1969. The uses of the *Sonata da Chiesa*, *JAMS*, xxii, No. 1. Boston, etc.

BORGHEZIO, G., 1924. La fondazione del collegio nuovo 'Puerum Innocentium' del duomo di Torino, *NA*, vol. i. Rome.

BREITENBACHER, ANTONÍN, 1928. *Hudební Archiv Kolegiátního Kostela Sv. Mořice v Kroměříže.* Kroměříž (Kremsier).

BRENET, MICHEL (BOBILLIER, MARIE), 1904. Deux comptes de la Chapelle-Musique des Rois de France, *SIMG*, vi. Leipzig.

——, 1909. Notes sur l'introduction des instruments dans les églises de France, *Riemann-Festschrift Gesammelte Studien.* Leipzig.

——, 1910. *Les musiciens de la Sainte-Chapelle du Palais.* Paris.

BRENET, MICHEL, 1917. French military music in the reign of Louis XIV, *MQ*, iii. New York.

BRIQUET, C. M., 1907. *Les filigranes. Dictionnaire historique des marques du papier*, 4 vols. Geneva.

BROSSARD, YOLANDE DE, 1965. *Musiciens de Paris 1535–1792* (part of the series *Vie musicale en France sous les rois Bourbons*). Paris.

BUCHNER, A., 1954. *Musical Instruments through the Ages*. London.

BUKOFZER, MANFRED, 1947. *Music in the Baroque Era*. New York.

BURNEY, CHARLES, 1773. *The present state of music in Germany, the Netherlands and United Provinces, or the journal of a tour . . . to collect those materials for a general history of music*, 2 vols. London.

——, 1782–9 (mod. ed. 2 vols., 1957). *A General History of Music*, 4 vols. London.

CAFFI, F., 1854. *Storia della musica sacra nella già capella ducale di S. Marco in Venezia dal 1318 al 1797*. Venice.

CART DE LAFONTAINE, HENRY, 1909. *The King's Musick*. London.

CHAMBERLAYNE, EDWARD, 1669 (5th ed. 1679). *Angliae Notitia, or the present state of England*, parts i and ii. London.

——, 1683. *The present state of England*, parts iii and iv. London.

CHAUVEAU, FRANÇOIS, and others (engravers), 1679–1743. (*Cabinet du Roi*, Paris, L'Imprimerie royale, 23 vols.)

CHERRY, NORMAN, 1961. A Corelli sonata for trumpet, violins and basso continuo, *BQ*, iv. Durham, New Hampshire.

CHURCHILL, W. A., 1935. *Watermarks in paper in the XVII and XVIII centuries*. Amsterdam.

CHYBIŃSKI, ADOLF, 1912. Polnische Musik und Musikkultur des 16. Jahrhunderts in ihren Beziehungen zu Deutschland, *SIMG*, xiii. Leipzig.

CLOSSON, E., 1935. *Le facteur des instruments de musique en Belgique*. Brussels.

CONLEY, PHILIP R., 1959. The use of the trumpet in the music of Purcell, *BQ*, iii, No. 1. Durham, New Hampshire.

(COUSSEMAKER, C. E. H. DE), 1877. *Catalogue de la bibliothèque et des instruments de musique de feu M. Ch. Edm. H. de Coussemaker*. Brussels.

CRUSSARD, CLAUDE, 1945. *Un Musicien français oublié: Marc-Antoine Charpentier, 1634–1704*. Paris.

CUDWORTH, CHARLES, and ZIMMERMAN, FRANKLIN B., 1960. The trumpet voluntary, *ML*, xli. London, Oxford.

DART, THURSTON, 1958. The repertory of the royal wind music, *GSJ*, xi. London.

DAVIDSSON, ÅKE, 1951. *Catalogue critique et descriptif des imprimés de musique des XVIe et XVIIe siècles conservés à la Bibliothèque de l'Université Royale d'Upsala*, vols. ii and iii (for vol. i *see* MITJANA, RAFAEL). Upsala.

——, 1952. *Catalogue critique et descriptif des imprimés de musique des XVIe et XVIIe siècles conservés dans les bibliothèques suédoises* (*Excepté la Bibliothèque de l'Université Royale d'Upsala*). Upsala.

DEAKIN, ANDREW, 1892. *Musical bibliography. A catalogue of the musical works . . . published in England during the fifteenth, sixteenth, seventeenth, and eighteenth centuries.* Birmingham.

DEGELE, LUDWIG, 1937. *Die Militärmusik . . . ihr werden und wesen, ihre Kulturelle und Nationale Bedeutung.* Wolfenbüttel.

DLABACZ, GOTTFRIED JOHANN, 1815. *Allgemeines historisches Künstler-Lexikon für Böhmen und zum Theil auch für Mähren und Schlesien,* 2 vols. Prague.

DUFORCQ, NORBERT, 1954. Concerts parisiens et associations de 'Symphonistes' dans les premières années du règne de Louis XIV, *RBM,* viii. Antwerp.

——, 1957 a. *Notes et références pour servir à une histoire de Michel-Richard Delalande . . . (1657–1726) . . .* Paris.

—— (ed.), 1957 b. *Larousse de la musique,* 2 vols. Paris.

DUTRIPON, F. P., 1837. *Concordantiae Bibliorum Sacrorum Vulgatae Editionis.* Paris.

ÉCORCHEVILLE, J., 1901. Quelques documents sur la musique de la Grande Écurie du Roi, *SIMG,* ii. Leipzig.

——, 1910–14. *Catalogue du fonds de musique ancienne de la Bibliothèque Nationale,* 8 vols. Paris.

EGAN, PATRICIA, 1961. Concert scenes in musical painting of the Italian Renaissance, *JAMS,* No. 2. Boston, etc.

EICHBORN, H., 1881. *Die Trompete in Alte and Neue Zeit. Ein Beitrag z. Musikgeschichte u. Instrumentenlehre.* Leipzig.

——, 1890. Girolamo Fantini, ein Virtuos des Siebzehnten Jahrhunderts, und seine Trompeten-Schule, *MfMg.* Berlin, Leipzig.

——, 1892. Studien zur Geschichte der Militärmusik, *MfMg.* Berlin, Leipzig.

——, 1894. *Das Alte Clarinblasen auf Trompeten.* Leipzig.

EINSTEIN, ALFRED, 1908. Italienische Musiker am Hofe der Neuburger Wittelsbacher, 1614–1716, *SIMG,* ix. Leipzig.

EITNER, ROBERT, 1871. Verzeichniss neuer Ausgaben alter Musikwerke . . . bis . . . 1800, *MfMg.* Berlin, Leipzig.

——, 1877. *Bibliographie der Musik-Sammelwerke des XVI. und XVII. Jahrhunderts.* Berlin.

——, 1881. Die Salzburger Musik-Kapelle um 1757, *MfMg.* Berlin, Leipzig.

——, 1895. Johann Krieger, *MfMg.* Berlin, Leipzig.

——, 1900–4. *Biographisch-Bibliographisches Quellen-Lexikon der Musiker und Musikgelehrten der christliche Zeitrechnung bis zur Mitte des Neunzehnten Jahrhunderts,* 10 vols. Leipzig.

ENSCHEDÉ, J. W., 1904. Joost van den Graft, Trompetenmaker, 1634, *Tijdschrift der Vereeniging voor Nederlandsche Musikgeschiednis,* vii.

EPPELSHEIM, JÜRGEN, 1961. *Das Orchester in den Werken Jean-Baptiste Lullys.* Tutzing.

294

EPSTEIN, PETER, 1924. Die Frankfurter Kapellmusik zur Zeit J. A. Herbsts, *AfMw*, vi. Bückeburg, etc.

FALLET, EDUARD M., 1929. Die Stadtpfeifer von Nürnberg im 16. und 17. Jahrhunderts, *Schweizerische Musikzeitung*, No. 69, pp. 42–5, 76–80. Zürich.

FANTINI, GIROLAMO, 1638 (facs. repr. 1934). *Modo per imparare a sonare di tromba* . . . Frankfort (facs. repr. Milan).

FEDERHOFER, HELLMUT, 1949. Die landschaftlichen Trompeter und Heerpauker in Steiermark, *Zeitschrift des historischen Vereines für Steiermark*, xi. Graz.

——, 1952. Alessandro Tadei, a pupil of Giovanni Gabrieli, *MD*, vol. vi. Rome, etc.

——, 1959. Unbekannte Kirchenmusik von Johann Joseph Fux, *Kirchenmusikalisches Jahrbuch*, 43. Regensburg, Cologne.

FELLOWES, EDMUND H., 1931. The Philidor manuscripts: Paris, Versailles, Tenbury, *ML*, vol. xii. London, Oxford.

——, 1934. *The Catalogue of Manuscripts in the Library of St Michael's College, Tenbury*. Paris.

FÉTIS, F. J., 1877–80. *Biographie Universelle des Musiciens*, 2nd ed. Paris.

——, 1878–80. *Supplément et Complément* [to the above] *publié sous la direction de Arthur Pougin*, 2 vols. Paris.

FINCK, HERMANN, 1556. *Practica Musica*. Wittenberg.

FISCHER, G., 1903. *Musik in Hanover*. Hanover.

FISCHER, KURT, 1910. Gabriel Voigtländer. Ein Dichter und Musiker des 17. Jahrhunderts, *SIMG*, xii. Leipzig.

FLOOD, W. H. GRATTON, 1909. Dublin 'City Music' from 1456 to 1786, *SIMG*, x. Leipzig.

——, 1913. Gild of English minstrels under King Henry vi, *SIMG*, xv. Leipzig.

FORKEL, J. N., 1802. *Ueber Johann Sebastian Bachs Leben, Kunst und Kunstwerke*. Leipzig.

FRANQUIN, M. J. B., La Trompette et le cornet, *Encyclopédie de la Musique et Dictionnaire du Conservatoire* (ed. L. de La Laurencie), pp. 1597–1637. Paris.

FULLER-MAITLAND, J. A., and MANN, A. H., 1893. *Catalogue of the music in the Fitzwilliam Museum*. Cambridge, London.

FÜRSTENAU, M., 1861–2. *Zur Geschichte der Musik und des Theaters am Hofe der Kurfürsten von Sachsen*. Dresden. Also published in the same years and place under the title *Zur Geschichte der Musik und des Theaters am Hofe zu Dresden*.

——, 1871. Fürstliche Gottesdienst in 17. Jahrhunderts. *MfMg*. Berlin, Leipzig.

GÁL, HANS, 1941. *Catalogue of manuscripts, printed music and books on music up to 1850 in the library of the music department at the University of Edinburgh (Reid Library)*. Edinburgh.

GALILEI, VINCENZO, 1581. *Dialogo della musica antica, et della moderna.* Florence.

GALPIN, FRANCIS W., 1906–7. The sackbut, its evolution and history, *PMA.* London.

——, 1910 (4th ed. rev. Thurston Dart, 1965). *Old English Instruments of Music.* London.

——, 1937. *A Textbook of European Musical Instruments.* London.

GASPARI, GAETANO, 1869. *Ragguagli sulla capella musicale della basilica di S. Petronio in Bologna.* Bologna.

——, 1878. *Dei musicisti Bolognesi al XVII secolo.* Modena.

——, 1890–1905. *Catalogo della Biblioteca del Liceo Musicale di Bologna.* Bologna.

GAUSSEN, FRANÇOISE, 1960. Actes d'état-civil de musiciens français, 1651–1681, *RMFC,* vol. i. Paris.

GEIRINGER, KARL, 1954. *The Bach Family.* New York.

——, 1955. *Music of the Bach Family.* Cambridge, Mass.

GIEGLING, FRANZ, 1949. *Giuseppe Torelli, ein Beitrag zur Entwicklungsgeschichte des italienischen Konzerts.* Kassel.

GOLDSCHMIDT, HUGO, 1895. Die Instrumentalbegleitung der italienischen Musikdrama in der ersten Hälfte des XVII. Jahrhunderts, *MfMg.* Berlin, Leipzig.

——, 1900. Das Orchester der italienischen Oper im 17. Jahrhundert, *SIMG,* ii. Leipzig.

GROUT, DONALD JAY, 1960. *A History of Western Music.* New York and London.

HAAS, ROBERT, 1927. *Die Estensischen Musikalien. Thematisches Verzeichnis mit Einleitung.* Regensburg.

HAASE, KARL, 1929. Die Instrumentation J. S. Bachs, *BJ.* Leipzig.

HAENSEL, R., 1954. Der Stadtpfeifer und die Stadtkapelle in Lobenstein, *Festschrift zu Ehrung von Heinrich Albert (1604–1651).* Weimar.

HAKE, ROBERT, c. 1854. *Catalogue of music belonging to the Music School* (now in the Bodleian Library, Oxford); MS. copy in Duke Humphrey's Library.

HALFPENNY, ERIC, 1951. Musicians at James II's coronation, *ML.* xxxii. London, Oxford.

——, 1960. William Shaw's 'harmonic trumpet', *GSJ,* xiii. London.

——, 1962. William Bull and the English Baroque trumpet, *GSJ,* xv. London.

——, 1963. Two Oxford trumpets, *GSJ,* xvi. London.

——, 1969. Four seventeenth-century British trumpets, *GSJ,* xxii. London.

HAMMERICH, A., 1911. Musical relations between England and Denmark in the seventeenth century, *SIMG,* xiii. Leipzig.

HAMMERICH, A., and ELLING, C., 1893. Die Musik am Hofe Christians IV von Dänemark, *Vierteljahrschrift für Musikwissenschaft,* ix. Leipzig.

HÄNSEL, R., 1957. Ein Trompeter-Lehrbrief aus Auma, *Jahrbuch des Kreismuseums Hohenleuben-Reichenfels.* vi. Hohenleuben (Thuringia).

HARRISON, FRANK LL., and RIMMER, JOAN, 1964. *European Musical Instruments*. London.

HAWKINS, SIR JOHN, 1853. *A General History of the Science and Practice of Music . . . A new edition with the author's posthumous notes*, 2 vols. London.

HEAWOOD, EDWARD, 1950. *Watermarks, mainly of the 17th and 18th centuries*. Hilversum.

HENDERSON, HUBERT, 1949. *A Study of the Trumpet in the 17th century: Its History, Resources and Use*. MS. music thesis. University of North Carolina.

HEUSS, A., 1903. Die venezianischen Opernsinfonien, *SIMG*, iv. Leipzig.

HIFF, ALOYS, 1919. *Catalogue of printed music published prior to 1801 now in the library of Christ Church, Oxford*. London.

HIRZEL, BRUNO, 1909. Dienstinstruktion und Personalstatus der Hofkapelle Ferdinand's der Erste aus dem Jahre 1527, *SIMG*, x. Leipzig.

HITCHCOCK, H. WILEY, 1955. The Latin oratorios of Marc-Antoine Charpentier, *MQ*, xli. New York.

HOEHLBAUM, KONSTANTIN (ed.), 1910. *Mitteilungen aus dem Stadtarchiv von Köln*, xi, 28–29.

HORMAN, WILLIAM, 1519. *Vulgaria viri doctissimi*. London.

HORNBOSTEL, E. M. VON, and SACHS, CURT, 1914. Systematik der Musikinstrumente. Ein Versuch, *Zeitschrift für Ethnologie*. Berlin.

HORNEFFER, AUGUST, 1899. Verzeichnis der Werke Johann Rosenmüller, *MfMg*. Berlin, Leipzig.

HORSLEY, IMOGENE, 1960. Wind techniques in the 16th and early 17th centuries, *BQ*, iv. Durham, New Hampshire.

HUGHES-HUGHES, AUGUSTUS, 1906–9. *Catalogue of manuscript music in the British Museum*, 3 vols. London.

HUTCHINGS, ARTHUR, 1961. *The Baroque Concerto*. London.

IGARASHI, JUICHI, and KOYASU, MARSARU, 1953. Acoustical properties of trumpets, *JASA*, 25. New York.

ISRAËL, CARL, 1881. *Übersichtliche Katalog der Musikalien der Ständischen Landesbibliothek zu Cassel (Zeitschrift des Vereins für hessische Geschichte und Landeskunde. Neue Folge. vii. Supplement)*. Kassel.

JACQUOT, ALBERT, 1882. *La musique en Lorraine*. Paris.

JACQUOT, JEAN (ed.), 1955. *La musique instrumentale de la Renaissance*. Paris.

JAHN, FRITZ, 1925. Die Nürnberger Trompeten- und Posaunenmacher im 16. Jahrhundert, *AfMw*, vii. Bückeburg, etc.

JEANS, JAMES, 1961 (first pub. 1937). *Science and Music*. Cambridge.

JEFFREYS, John, 1951. *The Eccles Family, a little-known family of XVII-century English musicians*. Ilford, Essex.

KADE, OTTO, 1889. Die älteren Musikalien der Stadt Freiberg in Sachsen, *MfMg*. Berlin, Leipzig.

KADE, R., 1889. Die Leipziger Stadtpfeifer, *MfMg*. Berlin, Leipzig.

KAHL, WILLI, and LUTHER, WILHELM-MARTIN, 1953. *Repertorium der Musikwissenschaft*. Kassel, Basel.

KARSTÄDT, GEORG, 1958. *Die Sammlung alter Musikinstrumente im St. Annen-Museum, Lübeck 1958*. Berlin.

KING, A. HYATT, and HUMPHRIES, CHARLES, 1951. *Catalogue of printed music in the British Museum, Accessions part 53 . . . music in the Hirsch Library*. London.

KLEEFELD, WILHELM, 1900. Das Orchester der Hamburger Oper, 1678–1738, *SIMG*, i. Leipzig.

KLENZ, WILLIAM, 1962. *Giovanni Maria Bononcini of Modena*. Durham, N. Carolina.

KNICK, BERNHARD, 1963. *St Thomas zu Leipzig*. Wiesbaden.

KÖCHEL, LUDWIG RITTER VON, 1869. *Die Kaiserliche Hof-Musikkapelle in Wien von 1543 bis 1867*. Vienna.

KOCZIRZ, ADOLF, 1920. Das Kollegium der sächsischen Stadt- und Kirchenmusikanten von 1653, *AfMw*, ii. Bückeburg, etc.

——, 1964. Zur Lebensgeschichte Johann Heinrich Schmelzers, *SzMw*, 26. Vienna.

KÖNIG, ERNST, 1957. Neuerkentnisse zu J. S. Bachs Köthener Zeit, *BJ*, 44. Leipzig.

KRETZSCHMAR, HERMANN, 1902. Das erste Jahrhundert der deutschen Oper, *SIMG*, iii. Leipzig.

KUKA, M. J., 1958. *A study of the acoustical effects of mutes on wind instruments*, musical thesis, University of S. Dakota.

KÜSTER, G. G., 1733. *Collectio Opusculorum Historiam Marchiam illustrantium . . .* Berlin.

LAFONTAINE, HENRY CART DE. *See* CART DE LAFONTAINE.

LAMBERTINI, M., 1914. *Catalogue museo instrumental*. Lisbon.

LANGER, WILLIAM L., 1952 (4th rev. ed. 1968). *An Encyclopedia of World History*. Boston.

LANGWILL, LYNDESAY G., 1962 (2nd, enlarged ed.). *An Index of Musical Wind-Instrument Makers*. Edinburgh.

LAURENCIE, LIONEL DE LA, 1906. Une dynastie de musiciens aux XVIIᵉ et XVIIIᵉ siècles, *SIMG*, vii. Leipzig.

LEMOINE, H., 1951. Les fêtes de nuit à Versailles; autrefois et aujourd'hui, *Revue l'histoire de Versailles et de Seine-et-Oise*, l. Paris.

LESURE, FRANÇOIS, 1955. La traité des instruments de musique de Pierre Trichet: les instruments à vent, *AM*, iii. Paris.

LIESS, ANDREAS, 1946. *Wiener Barockmusik*. Vienna.

LIGI, B., 1925. La capella musicale del duomo d'Urbino, *NA*, ii. Rome.

LINCOLN, STODDARD, 1963. *John Eccles, the last of a tradition*, D.Phil. thesis, Oxford University.

LONG, T. H., 1948. On the performance of cup mouthpiece instruments, *JASA*, xx. New York.

MACCLINTOCK, CAROL, 1961. Giustiniani's 'Discorso sopra la Musica', *MD*, xv. Rome, etc.

MADAN, FALCONER, and others, 1922–53. *A Summary Catalogue of Western Manuscripts in the Bodleian Library at Oxford*, 7 vols. (some in 2 parts), including index and conspectus. Oxford.

MAIER, JULIUS JOSEPH, 1879. *Die musikalischen Handschriften der K. Hof- und Stadtsbibliothek in Muenchen*. Munich.

MANTUANI, JOSEPH, 1897 and 1899. *Tabulae Codicum Manu Scriptorum . . . In Bibliotheca Palatina Vindobonensi Asservatorum*, vols. ix (Codicum musicorum pars I) and x (ditto pars II). Vienna.

MARPURG, FRIEDRICH WILHELM, 1757. *Historisch-kritische Beyträge zur Aufnahme der Musik*, vol. iii. Berlin.

MAYER-REINACH, ALFRED, 1904. Zur Geschichte der Königsberger Hofkapelle in den Jahren 1578–1720, *SIMG*, vi. Leipzig.

MEINECKE, LUDWIG, 1903. Michael Altenburg. Ein Beitrag zur Geschichte der Evangelischen Kirchenmusik, *SIMG*, v. Leipzig.

MENDEL, ARTHUR, 1950. More for the Bach Reader, *MQ*, xxxvi. New York.

MENKE, WERNER, 1934. *History of the Trumpet of Bach and Handel*. London.

MERSENNE (MERSENNUS), MARIN, 1635, 1636a. *Harmonicorum Liber Secundus*. Paris.

——, 1636b. *Harmonie universelle* (Libre Cinquiesme des Instruments à vent). Paris.

——, 1957 (trans. Roger E. Chapman). *Harmonie universelle: the books on instruments*. The Hague.

MEYER, ERNST, 1934. *Die mehrstimmige Spielmusik des 17. Jahrhundert in Nord- und Mitteleuropa*. Kassel.

——, 1946. *English Chamber Music: the history of a great art*. London.

——, 1956. Die Bedeutung der Instrumental-Musik am fürstbischofliche Hofe zu Olomouc (Olmütz) in Kroměříž (Kremsier), *Mf*, ix. Kassel.

MEYER, KATHI, and HIRSCH, PAUL, 1928–47. *Katalog der Musikbibliothek Paul Hirsch*, 4 vols. Berlin (vols. iii and iv Cambridge).

MITJANA, RAFAEL, 1911. *Catalogue critique et descriptif des imprimés de musique des XVIᵉ et XVIIᵉ siècles conservés à la Bibliothèque de l'Université Royale d'Upsala*, vol. i (for vols. ii and iii *see* DAVIDSSON, ÅKE). Upsala.

MÖRTZSCH, OTTO, 1921. Die Dresdener Hoftrompeter, *Musik im alten Dresden*, *Verlag des Vereins für Geschichte Dresdens*, No. 29. Dresden.

MOSER, HANS JOACHIM, 1959 (trans. C. F. Pfatteicher). *Heinrich Schütz: his Life and Work*. Saint Louis.

MÜNNICH, RICHARD, 1902. Kuhnau's Leben, *SIMG*, iii. Leipzig.

NAGEL, WILLIBALD, 1895. Annalen der englischen Hofmusik, 1509–1649, *MfMg*. Berlin, Leipzig.

NAGEL, WILLIBALD, 1900. Zur Geschichte der Musik am Hofe von Darmstadt, *MfMg*. Berlin, Leipzig.

——, 1905. Johann Heugel (ca. 1500–1584/5), *SIMG*, vii. Leipzig.

NAUMANN, EMIL, 1880–5. *Illustrirte Musikgeschichte*. Berlin, Stuttgart.

NEF, KARL, 1902. *Zur Geschichte der deutschen Instrumental Musik*. [*Beihefte der Internationalen Musik Gesellschaft (no. 5)*]. Leipzig.

——, 1909a. Die Musik in Basel, *SIMG*, x. Leipzig.

——, 1909b. Die Stadtpfeiferei und die Instrumentalmusiker in Basel (1385–1814), *SIMG*, x. Leipzig.

——, 1921. *Geschichte der Sinfonie und Suite*. Leipzig.

NETTL, PAUL, 1921. Die Wiener Tanzkompositionen in dem zweiten Hälfte des 17. Jahrhundert, *SzMw*, 8. Vienna.

——, 1921–2a. Weltliche Musik des Stiftes Ossegg (Böhmen) im 17 Jahrhundert, *ZfMw*, iv. Leipzig.

——, 1921–2b. Zur Geschichte der Musikkapelle des Fürstbischofs Karl Liechtenstein-Kastelkorn von Olmütz, *ZfMw*, iv. Leipzig. Reprinted in Nettl, 1927.

——, 1927. *Beiträge zur böhmischen und mährischen Musikgeschichte*. Brno.

——, 1929–32. Zur Geschichte der kaiserlichen Hofkapelle von 1636 bis 1680, *SzMw*, 16–19. Vienna.

NEUMANN, WERNER, 1947 (rev. ed. 1967). *Handbuch der Kantaten Johann Sebastian Bachs*. Leipzig.

NEWMAN, WILLIAM S., 1959. *The Sonata in the Baroque Era*. Chapel Hill.

NIEMANN, WALTER, 1903. Die schwedische Tonkunst, ihre Vergangenheit und Gegenwart, *SIMG*, v. Leipzig.

NOACK, ELISABETH, 1925. Die Bibliothek der Michaeliskirche zu Erfurt (now in D.S.B., Berlin), *AfMw*, vii. Bückeburg, etc.

NORLIND, TOBIAS, 1900. Die Musikgeschichte Schwedens in den Jahren 1630–1730, *SIMG*, i. Leipzig.

——, 1905. Ein Musikfest zu Nürnberg im Jahre 1649, *SIMG*, vii. Leipzig.

——, 1918. *Svensk Musikhistoria*. Stockholm.

OREL, ALFRED, 1953. *Musikstadt Wien*. Vienna.

OSTHOFF, WOLFGANG, 1956. Trombe sordine, *AfMw*, xiii. Bückeburg, etc.

PARIGI, LUIGI, 1951. *I Disegni Musicali del Gabinetto degli 'Uffizi' e delle minori collezione pubbliche a Firenze*. Florence.

PASQUÉ, ERNST, 1897. Die Weimarer Hofkapelle im XVI Jahrhundert, *MfMg*. Berlin, Leipzig.

PAZDIREK, F., (n.d.). *Manuel universel de la littérature musicale*. Paris.

PEDRELL, FELIP, 1903. La musique indigène dans le théâtre espagnol du XVIIe siècle, *SIMG*, v. Leipzig.

PEDRELL, FELIP, 1908–9. *Catàlech de la Biblioteca Musical de la Diputació de Barcelona*, 2 vols. Barcelona.

PEPYS, SAMUEL, 1893–9 (ed. H. Wheatley). *Diary*. London.

PERESS, MAURICE, 1961. A Baroque trumpet discovered in Greenwich Village, *BQ*, iv. Durham, New Hampshire.

PIERRE, CONSTANT, 1893. *Les facteurs des instruments de musique*. Paris.

PRAETORIUS, ERNST, 1906. Mitteilungen aus norddeutschen Archiven über Kantoren, Organisten, Orgelbauer und Stadtmusiker älterer Zeit bis ungefähr 1800, *SIMG*, vii. Leipzig.

PRAETORIUS, MICHAEL, 1614–19. *Syntagma Musicum*, 3 vols. Wolfenbüttel; facs. repr. (ed. W. Gurlitt), 1958–9. Kassel.

PROUT, EBENEZER, 1871 (May). The Imperial family of Austria, and its relations to music and musicians, *MMR*. London.

QUITTARD, HENRI, 1905. Note sur un ouvrage inédit de Marc-Antoine Charpentier (1634–1704), *ZdIM*, vi. Leipzig.

QUOIKA, RUDOLF, 1956. *Die Musik der Deutschen in Böhmen und Mähren*. Berlin.

RASMUSSEN, MARY, 1960. Gottfried Reiche and his 'Vier und zwanzig Neue Quatricinia' (Leipzig 1696), *BQ*, iv. Durham, New Hampshire.

——, 1962. New light on some unusual seventeenth-century French trumpet parts, *BQ*, vi. Durham, New Hampshire.

RHODES, EMILE, 1909. *Les Trompettes du Roi*. Paris.

RICHARDSON, E. G., 1929. *The Acoustics of Orchestral Instruments*. London.

RICHENTAL, ULRICH VON, 1874. *Concilium Constantiense, 1414–18* (36 plates in lithographic facsimile from the MS., with descriptive letterpress in Latin, French and German). St Petersburg.

——, 1881. *Ditto*, ed. H. Sevin. Karlsruhe. (Only 40 copies issued.)

RIEMANN, HUGO, 1959–61 (12th edn ed. by W. Gurlitt). 'Personenteil' in *Musik-Lexikon*, 2 vols. Mainz.

ROKSETH, YVONNE, 1960. The instrumental music of the Middle Ages and early sixteenth century, *NOHM*, vol. iii. London.

ROSENTHAL, KARL AUGUST, 1930 and 1932. Zur Stilistik der Salzburger Kirchenmusik von 1600 bis 1730, *SzMw*, 17 and 19. Vienna.

RUDHART, FRANZ MICHAEL, 1865. *Geschichte der Oper am Hofe zu München . . . Erster Theil: Die italienischen Oper von 1654–1787*. Freising.

SACHS, CURT, 1908. *Musikgeschichte der Stadt Berlin bis zum Jahre 1800*. Berlin.

——, 1909. Die Hofmusik der Fürsten Solms-Braunfels, *SIMG*, x. Leipzig.

——, 1909–10. Die Ansbacher Hofkapelle unter Markgraf Johann Friedrich (1672–1686), *SIMG*, xi. Leipzig.

——, 1913. *Real-Lexikon der Musikinstrumente*. Berlin.

——, 1920. *Handbuch der Musikinstrumentenkunde*. Leipzig.

SACHS, CURT, 1922. *Sammlung Alter Musikinstrumente bei der Staatlichen Hochschule für Musik zu Berlin*. Berlin.

——, 1929. *Geist und Werden der Musikinstrumente*. Berlin.

——, 1940. *The History of Musical Instruments*. New York.

——, 1950 (Jan.). Chromatic trumpets in the Renaissance, *MQ*, xxxvi. New York.

SANDFORD, FRANCIS, 1687. *The History of the Coronation of . . . James II . . .* London.

SARTORI, CLAUDIO, 1952. *Bibliografia della musica strumentale italiana stampata in Italia fino al 1700*. Florence. Second edition with additions, revisions and corrections, 1968.

——, (ed.), 1963–4. *Enciclopedia della musica*, 4 vols. Milan.

SCHAAL, RICHARD, 1964. Biographische Quellen zur wiener Musikern und Instrumentenmachern, *SzMw*, 26. Vienna.

SCHENK, ERICH, 1964. Beobachtungen über die modenesische Instrumentalmusikschule des 17. Jahrhunderts, *SzMw*, 26. Vienna.

SCHERING, ARNOLD, 1905, 1927. *Geschichte des Instrumentalkonzerts bis auf die Gegenwart*. Leipzig.

——, 1918. Zu Gottfried Reiches Leben und Kunst. *BJ*, 15. Leipzig.

——, 1918–19. Die alte Chorbibliothek der Thomasschule in Leipzig. *AfMw*, i. Bückeburg, etc.

——, 1921. Die Leipziger Ratsmusik von 1650 bis 1775, *AfMw*, iii. Vienna.

——, 1926, 1941. *Musikgeschichte Leipzigs*, vols. ii and iii. Leipzig.

——, 1931. *Geschichte der Musik in Beispielen*. Leipzig.

SCHEURLEER, D. F., 1905. *Het Muziekleven van Amsterdam*. Amsterdam.

SCHIEDERMAIR, LUDWIG, 1904. Die Anfänge der Münchener Oper, *SIMG*, v. Leipzig.

SCHLESINGER, KATHLEEN, 1910–11. Various articles on musical instruments, in *EB*. Cambridge.

SCHLETTERER, HANS MICHAEL, 1884. *Geschichte der Spielmannszunft in Frankreich und der Pariser Geigerkönige* (Part II of *Studien zur Geschichte der französischen Musik*, 3 parts, 1884–5). Berlin.

SCHLOSSER, JULIUS, 1920. *Die Sammlung alter Musikinstrumente Beschreibender Verzeichnis*. Vienna.

SCHMIDL, CARLO, 1928. *Dizionario universale dei musicisti*, 2 vols. Milan.

SCHMIEDER, WOLFGANG, 1950. *Thematisch-Systematisches Verzeichnis der musikalischen Werke von Johann Sebastian Bach*. [*Bach-Werke Verzeichnis (BWV)*]. Leipzig.

——, 1954–64. *Bibliographie des Musikschrifttums 1950 . . . 1959*, 5 vols. to date. Frankfurt.

——, 1958. Das Bachschriftum, *BJ*. Leipzig.

SCHNAPPER, EDITH B., 1957. *The British Union-Catalogue of Early Music printed before the year 1801*, 2 vols. London.

SCHNEIDER, MAX, 1906. Die Einweihung der Schlosskirche auf 'Friedenstein' zu Gotha im Jahre 1646, *SIMG*, vii. Leipzig.

——, 1907. Thematisches Verzeichnis der musikalischen Werke der Familie Bach: I. Teil, Die Werke Heinrich, Joh. Michael und Joh. Christoph Bachs, *BJ*. Leipzig.

——, 1918. Die Bedeutung der vielstimmiger Musik des 17. und 16. Jahrhunderts, *AfMw*, i. Bückeburg, etc.

SCHNOEBELEN, ANNE, 1969. Performance practices at San Petronio in the Baroque, *AM*, xli. Basel.

SCHÖNEICH, FRIEDRICH (ed.), 1955. *Historia von der Geburt . . . Jesu Christi*, vol. i. Kassel.

SCHÜNEMANN, GEORG (ed.), 1936. Trompeterfanfaren, Sonaten und Feldstücke, *EDM*, vii. Kassel.

SCOTT, HUGH ARTHUR, 1936. London's earliest public concerts, *MQ*, xxii, No. 4.

SEIFFERT, MAX, 1900. Matthias Weckmann und das Collegium Musicum in Hamburg, *SIMG*, ii. Leipzig.

——, 1908. Die Chorbibliothek der St Michaelsschule in Lüneberg zu Seb. Bachs Zeit, *SIMG*, ix. Leipzig.

SHERRINGTON, UNITY, and OLDHAM, GUY (ed.), 1961. *Music Libraries and Instruments*. London, New York.

SITTARD, JOSEPH, 1887. Den Trompetern, Pfeiffern und Lautenschlägern wird vom Grafen Ulrich v. Württemberg 'ihre gemachte Gesellschaft bestetig' 1458, *MfMg*. Berlin, Leipzig.

——, 1890. *Geschichte der Musik und des Konzertwesens in Hamburg*. Hamburg.

SMEND, FRIEDRICH, 1952. *Bach in Köthen*. Berlin.

SMIJERS, ALBERT, 1919–22. Die Kaiserliche Hofmusik-Kapelle von 1543–1619, *SzMw*, 6–9. Vienna.

SMITH, WILLIAM C., 1940. *Catalogue of printed music published before 1801 now in the British Museum, second supplement*. London.

——, 1948. *A bibliography of the musical works published by John Walsh during the years 1695–1720*. London.

SMITHERS, DON, 1965. The trumpets of J. W. Haas: a survey of four generations of Nuremberg brass instrument makers, *GSJ*, xviii. London.

——, 1967 (Oct.). Seventeenth-century English trumpet music, *ML*.

——, 1970 (Apl.). Music for the Prince-Bishop, *Music and Musicians*.

——, 1971. The Habsburg imperial *Trompeter* and *Heerpaucker* privileges of 1653, *GSJ*, xxiv. London.

SPEER, DANIEL, 1697. *Grund-richtiger, Kurtz-Leicht- und Nothiger jetzt Wolvermehrter Unterricht der musikalischen Kunst . . .* Ulm.

SPRINGER, HERMANN, SCHNEIDER, MAX, and WOLFHEIM, WERNER, 1912–16. *Miscellanea Musicae Bio-bibliographica Musikgeschichtliche Quellennachweise als Nachträge und Verbesserungen zu Eitners Quellenlexikon*, 10 annual *Hefte*. Leipzig.

SQUIRE, WILLIAM BARCLAY, 1903. Purcell's music for the funeral of Mary II, *SIMG*, iv. Leipzig.

——, 1909. *Catalogue of printed music in the library of the Royal College of Music, London.* London.

——, 1912. *Catalogue of printed music published between 1487 and 1800 now in the British Museum*, 2 vols. London.

——, 1927–9. *Catalogue of the King's Music Library* (in the British Museum), 3 vols. London.

STAHL, WILHELM, 1925. Franz Tunder und Dietrich Buxtehude, *AfMw*, viii. Bückeburg, etc.

STARKE, REINHOLD, 1900. Tobias Zeutschner, *MfMg*. Berlin, Leipzig.

STEIN, WALTER, 1894–5. *Akten und Geschichte der Verfassung und Verwaltung der Stadt Köln in 14. und 15. Jahrhundert*, 2 vols. Bonn.

STIASSNY, ROBERT, 1919. *Michael Pachers St Wolfganger Altar.* Vienna.

STIEHL, CARL, 1889. Die Familie Düben und die Buxtehude'schen Manuscripte auf der Bibliothek zu Upsala, *MfMg*. Berlin, Leipzig.

——, 1894. Die Lübeckischen Stadt- und Feldtrompeter, *Mitteilungen des Vereins für Lübeckische Geschichte und Altertumskunde*, vi. Lübeck.

——, 1895. *Katalog der Musik-sammlung auf der Stadtbibliothek zu Lübeck.* Lübeck.

STOKVIS, A. M. H. J., 1888–93. *Manuel d'histoire, de généalogie et de chronologie de tous les états du globe, depuis les temps les plus reculés jusqu'à nos jours*, 3 vols. Leiden.

STOW, JOHN, 1618. *The Survey of London . . . written in the yeere 1598 . . .* , (enlarged by Anthony Munday). London.

STRADANUS, J., (n.d.). *Encomium musices (text by Bochius)*. Antwerp.

SUSATO, TIELMAN, 1551 (mod. ed. 1936). *Danserye*. Antwerp (mod. ed. Mainz).

TALBOT, JAMES, 1948. Notes on Musical Instruments, ed. A. Baines and others from MS. 1187 (*c.* 1695) in the Library of Christ Church, Oxford, *GSJ*, i. 1948.

TANNERY, P., and DE WAARD, C. (ed.), 1946. *Correspondance du P. Marin Mersenne*, vol. ii. Paris.

TERRY, CHARLES S., 1932. *Bach's Orchestra.* London.

TILMOUTH, MICHAEL, 1959. The technique and forms of Purcell's sonatas, *ML*, xl, No. 2.

——, 1961–2. A calendar of references to music in newspapers published in London and the provinces (1660–1719), *RMARC*, vols. i and ii. London.

——, 1964. Corelli's trumpet sonata, *MMR*, 90. London.

TISCHER, G., and BURCHARD, K., 1902. Musikalienkatalog der Hauptkirche zu Sorau N./L., *MfMg*. Berlin, Leipzig.

TITCOMB, CALDWELL, 1956. Baroque court and military trumpets and kettle-drums: technique and music, *GSJ*, ix. London.

——, 1957. Carrousel music at the court of Louis XIV, *Essays on music in honor of Archibald Thompson Davidson by his associates.* Cambridge, Mass.

TRECHSEL, JOHN MARTIN, 1736. *Verneuertes Gedächtnis des Nürnbergischen Johannis-friedhofs.* Nuremberg.

VALE, G., 1930. La capella musicale del duomo di Udine dal secolo XIII al secolo XIX, *NA*, vii. Rome.

VALENTI, TOMMASO, 1926. Contratto di un maestro di tromba di Trevi dell' Umbria, *NA*, iii. Rome.

VAN DEN BORREN, CHARLES, 1924-7. Le manuscrit musical 222 C. 22 de la Bibliothèque de Strasbourg (xve siècle) brulé en 1870, et reconstitué d'après une copie partielle d'Edmond de Coussemaker, *Annales de l'Académie royale d'archéologie de Belgique*, vol. lxxi (1924), p. 343; lxxii (1924), p. 272; lxxiii (1925), p. 128; lxxiv (1927), p. 71. Antwerp.

VAN DER STRAETEN, EDMOND, 1867-88. *La musique aux Pays-Bas avant le XIXe siècle*, 8 vols. Brussels.

VATIELLI, F., 1927. *Arte e vita musicale a Bologna.* Bologna.

VIRDUNG, SEBASTIAN, 1511 (facs. rep. 1882). *Musica getutscht und ausgezoge . . .* Basel (fac. rep. Leipzig.)

VIZANI, 1602. *Descrittione della città contato, governo et altre cose notabili di Bologna.* Bologna.

VOGEL, PHILIPP EMIL, 1890. *Der Handschriften nebst älteren Druckwerken der Musik-Abteilung* (Wolfenbüttel). Wolfenbüttel.

VUILLEUMIER, H., 1893. Les trompettes d'église, *Revue historique vaudoise*, i. Lausanne.

WALDNER, FRANZ, 1897. Nachrichten über die Musikpflege am Hofe zu Innsbruck nach archivalischen Aufzeichnungen, *MfMg*. Berlin, Leipzig.

WEAVER, ROBERT, 1961. Sixteenth-century instrumentation, *MQ*, xlvii. New York.

WEBSTER, JOHN, 1948. Trumpet intonation differences due to bell taper, *JASA*, xx. New York.

——, 1949. Internal differences due to players and the taper of trumpet bells, *JASA*, xxi. New York.

WEED, WALTER HARVEY, 1907. *The Copper Mines of the World.* London.

WEINMANN, KARL, 1918. Andreas Hofer, *AfMw*, i. Bückeburg, etc.

WELLESZ, EGON, 1909. Die Opern und Oratorien in Wien von 1660-1708, *SzMw*, 6. Vienna.

——, 1914. *Die Ballett-Suiten von Johann Heinrich und Andreas Schmelzer.* Vienna.

——, 1940 (June). Italian musicians at the Austrian court, *MMR*. London.

WERNER, ARNO, 1900. Samuel und Gottfried Scheidt, *SIMG*, i. Leipzig.

——, 1905. Die thüringer Musikerfamilie Altenburg, *SIMG*, vii. Leipzig.

——, 1911. *Städtische und fürstliche Musikpflege in Weissenfels bis zum Ende des 18. Jahrhunderts.* Leipzig.

——, 1912. Neue Beiträge zur Scheidt-Biographie, *SIMG*, xiii. Leipzig.

——, 1918. Zur Musikgeschichte von Delitzsch, *AfMw*, i. Bückeburg, etc.

WERNER, ARNO, 1922. *Städtische und fürstliche Musikpflege in Zeitz bis zum Anfang des 19. Jahrhunderts*. Bückeburg, Leipzig.

——, 1926. Die alte Musikbibliothek und die Instrumentensammlung von St Wenzel in Naumburg, *AfMw*, viii. Buckeburg, etc.

——, 1932–3. Johann Ernest Altenburg, der letzte Vertreter der heroischen Trompeter- und Paukerkunst, *ZfMw*, xv. Leipzig.

WESSELY, OTHMAR, 1956. Archivalische Beiträge zum Musikgeschichte des maximilianischen Hofes, *SzMw*, 23. Vienna.

WESTRUP, J. A., 1933–4. The originality of Monteverdi, *PMA*, xl. London.

——, 1937. *Purcell*. London.

——, 1940. Monteverdi and the orchestra, *ML*. xxi. London, Oxford.

WHISTLING, K. F., 1828. *Handbuch der musikalischen Literatur*. Leipzig.

WINTERNITZ, EMANUEL, 1963. On angel concerts in the fifteenth century: A critical approach to realism and symbolism in sacred painting, *MQ*, xliv. New York.

WORSTHORNE, SIMON TOWNELEY, 1954. *Venetian Opera in the Seventeenth Century*. Oxford.

WÖRTHMÜLLER, WILLI, 1954. Die Nürnberger Trompeten- und Posaunenmacher des 17. und 18. Jahrhunderts. Ein Beitrag zur Geschichte des Nürnberger Musikinstrumentenbaus, *Mitteilungen des Vereins für Geschichte der Stadt Nürnberg*, 45. Nuremberg.

——, 1955. Die Instrumente des Nürnberger Trompeten- und Posaunenmacher, *Mitteilungen des Vereins für Geschichte der Stadt Nürnberg*, 46. Nuremberg.

WOTQUENNE, ALFRED, 1905. *Thematisches Verzeichnis der Werke von Carl Philipp Emanuel Bach*. Leipzig.

WUSTMANN, RUDOLF, 1909. *Musikgeschichte Leipzigs*, vol. i. Leipzig.

YOUNG, ROBERT W., 1948. On the performance of cup mouthpiece instruments, *JASA*, xx. New York.

ZAHN, JOHANNES, 1889–93. *Die Kirchenmelodien der deutschen evangelischen Kirchenlieder*, 6 vols. Gütersloh.

ZEDLER, JOHANN HEINRICH (ed.), 1732–54. *Grosses vollständiges Universal Lexicon*, 64 vols., with supplements. Leipzig.

ZIMMERMAN, FRANKLIN B., 1963. *Henry Purcell, 1659–1695. An analytical catalogue of his music*. London.

ZULAUF, E., 1902. *Beiträge zur Geschichte der Hofkapelle zu Cassel*. Leipzig.

INDEX

INDEX

See also Appendix, 'Inventory of Musical Sources for Baroque Trumpet'